THE CULTURE OF THE BOOK IN TIBET

THE CULTURE OF THE BOOK IN TIBET
Kurtis R. Schaeffer

COLUMBIA UNIVERSITY PRESS

NEW YORK

COLUMBIA UNIVERSITY PRESS
Publishers Since 1893
New York   Chichester, West Sussex

Copyright © 2009 Columbia University Press

Library of Congress Cataloging-in-Publication Data

Schaeffer, Kurtis R.
    The culture of the book in Tibet / Kurtis R. Schaeffer.
        p.   cm.
    Includes bibliographical references and index.
    ISBN 978-0-231-14716-3 (cloth : alk. paper)
    ISBN 978-0-231-51918-2 (electronic)
    1. Buddhist literature, Tibetan—History and criticism. 2. Buddhism and
culture. 3. Tibet (China)—Civilization. I. Title.

    BQ7622.S35   2009
    002.0951′5—dc22

                                                              2008036987

∞ Columbia University Press books are printed on permanent and durable
acid-free paper.
This book was printed on paper with recycled content.

Printed in the United States of America
c   10 9 8 7 6 5 4 3 2 1

References to Internet Web sites (URLs) were accurate at the time of writing.
Neither the author nor Columbia University Press is responsible for URLs that
may have expired or changed since the manuscript was prepared.

DESIGN BY MARTIN N. HINZE

CONTENTS

PREFACE

*W*hat was the cultural, social, and economic significance of the book in Tibet? How did scholars in Buddhist traditions edit works of religion, literature, art, or science? How was the written word implicated in the construction of power and authority in Buddhist societies? The present book is an attempt to address these questions— issues of broad significance for understanding Buddhist cultures throughout Asia—by looking at a single cultural location, Tibet, from the mid-thirteenth to the mid-eighteenth centuries. A motivating conviction is that what has been referred to as a "cult of the book" in Indian and other Buddhist cultures is more productively conceived as a culture of the book in Tibet, for the devotional practices that have been highlighted in India can, in the case of Tibet, be viewed as but one part of a set of interrelated material and cultural practices. The book in Tibet is variously the embodiment of the Buddha's voice, a principal tool in education, a source of tradition and authority, an economic product, a finely crafted aesthetic object, a medium of Buddhist written culture, and a symbol of the religion itself. From the earliest examples of Tibetan writing upon imperial stele to the mass production of printed canons a thousand years later, Tibetan scribes, scholars, and kings have explicitly made reference to the importance of books and the written word in areas of life from social authority to soteriology. Tibetan scholars of the five traditionally classified forms of knowledge (arts and crafts, medicine, language, logic, and the "inner art" of Buddhism) have exhibited passionate involvement with written culture—editorial theory; translation practices; forging authoritative transmissions of knowledge, practice, and lineage. Yet relatively little is known about the specific contours of the culture of the book in Tibet, such as the roles of patronage in the production of texts, the economic and social implications of producing the massive canons of Buddhist literature on the Himalayan plateau, the position of the scribe in society, and working life in a Buddhist scriptorium.

Every work is the work of many things besides an author.

—PAUL VALÉRY

The present work concentrates on the book—be it a handwritten manuscript or a printed volume—and more broadly the written word (inscription, charm, carved mantra, etc.) as a locus of cultural and social practices. It is a contribution to the loosely defined area of inquiry known as the history of books.[1] It is in no sense a comprehensive narrative history of the Tibetan book (a project for the next generation), but rather a set of linked case studies highlighting central themes in the study of written culture in Tibet. The temporal focus begins in the fourteenth century and the formative period of text-critical literature at Shalu monastery in west-central Tibet. From there the chapters trace an arc through the intervening centuries to the eighteenth century and the editors of Degé in eastern Tibet, plotting important points in the history and culture of the book in central, western, and eastern Tibet. This temporal range suggests a constructive unity, for this five-century period marks the age of the Buddhist canons (the Kangyur and Tengyur). Within this framework the central chapters offer detailed description and analysis of select moments in the cultural history of books, all of which are united by the intersection of explicit references in the sources to textual scholarship, the production of Buddhist culture, and the social and economic roles of books in Tibet. The book is a particularly rich focal point in the study of Tibetan cultural history, for it is a nexus of intellectual, religious, social, artistic, and economic aspects of life. A physical instantiation of learned culture and tradition, the book serves as a principal point for debating culture, whether the role of libraries in religious institutions, the relative merits of oral and written teachings, or the price of translated literature. The study of this single yet immensely important object of material culture, offers greater understanding of the cultural and social history of Tibet and of Buddhism.

In what follows I have sought a balance between thematic presentation and specific case studies of books, their makers, and their times and places. Each chapter centers on the activities of a few particular times and places while introducing a particular theme. To a greater or lesser extent, most chapters focus on the scholars who were engaged in work on language, literature, translation, editing, and book production. Some chapters dwell on the technical skills of editing manuscripts; others look more closely at the roles that writing and book production have played in the social and cultural life of Tibet or highlight the place of textual scholarship in the formation of individual scholars' identities.

Chapter 1 surveys the material aspects of the book, principally what traditional sources have to say about the paper, ink, wood, and fabric out of which books are fashioned. Chapter 2 looks first to two letters to editors of Buddhist canons, works whose brevity belies the rich and detailed sketches they draw of the making of Buddhist scriptural volumes. The first letter—and the more important for the subsequent history of book production—was written in the fourteenth century by the great scholar Butön Rinchendrup. It contains instructions to managers at the scriptorium of Shalu monastery and includes vivid details of scribal practice. The second was composed in the early seventeenth century by the twenty-fifth abbot of Drikung monastery, Chökyi Drakpa, and offers advice on the management of a team of scribes and details the methods to be followed in planning, designing, and executing the production of books. The final section of the chapter shifts focus from Tibetan scholars concerned with canonical literature to those involved with the compilation and reproduction of a single Tibetan writer's oeuvre—in this case, the famous abbot of Labrang monastery in the Amdo region of northeastern Tibet, Jamyang Shepé Dorjé. Chapter 3 moves to the late fifteenth and early sixteenth centuries to chronicle the career of a paradigmatic textual scholar, the translator and editor Shalu Lotsawa Chökyong Zangpo, who followed closely in the footsteps of Butön at Shalu. The second half of the chapter looks to the book-making activities of Shalu Lotsawa's contemporary, Tsangnyön Heruka, the "Madman" of Tsang, famous for redacting and printing the most popular version of the life story of that ubiquitous Tibetan hermit-saint, Milarepa. At first glance Shalu Lotsawa and Tsangnyön might seem irreconcilable opposites—the consummate scholar-monk and the ultimate hermit. When viewed from the perspective of their efforts in textual production and the promotion of the culture of the book, they have more in common than might have been imagined. Chapter 4 moves a step away from canonical literature to take up the themes elaborated in previous chapters in a new context: the debates over the proper place of textual scholarship in the medical traditions of Tibet, recounted and fueled principally in the late seventeenth century by Sangyé Gyatso, regent to the Fifth Dalai Lama and scholar extraordinaire of the arts and sciences. Chapter 5 introduces the two figures who might be considered the central characters of the book, Shuchen Tsültrim Rinchen and Situ Chökyi Jungné, the famous editors of mid-eighteenth-century Degé, chronicling their relationships with their patrons, the kings of Degé; the financing and production of the Buddhist canons by these patrons and scholars; and their editorial methods, revisiting persistent themes of earlier chapters in a new setting. The chapter also briefly compares the book production activities occurring elsewhere at the same time by looking to the manuscript canon produced by the leader of the central Tibetan government, Polané, as a memorial for his mother. Lastly, chapter 6 offers an explanation for the importance of the book in the economic, social, and cultural spheres of Tibetan life as an integral whole by suggesting that its immense symbolic potential works in concert with its aesthetic richness and material value to perpetuate the culture of the book. The chapter ends by returning one last time to Degé to hear the comments of Situ and Shuchen regarding the personal, social, cultural, and soteriological implications of their work as textual scholars—architects of the culture of the book— for while this work was often praised by their patrons, their kings, their students, and colleagues, it also became at times a cause for the king's censure and the scholar's lament. The epilogue offers without interpretation a story that recounts in a popular style the material, economic, and symbolic aspects of book culture in Tibet highlighted here. "The Boy Who Wrote *Sūtras* on the Sky" forms chapter 13 of a collection known as *Benefits of the Diamond Cutter Sūtra*, which contains fifteen miracle tales depicting the wondrous fate ensured for those who recite that famous *sūtra*.

◉

This book has developed over a decade and in a variety of venues. My interest in traditional editorial theory began in a class on the textual criticism of Indian texts led by William Arraj at the University of Washington in 1994, and developed in Richard Salomon's seminar on the history of Sanskrit as well as his sometimes quadrilingual reading seminars in Indian Buddhist literature. The tools of traditional scholars' trades became an ongoing interest in Leonard van der Kuijp's ever-rewarding seminars on Tibetan philology (out of which arose many unanswered and thus still productive questions) at both the University of Washington and Harvard University. My shift in focus from textual criticism toward the history of the book came about in the late 1990s with the growing feeling that, prior to (and as an integral aspect of) studying the social and cultural settings of their discursive content, I would do well to become acquainted with the processes by which the thousands of volumes of Tibetan literature at my disposal as a contemporary student of Buddhism and Tibetan culture came to be formed. The methodological challenge motivating this interest is perhaps best expressed in succinct terms by D. F. McKenzie, who argues that "new readers make new texts, and their new meanings are a function of their new forms."[2] It was also during this time that Roger Chartier called upon historians to take the material reality of their literary sources as worthy of cultural analysis: "To concentrate on the concrete conditions and processes that construct meaning," he argued, "is to recognize, unlike traditional intellectual history, that minds are not disincarnated, and, unlike hermeneutics, that the categories which engender experiences and interpretations are historical, discontinuous, and differentiated."[3] Equally provocative was the work of Armando Petrucci, who suggests: "Studying the participation of the author in the work of writing his or her own text and analyzing when and how such participation changed over time would constitute a notable contribution both to better understanding the processes by which complex texts are produced and to the criticism of those texts." For Petrucci this attention to detail has far-reaching implications, for "such studies . . . can also serve to make more precise for each historical epoch and situation what were the relationships between writing and reading, and between book and text, that constitute the deepest nature of any higher written culture." Although that phrase might suggest an unproductive reductionism if it were not made in the context of his detailed epigraphic studies, his careful work inspired my interest in the social and cultural locations of textual production.[4] In my own studies, the Tibetan book became not merely a source of discourses and practices but a crafted symbolic object itself formed by important discourses and practices, fully and simultaneously enmeshed in the economic, social, and cultural practices of Tibet. Rather than an inert container that adds nothing to the data "contained within" it, the book as such suddenly became "full" of data about—and a principal source for—the cultures in which it was involved. The container, so to speak, had become the content; the material had become the cultural.

Almost all of the work that forms the present book grew out of essays initially drafted for public presentation between 1997 and 2006. Sections of several chapters have been previously published; they are listed in the order in which they were first presented before a public audience. An early version of the final section of chapter 2 was first presented at a conference on Amdo at Harvard University in May 1997, and later published as "Printing the Words of the Master: Tibetan Editorial Practice in the Collected Works of 'Jam dbyangs bzhad pa'i rdo rje I (1648–1721)," *Acta Orientalia* 60 (1999): 159–177. An early version of the portions of chapter 2 dedicated to Butön's letter to editors was first presented at Harvard University in December 1997. An expanded version was later published as "A Letter to Editors of the Buddhist Canon in 14th-Century Tibet," *Journal of the American Oriental Society* 124, no. 2 (2004): 1–17. Portions of chapters 5 and 6 treating the Degé editors Situ Chökyi Jungné and Shuchen Tsültrim Rinchen were first presented at Harvard University in March 1998, and in July of the same year at the eighth seminar of the International Association for Tibetan Studies at Indiana University in Bloomington. A subsequent rendition was given in November 2004 at the School of Oriental and African Studies in London. Early versions of chapter 4 were first presented at Harvard University in October 2001 and at McMaster University in January 2003, and subsequently published as "Textual Scholarship, Medical Tradition, and Mahāyāna Buddhist Ideals in Tibet," *Journal of Indian Philosophy* 31, no. 5–6 (2003): 621–641. Parts of chapter 3 dedicated to the life of Shalu Lotsawa were first presented at the University of Virginia in March 2003. Sections of chapters 1 and 6 on book culture in the *Blue Annals* and the symbolic and economic aspects of books were first presented at the University of Virginia in March 2004. Finally, portions of chapter 3 having to do with the tradition of Tsangnyön Heruka were first presented at the eleventh seminar of the International Association for Tibetan Studies in Königswinter in September 2006.

I would like to thank everyone involved with those events, particularly Phyllis Granoff, Leonard van der Kuijp, Ulrich Pagel, and Eliot Sperling. Other people have generously shared their knowledge, advice, and texts, including Benjamin Bogin, Cristoph Cüppers, Jacob Dalton, Helmut Eimer, Franz-Karl Ehrhard, Natalie Gummer, Janet Gyatso, David Hall, Amy Heller, Martin Jaffee, Matthew Kapstein, Dan Martin, Susan Meinheit, Burkhard Quessel, Andrew Quintman, Jann Ronis, Sam van Schaik, and Gene Smith. I would like to thank each for their kind support. Final rewriting was undertaken during a research leave in the spring of 2007, for which I thank the Dean of the College of Arts and Sciences at the University of Virginia. The chairs of the two departments in which I have had the privilege of working, Russell McCutcheon at the University of Alabama and Paul Groner at the University of Virginia, have been immensely gracious during the writing of this book. It is rare to have managers who are mentors, and mentors who are friends; I have been twice graced. I would also like to thank my colleagues Bryan Cuevas, David Germano, and Gray Tuttle for scholarly encouragement offered through advice and example and—more importantly—for company and good cheer offered in unlikely places around the world over the past decade.

This book is dedicated to my family—Heather, Ruby, and Maxwell. May their love of books not decrease because of this one.

1 THE STUFF OF BOOKS

MAY THE GODS CRACK OPEN THEIR HEADS

In the conclusion to one of his many works on esoteric Buddhist practice, Butön Rinchendrup, the great fourteenth-century scholar of Shalu monastery in west-central Tibet, recounts a story that one of his masters, Lama Pakpa Ö, had related to him. It was a cautionary tale about books.[1] When Pakpa Ö was himself a student, his master, having grown quite old, had become unable to memorize teachings correctly. The master ordered Pakpa Ö to write down a certain text for him so he might read the work that now lay beyond his mnemonic abilities. Pakpa Ö had been explicitly ordered by another master never to write these teachings down, so this placed him in the difficult position of having to break one command in order to fulfill another. He resolved the dilemma by writing only an outline of the teachings for his aging mentor. As Pakpa Ö related the tale, Butön asked that such a ban not be placed upon him, for he wished to compose a more extensive treatise on the practice. Pakpa Ö, seeing that he had not impressed upon his disciple the gravity of this ban on recording the teachings on paper, then offered a sort of commentary on the episode. "Writing down the instructions of an oral lineage," he began allegorically, "is like the king descending to the common people or wandering about a village. The negative consequences are manifold." And he listed the harmful costs: "The power and benefits of the instruction become vitiated. After the text exists, the practical instructions will not be sought after, and people will come to know the instruction only by obtaining the text. In the end it will become merely a reading transmission and thus the lineage of the real instruction will be severed." Yet despite these concerns, Pakpa Ö consented to let Butön write: "If [you] wish to do so, by all means do." But, he cautioned, "do not let the profound instructions become merely a reading transmission." The problem was not the act of putting the oral instructions down on paper per se, but rather the danger that the transformation to a more permanent and portable communication medium might render direct master-disciple relationships unnecessary in the minds of those seeking instruction. "Do not give the teachings," he went on, "to those who have not thought of taking them into their experience and thus only amass authorizations to teach ever greater numbers of texts, desiring thereby to show to the world that they have learned the teachings, meditate, and are knowledgeable." In other words, Pakpa Ö feared that the ready availability of written texts would allow charlatans to claim the authority of spiritual teachings for themselves.

For a time Butön was convinced to give up his wish to write down the teachings. But he gave way when another prominent religious leader of the day, Lama Dampa Sönam Gyeltsen, requested from him a written version of the same teachings. Feeling that he could not refuse this powerful leader, Butön had a scribe write them down, with the proviso that the text be shown to no one who was not practicing the meditation instructions. The text of the oral teachings was now readily at hand, physical proof that Butön had disregarded the better judgment of his master and others before him. In a final effort to protect the teachings from the potential harmful effects of being set down in a book, Butön offered a closing prayer in the ending lines of the text, and a last warning. He prayed that practitioners of the esoteric contemplative system may attain the status of the Buddha Vajradhāra—a common enough entreaty. But for those who violate the spirit of the prohibition against writing Butön wished a different fate: "As for those who give the reading permission to people who are not actually practicing, may Vajradhāra himself crack open their heads!"

This minor episode from Butön Rinchendrup's career (which ranks among the more explicit Tibetan discussions of the relationship between orality and writing in the context of esoteric instructions) evokes the complex tension between the felt need to preserve tradition in the relatively permanent medium of writing and the sense that the efficacy of esoteric teachings must be protected through closely guarded oral transmission. Certainly other references to debates about orality and literacy—or in Buddhist terms, what might be conceived as a debate about contemplative versus scholastic means—are well known, even if they are usually found as asides in the context of larger works. An eleventh-century leader chastised his students for studying too much and not meditating enough,[2] while one of his students in turn gave books to disciples, urging them to study early and med-itate later lest demons get the best of them.[3] Another eleventh-century figure lamented that he had studied the great texts even though none would be of any help at the hour of his death. He encouraged his disciple not to study books, but to learn more practically oriented precepts.[4] Another yogin refers to himself as a beggar who has abandoned existence, "for whom writing is no longer needed."[5] By contrast, one master tells his student that "the meditation of those who have not studied [books] even the slightest is shallower than an armpit!"[6] Whether in favor of the written word as a medium of religious expression or against it, such anecdotes share a sense of disquiet regarding the social sig-nificance of writing and the culture of the book.

A further example illustrates the complex roles the book plays in these debates. A disciple asks his master for certain teachings, but the master gives him only part of them. When asked why he did not make public the teachings in their entirety, the master complains, "There were many men at the residence and all could have copied them, therefore I did not give them. Also they do not respect their teacher and simply look after books."[7] Here the master maintains a healthy respect for the reproductive power of writing; if anyone were to copy down his words, that person might compromise the value of his own oral teachings by giving them a life beyond his control. If orality was a part of the rheto-ric of authenticity and efficacy, it was also a powerful defense of intellectual property, against which books were potentially a seri-ous threat. At stake was the propriety of two different technolo-gies for the perpetuation of tradition, and the relative authority of those who promoted one over the other.

The present book is about those who brooked having their skulls cracked by Vajradhāra, who spent their lives putting the teachings—exoteric and esoteric alike—into writing. It is about traditions of textual scholarship and the social and cultural con-texts in which they flourished. The volumes of Tibetan literature that today crowd libraries around the world speak to centuries of such scholarship and the efforts of scribes, scholars, editors, and artisans who spent their lives working with ink, paper, wood, and chisel. The making of books was such a prominent aspect of Tibetan cultural life that it could even come to define a person, as in the autobiography of the early twentieth-century printer Ding-riwa Chökyi Gyeltsen—a work that reads more like a resume of his printing projects than the story of his life.[8] To a greater or lesser extent, the same could be said of each of the figures portrayed in the following chapters. Contemporary scholars of Buddhism benefit from the labors of these textual scholars every time we use an eighteenth-century Tibetan edition of a third-century Indian text, pick up an anthology of spiritual songs sung by a master and redacted by his student, or casually browse through the topically organized volumes of a Tibetan author's collected works. Yet rarely does one hear from the editors themselves about their work. Only with difficulty are contemporary researchers able to gain a glimpse into the workshops of these scholars from centuries past. This book looks to the rich biographical, autobiographical, epistolary, poetic, documentary, and historical literature of Tibet to envision the efforts of those who courted the crushing wrath of the gods to make books.

The majority of these characters are portrayed in the literature as ardent enthusiasts about the technology of writing, and this aspect of the stories told by and about them will be of primary focus. Their narrative identities as textual scholars are best read while keeping in mind the debates expressed in the preceding anecdotes over the relationship between Buddhist teachings and the media of their transmission as a sort of subtext, for even the most ardent proponents of textual scholarship in Tibetan history express grave doubts about its potential effects on soteriological matters. Butön himself, so concerned about putting the esoteric teachings he had received from his master into written form, was passionate about the value of philology in Buddhist practice. And Shuchen Tsültrim Rinchen—the famous "Great Editor" of Degé monastery in the eastern Tibetan cultural region of Kham, whose story will serve as a touchstone in the final chapters of this book—spent long years working with texts while still lamenting that it might have been a wasted effort, of little value for his spiritual development.

THE BUDDHIST BOOK IN TIBET

The production of books was a central aspect of the introduction of Buddhism to Tibet, and has been featured in understandings of the country's past since the beginning of Tibetan historical writing. In the earliest examples of historiographic literature from the Tibetan renaissance of the eleventh through thirteenth centuries, such as the *Testament of Ba*, paper and ink are among the necessary materials for the founding of the first monastic complex in central Tibet.[9] A common tale of the origins of Buddhism in Tibet finds several books of Buddhist scripture along with a silver *stūpa* falling from the sky upon the castle of the Tibetan King Lhatotori. A prophetic voice resounded from above when the book hit the castle, assuring that a Tibetan king would rise in five generations' time to make the books understood to the people and thereby spread Buddhism in the Land of Snows.[10] Such mythic understandings of the importance of scriptural volumes for Buddhist origins in Tibet find corroboration in the mundane details of old Tibetan contracts dating from imperial Tibetan control of central Asia, which explicitly relate that writing paper was itself a valuable commodity worthy of contracted exchange, and that the copying of Buddhist texts was an important economic and cultural practice.[11]

The intense importance of the reproduction of Buddhist literature in Tibet ultimately hails back to the cult of the book attested to more than a millennium earlier in the formative period of Indian Mahāyāna Buddhism. The *Lotus Sūtra* (which would be quoted by Tibetan writers in support of the worship of scriptural volumes), for instance, includes the following injunction regarding books: "If a good man or good woman shall receive and keep, read and recite, explain or copy in writing a single phrase of the *Scripture of the Dharma Blossom* . . . that person is to be looked up to and exalted by all the worlds, [and] showered with offerings fit for a Buddha. . . . Let it be known that that person is a great bodhisattva."[12] Such emphasis on the material and soteriological benefits of the word of the Buddha in its written form was a powerful rationale for funding the production of books in Tibet. By doing so, the patron, his or her region, and its inhabitants were guaranteed to be blessed by the Buddha himself, assured merit for themselves and their communities.[13] The conviction that the salvific power of writing out the words of the Buddha was an end in itself is perhaps given its ultimate form in the practice of printing on water—in which a Buddhist charm slapped down on streams and rivers leaves no physical trace, yet through the very act of momentarily imprinting the water with the Buddha's word distributes blessings—or perhaps in the shepherd's realization in "The Boy Who Wrote *Sūtras* on the Sky" that writing the *Diamond Cutter* in the air was as every bit as efficacious as writing it on paper. The printing of the canon and printing on water may be placed along a continuum in which devotional practices combine with the belief that the graphic word is inherently powerful. For in addition to what good comes to those who provide a permanent foundation for the word of the Buddha—printed texts that last a long time—the very act of printing was intrinsically meritorious. In social terms, the patron and the patron's region had the opportunity to achieve increased public renown by promoting the culture of Buddhism through books, an effect acknowledged by the *Lotus Sūtra* when it states that the patron is "exalted by all the worlds."

The same qualities are attributed to Buddhist volumes in accounts of other textual practices, of which reading and scribal work are primary examples. Learning to read scripture is a basic feature of accounts of childhood in almost any intellectual biography in traditional Tibet, as examples from that vast biographical compendium, Gö Lotsawa's *Blue Annals*, suggest.[14] People learned to write anywhere between the ages of four[15] and twelve,[16] from their father,[17] mother,[18] or elder brother.[19] Because Gö Lotsawa's subjects are almost always elite leaders, accounts of their education more often than not emphasize the extraordinary rather than the mundane. A ubiquitous feature in stories of the young lives of religious masters is the ability to learn reading and writing with little or no effort.[20] At age seven, one young savant was able to read through the various and massive *Perfection of Wisdom Sūtras* and grasp their meaning.[21] Another scholar is praised as a youth for being able to "learn by heart every morning texts the length of the *Sañcayagāthā* after reading them only once."[22] The Fourth Karmapa "kept many books around him, and was able to read them in his dreams and grasp their meaning."[23] Because reincarnated religious leaders have by definition already studied reading and writing in previous lives, they seldom need to do it again and are seen as youths miraculously reading without instruction.[24] In the case of those destined to be translators or travelers, they might also possess knowledge of Indian scripts[25] and be able to distinguish different forms of Tibetan and Indic scripts, and even different regional painting styles.[26]

In Gö Lotsawa's biographical vignettes, reading the *sūtras* and the tantras could be an experience of great transformation, and conversion experiences are often prompted by the faith produced through reading.[27] After reading the *Ratnakūṭa Sūtra*, Master Ling Repa decided that he was a reincarnation of a bodhisattva who had been present when the Buddha taught.[28] Reading the lives of holy men could produce immediate and profound results,

as when one yogin became cognizant of his dreams after reading a hagiography.[29] When another yogin recited a line from the
Perfection of Wisdom, he fell into a trance.[30] One twelfth-century
Kadampa master read through a tantric commentary, was overcome with faith, and thus beheld his own body as a mandala for
six days. The same figure read a philosophical work and then perceived all objects as rainbows.[31] In these scenes from the lives of
scholars and hermits alike, the act of reading scripture is praised
for holding transformative power in much the way contemplative
practice is so often praised.

Like reading, scribal work could be taken as a sign of intellectual mastery gained over the course of lifetimes. As a young
incarnation, Phakmodrüpa Dorjé Gyelpo was proficient in
writing without having studied it, and copied one volume of
a 100,000-line *Perfection of Wisdom Sūtra* for his master.[32] One
quick-handed incarnation of 11 years could copy a life story in a
single day.[33] Yet other references to copying texts in the *Blue Annals* provide some impression of the social circumstances of such
work.[34] Copying could be a local and small-scale affair between
two people, as when one student slowly copied one leaf in four
days as a sort of penance for disregarding his master's wishes.[35]
At other times he copied the works of his master, or edited books
copied by the poor among his religious brethren.[36] Books were
copied for specific teaching needs[37] and for funeral ceremonies.[38]
Books could be copied first by fathers and then by sons as part of
a family industry.[39] Finally, copyists are portrayed in the *Blue Annals* as participants in intellectual culture, not merely as laborers,
as when a certain yogin asked a group of scribes copying *Perfection of Wisdom* texts for their opinions on the greatest teacher of
the *Guhyasamāja Tantra*.

The early centuries of the later spread of Buddhism in Tibet—
that is, from the late tenth century on—saw the production of
beautiful manuscripts of both canonical Buddhist scripture and
indigenous Tibetan literature. Unfortunately, few of these now
survive.[40] Prior to 1411, when the first wood-block print edition
of the Kangyur was produced in Beijing, all Buddhist canonical
collections were produced and reproduced as handwritten manuscripts (despite the fact that Tibetan works had been printed
since at least the mid-twelfth century, as discussed below).
Scribal publication was a costly and laborious process in which
an equally great expenditure of funds and resources was needed
for each and every copy desired. Descriptions of the material

resources poured into such books are relatively infrequent and usually quite brief.[41] A sixteenth-century work provides a few enticing details regarding the paper, ink, and decorative minerals utilized to make a Tibetan book: Mongol paper is found in both smooth and coarse varieties, Indian paper is generally soft, while the paper produced in the Mönpa regions south of central Tibet is preferred for its smoothness and pliancy. When gold ink is required, gold dust from rivers is good, gold from Garlok regions is quite red, and mixed white and yellow gold is best. Books illustrated with flowers drawn with beryl bitumen are known as "beryl books."[42]

According to the fifteenth-century scholar Taktsang Lotsawa, the quality of the materials used to produce paper and ink for Buddhist books is of the utmost importance: "The birch or [other] tree bark, white or dyed paper [should be of] clear complexion," he says of the writing surface, and "the best ink is refined out of gold or silver, either highly refined or semi-refined." "Ordinary ink," he allows, "is also fine"—though he does not go on to specify exactly what this is. One of the clearest descriptions of papermaking is provided by Samuel Turner, who witnessed its manufacture in Bhutan (a major exporter of paper to Tibet)[43] in 1783. His observations are worth citing in full:

> When a sufficient quantity of bark is collected and boiled in a lixivium of wood ashes, it is then taken up, and laid in a heap to drain; after which it is beaten upon a stone, with a wooden mallet, until it is reduced to an impalpable pulp; it is then thrown into a reservoir of water, where, being well stirred about, and cleansed from the coarse and dirty part, which floats upon the surface, it is still further depurated in another large reservoir of clean water. When the preparation is complete, the parts are finely broken, and that which sinks in the water appears mucilaginous to the touch. All that now remains is to form it into sheets, which is done upon small reeds set in frames. The labourer dips the frame in the water, and raises up a quantity of the pulp, which, by moving the frame in the water, he spreads, until it entirely and equally covers the surface of the reeds; he then raises the frame perpendicularly, the water drains off, and the frame is hung up till the sheet is nearly dry: it is then taken off, and suspended upon lines.

"The paper thus prepared," Turner concludes, "is of a much stronger texture, than that of any other country with which I am acquainted."[44]

Taktsang Lotsawa continues his account by emphasizing that both the tools and the craftsmanship should be of good quality: "Tools such as the pen and the knife should be the same size. Work must not be done carelessly: study as ever, then write." (Elsewhere one reads that a good pen and ink could be among the personal effects of learned people, allowing them to write wherever they wished.)[45] And if there were aesthetic standards for the materials going into the book, the size of the book itself appears to have been less regulated. "It is said in some of the tantras," Taktsang continues, "that [books] should be hidden in the hair or under the arm, they should be between twelve and sixteen finger widths." Taktsang Lotsawa, incidentally, appears to have taken most of these details from the *Hevajra Tantra*.[46] Yet, he notes, "in the conclusion to the [*Perfection of Wisdom in*] *Eight-Thousand Lines* it states that one should write clear script in a very large book." Therefore, he concludes, "one should [produce books] according to context." Details of the page layout were also variable, in Taktsang's opinion. The decorative hole found in many early Tibetan books could, for instance, be adapted in a variety of ways: "In Indian books there is either one hole or two," and therefore Tibetan book producers could be allowed some freedom in how they formatted the page: "In the first case, [place the hole] at the line between the second and third fifths of five parts. In the second case, divide [the page] in thirds and place the hole there. A round or a square hole [should be] neither too big nor to small, but attractive."[47]

While the production of handwritten manuscripts never ceased to be an essential craft, the rise of printing in Tibet was an event of the utmost importance for Tibetan cultural and intellectual life. A major canonical collection is not known to have been printed until 1411, when that first Kangyur was printed with Ming imperial patronage. Yet printing had been utilized for Tibetan-language publications centuries before. The earliest Tibetan-language wood-block print currently known is a small prayer printed in Khara Khoto in 1153,[48] and the earliest datable major Tibetan work currently known was printed in China under Mongol patronage no later than the 1270s.[49] This was an annotated edition of the *Hevajra Tantra* produced by Pakpa Lödrö Gyeltsen (1235–80) with the patronage of the Mongol court. Pakpa was the premier Tibetan priest of the Mongol Khans, working under Chinggis Khan (1169–1227) as well as his grandson Qubilai Khan, first emperor of the Yuan dynasty of China (reigned 1260–94).[50] Pakpa is perhaps most famous for devising the "Pakpa Script" for the official use of the Yuan imperial government, an endeavor he completed while residing in Peking in 1269, and in connection with which he was awarded the title of Imperial Preceptor. In the previous year he had traveled from his home institution of Sakya monastery in west Tibet to Beijing. After embarking on the return journey, Pakpa resided in Lintao for three years, from early 1271 to the beginning of 1274.[51] During this period, in 1273, he had his edition of the *Hevajra Tantra* (annotations to which he likely composed in 1265 at Sakya monastery) carved into blocks by both Tibetan and Chinese craftsmen. Urged by the glorious and thoughtful Jibig Temor (son of Goden Khan),[52] Mongol leaders Yesu Boga and Hayimdu sponsored the production. No fewer than 1,000 prints were made from the newly carved blocks, which suggests that the potential of wood-block printing to enable mass distribution was already being taken advantage of in the earliest stages of Tibetan printing.[53] Pakpa's involvement with book production continued through the 1270s, and the concluding chapter of this book will return to his metaphorical evocations of the book as the body of the Buddha.[54] At any rate, he played a significant role in the rise of Tibetan printing under the Mongols. Of the rise of printing in central Tibet far less is known: there are scattered reports of early wood-block printing efforts in Ü and Tsang during the thirteenth century, such as the spells (*dhāraṇī*) reported to have been printed at Nartang monastery in Tsang during the abbacy of Chim Namkadrak (1210–85).[55] But it was not until the beginning of the fifteenth century, in 1418, that block printing was carried out in central Tibet on a wide scale.[56]

In the absence of thorough quantitative studies, it is difficult to assess how many blocks were produced in the various regions of Tibet. Tibetan institutions did keep lists of printing blocks held within their confines, but for the most part surveys beyond individual monasteries and temples were not done. One very useful list was completed by the central Tibetan government in 1957. It provides a thought-provoking, if incomplete sketch of the massive scale of block printing by the middle decades of the twentieth century.[57] This catalog lists blocks held in approximately 110 monasteries, monastic colleges, temples, and hermitages in central and (to a lesser extent) western Tibet. Because it was produced by the state, the institutions included are largely part of the Geluk tradition, and only those in the regions of Ü and Tsang are counted. As the conclusion to the list itself makes clear, the monasteries of Upper and Lower Dokham—the regions of Amdo and Kham, which make up the larger part of eastern Tibet—are not treated. Sakya, Kagyu, and Nyingma monasteries are represented, though only poorly, and Bönpo monasteries are not considered at all. Nevertheless, a crude sense of the sheer productivity of printing houses emerges when one considers that this list provides detailed figures for some 260,000 printing blocks, or well over half a million printable pages. To this number the list also adds (without giving precise numbers of blocks) several hundred more volumes of canonical and indigenous literature (such as the Nartang Tengyur), which must have amounted to as many as 100,000 blocks. Many of these 350,000-odd blocks were housed in the two principal state printeries located in the Zhöl village at the base of the Potala in Lhasa, with 92,441 blocks at the Kangyur Printing House at Zhöl village and 36,287 at the Eastern Zhöl Printing House.[58] The large monasteries around Lhasa also contained substantial collections, with 48,480 at Drepung, 15,619 at Sera, and 7,534 at the Phurbuchok Hermitage and 7,769 at Tashichöling monastery (both of which are located to the north of Sera). Tashilhunpo monastery, the main Geluk institution of the Tsang region, also had a large holding of 45,346 blocks. Interestingly, the state-sponsored list also includes the names of four private printers, including the well-known early twentieth-century carver of illustrated scriptures, Chökyi Gyeltsen, who is personally credited with 3,196 blocks.[59]

Wood-block printing as practiced by Tibetans consists of several steps.[60] First, a manuscript of thin paper is prepared by a scribe and placed face down on a blank wood block evenly covered with paste. After the paste dries the paper is moistened and removed from the block, leaving in ink the reversed letters. This reverse-image page is then relief-carved to make the printable surface. The finished block is smeared with ink, and then a blank paper is laid on top of the block and firmly impressed with a roller. As shall be seen in more detail below, the initial process of making a set of blocks requires a full work force of scribes, just the same as any handwritten manuscript project, as well as a massive contingent of carvers and printers. Carving was the most expensive part of the operation, more than doubling the cost of producing a manuscript, but then of course allowing for multiple copies to be made with far less effort. However, even if the makers of canons after 1411 did know about printing, it appears that for these largest of literary endeavors manuscript production was often the more viable alternative, for manuscript canons continued to be produced alongside printed editions right into the twentieth century.[61]

THE BUDDHIST CANONS IN TIBET

In the reproduction of the Kangyur and the Tengyur, often referred to collectively as the "Tibetan Buddhist canon," book production in Tibet achieved a scale of mammoth proportions. From the end of the thirteenth century these volumes were constantly produced for major institutions, with massive economic resources poured into their making.[62] Much of what follows in the ensuing chapters therefore deals with the making of these canons, so before entering into the printing houses, scriptoria, and scholarly workshops of Tibet it will be useful to briefly survey the development of Buddhist canonical collections. The Kangyur contains the Buddha's word in translation, and the Tengyur contains the exegetical treatises in translation. Despite one scholar's insistence that "it would be a triumph of understatement to say that our knowledge of the history of the Tibetan canon is still very imperfect,"[63] the recensional history of the Kangyur—and to a lesser extent the Tengyur—is by now reasonably well known. A handful of scholars have traced the textual history of what has come to be seen as an open and constantly changing canon. From the ninth century to the beginning of the twentieth century, literature translated from Sanskrit and other Indic languages, from Chinese, Korean, and Khotanese has been continually edited, categorized, compiled, reproduced, read, recited, and worshipped. During the first half of the fourteenth century, in the wake of nearly six centuries of translation and transmission of Buddhist literature from India and elsewhere to Tibet, the intertwining processes of collation, authentication, and canonization were in full swing. This was the era of the prolific and indefatigable textual scholar Butön Rinchendrup, who was instrumental in producing Buddhist canonical collections at his institution and home of over three decades, Shalu monastery in Tsang. Recent scholarship has drawn a complex picture of the proliferation of canonical collections from Shalu, based primarily on the text-critical study of the relationships between the various recensions of the collections.[64] One scholar has recently likened the passage of the multitude of Buddhist manuscripts through

Shalu and other monasteries to the shape of an hourglass;[65] at these centers of learning were gathered copies—some commonly available and some very rare—of *sūtras*, tantras, poetic songs, and treatises on logic and epistemology from all around Tibet, and through the efforts of scholars like Butön, they were transformed into a highly organized body of literature that could then, in a manner of speaking, be mass-produced and reintroduced into the region at large.

Much of the intellectual labor of classifying and organizing Indian Buddhist literature in central Tibet was carried out in the two or three generations preceding Butön's maturity at the nearby Nartang monastery. The separation of the Kangyur and the Tengyur into two distinct classes of literature, and thus into two physically separate collections, was by all accounts undertaken by the scholar Chomden Reldri and his students (and perhaps more by them than him) at Nartang in the latter decades of the thirteenth century. This is evident in the vast difference between canonical catalogs produced by this group: in 1268 Chomden Reldri completed a survey of Indian Buddhist literature in Tibetan translation, in which a rigid separation between the word of the Buddha (*bka'*) and the treatises of subsequent Indian Buddhist writers (*bstan bcos*) was not the guiding organizational strategy. Rather, after largely recapitulating the order of two well-known lists from the imperial period of the early ninth century, Chomden organizes his list according to translator. Famous personalities of the past, such as the translator Rinchen Zangpo, take pride of place, with genre playing only a secondary organizational role. It is likely, in fact, that Chomden Reldri was not making a catalog of a new physical collection of literature but rather compiling a list of titles that would eventually form the basis for the production of a canon. Decades later, perhaps in the last decade of the thirteenth or the first decade of the fourteenth century, Chomden Reldri's student Üpa Losel compiled a catalog of Buddhist treatises in translation, quite separate from the *sūtras* and tantras that make up the Buddha's word. This appears to be the first such record of a collection that would become known throughout Tibet as a Tengyur, "treatises in translation." Moreover, it is clear from the reference to volume numbers that Üpa Losel was not merely making a list of titles but actually cataloging a physical collection of books.[66]

With these groundbreaking labors at Nartang monastery forming a basis for the separation of the word of the Buddha from the commentaries and works of his spiritual descendants, the two collections have had very different lives in Tibet from the middle of the fourteenth century to the present. The Kangyur has been by far the more popular of the two, surely because these *sūtras* and tantras are the teachings of the Buddha himself, but perhaps also because the Kangyur is roughly half the size of the Tengyur, making its reproduction a relatively more manageable affair. While Kangyurs have often been produced separately, Tengyurs are almost always produced following on the heels of a Kangyur, as will be seen in the cases of the printed Tengyurs at Degé, Choné, and Nartang throughout the eighteenth century and the Lhasa Kangyur and the (as yet unfinished) Lhasa Tengyur in the twentieth and twenty-first centuries.

The canonical collections known today have retained the basic format and organizational features developed from the late thirteenth to the mid-fourteenth centuries at Nartang and Shalu monasteries. But this is not to say that the Kangyur and Tengyur were static literary relics for the next six hundred years, for neither was ever treated as a closed canon; they were added to, edited, and rearranged constantly as scholars made minor adjustments or major organizational overhauls. Individual texts were reworked, retranslated, or omitted depending on time, place, and the preferences of their many redactors, and whole sections were placed earlier or later in the collections for the same reasons. There are well over twenty independently produced Kangyur redactions, all created at different times and in different regions of Tibet and China, and more are continually coming to light.[67] Although most of these descend in part from efforts of Chomden Reldri and his students at Nartang, each one bears witness to the efforts of local scholars and artisans in terms of content, arrangement, and the physical, or perhaps aesthetic, aspects of the books themselves.[68]

Much of the following deals explicitly with the production of Buddhist canons throughout Tibet over roughly a 500-year period, even when not discussing canon production as such. Readers may therefore wish to review the contents of the Buddhist canons, for this is the principal literature with which the scholars whose stories I recount worked. Because each of the major Kangyurs and Tengyurs differs from the others to a greater or lesser extent, it is not possible to describe an organizational structure that accurately represents all of them. Still, the differences are not absolute, and a single example does reveal much about the Kangyurs and Tengyurs taken as a whole. Appendix 2 offers a sketch of the contents of the Kangyur and Tengyur produced at Degé in the 1730s and '40s. This should provide useful background for what follows, and may also serve as a rough guide to the canons more generally.

FROM CONTENT TO CULTURE

Although it is possible to outline the recensional history and the contents of the Tibetan canonical collections, the actual circumstances of their production—the day-to-day activities that went into the creation of such enormous bodies of Buddhist literature—are far less clear. This book focuses on select moments and places in the centuries-long process of canonical production in order to inquire about the social and cultural significance of these volumes and their manufacture. It does not primarily look to the canons themselves, as a textual critic interested in recension must do, but to biographical, historical, and critical literature by and about the figures involved in their making.

Several chapters focus in part on the ways the editors of Buddhist canons made use of the textual materials at their disposal. In asking what these scholars can narrate in their own words about editorial theory and method, I have two goals: one, far less immediately tangible, is that through a greater appreciation of the practices of Tibetan editors themselves, contemporary scholars may enhance their own efforts in editing—as well as reading—Tibetan literature. For as one theorist of textual scholarship has recently said, "We are . . . part of the long tradition of . . . suspicious readers, and before embarking on the specific task of interrogating a text by producing a scholarly edition, it is as well if we are aware of this tradition, of those readers who have preceded us in the role."[69] But this is secondary to my first goal: to convey a more concrete sense of the production of Tibetan literature and, more generally, of textual scholarship within the social and cultural history of Tibet.

To understand a literary culture such as that of Tibet, where the medium was the handwritten manuscript or hand-carved wood-block print, it is important to examine the many stages that a work may be taken through as it passes from the author's hand (or mouth) to scribes and finally to the xylograph print, for these are, in a very concrete sense, the moments in which the work comes into existence. Of what steps did the actual work of editing, copying, and proofreading consist?[70] If Butön was renowned for his textual scholarship, which included making new translations, revising or editing translated works, and filling in gaps in faulty texts,[71] under what social circumstances and with what material resources did he go about these activities? How many laborers were involved, of what sorts, and how might the systems of management necessary for the successful completion of such a large project have been organized? Further, what significance did the making of a canon hold for its patrons, its readers, its editors and scribes, and the laborer who delivered the paper to the monastery? In short, what does the history of Tibetan Buddhist literature look like on the ground and in the printing house?[72] Such questions shift attention from the canons themselves to the conditions of production and reproduction in which they came into being and were used.

Given such concerns, this study is concerned less with the recension history of the canons—or even with the production of paper or other materials that go into making books (as a historian of technology or an art historian might be)—than with records of such material goods and practices relating to them. It takes mention of material resources—paper, ink, printing, or any other material that makes up the book as a fabricated object—in Tibetan scholarly works to be significant and purposeful, not incidental or casual. When a material object is mentioned in a biography, an autobiography, or a letter, it has passed from the realm of craft—and thereby largely been deemed in Tibetan intellectual circles to be in need of no commentary—and entered the realm of methodological, theoretical, and even theological debate. It has passed from being part of a book to being part of a culture of the book. For in the context of the close link between buddhas and books, paper is an integral part of Buddhist culture. To the religious centers where Buddhist canons were produced flowed vast amounts of intellectual and economic energy that, once transformed, spread back out to the surrounding regions. Wood, paper, and ink were transmuted into the words of the Buddha through a most amazing act of communal religiosity, in communities that brought together—amicably or not—aristocrats, laborers, artists, woodcutters, painters, scholars, hermits. Viewed in this light, the book comes to have a "social life," as the economic and symbolic potential of fabricated objects has recently been characterized.[73] And when the Buddhist canon is considered as an economic product, an object of tribute, or a valid form of tax payment, it may be seen not as a repository of sacred texts or as some rarefied holy object but as an important locus of social and cultural formation and contestation.

With these considerations in mind, in this study of books, their defenders, and their producers in Tibet, the phrase "book culture" delimits a set of representations and practices related to a specific set of materials and technologies. As an object of contemporary academic concern, the book is a rich focal point for the study of history, society, and culture, because this single object (defined for our purposes by that which can be denoted by the terms *dpe cha* and *glegs bam*, or the more recent *deb*) represents material, intellectual, and social values. It is a container of intellectual tradition, a finely crafted work comparable to painting or sculpture (though with its own techniques and traditions of manufacture), a significant commodity within the premodern Tibetan economy, a symbol of Buddhist notions of salvation and soteriology. By combining the term "book" with the term "culture," I seek to highlight possible interrelations among these areas rather than separate them. In other words, the study of the culture of the book in Tibet is the study of discourse about books in the region's history, that discourse's attendant practices, and the communities and institutions formed by that discourse and in which it is debated and contested.[74]

The contours of book culture in Tibet are delineated in part by the well-known ideological significance of volumes of scripture in the Indian Buddhist *Perfection of Wisdom* literature. Here just one passage of this type from the conclusion to the *Perfection of Wisdom in Eight Thousand Lines* may be cited: "Well written, in very distinct letters, in a great book," the *sūtra* speaks of itself. "One should honor, revere, adore, and worship it." "One should know," it continues, "that those beings are living in the presence of the Tathāgata who will hear this *perfection of wisdom*, take it up, study, spread, repeat and write it."[75] These particular lines were quoted by a fifteenth-century theorist of the arts and sciences in a discussion of book arts composed near the time of the *Blue Annals*, but one could cite any number of texts, from the ubiquitous *sūtras* of Dunhuang with their colophons dedicating the merit gained through textual reproduction to various goals, to the great catalogs of printed Kangyurs and Tengyurs of the eighteenth century, in which large-scale state-funded printing projects are justified with *Perfection of Wisdom* rhetoric at great length. Materials and technologies that have a variety of possible uses, such as wood and carving, papermaking, weaving, blacksmithing, writing, and textual editing, are specifically associated with an ideology of salvation, or at the very least an aura of numinous and beneficent power. Yoked with this specific sort of ideological strength, books have a multifaceted social and cultural significance and authority. To begin charting the manifold ways Tibetan writers integrated and transformed this discourse, there is no more perfect character than the editor largely credited with popularizing the broad outlines of the Buddhist canonical collections in Tibet during the early fourteenth century, Butön Rinchendrup of Shalu monastery.

LETTERS TO EDITORS

In the summer of 1364, at the monastery of Shalu in midwestern Tibet, Butön Rinchendrup—scholar, artist, teacher, abbot, and zealous collector of manuscripts containing the word of the Buddha—passed away at the age of seventy-four.[1] During the elaborate rituals of homage and mourning the Kangyur was recited three times. There could have been no more appropriate act of devotion toward Butön, for he had dedicated a large part of his life to the compilation and production of Buddhist canonical collections and had designed the temple at Shalu in which the Kangyur was housed.[2] While his physical remains were distributed as relics throughout Tibet, India, China, and Nepal, the physical manifestations of his scholarly efforts were eventually to spread in the form of the Tibetan Buddhist canons.

Butön's love of learning and his desire to propagate the teachings of the Buddha and the Buddhist masters through textual scholarship—just one facet of his contributions to the spread of Buddhist culture in Tibet—are thematized by his biographer and close disciple Dratsepa Rinchen Namgyel (1318–88) in *A Handful of Flowers*. Dratsepa repeatedly stresses his master's passion for and expertise in such matters. At the age of four or five, he learned to read the Tibetan printed script perfectly under the tutelage of his mother, not by using a spelling guide as seems to have been the norm, but through copying out and thereupon immediately reciting a Buddhist scripture, the *Atajñā Sūtra*.[3] The five-year-old Butön then strove to learn the cursive script, and was so distraught when he could not do so that his patron deity, Mañjughoṣa, showed him favor and blessed him with the ability to read this version of written Tibetan.[4]

Dratsepa elaborates on the theme of textual learning and scholarship in Butön's life story in a number of ways. He evokes visions of a scholar at work amid his entourage: "Even surrounded by all the scribes and creating many different types of translations and compositions, Butön dictated without faltering so that the hand of each scribe was not empty."[5] In particular, he focuses on the increasing importance of editorial activities for Butön. In 1332 he was called upon in a vision by the master of the Sakya school, Jetsün Drakpa Gyeltsen (1147–1216), who urged Butön not only to compose commentaries on the *sūtras* and tantras but also to "Edit the word of the Buddha and the treatises in general, and the tantras in particular." Drakpa Gyeltsen lamented to Butön that he had not been able to complete his own efforts: "Earlier I thought to edit my own works, but I did not finish. Now you must edit them."[6] Butön took his Sakyapa ancestor's injunction to heart, placing editorial work at the center of his scholarly activities. Dratsepa later praises his master's work as a mature scholar in his fifties, writing: "Through translation and editorial work he has grown the magnificent life-giving tree, the foundation of the Buddhist teachings."[7] Indeed, references to books, editing, translating, and textual scholarship abound not only in this biography by Dratsepa but also in songs in praise of Butön by later Tibetans. Writing in 1485, Shakya Chokden (1428–1507) eulogizes Butön for editing the words of the Buddha anew and for setting the Himalayas ablaze with the light of the Buddha's kindness by producing canonical volumes.[8]

Just three years prior to his death, Butön exhorted Dratsepa to undertake the editorial revision of several of his own manuscripts, with concern that the work he had initiated at Shalu monastery continue, and, it sounds, with an almost manic concern that his reputation as a textual scholar not be tarnished after his death. Dratsepa relates how, in a short-tempered mood, his mentor issued these words of warning to him: "My own collection of manuscripts—the grammatical and tantric works—must be brought to completion, [for] if I should die, when scholars and peers look at them they will say, 'These manuscripts of his were not even edited once!' and they will scoff. When the ignorant look at them, they will scurry about as if their bladders are filled with urine!"[9]

It is perhaps fitting, then, that one of the earliest and most detailed works describing the process of editing and copying Buddhist manuscripts in Tibet presently known is a brief letter written by Butön. The two-page letter, containing detailed instructions to the "virtuous friends," the *kalyāṇamitras*—the editors-in-chief, if you will—and distinguished scholars overseeing a manuscript-copying project, is undated and contains no proper names. Though it is impossible to say with certainty to whom Butön addressed his instructions, it is quite likely that he was in correspondence with managers in charge of copying the reorganized Tengyur at Shalu monastery. In the catalog to this Tengyur, Butön recounts that in mid–1334 the secular ruler of the Shalu region, the nobleman Kushang Kunga Döndrup,[10] funded the project and "invited the most learned scribes in the regions of Central and Mid-western Tibet." Three *kalyāṇamitras*, Shakya Sengé, Darma Jangchup, and Shönu Pel, thus came to Shalu to oversee the endeavor.[11] In all likelihood, these same scholar-craftsmen, in charge of instructing and managing the workers involved, were the initial recipients of Butön's letter.[12]

IN THE SCRIBAL WORKSHOP

This small correspondence provides a window into the workshop of the creators of a collection of Buddhist literature that would exert a profound impact on the history of Buddhism in Tibet for the next six hundred years, and it therefore repays a close look. The letter is terse and moves quickly from topic to topic, as a reading of it with commentary illustrates well. Butön styles his letter "An appeal to the ear of virtuous friends, the religious stewards and distinguished scholars who are producing the great treatises, and a request that you work in accordance with the instructions I have given," and he makes the first of several calls for scholarly rigor: "Through looking them over sufficiently, the guidelines of my advice will come fully to distinguished scholars. Take them to heart; it is extremely important that those distinguished scholars listen." After these firm yet conciliatory remarks, Butön moves quickly to a detailed description of the process of emending problematic passages in manuscripts the scribes and proofreaders were copying and editing.

Here, as in the rest of the letter, he offers polite instructions to the *kalyāṇamitras* on how to direct the workforce of scribes and proofreaders. Many types of manuscripts would have been gathered to the scriptorium at Shalu: some old and brittle, some abounding in spelling mistakes, some in barely legible scribal hands, and some perhaps exquisitely penned in gold ink upon black paper. Some of these would have been well edited and would have required little editorial effort from the scribes and scholars of Shalu; others would have required more drastic intervention, in which case Butön advises the chief editors to "have [the scribes] insert missing words to be added in [their] original place; affix a paper patch right upon that [spot] on the thin paper [of the original manuscript, and] write upon that [patch]." It is clear that Butön upheld a strict set of aesthetic guidelines concerning the look of the written page, guidelines that were inextricably connected with orthographic issues such as the dense contraction words that so plague editors. "Do not write contractions," he continues. "Even those [contractions] present in the original [manuscript] should be expanded. In spots where insertions of missing words are needed, repeatedly look over each small passage [of text] previous [to those spots] when you proofread." These aesthetic guidelines extend to the page layout more generally, for scribes must attend to the margins of the page ("See whether or not the small marginal numbers and notations are legible, and have [the workers] insert [them] so as to make those that are illegible or unintelligible, intelligible") as well as to the line as a coherent visual unit ("See whether or not the size of the letters and the slash and dot [punctuation marks] are consistently spaced, and whether or not each line contains 115 to 120 letters. Please instruct [the scribes] that incomplete [lines] must be written out completely").

Butön then touches on several points quickly, all having to do with the copying and checking of the newly created manuscripts. When overseeing a copying project, scribal managers should "instruct the writers of printing-style letters to make [them] small, complete, joined, and firmly printed." In addition, they should tell "the writers of cursive letters to make [them] such that they don't exceed proper orthographic dimensions, [to make them] smooth, generally even, and correctly spelled." When a manuscript has been copied, it must be proofread, an oral process that involves collaboration between a reader intoning the text out loud and scribes listening and reading along. Butön briefly touches on this, informing his audience that "During proofreading, [the text] should be read out loud slowly and with clarity by the recitator, and the scribes should certify that reading with the certifier in between work [periods]. At the end of completed texts [the scribes] should write a full [record of certification]. Please instruct [the workers] to make no omissions or additions."[13]

At this point Butön enters into detailed discussion regarding the proper punctuation of the new manuscripts. He is concerned with employing punctuation for major divisions of a given work or to separate clearly commentarial passages from primary text, or *sūtra* passages. According to Butön, two primary divisions are used in canonical literature: "[The text division called] *bam po* marks the beginning [of a section], and the [text division called] *le'u* marks the end [of a section], and therefore [these cases] require a blank space." Within the passages set off by these breaks, scribes must be able to divide the text clearly using only a few punctuation marks: "Please instruct [the workers] to make a detailed analysis of the [punctuation marks:] single slash, double slash, quadruple slash, and the dot-and-slash." These must be used to mark different registers of language, such as verse, prose, and quoted material, and Butön would have scribes "add a double slash after such phrases as 'In the *sūtra* . . .' and after the completion of root verses [within a commentary]." Further, they should add them "in between commentary and a second [quote from the root verses], [after] phrases such as 'So it is said . . .,' [and after] reduplicated letters." Finally, scribes should "add a dot-and-slash in between commentarial words following those [root verses]." It is not clear whether Butön is describing a system of punctuation already well established or prescribing a system that might strike his contemporaries as innovative. However, a style of punctuation and page layout like this was to prevail for hundreds of years after his time.[14] One has only to look at the page layout of the edition of Butön's collected works published in the early twentieth century under the auspices of the Thirteenth Dalai Lama to see that the parameters laid down at Shalu were in many ways definitive until the broad deployment of Tibetan moveable type in the mid-twentieth century.

Following this discussion, Butön devotes a single sentence to the hermeneutics of textual emendation; this hints that the editorial process known in classical scholarship as conjectural emendation was in use in fourteenth-century Tibet as well. Butön advises the editors that "Since an understanding of the word and the meaning are dependent upon one another, when some doubt arises, understand the meaning from the word by looking at [the word] analytically, and the [correct] graph will be understood from the meaning." In other words, the text should make sense, and if it does not the editor is encouraged to emend it in accordance with his reasoned understanding of what the text *should* say. The act of editing was for Butön an act of personal interpretation, at least in part. This method no doubt led to many problems, and not a few anonymous editors have been accused of fabricating meanings in their efforts at conjectural emendation. Indeed, one of the most serious charges against authors and editors alike is that the texts they produce are self-made (*rang bzo*), and therefore not in accordance with tradition. Butön's positive assessment of conjectural emendation constitutes a significant difference between him and many later editors, who considered it to be a major source of textual error.

Butön's letter next addresses the proper writing of Sanskrit mantras in the Tibetan script, asking editors to "distinguish the orthography of [Sanskrit] mantras from that of Tibetan. Also, write the long and short [vowels] and the aspirated and unaspirated [consonants] in mantras with no mistakes, according to the manner adhered to in each individual *sādhana* evocation ritual." "Don't," he concludes somewhat cryptically, "make the mistake of patterning your hat after your boot!" Here it appears that Butön was concerned that each tradition of *sādhana*, or the ritual of deity evocation, retain the proper pronunciation of its unique mantra, so as not to vitiate the efficacy of the ritual. As on paper, so in the spoken word of the ritual performance; for Butön it was vital that the scribes write down these "words of power" according to exacting traditional specifications, the intricacies of which he no doubt knew well, having himself compiled nearly 350 mantras.[15] "Don't pattern your hat after your boot" stresses by analogy the importance to the scribe of not taking just any *sādhana* (a boot) as the model for the mantra at hand (the hat).[16] And for those looking for a correct model, Butön dispenses some advice: "Since there are many different manuals on spelling, work according to the correct [manuals] I have composed as well as the *Imperial Decree* and *Gyelzang*[17] [linguistic guides]. Though there are correct [instructions] in all manuals, since there is the possibility for incorrect [points] in even the best spellers, [they] are not reliable."

Although Butön here shows a fairly ecumenical distrust for all manuals but his own, he does give precedence to those developed under imperial patronage in central Tibet during the early ninth century. "Imperial decree" (*bka' bcad* or *bkas bcad*) refers to both the *Mahāvyutpatti* (*Bye brag tu rtogs par byed pa*) and its commentary, the *Madhyavyutpatti* (*Sgra sbyor bam po gnyis pa*),[18] but also has a wider definition that includes three periods of translation and revision. The *Li shi'i gur khang*[19] of Kyogtön Rinchen Tashi (c. 1495–after 1577)[20] divided early Tibetan translation history into three periods of imperial patronage and direction: that of King Trisong Detsen; that of King Tri Relpachen; and that of the west Tibetan King Lha Lama Yeshé Ö.[21] We can trace this scheme—and indeed the entire passage devoted to the three imperial decrees in the *Li shi'i gur khang*—to the end of the thirteenth century; writing a generation before Butön, Chomden Reldri (1227–1305) describes the three imperial decrees in his treatise on linguistics.[22] It is possible that Butön also had in mind this wider sense of *bkas bcad* as the major historiographic periods of translation when he used the term in his instructions. It continued to have significance in literature on the language arts in the following centuries. Writing in 1514, Butön's scholarly descendant Shalu Lotsawa Chökyong Zangpo (1441–1527) also refers to the imperial decree in the concluding verses of his own influential linguistic survey, where he appears to mix both senses of the term.[23] Centuries later Longdöl Lama Ngawang Losang (1719–94) uses the term with yet a different implication, though still related to book production. He refers to an imperial decree by the "dharma kings" of Tibet stating that large scriptural volumes should be written in large, headed letters (*dbu can*), the standard printed script; Indian treatises in a mid-sized script; and Tibetan treatises in a small script.[24] The notion that the conventions of textual production hailed back to imperial mandate was thus long-standing, and Shalu monastery holds a central position in this tradition.

Butön then takes a step back from the intricacies of the copying and proofreading process to address the realities of managing a work team, in which there was an unambiguous hierarchy of labor. Schedules were firmly enforced, managers were given leave to mete out punishments as they saw fit, and scribes were compelled to work quickly yet required to uphold a high standard of quality. Butön warns: "Again, for every single letter have [the workers] make a detailed inspection." (In an apparent aside, he also orders that the old colophons should be replaced by new ones, thereby erasing the previous history of individual manuscripts collected at Shalu in favor of a more formalized presentation: "Please instruct them to write new writer's colophons, and to not write the old [colophons], even if patrons wrote them"). And when workers do not meet expectations, they should be reprimanded, for "if [the scribes] are not producing letters both distinct and complete, or if they are not listening to instructions, the religious steward must have a word with them." If scribes are not receptive to changes, they should be docked pay: "Kindly inform the scribes and proofreaders of the scriptorium that the fine will be half an ounce of tea if they do not come in when the break-time bell has sounded."

Finally, Butön once again stresses the importance of their task as well as the magnitude of the undertaking. He concludes, "In short: this is not just writing down some village family's little *sūtra*. These are the manuscripts of the Nobleman [of Shalu], and therefore care is vital for everyone. Great efforts should go into attaining provisions [for the workers]. Since we will handsomely provide wages and bonuses afterward as befits the qualifications [of the different workers], care is vital for everyone, so very vital. Be well." Clearly for Butön the production of a manuscript version of the Buddhist canon was big business, and everyone must act accordingly. Once again the letter provides a unique glimpse into the social aspects of book production, for from these last passages one can infer several things. First, the craftsmen were generally respected, at least to the extent that they were paid well upon the completion of their duties. This accords with other prescriptions regarding the treatment of scribes and craftsmen involved in producing canonical literature.[25] Disciplinary problems were not unknown in the scriptorium, however, and one wonders to what extent such reprimands as the docking of tea were enforced. Second, Butön clearly considered this manuscript canon to be the property of Kushang Kunga Döndrup, the ruler of the Shalu region, not that of the monastery or its abbot. The canon belonged to the patron. Finally, in addition to large-scale manuscript copying enterprises such as this, there was also an economy of local, household book making, in which the "little *sūtras* of village families" were copied. It is likely that many of the scribes in the scriptorium at Shalu were employed in such small-scale ventures when not working on canonical projects backed by heavy patronage.

Butön does not mention every type of craftsman who would have been involved in this enterprise. Fortunately a longer list of workers is available: a Tengyur catalog composed 28 years after Butön completed his own project. Beginning June 8, 1362 and finishing November 4 of the same year, three scholars directed a group of craftsmen at Shalu under the patronage of the Phagmodru leader Tai Situ Jangchup Gyeltsen (1304–64). The catalog mentions directors (*zhal ta ba*), scribal managers (*yig gnyer ba*), proofreaders (*zhus dag pa*), chief scribes (*gtso bo yig mkhan*) (also known as "distinguished scholars," the same appellation given

to the recipients of Butön's letter), papermakers (*shog bzo ba*),
engravers (*rkos mkhan*) (presumably working on the book covers), goldsmiths who worked on the book covers (*gdong rkos kyi
gser bzo mkhan*), page numberers (*grangs yig pa*), collators (*gras
mkhan*), book-strap makers (*sku rags mkhan*), and blacksmiths
who made the buckles for the straps (*sku rags kyi chab ma'i mgar
ba*).[26] There is also no specific number of workers listed in Butön's
letter, but based upon other projects at the time, it seems likely
that the workforce ran into the hundreds. To cite one example
from the fourteenth century: sometime between 1354 and 1363,
Chökyi Gyelpo (1335–1407), the tenth abbot of Drikung monastery, employed 400 scribes to create a Kangyur for his establishment.[27] Again, this was big business, in which a workforce the
size of a large village could be employed for months at a time.

Neither does Butön reveal much about the primary materials
used to make these volumes of scripture—the paper and ink that
were to embody the word of the Buddha. From other sources it
is apparent that throughout the fourteenth century in Utsang,
Kangyur and Tengyur manuscripts were made with both black
ink on white paper and gold or silver ink on blue-black paper, and
it is tempting to think that the canons at Zhalu were produced
with similar materials. Butön himself had three *Prajñāpāramitā*
works made with gold lettering sometime between 1332 and
1344.[28] According to Tselpa Kunga Dorjé, in the winter of 1335,
Karma pa III Rangjung Dorjé (1284–1339) donated the materials
for, commissioned, and consecrated a "golden Tengyur"—that is,
a manuscript with gold lettering on dark blue or black paper—at
Tsel.[29] This would have been just one year after Butön completed
the Tengyur at Shalu. Between 1314 and 1334 the ninth abbot of
Drikung, Dorjé Gyelpo (1284–1351), is said to have produced
many *sūtra* and *vinaya* collections in gold ink on blue-black paper.[30] During a three-month period in 1389 the tenth abbot of Drikung, Chökyi Gyelpo, completed a Tengyur and a set of Kagyupa
hagiographies written in black ink on white paper.[31] A colophon
from the Tselpa Kangyur (as preserved in the Litang Kangyur)
completed in 1349, just fourteen years after Butön's Tengyur, provides a brief vivid description of the materials used; the paper
was soft and white like the base of a conch, and the bright and
clear ink from China was the color of a blue lotus.[32] Finally, the
verse catalog of the Kangyur completed in 1431 at Gyantsé under the sponsorship of Situ Rapten Kunzang Pakpa (1389–1442)
tells that Kunzang Pakpa commissioned black-on-white and

gold-on-black Kangyurs as well as a black-on-white Tengyur.[33] The aesthetic qualities of such volumes were important to their makers and patrons, but were also important enough as symbolic elements that later historians saw fit to include such details in accounts of their Buddhist past.

Although it is difficult to trace the specific influence of this letter on later editors, a few examples from biographical literature will suffice to show that the influence of Butön as a model textual scholar and bibliophile was great. For example, Bodong Panchen Choklé Namgyel (1375–1451) was said to have received a visionary exhortation by Butön to compose his massive *Compendium of Knowledge*.[34] Two sections of the *Compendium*, the *Introduction for Novices* and the *Explanation on Creating the Three Supports [of the Dharma] According to the Treatises*, contain brief but detailed descriptions of the scribe's craft and its materials.[35] In the fifteenth and sixteenth centuries the great editor and textual scholar of Shalu and Pelkor Dechen, Shalu Lotsawa Chökyong Pelzangpo, carried on the tradition of Butön, both as abbot of Shalu and as a well-known editor and translator of scripture. Writing in 1517, his student and biographer, Kyogtön Lotsawa Rinchen Tashi, relates that he performed the duties of the abbatial see just as described in Butön's *Testament of Advice to Abbots*. He frequently read Butön's testaments (*bka' chems*) to the community at Shalu.[36] Though there appears to be no reference to Butön's letter to editors in Shalu Lotsawa's biography, these small testaments are located in Butön's collected works very close to the letter (at least in the Lhasa edition), suggesting that Shalu Lotsawa in all likelihood knew of and read it as well. In a touching aside, Rinchen Tashi Lodrö reveals that his master wept when reading of the death of Butön in Dratsepa's biography.[37] It is thus clear that both the teachings and the life story of Butön had enormous impact on Shalu Lotsawa's development as a scholar and institutional leader. How this impact was portrayed by Shalu Lotsawa's biographer will be a subject of the following chapter.

Butön's letter also caught the eye of later scholars such as Yongdzin Yeshé Gyeltsen (1713–93),[38] who in 1779 made specific reference to it in his catalog of the edition of Butön's collected works kept at Tashi Samten Ling monastery in Kyirong, far to the southwest. The fact that Yeshé Gyeltsen explicitly mentions the letter is significant, for he does not list the rest of Butön's many epistles separately. This suggests that Yeshé Gyeltsen held the letter to be of particular importance in relation to the others in this section.[39] That he names it is all the more significant in light of the fact that earlier catalogs of Butön's collected works by Dratsepa and Butön himself do not mention it.[40] Further evidence that Yeshé Gyeltsen relied explicitly upon Butön's scholarly efforts is to be found in a fascinating passage from the biography of Yeshé Gyeltsen by the Eighth Dalai Lama, Jampel Gyatso (1758–1804).[41] In 1792, during his last year as tutor to the Dalai Lama (and the last year of his life), Yeshé Gyeltsen undertook the editing of Tsongkhapa Lobsang Drakpa's (1357–1419) commentary on the difficult points in the *Pradīpodyotana* commentary of the *Guhyasamāja Tantra*.[42] According to the Eighth Dalai Lama, copies of Tsongkhapa's commentary existed at both Tashilhunpo and Drepung monasteries, though unfortunately they had many orthographic errors introduced by bad practices: broken verses, commentarial annotations confused with lines of the basic text, faulty punctuation, and unclear word separation. Yeshé Gyeltsen set about creating a corrected edition of Tsongkhapa's work with methods comparable to those of Butön. First he collected a number of witnesses, including many old prints of the *Guhyasamāja Tantra* itself and old xylograph prints of the *Pradīpodyotana* from the monasteries of Drepung, Tashilhunpo, Riwo Dangchen, and Nartang. He utilized a number of Tibetan commentaries, including one by Butön.[43] He also used a manuscript copy of the *Guhyasamāja Tantra* believed to be the actual manuscript of Tsongkhapa himself, as well as a manuscript belonging to the Seventh Dalai Lama, Kelsang Gyatso (1708–57). To correct grammatical errors Yeshé Gyeltsen used the basic Tibetan grammatical treatises attributed to the imperial linguist Tönmi Sambhota (*Sum rtags*, or *Sum cu pa* and *Rtags kyi 'jug pa*) and unidentified commentaries upon them. He "eliminated the orthographic errors that had been mixed in with and corrupted the Buddha's teachings," and he "edited the tantra itself, as well as Tsongkhapa's smaller commentary."[44]

Like Butön's efforts at Shalu monastery, Yeshé Gyeltsen's textual production went beyond purely editorial concerns to the physical qualities of the finished volume. Yet where Butön created finely crafted books for the nobleman of Shalu, Yeshé Gyeltsen created them for his pupil and leader, the Eighth Dalai Lama. "As a visual aid and meditation support," Yeshé Gyeltsen had the *Tantra* itself, the *Pradīpodyotana*, and Tsongkhapa's two commentaries bound in a single ornate volume written in gold ink on good black paper. This "specially produced" volume was covered in silk brocade; had a title flap of well-aged material and book boards with the eight auspicious symbols written upon them in gold ink; and was bound by a silk strap with a silver buckle. Linking editorial activity, book production, patronage, and the power attributed to finely crafted volumes of scripture, the Eighth Dalai Lama states that Yeshé Gyeltsen's finished volume is "a visual aid for us, aglow with the luster of blessings." Yeshé Gyeltsen's choice to reproduce Tsongkhapa's commentaries is interesting in light of the fact that the earliest known printed works in central Tibet were prepared by Tsongkhapa himself between 1418 and 1419, and were none other than the *Guhyasamāja Tantra* and the *Pradīpodyotana*.[45] Could they have been among the prints at Drepung? And yet, even in the "golden age" of Tibetan xylograph printing during the eighteenth century, Yeshé Gyeltsen produced a handwritten manuscript of his editions. This four-part volume was not, after all, intended for mass dissemination, but as an ornate and unique offering to the Eighth Dalai Lama. The close connection between the aesthetics of book production and patronage first encountered in Butön's letter to editors in the mid-fourteenth century was alive and well four centuries later, at the close of the eighteenth century.

Instructions to editors and scribes continued to be produced in the centuries following the making of the canon at Shalu monastery. Works such as Desi Sangyé Gyatso's 1681 *Clear Crystal Mirror: A Guideline for Clarifying Regulations and Prohibitions in Twenty-One [Chapters]* contain instructions to court scribes on the proper writing, editing, and rewriting of official documents, making evident that talk of scribal practice was not limited to the monastery scriptorium.[46] The production of canonical volumes also merited continuing advice throughout the centuries, as another letter shows. It was composed almost 300 years after Butön's by the twenty-fifth abbot of Drikung monastery, Chökyi Drakpa, who served as the leader of that central Tibetan institution from 1626 to his death in 1659.[47] Twelve papermakers and 110 scribes labored throughout 1640 to produce a Kangyur in 120 volumes. The collection was catalogued by Chökyi Drakpa and included 13 volumes of *vinaya*, 36 volumes of *Perfection of Wisdom* literature (counting the four-volume *Avataṃsaka* and the six-volume *Ratnakūṭa* collections), 32 volumes of *sūtras*, 18 volumes of "new tantras," two volumes of spells, one volume of mantras, and 20 volumes of "ancient tantras."[48] Butön would likely not have been party to the production of so many tantras

of the Nyingma school, but this Drikung Kangyur reflected the
synthesis of old and new schools of thought that had taken place
by the mid-seventeenth century. Butön and Chökyi Drakpa did
share a passion for textual scholarship and, like Butön several
centuries before him, Chökyi Drakpa provided instructions to
his chief scribes on the art of managing a scriptorium. This short
work is titled "Guidelines for Chief scribes During the Production of a Kangyur" in Chökyi Drakpa's collected works.[49] He
writes that his audience must "have certainty in their minds"
when they conduct their work, for while "the worldly goods are
of high value" and thus "the fool will look at nothing but the style
of its pleasing form," this Drikung Kangyur must also serve as "a
visual ornament of the teaching in the future." In this capacity it
must "be suitable as an original" to be copied itself at a later date.
To this end, the material features of the volumes must be of the
highest quality, and the editing within the volumes must also be
"a complete delight to the scholar possessed of an intelligent and
discriminating eye."

In particular, the managing scribes must be continually vigi-
lant for writing too hastily jotted down and therefore "without
good form and clean manner." They should ensure that the
scribes under them are fully aware that "white and black must be
balanced; the copy [must] follow after the original. Letters that
are spaced too wide should be clumped in the copy, and clumped
[letters] in the original should be slightly spaced." To this end,
Chökyi Drakpa stresses the details of proper orthography:

> For every seven letters, there [should be] no space or cramping.
> Do not confuse [letters] with no crooks or curves for straight [let-
> ters], there should be no unknown contractions proliferating from
> the regularity of individual letters. Especially, while the reverse i
> [vowel] is not possible in Tibetan, thinking of space consider-
> ations, scribes execute them in some original [manuscripts]; but
> do not do them in this case. Place the i, u, and o [vowels] above
> the actual letter [of] significance. . . . Account for [each] space, and
> do not make confusion. Except where small syllables are inserted
> as a group, do not insert omissions.

Like Butön, Chökyi Drakpa offers clear instructions for punctuation marks,[50] but he then segues to a trenchant sermon on the
ethos of scribal work. He cautions, "Even those who know writing should not become arrogant and careless, and should write

after investigating the meaning of the word." Young scribes who
are not learned in orthography "should not write according to
what appears to be a suitable example, but should ask those who
are experienced and then write." And every scribe, regardless
of experience, "should not simply copy whatever is in the original, but analyze the meaning of the words and only then write it
down." If they are not able to decide upon a reasonable textual
emendation, they should exercise a judiciously light editorial
hand: "Where some doubtful passages occur in the original, do
not write what you cannot figure out on the paper; just leave it as
in the original."[51] Here Chökyi Drakpa argues for a more conser-
vative editorial policy than the conjectural emendation allowed
by Butön.

If scribes are unable to follow these general guidelines in their
work, they run the risk of fulfilling the promise of a bit of folk
wisdom cited by Chökyi Drakpa: "For the most part scribes are
executioners of the Buddhist teaching!" Therefore, if they write
down scripture in haste and with inaccuracy, people will surely
forsake Buddhism when they hear or see such inferior products. They will think of the teachings only as a set of rules to be
obeyed, just as "the young listen to the words of the old and consider them to be like regulations from some old work foreman."
This in turn will lead, Chökyi Drakpa warns, to a more general
state of moral and social decay, in which "internal and external
preparations are not made, there is fighting over material items,
[people are] drunk, abusive, and unruly. What is more important
than to perform these in the proper way?" he asks rhetorically.
And with the very foundations of Buddhist society based upon
the properly executed volume of scripture, what scribe, what editor, would dare to produce sloppy work?

Aside from the provocative picture of life in a scriptorium
sketched out in these small letters, what strikes the reader is the
vehemence with which both Butön and Chökyi Drakpa impart
their at times rather technical instructions on the details of working with texts. This passion may have been motivated in part by
the importance of such craftsmanship for the preservation and
propagation of Buddhist literature, Buddhist doctrine, in Tibet. Editing, proofreading, and copying was for Butön religious
work, as important as the painting of mandalas or the construction of *stūpas*, both of which he was involved in as well. His work
in the planning of murals can be fruitfully compared with his
instructions to editors; in both cases he appears to have been a

sort of executive producer more than a hands-on craftsman.[52]
Manuscript production was a practical manifestation of the second of the triad of foundations for Buddhist religious life—the
foundations for the enlightened body (*sku rten*), speech (*gsung rten*), and mind (*thugs rten*) of the Buddha himself, manifested
in statues, scriptures, and *stūpas* respectively—and for this reason, as Butön states at the close of his letter, in editing, "Care is
vital for everyone, so very vital." His zeal for developing rules for
scriptoria bears comparison with the emphatically prescriptive
verses in praise of the early medieval European scriptorium by
Alcuin (c. 735–904), central figure of the Carolingian renaissance
under Charlemagne: "May those who copy the pronouncements
of the holy law and the hallowed sayings of the saintly Fathers sit
here. Here let them take care not to insert their vain words, lest
their hands make mistakes through such foolishness. Let them
resolutely strive to produce emended texts and may their pens fly
along the correct path."[53]

In Butön's letter—but not in that of Chökyi Drakpa—there
is another, perhaps more immediate reason for careful work,
namely that the manuscripts, indeed the whole venture, were in
fact the property of the Lord of the Manor at Shalu. At the close
of the letter, just where one might expect a call for treating the
sacred word of the Buddha with respect, there is instead a call to
treat the property of the one who is meting out the wages with all
the respect that such an employer deserves! In broad terms, the
importance Butön places on ownership resonates well with the
notion that for the rulers of Tibet "possession of the canon signified the incorporation into the monarch's domain of the well-ordered empire of enlightened reason."[54] For Chökyi Drakpa, a
poorly produced book signified a poorly ordered moral universe.
And from Butön's letter it is clear that he did much more than
add a thousand works to the emerging Tengyur, the achievement
for which he has been primarily known; he developed, or at the
very least clearly articulated, an aesthetic for canonical volumes.
Moreover, this drive for aesthetic sophistication and symmetry
was directly related to both patronage (for Butön) and social welfare (for Chökyi Drakpa).[55]

Butön's letter illustrates that a broad spectrum of concerns—
economic, religious, social, and personal—played a role in his
plea for fine and detailed work. In this fascinating undertaking
of 1334, we witness an interface among several spheres of Buddhist life: scholastic and practical arts, devotional practice, and

the economic importance of the patron–patronized relationship. Beginning with the written letter on paper and spiraling outward from this material foundation in expanding circles of religious practice and social life, the letters of Butön and Chökyi Drakpa provide a rare glimpse into the realities of Buddhist book production in traditional Tibet, and more broadly into Buddhist literature in its most physical sense. And if these missives focus overmuch on the work of the scribe and the editor and less on a portrait of the textual scholar himself, the story of the famous translator Shalu Lotsawa Chökyong Zangpo, detailed in the next chapter, does the opposite. But before turning to Shalu Lotsawa's portrait, it may be useful to hear from other intellectual descendents of scholars such as Butön, to gain a different perspective on the editorial issues highlighted in the letters to editors.

THE WORK OF COLLECTED WORKS

The collected works of Jamyang Shepé Dorjé I, Ngawang Tsondrü (1648–1721), the well-known founder of Labrang Tashikyil monastery in Amdo, provide an excellent opportunity to expand upon the issues of Tibetan editorial practice raised so far, though in a more restricted context—the works of a single author—and in a different region of Tibet, the northeastern area of Amdo.[56] The ready availability of fine exemplars of Jamyang Shepé Dorjé's writings is due to the great efforts of the scholars and craftsmen at Labrang Tashikyil, who were involved in collecting and editing manuscripts and carving wood blocks for the ordered presentation and printing of his *Collected Works*. The practices by which the editors of such collections brought individual works from singular manuscript to block-printed collection are important for our understanding the form of the texts available to contemporary readers, as well as for twenty-first century scholars editing the texts of Buddhist authors writing in the seventeenth and eighteenth centuries. Unlike Büton and Chökyi Drakpa, these editors did not leave letters describing their editorial practices and prescribing those of others. They did, however, provide glimpses of their techniques in the printing colophons at the close of many of the works they edited.[57] From these brief passages, lodged in the cracks of Jamyang Shepé Dorjé's literary corpus, a rich sense of these practices may be gathered.

The Tashikyil wood-block redaction of the *Collected Works* includes approximately 143 individually titled works, totaling 6,343 folios, or 12,686 separately carved wood-block sides. The exact date on which this rather large printing project (larger than the total output of Lhatsün Rinchen Namgyel at Drakar Taso—summarized in the next chapter—yet much smaller than the massive Tibetan Buddhist canonical collections) was inaugurated is difficult to pin down, though based on evidence internal to the colophons it appears to have taken place sometime after 1758, no less than 37 years after the death of Jamyang Shepé Dorjé, and sometime before 1791, the year Jamyang Shepé Dorjé II, Könchog Jigmé Wangpo (1728–91) passed away. This was not the first time that works of Jamyang Shepé Dorjé were carved into blocks, however; several of his larger writings were block-printed sometime before 1738 by his student and successor, Trichen Ngawang Tashi (1678–1738).[58] Some 20 colophons form a rather rich source from which to sketch the editorial labors leading to the block printing of his works. These include notices written by the editors, the scribes, and the author himself. They provide information on where, when, and how the works were composed; how they achieved their final form before block printing; and the individuals involved in the often difficult process of bringing a work from composition to print.

Jamyang Shepé Dorjé appears to have actually written down the majority of his works himself. If we can judge from his detailed work on the history and practice of composing letters, as well as the etiquette of sending and receiving written correspondence, he was in his day considered an authority on the art of writing.[59] The Mongolian scholar Alasha Ngawang Tendar (1759–c. 1839) informs us that Labrang Tashikyil monastery was well known for developing a widely used style of cursive writing, and it is probable that Jamyang Shepé Dorjé I stands at the beginning of this tradition.[60] His skill in writing and reading was certainly not taken for granted by his successors, as is clear from the small anecdote about his formative years related by Könchok Jigmé Wangpo, who writes: "When the Master had reached seven years of age, his uncle, the monk Sönam Lhündrup, who was proficient in reading of all types, took the youth on his lap and taught him the alphabet. [The Master] said, 'You don't know how to teach! Write out a sample, and I'll study it.' Everyone was horrified that he said this, but [his uncle] the monk wrote out a sample and he studied it, and within the day he knew the alphabet pretty well. In no time at all he became adept in all reading and writing."[61]

The works of Jamyang Shepé Dorjé largely constituted a textually based literary corpus from the moment of their composition to the final printed product, as suggested by the fact that many of the colophons employ verbs that specifically mean "writing." His was not an oral tradition; primary authority resided in the manuscript, not the spoken word.[62] Given this fact, the crucial prerequisite of the editorial task was the acquisition of an autograph manuscript penned by Jamyang Shepé Dorjé himself on which to base all editorial decisions. In cases where no autograph was forthcoming, the search was extended to manuscripts written down by Jamyang Shepé Dorjé's immediate disciples, such as Trichen Ngawang Tashi. The autograph did not wield carte blanche authority, however, for several of the colophons tell of corrupt original manuscripts that were in need of emendation.

Within this editorial process Jamyang Shepé Dorjé himself was in some cases the editor of his own work, transforming earlier drafts and proofreading his earlier writings. The three versions of his famous *Explication of Philosophical Tenets*[63] and the two versions of the eighth chapter of his commentary on the *Abhisamayālaṃkāra*[64] are good examples of this. The subsequent value placed on Jamyang Shepé Dorjé's editorial efforts is evident from the fact that the compilers of his *Collected Works* included these multiple versions at all, rather than choosing what they considered to be the best text and relegating the others to posterity. Finally, it is apparent from his edition of the *Amarakośa* that he also had a hand in revising, updating, and editing the translations and philological efforts of other scholars. The remainder of the chapter will analyze first the colophons written by Jamyang Shepé Dorjé himself (the *mdzad byang*) and second the print colophons written by editors (the *par byang*).

The corpus of Jamyang Shepé Dorjé's works was not, as some Tibetan literature is or claims to be, an oral corpus first and only a written collection second. Writing came first. Of 143 separately titled works in the *Collected Works*, 106 have authorial colophons, and of these 39 use the word "written" (*bris pa*) to refer to the way the work was created.[65] An additional 10 include editorial colophons that make clear that the work was penned by Jamyang Shepé Dorjé himself, while two colophons use the phrase "put into writing" (*yi ger bkod pa*). Thus no less than 50, or well more than one third, of the works are explicitly said to have been composed in a written format, whereas a mere eight works are specifically said to have been spoken (*gsungs pa* or *smras pa*), or perhaps dictated, by the master. Though very few of these colophons tell us anything more about his composition habits, several phrases are quite suggestive and worthy of note.

The first of these mentions that Jamyang Shepé Dorjé "jotted works down quickly."[66] Another claims that on one occasion he "extemporaneously composed" a liturgical manual for the benefit of his many students.[67] We also find him writing during the intermission of a musical performance.[68] In several colophons he refers to his works as notes or drafts (*zin bris*), and once as rough notes (*gsung rjen zin bris*).[69] Notes are used as an aid to memory, as when he jots down the words of past masters (*zin bris su btab pa*)[70] for fear of their being forgotten. Such notes and hastily written works could form the basis for further and more refined writings, as for instance when our author first checks (*zhus gtugs*) earlier Tibetan manuals and Indic texts regarding the old ritual cycle known as the *One Hundred Rituals of Bari Lotsawa*, making notes (*zin bris byas pa*) and subsequently writing down the rituals (*sug bris byas pa*).[71] In this Jamyang Shepé Dorjé edited both his own written works and those of others, an activity also noted in another colophon, where the reader is told that a teaching on logic given at Tashi Gomang was later proofread (*zhus dag byas pa*)[72] at Labrang Tashikyil monastery. Finally, one remark is not concerned with writing time or format, but rather with Jamyang Shepé Dorjé's personal use of writing: at the end of a work dedicated to dealing with troublesome serpent deities, he states, "May this [work] written down by Jamyang Shepé Dorjé extemporaneously for my own use be of benefit for all."[73] More than a vehicle for teaching, writing was a personal tool for intellectual development, the dissemination of which was beneficial but not always the prime motivation.

The editorial activities carried out by Jamyang Shepa's successors at Labrang monastery included locating at least one autograph manuscript or some other reliable witness for any given work; comparing, analyzing and proofreading these manuscripts; and lastly, ornamenting and segmenting the text through the insertion of punctuation. These activities occurred within the larger endeavor of bringing the works to print, which included a number of participants. A printing notice to a short work on the Four Noble Truths provides a relatively detailed list of the people involved with the project: "All the materials were assembled by the faithful Darhan Chöjé (i.e., funded by him), and then this [text] was created by the proofreaders . . . the supervisors . . . the scribe . . . and the carver.[74] As a printing notice to the block print [this] was composed by the Yellow-Hatted Buddhist monk Kön-chok Jigmé Wangpo."[75] In this passage five specific roles in the printing process are mentioned: patron, proofreader, supervisor, scribe, and carver. There are many more aspects to the editorial process that received no explicit mention, not the least of which is the categorization and arrangement of many disparate types of written works into a single compendium, the *Collected Works* itself. Nevertheless, the single greatest concern noted in the colophons themselves is the acquisition of an autograph on which to base editorial decisions. This was of course not a issue for Butön and Chökyi Drakpa, who both worked exclusively with Indian works in translation.

Editorial notices that discuss autographs of Jamyang Shepé Dorjé can be divided into two groups: those in which a manuscript penned by the master himself was located, and those in which no such original was forthcoming. In the first case the editorial process was often greatly simplified, for a direct copy could then be made, for instance the extant version of Jamyang Shepé Dorjé's annotated edition of Saraha's *Dohākośa*, which is said to have been "copied from a faultless autograph of the Master and block printed."[76] Elsewhere, in an editorial notice internal to one of several collections of miscellaneous writings found in the *Collected Works*[77] and again at the close of Jamyang Shepé Dorjé's encomium to one Lama Könchok, we are told that the works were "copied from an original autograph of the Master himself."[78]

Occasionally, however, it was deemed necessary to cast a critical eye toward the autographs of the master, a situation that seems to have caused the editors some anxiety. In several cases the editors relate that the original manuscript was in some way faulty, yet emendations were either severely limited or altogether not attempted. When dealing with Jamyang Shepa's notes on meditation practices involving the deity Cakrasaṃvara, the editors took a hands-off approach, stating that "even though there are several suspect cases in these notes on . . . the generation phase [of meditation] upon Cakrasaṃvara, since no original manuscript was obtained but the one, [they] have been retained without venturing an interpolation."[79] A similar approach was taken with the master's annotated edition of a canonical instruction on ritual practices dedicated to the deity Raktayamāri practice, where it is lamented that "another original manuscript for this [work] was not found, and because the master's autograph is quite corrupt, detailed corrections were not attempted."[80] The editors were in a difficult position; they felt it necessary to point out that the text they were putting into print was corrupt, as a warning or perhaps as an apology, while there appear to have been strictures against meddling with even a corrupt autograph. As in the case of Chökyi Drakpa, this policy stands in opposition to Butön's more liberal policy of conjectural emendation.

Elsewhere, however, there was apparently some license to alter the original, as in the case of a commentary on Tsongkhapa's answers to the queries of sometimes teacher, sometimes colleague Rendawa, at the end of which it is recorded that a fine original (*phyi mo dag pa*) was located and then critically proofread (*dpyad pa byed par zhu*).[81] For Jamyang Shepé Dorjé's record of teachings received (*gsan yig*) the autograph was but one of several problematic witnesses employed for the establishment of a readable printed version. The editorial notice runs: "Here, as several manuscripts were missing folios, and as there were also several questions remaining, at the break between sections a fourfold slash or a serpent slash was added, and it was proofread according to the original."[82]

In cases where no autograph by Jamyang Shepé Dorjé was forthcoming, the next best thing was an autograph of his secretary, one of his disciples, or another teacher. In the notice to an unfinished commentary on Tsongkhapa's *Great Stages of the Path*, the editors tell of one such situation: "While it is said in the Master's biography that there is a fragment of the *Great Stages of the Path Commentary* given by the Master, in later times the original text has not been located. Later, from among the autographs of Pönlop Sönam Gyatso, the minister of Trichen Ngawang Tashi, one was found, so it was copied, small errors were corrected, and it was block printed."[83]

The abbot of Labrang monastery, Trichen Ngawang Tashi, played a prominent role in the preservation of Jamyang Shepé Dorjé's works. Ngawang Tashi was a prodigious author of notes (*zin bris*), both on his own lectures and on the works of his teacher. Writing in 1800, Welmang Könchok Gyeltsen lauds him for composing analytical writings (*brtsi bzhag*) on at least four chapters of Jamyang Shepé Dorjé's massive eight-chapter commentary on the *Abhisamayālaṃkāra*.[84] These analytical summaries were later compiled and arranged into notes.[85] Despite his best efforts, however, the original manuscript of the seventh chapter of the master's commentary was lost during a violent time in the Kokonor region of Amdo.[86] It was apparently supposed to have been among the manuscripts of Jamyang Shepé Dorjé's secretary,[87] but was found missing. Welmang Könchok Gyeltsen relates that, according to his teacher, the fifteenth abbot of Labrang Tashikyil, Trichen Sönam Wangyal (born 1726),[88] the existing seventh chapter was not composed by Jamyang Shepé Dorjé but was an addition written by Trichen Ngawang Tashi himself. [89]

Trichen Ngawang Tashi was also responsible for printing no fewer than nine of Jamyang Shepé Dorjé's works, and it is probable that this was the first effort at printing the master's writings.[90] These include the large manuals on Middle Way philosophy,[91] *Perfection of Wisdom* scriptures,[92] monastic conduct,[93] and the *Great Exposition of Tenets*. These works were to achieve great prominence as textbooks in the curriculum of Gomang college of Drepung monastery in Central Tibet,[94] and it would thus not be surprising if they were among the first works of the master to be printed for distribution. Still, it remains an open question whether their popularity was more a cause or a result of Ngawang Tashi's printing efforts. This notice also provides the earliest possible date *after* which the *Collected Works* as a whole could have been printed, for Könchok Jigmé Wangpo's life story of Jamyang Shepé Dorjé I was completed in 1758.[95] Given that Trichen Ngawang Tashi died in 1738, there was at least a twenty-year hiatus between the first printing of Jamyang Shepé Dorjé's manuals and the formation of a printed edition of his *Collected Works*.

In the colophon to a short work on logical argumentation, an editorial reticence in the face of many differences of opinion on the correct reading of the master's work can be discerned. The notice complains that "in the polemics stemming from the individual claims of scholars there are many doubtful points regarding the difficult spots of these words bequeathed by Jamyang Shepa, and a reliable original manuscript was not found, so [this text] must be analyzed again."[96] It is clear that even though the work was being carried through to block print, this was not considered to be a definitive version. Here (and in one other notice, examined below) the editors invited future scholars to improve upon their work, to succeed where they felt they had failed.

Lastly, it should be noted that editors were not exclusively involved in bringing manuscript works into print, but also spent time improving already printed works. A long printing colophon attached to Jamyang Shepa's *Religious History of Vajrabhairava* (composed in 1718 at Labrang monastery) states that the initial xylograph of the work was found wanting, and as a result a revised block-print edition was undertaken. Despite the fact that "the Second Omniscient One [Könchok Jigmé Wangpo] proofread [the work] in detail, Harchen Ratnasiddhivada patronized [it],[97] and this *Religious History of Glorious Vajrabhairava* . . . was block-printed," it was deemed necessary to carve new blocks for the work. "Nevertheless," the editors argue, "as there were still some small orthographic errors, in accordance with the teachings of the Second Omniscient One himself, an autograph of the secretary of the former Omniscient One, Samlo Gompa Rinchen Tenzin, was acquired and corrected, and [this work] was again block printed at Ganden Tashikyil [i.e., Labrang monastery].[98]

Finally, an extended printing notice of a Tibetan script version of the Indian lexicon known as the *Amarakośa* is included in the *Collected Works*. Within this notice all of the moments and concerns of the editorial process discussed by the editors of Jamyang Shepé Dorjé's works are recapitulated—albeit in the limited scope of a single problematic text. The history of the *Amarakośa* in Tibet has been in large part a series of attempts to translate, revise, and successfully present this linguistically and graphically challenging work.[99] The Labrang monastery editors' final call for future generations to continue working on this difficult project is a testament to their commitment to scholarship. The colophon begins with a brief quote from Könchok Jigmé Wangpo's biography of the master[100] and proceeds to give a brief printing history of the *Amarakośa* at Labrang.[101] "Around the age of 67 or 68," the colophon begins, "Jamyang Shepé Dorjé went to Amdo, and according to [his] *Life Story*, 'He said that there were some gaps left and also several translation errors in the old translation of the *Amarakośa*, and so, on the basis of a manuscript in the *nāgarī* [script], he translated an authoritative [version from] beginning [to] end.'" The editors claim that "Since there were plans to block print an original autograph of a multilingual *nāgarī* manuscript that came from the second [Jamyang Shepé Dorjé] incarnation, the Protector [Könchok Jigmé Wangpo], [this manuscript] was proofread, but [the project] was not completed." And unfortunately, the results of his efforts were lost: "There did exist an authoritative text of the *Amarakośa*, which was cited by the Glorious Candrakīrti in the *Pradīpodyotana*,[102] as well as more particularly a revised translation by the Omniscient Master [Jamyang Shepé Dorjé] that was considered to be extremely important." All that could be found was a secondary manuscript, for "through subsequent searching no manuscript surfaced other than that of Kewang Yigkya Rapjampa Jamyang Pelden." The editors would have liked to utilize the revised translation made by Shalu Lotsawa, which in turn was edited on the basis of the translation of Yarlung Lotsawa Drakpa Gyeltsen and Yarlung Drakpa Tayé, yet again, "an extra manuscript of that [version] was not located." As a result, the editors apologize, "the particular differences between [our manuscript] and that one, or whether it is complete or incomplete, are uncertain."

But these difficult circumstances did not deter the editors in the end: "for fear of wasting even this unique manuscript, whatever annotations and indications of word division and so forth there were in the [manuscript of Jamyang Pelden] have been kept in place, minor proofreading has been carried out, and it has been carved into blocks." Although they did produce a printed version from this single manuscript, they felt the need to plea for tolerance from their future peers, suggesting that "if someone skilled in research and analysis were to once again diligently search for that multilingual *nāgarī* autograph of the Omniscient Master, and there was a chance for comparison, this would be quite good." The request was echoed in 1800 by Welmang Könchok Gyeltsen, which suggests that no progress had been made in locating the master's works by the beginning of the nineteenth century, more than eighty years after his death.[103] And as much as a century after the printing of the master's works (which could have taken place no earlier than 1768), Könchok Tenpa Rabgyé (1800/1–66) contends in his 1865 opus on the history of Buddhism in Amdo that many writings by the master were not included in the *Collected Works*, and goes on to ask that people make an earnest effort to locate such lost manuscripts.[104] Again it is apparent that if a single work—or even an entire collection—was printed, for its editors this was not necessarily *the* definitive edition. The exigencies of time, place, chance, and the right tools in the creation of not only the physical text, but also the meaning were not lost on them. For these scholars the block print was merely provisional, just one imperfect version; it was not indelible, and not considered to be categorically superior to scribal publication. More than the technology of reproduction, what made a text good was the quality of its editors. Even in the case of an author as famous as the founder of Labrang monastery, the *Collected Works* as they were assembled in the second half of the eighteenth century—and as they are available today—were not considered by their editors to be the final word.

To a great extent this constant refrain in editorial postfaces may be heard as a genuine call for scholars in subsequent generations to improve upon the work presented before an audience in print. It may also be taken as an anticipatory defense of the editors, for who can wholly blame the scholar who readily admits his own imperfections? These editors were concerned with their reputation every bit as much as their more famous forbearer, Shalu Lotsawa, for whom "Those who are renowned as scholars are only those reputed to be so at the King's court." The next chapter surveys the public image of scholars and their books from two different vantage points by looking to this archetypal grammarian and translator and his (seeming) counterpart, Tsangnyön Heruka—the "Madman" of Tsang—to investigate their shared concern with the culture of the book.

*I*n the second decade of the fifteenth century, Shalu Lotsawa Chökyong Zangpo held a teaching seminar at Riphuk, the retreat center on the slopes above Shalu monastery. As he read the life story of his predecessor, Butön Rinchendrup, out loud for the benefit of his students, rainbows appeared in the sky. They rose above onlookers' heads, "just as in the paintings," in ornate patterns and as finely wrought holy objects. And as he finally began, amid this miraculous display, to read of Butön's death, he wept,[1] mourning the former abbot of Shalu, now dead more than a century and a half. He wept for a man who is claimed to have worried intensely about how he would be remembered and who complained to his student that if his personal manuscripts were not revised before his death he would be ridiculed after his passing. Shalu Lotsawa wept for a scholar, a man of books, in whose shadow he now stood and under whose multicolored display of wonders he now taught.

The culture of the book in Tibet may be viewed in wide perspective through the lens of the biographies of Shalu Lotsawa, the most important of which is that by Rinchen Tashi, a famous translator in his own right who learned his craft under the scholar from Shalu.[2] This biography offers many paths of inquiry. It is an important source for the history of language arts in Tibet, cataloging the hundreds of titles received, taught, or edited by Shalu Lotsawa, his teachers, and his students. It recounts fascinating details about the development of the Tibetan Buddhist canons in the century following their codification at Nartang and Shalu monasteries. It will also certainly play a part in an eventual history of central Tibet monastic institutions during the fifteenth and sixteenth centuries, as it mentions some sixty institutions of greater and lesser renown. This chapter attempts far less than this. After a brief resume of the life of Shalu Lotsawa, it illustrates how Rinchen Tashi's biography not only describes the career of a translator but also prescribes the conduct and skills becoming to scholars more generally. The chapter then looks at the role of book printing (and dreams thereon) in the life story of the famous adept Tsangnyön Heruka. Tsangnyön, the "Madman of Tsang," who may be regarded as the intellectual antithesis and competitor of Shalu Lotsawa, was equally at home in the social, economic, and rhetorical practices that make up the culture of the book. I conclude with a few remarks on possible implications that might be drawn from such life stories for studying the cultural history of scholarship in Tibet.

JOURNEYMAN SCHOLAR IN CENTRAL TIBET

Shalu Lotsawa's career may be divided into three main periods, though these overlap more than is possible to represent here. The first period includes his education and apprenticeship and roughly spans the years 1450 to 1480. In the second period, between the ages of thirty-five and fifty, he traveled extensively as an itinerant translator. Finally, from 1495 until his death in 1528, he worked intermittently as an abbot and religious leader—first at Dratang monastery in central Tibet and later at his home institution of Shalu. He was born in 1441 at Shalu, and his father seems to have been a military leader loyal to the rulers of nearby Gyantsé. When he was seven years old his father died in a fierce battle near Nartang between the Sharkawa rulers of Gyantsé and the Rinpungpa rulers. After this his elders felt that he should train in secular affairs. He was thus invited to work for the former Gyantsé ruler, Tashi Pakpa (born 1395), and subsequently became close with the ruling family of Gyantsé, though certainly in a different function from that of his father. This relationship was important in Shalu Lotsawa's development as a scholar. As an apprentice in secular affairs he learned to read and write, though Rinchen Tashi relates that his studies were difficult going at first due to his limited predisposition for language study—a statement that is humorously ironic given his later expertise. Back at Shalu the young student appears to have developed an interest in the language of religion, where he had not in the language of administration. He found joy in gazing at the Indic inscriptions upon the temple murals and began to read and write Indic scripts under a Nepalese artisan. As a teenager he made fervent prayers to the Buddha, and at the sight of a statue of Buddhism's founder he would burst into "tears of unpretentious faith." He decided to enter monastic life, and in 1462 he took novitiate vows at Pelkor

Dechen monastery back in Gyantsé. Following his teenage gravitation toward foreign languages, he quickly undertook an extensive education in Indian and Tibetan language arts, working under scholars at both Shalu and Gyantsé.

It is no wonder, then, that at the age of twenty-four Shalu Lotsawa was chosen to work on the Buddhist scriptures in production at Pelkor Dechen. For fifteen consecutive years he spent spring and summer translating at Gyantsé and fall and winter at Shalu furthering his education, writing, translating, and meditating in retreat. Gyantsé was at this time a veritable factory of Buddhist canons, producing many ornate volumes annually. According to Rinchen Tashi, the Gyantsé ruler Situ Rapten Kunzang Pakpa, who was active in the early decades of the fifteenth century,[3] had initiated the production of ten golden Kangyur volumes and thirteen Tengyur volumes in black and white each year. Now, in the late 1460s, the Gyantsé noble Dagchen Tashi Rapten felt that in order to improve this tradition of copying the scriptures, they should be edited. "Good editors are rare," the nobleman said to Shalu Lotsawa, "and because you are learned in religion, you must edit and take care of the teachings."

So the young translator seems to have been essentially conscripted. Again Rinchen Tashi gives voice to Shalu Lotsawa's reflection on the work of translation: "Generally it appears that inspecting the treatises entails gathering Indic manuscripts. Even though there are many scriptures produced, editorially sound [volumes] are rare indeed. So the work of editing will be of benefit to the teachings." And here Rinchen Tashi relates something of Shalu Lotsawa's editorial method. First he inspected the original, then he edited for meaning, and finally he edited the words in complete accordance with the Tibetan grammatical treatises. Checking with whatever Indic manuscripts he could find, he fixed omissions in the Tibetan text and emended unedited passages. Rinchen Tashi proudly claims that up to the present day— that is 1517, the year in which he completed his biography—the volumes produced by Shalu Lotsawa at Gyantsé were the most important examples of scripture around, at least in terms of their editorial quality.

Around 1477 Shalu Lotsawa's mother died while he worked on at Gyantsé. This caused him to redouble his efforts to promote the dharma, and the next scene in Rinchen Tashi's biography finds him paying a visit to Sakya, where he was fortunate enough to be able to inspect many Indic manuscripts. Wishing to translate several of these, he was given leave to take them back home to Shalu monastery. As he gained a reputation for rendering previously untranslated works into Tibetan, certain detractors felt his abilities to be exaggerated. Yet most, Rinchen Tashi assures the reader, had faith in his skill, so much so that he was deemed by some to be a manifestation of the great renaissance translator Rinchen Zangpo, or even of the great imperial grammarian Tönmi Sambhota.

At this point in the narrative Rinchen Tashi pauses to highlight a shift in scene. In 1480 his subject began his career in central Tibet, in Ü. For Rinchen Tashi it is no mere coincidence that Shalu Lotsawa spent so much time warming up in Tsang first, for just as Śāntideva and Atiśa were born elsewhere, yet flourished in Tibet, so did Shalu Lotsawa's early labors in Tsang come to full fruition only in central Tibet. He first traveled to Lhasa, and then to Samyé monastery, where he beheld the skull of Śāntideva and paid a visit to the Translator's Chapel located southwest of the main temple. This experience strengthened his resolve to "translate what had not been translated, to modernize the orthography of old translations, to improve bad translations, and generally to clarify the teachings."

From Samyé, Shalu Lotsawa made his way along the Yarlung Tsangpo river, eventually reaching the great center of Densatil monastery, the beauty and opulence of which amazed him. It appears that Shalu Lotsawa had a growing reputation already at this point in his life, for news of his talents had preceded him by word of mouth. Chenga Ngagi Wangchuk, the tenth Pakmodrupa Desi (the leader of the Phagmodru-controlled territory) (1439–95) had heard good reports, and sent a request to join him at the political center of Nedong. Now this was an important meeting for Shalu Lotsawa. It could make or break his career, for as he told himself: "Those who are renowned as scholars are only [those] reputed [to be so] at the king's court." So thinking, he resolved to make his status clear at court, "to eliminate naysayers, and to lead beings along the true path through scholarship."

He thus traveled to "the source of Tibetan kings," the court of the Phakmodru leaders, Nedong. There he translated several Sanskrit letters that had been sent to the eighth Pakmodrupa Desi, Kunga Lekpa, and offered several ornate verses to Ngagi Wangchuk. The ruler—being a discerning man himself, Rinchen Tashi hastens to say—was delighted, and knew that a scholar stood before him. But apparently some at court were less convinced of his skills. To test him, several monks learned in astrology and other arts spread many Indic manuscripts before Shalu Lotsawa and riddled him with questions. They also commanded him to read the Indic manuscripts in their presence, a challenge to which he readily agreed. First he read the text in "the Indian language"—Sanskrit or perhaps one of the Prakrit dialects—and then he proceeded to translate it into Tibetan line by line. Rinchen Tashi tells us that his interrogators were pleased, and proclaimed him to be just like the scholars of old—though it is not hard to imagine that they were less pleased about the young scholar from Tsang catching their lord's ear than Rinchen Tashi would have us believe. Nevertheless, from this point on his reputation was secure. Having proven himself at Nedong, he was henceforth known as "Great Translator."[4]

From Nedong, Shalu Lotsawa traveled south a short distance to Chingwa Taktsé, the center of the estate adjoining the old Tibetan imperial burial grounds (and future birthplace of the Fifth Dalai Lama). There he spent some time comparing the Chingwa Taktsé leader's canonical collection with that of Gyantsé and arranging for both collections to be supplemented with copies of the unique texts housed in each. He then began the journey back to Tsang. Along the way he spent time at Gongkar monastery engaged in further translation work, and this visit is what likely resulted in an edict issued from Gongkar strongly suggesting that he return to central Tibet. Throughout his travels thereafter, he routinely came into contact with the most important religious leaders of the day. During this trip of 1482 he met with the Fourth Shamarpa, Chökyi Drakpa (1453–1554), for the first of several times. He also traveled to Taklung monastery for the first time and met with the twelfth abbot, Ngawang Drakpa (1418–96). As the elderly leader was learned in grammatical studies, they spoke at length about the arts. In the course of their conversation the abbot said, "Yesterday a letter from the Nedong ruler came, which claimed that a great translator had visited there, translated works, and edited works such as commentaries upon the popular *Chanting the Names of Mañjuśrī*. At first I did not believe this, for the translators of old are no more, and today's translators do not know anything more than an outline of the *Kalāpa* [grammar]. Yet it appears that you are this great translator." Overjoyed at this compliment, Shalu Lotsawa stopped to serve at Taklung for a while. Throughout the 1480s and '90s, he traveled frequently from Tsang to Ü and back. In 1488 at Lhündrup Ling he met with the Fourth Shamarpa again and impressed the leader with his teaching abilities. The Shamarpa asked him to translate Indic manuscripts of *Abhidharmakośa* commentaries that had come into the hands of Namgyel Drakpa, Lord of Latö Jang, and had been in the possession of the great translator and historian Gö Lotsawa himself. The author of the *Blue Annals* history could not translate them due to failing health and bad eyesight, so Shalu Lotsawa began these at Lhündrup Ling and finished them while serving the Fourth Shamarpa on the road to Kongpo.

In 1495 Shalu Lotsawa's career turned from that of a journeyman scholar toward one of administrative leadership when he was asked to become abbot of Dratang monastery in central Tibet.[5] His tenure at Dratang is characterized as stable and orderly. Monks kept their vows, tantric yogins kept their commitments, householders worked on their purification rituals, and many people were set upon the path to liberation (and all this from teaching grammar!). Students from Ngari in the far west to Kham and Amdo in the east studied grammatical works under his leadership here. Just like Atiśa long before, Shalu Lotsawa "brought light to the teachings."[6] But this does not mean that he was stationary, for in the early decades of the sixteenth century he divided his time between abbatial duties and service to his superiors—a task for which he would travel continuously between major monasteries and secular institutions from Sakya in the west to Kongpo in the east. Sometime between 1501 and 1503 Shalu Lotsawa also found himself at Nedong teaching dharma to Dönyö Dorjé, the Rinpungpa leader of Central Tibet who, remarks Rinchen Tashi, "worked only for the benefit of others, without regard for his own fatigue or anguish."[7] While staying in Lhasa in 1503 with the Seventh Karmapa, Chödrak Gyatso,[8] he translated letters of invitation by the Karmapa to Indian scholars, as well as a letter to the Karmapa from Indian scholars, and even from the king of Kashmir.[9]

Shalu Lotsawa's career as an itinerant scholar and translator did eventually transform into a more sedentary mode. His second major abbacy was at Shalu itself, from 1514 to 1524.[10] Rinchen Tashi paints a lavish picture of his enthronement ceremony, emphasizing the historic significance of the event. Indeed, history remembers little between Shalu Lotsawa's abbacy and the tenure of his great predecessor, Butön himself. Rinchen Tashi makes the most of the comparison between the two figures, and as Shalu Lotsawa steps up to the abbot's chair, all onlookers praise him in a single voice: "Butön has returned to the throne!"[11] And it appears that the writings of Butön had a great influence on Shalu Lotsawa. Seeking inspiration for his role as abbot, Shalu Lotsawa read Butön's final testament many times and attempted to perform his duties according to his predecessor's instructions. He gave teachings on works by Butön, including even his famous *History of Buddhism*.[12]

In the last year of his life Shalu Lotsawa was called upon once again to serve as abbot of Dratang monastery. He was an elderly man of eighty-five or so, and he did not hold the see long. He died at Dratang in July 1528. The biographies are laconic about his death, revealing little regarding his funeral proceedings or the fate of his relics. He had entrusted the abbacy to his nephew, Pekar Lotsawa, the year before, and at the death of his uncle Pekar Lotsawa renovated Dratang and instituted annual rituals in honor of this "Great Translator" from Shalu.

THE SCHOLAR'S DREAM

Here Rinchen Tashi leaves his narrative of Shalu Lotsawa's career to undertake an alternative portrayal of the scholar, in which it becomes plain that his *Life of Shalu Lotsawa* is as much a laudatory defense of scholarly ideals and their value for patrons as it is the resumé of an individual figure. Shalu Lotsawa is very much a historically rooted personality in the biography, and no one would mistake him for another scholar. Yet he is also an ideal type, the ideal textual scholar, and much of Rinchen Tashi's account is designed to portray just how such a scholar should act. This portrait may be divided into four main components. First, the scholar must possess expertise in Indic and Tibetan grammatical systems. A related, but no less important aspect of this expertise is that it should be publicly displayed. Third, the scholar should be on a par with the scholars of the past, to whom Shalu Lotsawa is repeatedly compared. Fourth, the ideal scholar should, like him, be a leader of great character and a contemplative practitioner of great self-discipline. Shalu Lotsawa is also presented as a model bodhisattva.

From an early age Shalu Lotsawa is heard in the biography reflecting upon the skills of the textual scholar. During his grammatical studies at Shalu in the 1460s, he thinks: "to understand the words and meaning of the scriptures, first one must know the

words; one must know grammar. Since there have been some
bad translations, and many orthographic errors introduced by
scribes, if one does not look at the Indic texts, others will not be
able to understand [the text when it is translated]." Elsewhere
the biography seeks to persuade the reader that in order to be
a translator one must have the *Kalāpa*, the *Candrapa*, and other
Indic grammatical works memorized. One should have a firm
command not only of different languages but also of poetics, syn-
onomics, as well as a deep knowledge of the scriptures. The process of translation, Rinchen Tashi relates, involves several steps.
First one must understand the words and the sense of the Indic
text. Then one should translate the work into Tibetan in a way
that does not contradict the sense. "This procedure," he assures,
"will yield a good translation."[13] But this sounds easier than it is,
especially in Shalu Lotsawa's time, centuries after the glory days
of translators in the eleventh, twelfth, and thirteenth centuries.
The translators of old could ask an Indian scholar but these days
there are no Indian scholars, Rinchen Tashi laments, and Tibetan
translators must work by themselves.

Shalu Lotsawa is thus praised for his independence, his ability to translate without such help and overcome the limitations of
his day. If nothing else, Rinchen Tashi expresses true admiration
for his teacher's work on such technical treatises: "His editorial
work of the *Candrapa* is totally amazing," he exclaims. "When
you look at it, there is no other way he could have known how
to do it except for clairvoyance."[14] But to those who may wonder if there is any point to practicing translation in this late age,
Rinchen Tashi defends the work of the translator in his time. "If
one were to think that the [works] translated by the translators
of old are in no need of revision," he cautions, "this is not so. The
Great Translator [Shalu Lotsawa] has said, 'If minor translation
errors appear in the translations of scholars such as Kawa Peltsek,
Chokro, Rinchen Zangpo, Loden Sherap, or Shongtön Dorjé
Gyelpo, what need is there even to speak of [the translations of]
others?' And that is not all: subsequently, foolish Tibetan scribes
as well as commentators making things up themselves have made
many revisions. [Therefore,] editing is by all means valuable!
So the work of editing and restoring faulty translations is utterly
amazing."[15] It is no little irony that Rinchen Tashi here implicitly
criticizes the conjectural emendation recommended by Butön,
given the latter's profound influence overall upon Shalu Lotsawa
and the tradition of scholarship at Shalu monastery. He also

makes clear that, however important Butön was, his instructions need not be followed to the letter.

Despite possible detractors, Rinchen Tashi suggests that the work of translation was still a valued profession at the dawn of the sixteenth century. Shalu Lotsawa's services were in demand, and this brought him into contact with many leaders over a wide geographical region. The thoroughly social nature of his scholarship is an important theme in the biography and exemplifies the second crucial feature of scholarly expertise, that it be publicly recognized. As seen earlier, according to the biographies, "Those who are renowned as scholars are only [those] reputed [to be so] at the king's court." Yet the Nedong court was not the only place where Shalu Lotsawa dazzled his audience. Time and time again he engaged in great displays of virtuosity. While staying at Taklung in the early 1490s, he came across an Indic manuscript in the Sindhu script. Nobody had been successful in reading it, yet Shalu Lotsawa was able to both read and translate the unnamed work. This, Rinchen Tashi declares, clearly indicated his high rank among scholars—and illuminated the ignorance of a number of other people (likely critics and competitors) in the process.[16] While in the court of the Rinpungpa leader Ngawang Namgyel at Chushül, Shalu Lotsawa engaged in further feats of scholastic pyrotechnics, orally translating a Sanskrit text into Tibetan instantaneously while reading it, to the amazement of the ruler and his attendant monks. To top this off, a rain of flowers fell upon Chushül as he translated aloud.[17] Shalu Lotsawa is even held to have been famous in India for his skills in Sanskrit composition. When once he composed a Sanskrit verse of praise to the Mahābodhi temple and gave it to an Indian yogin with a request to place it upon the door of Vajrāsana, those gathered at the site of the Buddha's enlightenment remarked that the Sanskrit was good. "There are scholars in Tibet!" the people exclaimed. The Buddhists were overjoyed, Rinchen Tashi assures us, while the non-Buddhists began to tremble in fear at the rumor of such an adept Buddhist scholar in Tibet. For Rinchen Tashi this episode confirms that "there is no one more astute than this one from here to the river Ganga."

If Shalu Lotsawa was the greatest scholar in geographic terms, he was also the greatest translator since the famed translators of old. Rinchen Tashi routinely links Shalu Lotsawa to the past in a way that both praises his teacher and eulogizes the glories of days gone by. Shalu Lotsawa represents a golden age in which the translators were busy moving Buddhism from one language to another, from one world to another, all under the benevolent guidance of the great Tibetan kings. "He is Tönmi Sambhota." "He is a manifestation of Rinchen Zangpo." "He is a second Sakya Paṇḍita." "Butön has returned to the throne." Shalu Lotsawa represents each of these exemplary scholars, and his travels in central Tibet are likened to the missionary efforts of Atiśa himself.

For Rinchen Tashi the great translator's good works extend beyond textual matters, as one might expect. Shalu Lotsawa is presented as a man of all-around good character. As a student he was a good example for others in the college at Gyantsé. Rinchen Tashi relates, "He never engaged in idle chatter, and from dusk to dawn he could be seen with a book in his hand. What others needed months to learn he would master in days. His faculties were profound and his energy limitless." An intimate sketch of a day in the life of Shalu Lotsawa the teacher highlights his good character. In the morning he would meditate. During the day he would translate, edit, write, and teach. He would not get irritated at less intelligent students but would encourage them again and again, saying, "If you are able to listen, I am able to teach!" He would teach throughout the day, and during free moments he would look to his own manuscripts. Sometimes he would read the lives of Pang Lotsawa, Butön, or other past masters. At night he would say prayers, and "finally," the biography hints, "it is heard tell that when he has finished with the details of the day he sits in meditation on his bed."

But why stop there? What, one might ask, did a scholar of such dedication and renown dream of? Well, books, of course. A late sixteenth-century history of grammatical studies in Tibet contains what is claimed to be a small autobiographical resume by Shalu Lotsawa. It is primarily a list of texts that he edited, with a small note on method in which he laconically states: "I came to understand translation by following the methods of the translators of old." What else could he say? But at the close of the note Shalu Lotsawa invites the reader into his dreams "of Indian and Tibetan volumes, in gold with ruby-red letters, covered in silk and fine brocade decorated in with deities and letters"—those very objects by which his fame is measured. And if the scholar could dream of books, so could his counterpart, the hermit Tsangnyön Heruka. For the hermit also built a career through the production of books.

If the hagiographic record can serve as a guide, then it appears that the ready availability of the famous *Life of Milarepa* throughout the world may be traced to the dreams of two Tibetan publishers in the late fifteenth and early sixteenth centuries.[18] One night toward the end of his life (perhaps in the 1550s), Lhatsün Rinchen Namgyel—son of the ruler of the Gungtang kingdom in southwest Tibet—was visited by a woman in a dream. She commanded Rinchen Namgyel to print books. "Human, your previous activities have been beyond belief," she began, perhaps alluding to the nearly 4,000 folios of literature that his biographer claims he had printed up to that point. "Still, if now you were to print whatever texts you have at hand of the life and songs of Milarepa, this would be your final act." The dream directive was not without precedent; his biographer assures the reader that the better part of Rinchen Namgyel's printing projects had been inspired by exhortations from his patron deity.[19] So once more he took his nocturnal visions seriously and prepared to collect and print an anthology of the songs of Milarepa that had not been included in the massive *Hundred Thousand Songs of Milarepa* compiled by his teacher, Tsangnyön Heruka.

In dreaming of the printed word, Rinchen Namgyel was following in the tradition of his master Tsangnyön, who likewise received exhortations to print as he slept.[20] When Tsangnyön was in retreat at Dropuk in Nyanang, an important site for Milarepa, he had a vision—part dream and part luminous revelation—in which he beheld the Indian adept Nāropa as a giant, naked and bejeweled, his skin blazing with beautiful light. He was standing upon a white lion, with his hands in the gesture of instruction, speaking to innumerable hosts of gods and humans. The vision was the most wondrous that Tsangnyön had ever experienced, or had even heard about happening to someone else. He made an offering and a request for teachings to the giant Indian, who in response spoke to him—not in Tibetan but in Sanskrit. The language was beautiful, but unfortunately Tsangnyön did not understand a word of it. He made another offering, and this time Nāropa spoke in both Sanskrit and Tibetan, but Tsangnyön still had difficulty getting the point. Finally an Indian translator emerged from the crowd to assist the enthusiastic Tibetan yogin, and related Nāropa's command to Tsangnyön. "[Nāropa] counseled in Sanskrit," the Indian began, "that you should assemble the life and songs of Lord Milarepa from his birth up to his awakening. You should carve this into wood blocks, and you should print it. Distributing the prints will bring a prayer for Milarepa to wherever the teachings of the Buddha have spread." Tsangnyön responded, "But I do not have a patron for this." Nāropa replied, again in Sanskrit, and faced toward the Tibetan regions of Lowo, Gungtang, and Latö. The translator interpreted the gesture for Tsangnyön, saying, "He has indicated that they are your patrons." "But I cannot prepare wood, carvers, or scribes," complained Tsangnyön. Again Nāropa pointed, this time to five women seated nearby, who rose and vowed that they would aid in the preparations. After listening to songs in Sanskrit for a while longer, Tsangnyön awoke, inspired by this dream (despite his difficulty in actually understanding the Indian adept, a problem Shalu Lotsawa would not have faced) to print the life and songs of Milarepa.

It is well known that in creating his *Life of Milarepa*, Tsangnyön Heruka was drawing on a long literary tradition of an already important hermit-saint.[21] If one can judge from Gö Lotsawa Shönu Pel's late fifteenth-century *Blue Annals*, Milarepa's life (it is not clear in what forms Gö Lotsawa had in mind) was being used at the teaching center of Phakmodrü in central Tibet by the mid-twelfth century, only decades after his death.[22] In 1346, almost a century and a half before Tsangnyön's efforts, it could be said that Milarepa was the most famous holy man in Tibet.[23] In the mid-fifteenth century, festivals to Milarepa were being held in Kagyu monasteries such as Taklung, at which the faithful would gather to listen to his songs.[24] And as early as the beginning of the fourteenth century it was rumored that there were 127 different life stories of Milarepa.[25]

Tsangnyön capitalized on this popularity, and his promotion of Milarepa as a saint through print publication has earned him renown throughout the Tibetan cultural world—from the southwestern Himalayas to Amdo in the northeast. Using printed texts, paintings, and teachings composed in the style of Milarepa's famous songs, Tsangnyön spent much of his life promoting a cult of devotion. Such missionary work was to have lasting consequences. From the fifteenth to the nineteenth centuries, his telling of Milarepa's tale was carved in new wood-block editions no fewer than ten times, in southwest Tibet, Bhutan, Degé, Amdo, Mongolia, Lhasa, and Beijing.[26] And Milarepa's reputation was not limited to Kagyu circles: he was even considered to be a previous birth of the Gelukpa master Chankya Rölpé Dorjé, in whose biography explicit mention is made of Tsangnyön's efforts at composing and printing the life and songs.[27]

In the largest of three hagiographies dedicated to Tsangnyön,[28] Götsang Repa Natsok Rangdröl waxes long on the highly realized status of his master, combining classic Mahāyāna descriptions of enlightened beings with an explicit comparison to Milarepa: "With fierce effort that was no different from the Leader of Yogins, Mila Shepé Dorjé himself, in a single life [Tsangnyön] manifestly achieved the stature of Lord Vajradhāra, with the five wisdoms and four enlightened bodies."[29] Götsang Repa even goes so far as to style Tsangnyön as an incarnation of Milarepa.[30] During his relatively short life of fifty-five years, Tsangnyön enjoyed considerable prestige among rulers and wealthy patrons from central Tibet to Kathmandu. He was patronized by the most powerful leader of central Tibet during the late fifteenth century, Rinpungpa Dönyö Dorjé,[31] with whom he had occasion to discuss the life story of the saint.

Tsangnyön drew on a rich tradition of hagiographic materials to create his vision of Milarepa while adapting and transforming this tradition for a new audience.[32] Yet it is not just the new form of Milarepa's biography that makes Tsangnyön's effort so interesting, but the extent to which he self-consciously used the printed volume as a means to expand his network of patrons, disciples, and holy sites. Judging from his biographer's accounts, Tsangnyön developed an interest in promoting the tradition of Milarepa early in life. In his young adulthood Tsangnyön traveled to Ngatsa, the birthplace of Milarepa in southern Gungtang. He saw a small red temple and Mila's uncle's house in ruins, and at a renovated temple containing a statue of Milarepa he met a steward who asked him to compose verses in praise of Milarepa's life. Tsangnyön thus composed an encomium in the form of the twelve acts[33] of the Buddha.[34] In a fascinating passage, Tsangnyön's biographers write of the benefits of Milarepa's life story by attributing the following considerations to Tsangnyön himself:

> *There are currently many life stories and song collections of Milarepa. Still, since this extraordinary life story has not been a continuous tradition, it should be clarified and taught for the benefit of my disciples, for teaching its profound and vast dharma and spiritual instructions will surely lead to liberation. They will collect*

*merit. There are kings, ministers, nobles who think that they are
great people, and commoners, none of whom has time to practice
in accordance with the dharma. Then there are those who do have
the time and conceitedly think they are practicing the dharma,
but have not taken the spiritual instructions into their experience:
they are stirring up bubbles with words. There are those who are
conceited into thinking that they are masters who have found the
means to achieve the status of a Buddha in a single lifetime: in
them all virtue will be destroyed.*

Götsang Repa continues (again in Tsangnyön's voice), extolling
the benefits of printing Milarepa's life:

If this Life of Milarepa *were to be well known, sense pleasures
and things desired in this life would become supports for undertaking ascetic practice, while entertainments in which one wan-
ders would become supports for practicing single-pointedness.
[Milarepa's life] would become a perfect example for those who
doubt that buddhahood can be attained in a single lifetime, or believe that they are meditating at the wrong time. They will have
faith in the holy dharma of certain meaning, and will be liberated in this life or in the intermediate state. Even those of mediocre
capacity can have faith in those who are experienced and provide
material support for them. With a pure vow they can go into retreat, gain meditative experience in the next life, and based on
that, gain liberation. Even extremists will give up backward views
and develop extraordinary faith, and they will certainly come to
the end of samsara. Thus, printing [Milarepa's life] will be of benefit to all beings.*[35]

Here Tsangnyön's biographers characterize him as a reformer,
using Milarepa's life to counteract hypocrisy and conceit in his
own time. Milarepa's life story should be engaging for different
types of people and should encourage different responses. Block
printing is explicitly associated with mass dissemination of hagiographies, and thus with the goal of "benefiting humanity." According to Götsang Repa, the *Life of Milarepa* experienced unprecedented popularity due to Tsangnyön's efforts: in the years
immediately following the carving of the wood blocks, prints and
paintings were distributed in Mustang, Gungtang, and central Tibet, and Tsangnyön sent close disciples such as Sönam Drüpa on
a tour through Ü, Tsang, and Tsari with both paintings and block

prints "for the benefit of people," in other words, to prosletyze on behalf of Tsangnyön.[36]

The hagiographic tradition of Milarepa thus reached its height with the redaction of his life story by Tsangnyön Heruka. The immense popularity of this work also suggests this late fifteenth-century religious leader was arguably the most influential hagiographer of the Kagyu schools of Tibetan Buddhism. Not only did he promote the cult of Milarepa so successfully that it spread throughout Asia, he also initiated a tradition of printing that was to continue for the better part of a century after his death in 1507 and was to be remembered in southwestern Tibet into the twentieth century. In the late fifteenth and sixteenth centuries Tsangnyön and his disciples actively promoted their school by compiling numerous hagiographies of early Kagyu masters from the eleventh through the thirteenth centuries.[37] After Tsangnyön, the two most important figures in this tradition are his two principal disciples, Lhatsün Rinchen Namgyel (1473–1557) and Götsang Repa Natsok Rangdröl (died 1570). Rinchen Namgyel was active primarily at Drakar Taso, a hermitage in the Kyirong Valley at which Milarepa is held to have achieved enlightenment. Götsang Repa published some 12 works amounting to more than 700 folios at the hermitage of Rechungpuk, situated on the spur separating the Yarlung and the Chongyé valleys, just south of Tsetang. He wrote at Rechungpuk as well, but he also wrote in Kongpo to the southeast and in Lapchi to the southwest. In one case he composed a work (his history of the *Cakrasaṃvara Tantra* lineages in India and Tibet) at Lapchi and later had it printed at Rechungpuk.[38]

In terms of a broader history of printing in Tibet, Lhatsün Rinchen Namgyel achieves pride of place over Götsang Repa. Over the course of nearly 20 years (though the majority of the work was undertaken during the early to mid-1550s) Rinchen Namgyel published no fewer than 28 works totaling more than 1,500 folios.[39] Biographies of him typically list works that he had printed, but they are also usually incomplete compared to the list that may be assembled from presently extant works. One biography states that he alone produced more than 4,000 folios of printed literature, a figure that far exceeds the estimation we can make.[40] Traditional biographers therefore have underestimated the number of titles that he was responsible for printing while significantly exaggerating the number of pages he printed. Writing in the early nineteenth century, Drakar Taso's most prominent historian, Chökyi Wangchuk, was clearly proud of the fact that the many editions of the biography and the collected songs of Milarepa that had been printed between Tsangnyön's time and his own stemmed from Rinchen Namgyel's printing-house hermitage. According to him, the printing house at Drakar Taso was established by Rinchen Namgyel and renovated by Karma Lobsang in the late seventeenth or early eighteenth century. Chökyi Wangchuk had engaged in a philological study of several block-print editions of Tsangnyön's life of Milarepa from around Tibet. All, he declared, descended not from the edition produced by Tsangnyön Heruka but from the one produced by his student Rinchen Namgyel at Drakar Taso. This is an important philological claim with potentially far-reaching cultural consequences, for it places Drakar Taso at the center of one of the most widespread biographical traditions in the whole of the Tibetan cultural world.[41]

The publication of works of the Kagyu schools at Drakar Taso in Gungtang and Rechungpuk in the Tsetang region was part of a broader increase in printing throughout central and southwest Tibet, especially in evidence at Mangyul Gungtang.[42] This was taking place precisely during the era of both Shalu Lotsawa and Tsangnyön Heruka, though it appears that only Tsangnyön took advantage of it while Shalu Lotsawa worked throughout his life with texts in manuscript form. What is unique about the publishing at Drakar Taso is Richen Namgyel's distinctive and patient determination over twenty years to build a well-rounded corpus of Kagyu hagiographies, histories, songs, preaching guidebooks, and contemplative manuals (perhaps here a comparison can be made to Shalu Lotsawa's persistent efforts to translate and redact a relatively coherent body of literature, albeit consisting of Indian grammatical treatises). Taken together, their publications include works by and about more than twenty figures. Indian personalities include Vajradhāra, Saraha, Tilopa, Nāropa, and—though he does not belong to the lineage of the former siddhas—the late Indian yogin Mitrayogin, who traveled to Tibet in the twelfth century, as well as the great Kadampa preacher Potowa Rinchensel. Among the Tibetan masters represented in the printed works of Tsangnyön's tradition are Marpa, Milarepa, Rechungpa, Gampopa, Pakmodrupa, Ling Repa Pema Dorjé, Tsangpa Gyaré Yeshé Dorjé, Götsangpa Gompo Dorjé, Yangönpa, and, somewhat later, the yogin–poet Kodrakpa Sönam Gyeltsen. Figures from the late thirteenth through the mid-fifteenth cen-

turies are not represented, and the narratives resume with Tsangnyön Heruka's teacher, Shara Rapjampa Sangyé Sengé, and
move through Tsangnyön himself to his two principal disciples,
Lhatsün Rinchen Namgyel and Götsang Repa Natsok Rangdröl,
and finally to Sangyé Darpo, whose work of 1568 marks a convenient place to draw a close to the tradition. Sangyé Darpo was
the tradition's official historiographer, who composed a history
of Kagyu schools from the time of the Buddha up to Tsangnyön
Heruka, Götsang Repa, and Rinchen Namgyel. He was also a
patron of printing, sponsoring such works as the biography of
Yangönpa (printed not at one of the two more well-known printing houses, but at Tsibri). It is significant that there are no du-
plicate works published at both Dakar Taso and Rechungpuk,
suggesting that Götsang Repa and Rinchen Namgyel were aware
of each other's catalog of publications. In an apparent division of
major saints, Rinchen Namgyel seems to have secured Milarepa,
while Götsang Repa worked to a greater extent on the life of Milarepa's most famous contemplative disciple, Rechungpa Dorjé
Drakpa.

Aside from their value as examples of the rich poetic and
biographical literature that had reached a zenith among the Kagyu schools by the beginning of the sixteenth century, the prints
published by Rinchen Namgyel and Götsang Repa contain informative colophons authored by either the two editor/producers
themselves or a senior scribe (like the colophons in the works of
Jamyang Shepé Dorjé). A full colophon may include reasons for
composing or redacting the work, reasons for printing it, a list of
sponsors, a list of the artisans, and the date of the creation, carving, and consecration of the printed work. These important pub-
lisher's postfaces have to much say about the sponsors and what
they donated in particular. For any given major project, there
could be more than fifty sponsors—on occasion the scribe of the
colophon despairs at writing down all of their names! A broad
range of social positions is represented, including such intriguing
if otherwise unknowable figures as the army officer from Ngari
who donated to the publication of the brief biography of Rechungpa produced at Drakar Taso. Other types of people making
donations to the publication of Tsangnyön Heruka's biography of
Milarepa at Drakar Taso included monks, nuns, nomads, noble-
men and noblewomen, hermits, and people from western regions
such as Ngari and Dolpo. An extensive donor list is provided in
Rinchen Namgyel's re-carving of Tsangnyön Heruka's *Life of Mil-*

arepa, offering a vivid description of the rich economic and material life in which wood-block printing was enmeshed.[43] Materials donated include butter; Nepalese coins; domestic animals such as dri, yak, and dzomo; offering scarves; coral; green silk; white silk; Chinese silk; silver; saffron; cotton cloth in plain, dyed, and printed varieties; molasses; armor; barley; turquoise; wool cloth; monk's clothing; medicine; copper pots; tin plates; amulet boxes; vegetables; rice; tripod stoves; skins from wild goats and spotted deer (from Rechungpa's biography); yogurt (from Götsang Repa's biography of Tsangnyön Heruka); tea; conch shells; animal horns; helmets; horses; bells; knives; sapphires; salt; and—lest one forget that this is for book publishing—wood blocks for carving and paper for printing.

There is little doubt that the doctrines of karma and merit played an important role in encouraging people to donate—printing was good Buddhist work, and by the sixteenth century donating to a biography or collection of poetry authored by a Tibetan saint was every bit as meritorious as sponsoring a sūtra or a tantra. But people might just as well make an offering as a memorial to a person now deceased, or wish for the welfare of a particular place rather than a person. The biography of Tsangnyön Heruka's teacher, Sharawa, was authored and likely printed in 1559 by a student of Götsang Repa to fulfill the last wishes of Lhatsün (who died in 1557) and to prolong the life of Götsang (who would die in 1570). These were not uncommon purposes for publishing; projects undertaken at Sakya monastery in the 1540s were also carried out in accordance with the wishes of the deceased and for the longevity of prominent living figures. More interesting are the several works dedicated to peace and prosperity of reigning rulers over the region in which the work was printed. Rinchen Namgyel dedicated his 1550 publication of the life of the Indian adept Tilopa to the eventual enlightenment of his deceased mother and father, as well as to the long life of the Gongma (or leader) and the peace and prosperity of his kingdom. Although he does not mention this leader's name, he likely refers to the ruler of Mangyul Gungtang, Tri Kunzang Nyida Drakpa (1514–60),[44] who also happened to be his nephew. Thus the life story of a tenth-century Indian mystic came to be dedicated to the proper function of a sixteenth-century Tibetan principality. Rinchen Namgyel dedicated the publication of the life of Götsangpa to both the welfare of the Ngari region and his mother and father. It is clear that regional interests were strongly in mind when authors and editors printed works—a point that will be discussed again below.

As was the case at Shalu and other publishing houses, the artisans who carried out the work of printing were, at least in rhetorical terms, held in high esteem, and are mentioned in many of the publishers' conclusions. Scribes are accorded a place of respect in the list, and sometimes it is only they who are named, while the block carvers remain anonymous. In other cases the carvers are highly praised and are compared even to Viśvakarma, the divine architect of Indian myth. As many as thirteen carvers could work on a single project (as was the case for the small prayer to Milarepa carved at Rechungpuk), far fewer than the hundreds who would work on the massive canonical collections of the eighteenth century, but still a significant collection of laborers for a small retreat center. Artisans could participate in printing projects on an ongoing basis, and it is possible that they remained in residence at both Drakar Taso and Rechungpuk. The printer Chupön Dorjé Gyeltsen is one example: he worked at Drakar Taso as early as 1538 on Rinchen Namgyel's brief biography of Rechungpa, and he appears to have outlived Rinchen Namgyel himself, for he worked on the biography of the master after his death in 1557.

Scribes and carvers would work in teams and most likely simultaneously, each taking responsibility for a portion of the project. Two experienced scribes might split a work such as Tsangnyön Heruka's *Hundred Thousand Songs of Milarepa*, each completing half of the total text. The carvers would generally take on much less work per person than the scribes; 10 carvers, for instance, completed the 250 blocks of Milarepa's songs in 1555 at Drakar Taso (with their names listed throughout the edition at the bottom of the last folio for which they were responsible). In some cases scribe and carver might be the same person, like Chuwön Dorjé Gyeltsen, who acted as scribe for the second half of Milarepa's songs and also worked as a carver on the last 10 folios. Occasionally a scribe refers to himself in the first person in a colophon, thus making it plain that it was he and not Rinchen Namgyel or Götsang Repa who composed it. So while these two prominent figures are often referred to as the creators of these printed editions, they might better be thought of as the publishers or the executive producers, and the scribes working under them as the editors, producers, or project managers.

Printing continued after the death of Rinchen Namgyel, for his own treatise on the contemplative practices of the Great Seal tradition so popular among the Kagyu schools was printed in 1561, four years after his passing. However, though rightly famous for institutionalizing the printing of biographical and poetic works associated with Milarepa and similar figures, Rinchen Namgyel was not the first person after Tsangnyön Heruka to produce a new set of printing blocks for the life and songs of Milarepa. That honor goes to his contemporary Sönam Lodrö (c. 1460–1541), a fellow student of Tsangnyön. The 1544/1556[45] biography of Sönam Lodrö states that he waited on Tsangnyön for more than fifteen years, from around 1490 to Tsangnyön's death in 1507. Sönam Lodrö had prints made as early as the 1530s (and certainly no later than 1541, the year of his death). His most important contributions were reprints of three of Tsangnyön's works, the life and songs of Milarepa and the biography of Marpa. The story of these blocks is as follows. On one occasion Sönam Lodrö received offerings of tea, cups, iron, and fabric from disciples in a request that he produce new blocks of the biography and songs of Milarepa, for the old blocks had become worn. With donations from the several settlements around the Nyanang region of southwestern Tibet, he was able to complete more than 100 blocks from the *Hundred Thousand Songs of Milarepa* initially, and he completed the full work after gathering more donations. Shortly after that he completed new blocks for the biography of Milarepa as well as a short devotional work. Sönam Lodrö made sure (in what begins to be an all but required element in narratives of publishing projects) that the scribes and carvers were well paid, and as the blocks were consecrated, a rain of flowers fell—ever a sure sign that the forces of enlightenment are looking favorably upon one's labors. Finally, just after he published the biography of Marpa, he had many hundreds of prints made and gave them out as "dharma gifts" to the faithful around the region.[46] The blocks of Marpa's biography seem to have been dear to Sönam Lodrö, for they are one of the few items about which he gave specific instructions to his disciples upon his death. The blocks were to be moved to Dropuk, the old hermitage of Milarepa, the same place Tsangnyön Heruka had received the visionary command to publish the life of Milarepa, where this tradition's dreams of the printed word began.

BOOK, MONUMENT, AND PLACE

In the biographies of Shalu Lotsawa and Tsangnyön Heruka, the effusive praise of textual scholarship found throughout may distract from or obscure important interconnections among technical expertise, economic relations, and social identity. Why did rulers such as Rapten Kunzang Pakpa of Gyantsé pour resources into producing elaborate volumes of scripture that would seldom, if ever, be read? What did Rinpungpa Dönyö Dorjé, arguably the most powerful leader of central Tibet during the florescence of both Shalu Lotsawa and Tsangnyön Heruka, care about the editorial status of a Sanskrit grammatical treatise or the long cave-bound years of an eccentric hermit? The usual answer is that such patrons sought to accrue merit, but this explanation is based primarily on a Buddhist theological reading of human action. To answer such questions in social terms, it is useful to compare the book production efforts of Tsangnyön and Shalu Lotsawa to another activity with more immediately visible political implications. In 1504 Tsagnyön Heruka (only three years prior to his death) was involved with another major project that involved royal patronage, the restoration of Swayambhu Stūpa in the Kathmandu Valley of Nepal.[47] The story of his restoration efforts throws his and others' book production activities into greater relief, and highlights the interplay between political patrons and religious leaders in Buddhist cultural projects.

Preparations for the work of 1504 actually began three years earlier, in 1501. For the previous few years Ratnamalla, king of Yambu—the northern section of modern Kathmandu—since 1484, had sent repeated requests to Tibetan yogins who made pilgrimage to Swayambhu for their aid in restoring the *stūpa*. Tsangnyön had refused these pleas until 1501, when he received a donation of gold from a certain Tibetan patron. Encouraged by this auspicious financial sign, he agreed to mount a full-scale campaign to raise funds for the restoration, and sent his disciples to all reaches of the Tibetan cultural area in search of faithful donors. Many Tibetans contributed both gold and supplies to the restoration, and—just as in the colophon of a block-printed volume of scripture—Tsangnyön dutifully listed their names, ranks, and specific donations in a register that Götsang Repa reproduced in his biography. Offerings of gold, copper, silver, horses, grain, and labor came from rulers and ministers in Dakpo, Kongpo, Tsari, Gungthang, Guge, Yolmo, Mustang, Kailash, Ladakh—in short, all the major areas along the southern border of the Tibetan cultural world. Secular leaders were not entirely absent from this list; the ruler of southwest central Tibet himself, Rinpungpa Dönyo Dorjé, donated mules with saddles and other goods. News of Tsangnyön's efforts caught the attention of major religious leaders as well; the Seventh Karmapa, Chödrak Gyatso, commented that Tsangnyön was "carrying the great burden of the teachings by restoring Swayambhu Stūpa."

This process of fund raising took three years, and it was not until the autumn of 1504 that Tsangnyön felt ready to travel to Kathmandu and start the repairs. He set out from Chuwar, his primary retreat center, and traveled northwest to Dzongkar, where he was received by the lord of the region and given gold, barley, and corvee laborers to carry provisions to his next stop, Kyirong, some thirty miles north of the Nepal–Tibet border. At Dzongkar Tsangnyön also picked up travel documents and a travel manager, as well as a personal assistant and a treasurer. On his way south he enlisted two translators at Lajang, very close to the modern border, to aid him in communicating effectively with the citizens of the Kathmandu Valley (remember that he could not understand Nāropa, even in a dream). There he was first met by Newars, musicians from the valley who had trekked north to meet him. He was also given a Newar-style palanquin, which suggests that he was carried for the remainder of the journey. Upon his arrival in the valley in September 1504 he was met by King Ratnamalla's ministers, musicians, and hundreds of people from Yambu and Yangel, the traditional names of what are now the northern and southern areas of Kathmandu. Together with representatives of the king, Tsangnyön proceeded to Tham Bahil, the old Newar Buddhist monastic complex on the north edge of Yambu, where a feast was held on his behalf. After touring the city and paying homage to the protector deity Mahākāla, Tsangnyön went to the royal residence and met with King Ratnamalla.

After preliminary meetings with the king, in which the arrangements for laborers and funding were finalized, Tsangnyön met with priests to perform a ritual to begin the joint Newar–Tibetan undertaking. This was done in an ecumenical fashion; first the Newars performed the commencement ritual in the Newar style, and then Tsangnyön performed the same ritual in the Tibetan style. Just days before, Tsangnyön had had a vision in which he made preparations of another sort. He was visited by Viśvakarma, the divine architect of Indic mythology (who, recall, could serve as the mythic identity of wood-block carvers producing books), who appeared to him in the form of a Newar craftsman and beseeched him to finish the restoration of Swayambhu quickly. Tsangnyön agreed and enlisted the aid of the god. This was not the first time that Tsangnyön had been approached by the gods to work on the *stūpa*; years before, during an earlier journey to Kathmandu, the elephant-headed Ganeśa made the same request to him.

Having spent four years on preparations with leaders, monks, craftsmen, and gods, Tsangnyön commenced the restoration in October 1504. The workforce provided by Ratnamalla numbered more than 600 craftsmen and laborers, including 72 carpenters, 340 assemblers, 200 corvee laborers, 12 blacksmiths, 42 coppersmiths, and 12 goldsmiths. The restorations themselves included primarily decorative additions. Tsangnyön added window and door ornaments, numerous mirrors and bells, and—most importantly—a copper canopy to protect the *stūpa* from the rain, supported by four gold and copper-covered pillars. Much like Lhatsün Rinchen Namgyel at the printing house of Drakar Taso, during these labors Tsangnyön acted as a sort of executive producer, overseeing all aspects of the work. But his esoteric skills surpassed those of his student (or for that matter, his philologist competitor Shalu Lotsawa, who would have been translating another grammatical treatise at about this time), and his expertise as a spiritual adept was continually required to avert mishaps and maintain good relations with divine and natural forces. He routinely circumambulated the *stūpa* while performing rituals of protection for the workers. One day he skipped the ritual on the twelfth pass around the *stūpa*. Immediately a swarm of bees with stingers as sharp as weapons attacked the workers and stung them until they bled. Tsangnyön bellowed a command and the bees instantly disappeared. On another occasion the work was impeded by rain, so the master ordered Ganeśa to provide sunshine and keep away the rains until the work was finished. Each day from then on was clear and sunny, and productivity increased.

Throughout his stay in Kathmandu Tsangnyön was the guest of the king himself, who paid for all his food, including a liberal supply of beer, as well as his entertainment. In this instance he was the patronized, similarly to the craftsmen at Shalu or Degé receiving gifts for their services. At one point during his stay some 500 Newar women came to his residence to dance and play music for him—women who, the biographies say, made the mind swoon with their celestial loveliness. The project was not without its setbacks, however. A number of the Tibetans accompanying Tsangnyön became gravely ill, and many returned to Tibet for fear of being stricken down in the Kathmandu Valley. The financial aspects of the work were also problematic; gold and copper were running out, and there was not enough to complete the canopy. The king gave 40 large measures (*srang*) of gold, and when Tsangnyön hinted that the canopy might fall down if not properly done, gave 20 more. By the time they were finished Tsangnyön and his disciple Lhatsün had spent a total of three and a half months in Kathmandu, the restorations taking two months and 13 days. Work was completed toward the end of December 1504. The cost of the venture, which included gold, copper, wood, labor, food, lodging, entertainment for the workforce, and letters and gifts to patrons both before and after the restoration, amounted to 2,751 measures (*zho*) of gold.

Upon completion of the repairs there was, of course, a festival marking the auspicious conclusion of the project. The king invited Tsangnyön one last time to his palace, where the Tibetan master was dressed in ornate robes of silk and beautiful jewelry for the ceremony. On the night before, a miraculous wind swept through the city and cleaned every stone, brick, tree, and street. The following day people from Yambu and Yangel came out by the hundreds to participate, and the spotless lanes between city and *stūpa* were totally packed with revelers. The king himself was present at the consecration and ceremonial whitewashing of the *stūpa*, during which there were numerous miraculous events. Through the restoration the *stūpa*'s power to maintain order had been reinvigorated, and it was not limited to Kathmandu; at the time of the festival and the consecration good people all around the region were happy, and bad people received karmic retribution for their negative deeds. The action of the *stūpa* was quick, specific, and even deadly: at the moment of consecration, a particularly vile person in Kyirong—nearly 100 miles north—became ill, coughed up blood, and dropped dead due to the force of its effect. During these closing ceremonies all the gods were present, Ganeśa and Viśvakarma among them, to bear witness to the success of Tsangnyön's labors. The *stūpa* became a meeting point for the divine and the human as the king, the ministers, the people of Kathmandu and Tibet, and the gods and nonhumans of many realms came to circumambulate the white-domed monument.

Just as the Kathmandu Valley was a place where work on Buddhist monumental architecture could bring religious leaders in close contact with political leaders, institutions such as the monasteries of Dratang, Gongkar, Shalu, and the political centers of Rinpung, Gungtang, and Nedong were places where court reputations could be won or lost in displays of grammatical prowess or on-the-spot translation. The biographies of Shalu Lotsawa, Tsangnyön Heruka, and Tsangnyön's disciples are rich sources for studying perceptions of textual scholars in Tibet. Yet they are about more than the lives of a select few influential figures—they illustrate the lives of whole communities consisting of diverse types of social actors (the colophons often bring this into greater relief than the biographies themselves). In reading these life stories one is often drawn beyond the image of the protagonist—be he a scholar or a hermit—toward the networks of intellectual cooperation and contest, his patrons, his social world, and the places where he worked. The biographies by and about Tsangnyön Heruka show that the locations where printing was done were glorified by hosting the printed word. Shalu Lotsawa worked for several of the most powerful men in fifteenth-century central and southwestern Tibet—including the rulers of Gyantsé, Nedong, and Rinpung—as well as the Fourth Shamarpa, the Seventh Karmapa, and the abbot of Taklung monastery. Were it not for his popularity among these leaders, perhaps little if anything would now be known of his activities, and he almost certainly would not have been known in places south of the Himalayas such as Vajrāsana.

Likewise, Tsangnyön and his disciples were connected to the leaders of central Tibet as well as to those in Kathmandu. The Rinpungpa leader Dönyö Dorjé was sponsor to both Shalu Lotsawa and Tsangnyön Heruka, and both utilized their skills as editors, writers, publishers, and printers in his service. The biographies dwell upon relationships fostered between scholars and political leaders, but it is once again publishers' concluding remarks that vividly illustrate how important both scribally produced and printed books could be to writers, sponsors, and artisans alike (here the works of the Tsangnyön tradition offer clear advantages over the works associated with Shalu Lotsawa in terms of the abundance of social data provided). Indeed, one of the most interesting things about the Tsangnyön tradition of printing is not that it came into existence—there were other, less documented printing traditions beginning at this time—but that its members were compelled to record its occurrence so thoroughly in both biographies and publishers' postfaces. Clearly wood-block printing was a self-consciously significant affair, as was the renovation of religious monuments. Yet these publishers rarely speak to why printing was important in the first place, as opposed, say, to scribal publication, which was still a major form of text production in sixteenth-century Tibet. One obvious reason is to support proselytizing activities—a rationale laid out in Tsangnyön's long prolegomena to printing the *Life of Milarepa* quoted in full above, but never explicitly referred to in the colophons themselves. He certainly aimed such efforts at political leaders with some success, yet as a form of proselytizing, book production may in turn have been connected with the growth and reputation of locations where printing was undertaken. As the biographies and songs of famous Indian and Tibetan masters were disseminated from places such as Drakar Taso and Rechungpuk, these institutions would become known beyond their regions as centers of meritorious activity, perhaps worthy of a trip to pay homage to the memory of the masters portrayed in the biographies—like the visit of the Rinpungpa leader Dönyö Dorjé during Tsangnyön Heruka's funeral at Rechungpuk. Again, comparisons with monuments are instructive; the renovated *stūpa*, like the reproduced biography, was a good investment in regional reputation. These institutions are often praised as the beneficent domains of celestial significance that support the printing of Buddhist literature. The colophon to Götsang Repa's life of Rechungpa offers a good description of Rechungpuk: "The center of the long Yarlung Valley—a Dharmodaya temple piled five stories high, with green rice fields at its base, called Lomalori, with its peak as if covered with piles of jewels, prophesied by Milarepa, blessed by Rechungpa, the place at which Tsangnyön Heruka passed into the realm of reality."[48] And while Drakar Taso is claimed in a geopolitical sense as a region of Mangyul Gungtang, which is, according to Rinchen Namgyel, itself but a part of the larger western Tibetan region of Ngari, it is said in more cosmic terms to be a place that promotes the dharma in a degenerate time, even better than the limitless celestial Buddha fields for its ability to serve Buddhism. If a *stūpa* could provide the symbolic center for a polity, so could books or the production of books.

But again, if printing is important to missionary efforts and to personal or institutional promotion, this does not necessarily distinguish it from scribal publication in absolute terms. Shalu Lotsawa seems to have engaged only in scribal publication, but his efforts to promote himself through textual production are still comparable to Tsangnyön's printing projects. One turn of phrase that hints at the unique ability of printing is used only twice in the nearly sixty works from Drakar Taso and Rechungpuk consulted here: according to the colophon of Tsangnyön Heru-ka's famous *Life of Milarepa*, Tsangnyön had produced an "inex-haustible print." This expression suggests the unique capacity of the printing technology to reproduce vast quantities of the work, surely the most obvious technical and economic advantage over scribal publication. This was also an advantage of print publica-tion over monument restoration, for prints could be more easily disseminated as a sort of advertisement for the production loca-tion than could the *stūpa* (although models of *stūpa*s are known to have been distributed[49]). However, the appellation "inex-haustible" is perhaps more evocative than descriptive, for blocks do wear out—a simple fact of which the publishers themselves speak openly. Because Tsangnyön Heruka's blocks had "ben-efited humanity in such great measure," they had become some-what unclear, and for this reason, some sixty years after Tsang-nyön produced his, Rinchen Namgyel ventured to make a new set of blocks for what had already become a classic of Tibetan literature. So popular was this version of Milarepa's story that the new blocks in turn wore out due to extensive use, and a fresh set was once again produced by Rinchen Namgyel.

Like the publication (or republication) of a saint's biography or the translation of a complex grammatical treatise, the restora-tion of a Buddhist monument was a complex affair comprising many steps—the request of a central patron, the interest and availability of a religious specialist, the gathering of donations, the organizing of a large labor force, and the memorialization of the labors of both patrons and specialists. Preliminary rituals were needed to protect workers, mediating between humans in very real political situations and between gods and humans in more esoteric circumstances. The business of restoration cre-ated an opportunity for the religious leader and the king to come together in a joint project linking different regions of the Hima-layas in a peaceful alliance. The king enhanced the prestige and legitimacy of his rule by contributing to the maintenance of a Buddhist monument, while the religious leader was prominently seen as maintaining moral and spiritual order by caring for the concrete embodiment of the enlightened mind of the Buddha. In the process he received patronage that would allow him to undertake further religious activities. Donating to the restora-tion was not merely a way for disparate patrons to gain merit for themselves but also an important means to create political ties mediated by both *stūpa* and religious master. Surely that was also the case with the printing efforts at Drakar Taso and the varied causes to which the leader of central Tibet, Dönyö Dorjé, contributed as he patronized both the scholar and the hermit.

The study of a single biography or a limited corpus of printed works will not fully address how book production, *stūpa* restoration, or other activities normally described in doctrinal terms may be explained as social acts. That will entail entering into debates on the nature of kingship, the role of luxury goods and kingly prestige, and relationships among scholarly reputations, institutional reputations, and the economy in Tibet, to name but a few issues. Yet the beginnings of an answer may be discerned in Shalu Lotsawa's (or more accurately Rinchen Tashi's) statement as he approaches the court at Nedong: "Those who are renowned as scholars are only those reputed to be so at the king's court." Here, in the words of the biography itself, is the start of a social definition of scholarship. Scholars are those whose labors are publicly recognized by leaders, for only with such recognition could one continue to practice one's craft. And it might be said that "Those who are renowned as hermits and madmen are only those reputed to be so at the king's court," be that in central Tibet or in the Kathmandu Valley. Is it any wonder, then, that in this and other biographies scholars are profoundly concerned with public image? Butön laments his manuscripts at death, and Shalu Lotsawa weeps at the death scene in Butön's life story. Reputation makes a scholar, these works suggest, and reputation at court makes a great scholar, a great madman—or at least one who can afford to buy paper. For we can infer from the tests to which Shalu Lotsawa was put by the scholar-monks of the Nedong court that scholarship entailed competition—for resources, patronage, and prestige in the eyes of rulers and potential benefactors. Shalu Lotsawa and Tsangnyön were contemporaries (indeed, they could very well have been together in Gyantsé at Pelkhor Dechen monastery during the 1470s). Both competed as court intellectuals, though with very different personae. Yet both were proponents of the culture of the book.

And it may be that rulers competed for scholars as well, for (as Rinchen Tashi has argued, at least) Shalu Lotsawa was in demand, and King Ratnamalla had trouble finding someone to restore the *stūpa* of Swayambhu until he increased the amount he was willing to offer for the job. The objects produced by scholars and scribes—books, in this case—produced prestige for the patrons, and the expertise of scholars such as Shalu Lotsawa increased this prestige, as one might surmise from the scene in which the Gyantsé ruler employs Shalu Lotsawa to "improve" the already lavish canonical volumes at Pelkor Dechen through editing. Here editing is aesthetic, and the aesthetic is political. Perhaps having such a scholar and his products in one's court displayed the justness of one's rule, the civility of one's court, the sophistication of one's aesthetic sensibility. But the voices of rulers are seldom heard in biographies such as those of Shalu Lotsawa or Tsangnyön Heruka, and the interests of scholars, yogins, and kings did not always intersect. It is difficult to get at the ruling end of the patron–patronized relationship, so important for the socially oriented view of scholarship. One vantage point is offered in the work of a figure who was both a scholar and a leader, the last regent of the Fifth Dalai Lama, Sangyé Gyatso. His work on medical literature places great emphasis on the textual scholarship by which others like Shalu Lotsawa made their reputations, and it also explicitly connects such scholarship and the constitution of one of the principal patrons of Buddhist culture during the seventeenth century, the central Tibetan government of the Fifth Dalai Lama.

*V*ivid words of warning from the *Four Medical Tantras*—the primary work on the healing arts in Tibet—underscore the central place of textual learning in the practice of medicine:

> *The physician without a lineage*
> *Is like a fox that seizes the king's throne:*
> *He deserves no one's respect.*
> *The physician who does not understand the texts*
> *Is like a blind person to whom you show something:*
> *He can discern neither the disease nor the cure.*[1]

Textual expertise in its many forms is an integral part of the medical tradition in Tibet, or more precisely, of certain formulations of the medical tradition with a generalized emphasis on scholarship. For certain writers the *Four Tantras* were the subject of a heated scholarly debate, in great part about text critical issues. This chapter moves beyond the strictly Buddhist focus of previous chapters to explore what several important Tibetan writers have said about the role of textual scholarship in medical learning— the place of scholarly learning in a field dedicated (in an ideal sense) ultimately to practical application—and about the relationship between medical scholarship and the bodhisattva ideal of Mahāyāna Buddhism. Specifically, the following makes several points: first, debates about philological scholarship in premodern Tibet were not limited to discussions involving Buddhist literature but also went on in fields such as medical scholarship (as well as history, poetics, linguistics, etc.). Such debates were nevertheless framed by recourse to the Mahāyāna Buddhist ideal of the bodhisattva and the injunction that bodhisattvas study the five arts and sciences, including medicine. Second, reports of such debates were part of larger efforts to claim authority by certain groups of medical scholars at the expense of others, by casting doubt on both their ability to practice medicine and their adherence to bodhisattva ideals. Finally, this rhetoric linking the bodhisattva and the textual/medical scholar was part of an attempt to exert direct influence over the development of learning and culture by the newly formed Tibetan theocracy, the Ganden government of the Fifth Dalai Lama, at the end of the seventeenth century. In examining the actual debates about textual scholarship in Tibetan medical literature, these larger issues provide important context.

The principal character in this chapter is Sangyé Gyatso, the person traditionally credited with institutionalizing and systematizing the Tibetan medical tradition under the auspices of the Fifth Dalai Lama, Ngawang Lobsang Gyatso (1617–82),[2] and the Ganden government during the last decades of the seventeenth century.[3] We will also look to select figures in the earlier history of the *Four Tantras*, including Drangti Pelden Tshojé (thirteenth/fourteenth century), Zurkhar Lodrö Gyelpo (1509–c. 1573), Darmo Menrampa Lobsang Chödrak (1638–97/1700), and Namling Panchen Könchok Chödrak (1646–1718). Each had much to say on textual scholarship, and each had a profound impact on Sangyé Gyatso.

THE REGENT'S BOOKS OF MEDICINE

It is probably no exaggeration to say that Sangyé Gyatso, the most important regent to the great Fifth Dalai Lama, did more than anyone prior or since to promote medical learning in Tibet. Other than the Fifth Dalai Lama himself, medicine was Sangyé Gyatso's favorite topic, and his medical writings set the standard for generations to come. His detailed history of Tibetan medicine, the *Beryl Mirror*,[4] reveals much about his attitudes toward textual scholarship and its foundational role in medical learning and practice, particularly in several autobiographical passages that include remarks regarding his early studies in medicine, as well as his early efforts at editing and printing of the *Four Tantras*. This scholar's undertakings in the philology of medical texts were motivated by an understanding of the place of medicine in the traditional Buddhist domains of knowledge: practical arts, medical arts, linguistics, logic and epistemology, and the art of Buddhist learning and realization itself. Like the medieval physicians of Italy responsible for introducing Greco-Arab medical scholarship to Europe, Sangyé Gyatso held medical education to be intimately bound with these arts and sciences. Thus, the present chapter also touches on his more thematic remarks about the nature of medical learning, and suggests that his efforts in medical scholarship must be seen as well in relation to his leadership of the Ganden government.

The basis for much of the following discussion is the final chapter of the *Explanatory Tantra*, the second of the *Four Tantras*.[5] Chapter 31, the source of the verse quoted above, prescribes the qualities of the ideal physician.[6] The first lines of the chapter list six prerequisites: intelligence, altruism, honor, practical skill, diligence, and knowledge of worldly affairs. Intelligence, the first of the six, is defined at the outset in singular terms: "With great, firm, and fine intellect, learn deeply the medical treatises."[7] The sixth prerequisite of the physician, diligence, is in turn divided into four aspects, the first of which is the following injunction: "Learn writing and reading completely, for whether [you] are capable or incapable depends on these."[8] In his commentary to the *Four Tantras*, the *Blue Beryl*, Sangyé Gyatso elaborates on these lines by saying that competence in exposition, composition, and debate is based upon the ability to read and write.[9] The second aspect is reliance upon a skilled teacher, who is characterized in part as someone who has a deep knowledge of medical texts. While there are plainly many other qualities required of the well-trained physician, chapter 31 begins with an explicit emphasis on textual scholarship for both teacher and student. This emphasis may seem pro forma, and perhaps somewhat inconsequential compared to the massive therapeutic or *materia medica* chapters of the *Four Tantras*. Yet this passage from the *Explanatory Tantra* has far-reaching implications for the medical writers considered here; while Sangyé Gyatso's *Beryl Mirror* is typically conceived of as a work of history, it can also be usefully appreciated as an extended commentary on that chapter, and on these passages in particular.

From the age of eight, Sangyé Gyatso studied medicine under several of the finest medical scholars of the seventeenth century, all under the care of the Fifth Dalai Lama. During his relatively short life of fifty-two years, the regent of Tibet composed three major medical works. In 1687, at the age of thirty-five, he began the commentary known as the *Blue Beryl*, which he completed one year later, in 1688. Two years after this he began an extended commentary on the third of the *Four Tantras*, the *Instructional Tantra*. This extended survey of medical practice was completed in 1691. Eleven years later, in 1702, he began the final draft of what was to be his last medical work, the *Beryl Mirror*, more commonly known as the *Interior Analysis of the Medical Arts*.[10] This is explicitly based upon an earlier work by Drangti Pelden Tshojé (early/mid-fourteenth century). According to Sangyé Gyatso, Pelden Tshojé's *Elucidation of Topics* forms the basis for most medical historiography between the fourteenth and the seventeenth centuries.[11]

Sangyé Gyatso's survey of the medical tradition, the *Beryl Mirror* is a complex work, integrating medical history, a schematic presentation of the Buddhist teachings, a long prescriptive survey of the qualities of the ideal physician, and several autobiographical passages. He completed it in 1703, just two years before his death in 1705. It is likely, however, that he had been working on it for a number of years prior to this. At the close of the work is a small note relating the unfavorable circumstances of its creation. Up to age fifty, that is, until 1702, Sangyé Gyatso dictated to a scribe. He admits that this process was a major source of error, for his own words were often misconstrued and written down incorrectly. In 1702 Sangyé Gyatso considered the work to be only a collection of draft notes. Unfortunately, in the same year his eyesight began to fail. It became difficult for him to see fine objects in the morning and evening, and his ability to write for himself waned. His scribe, Chakarwa Pema Sönam, thus completed his work. It is tempting to speculate that the survey is unfinished as it stands.[12]

Perhaps the most interesting passages in Sangyé Gyatso's *Beryl Mirror* are the scattered autobiographical remarks on his medical education and subsequent efforts to promote medical learning and practice. His reminiscences lead through some of the most important years in the textual history of the *Four Tantras*. In his own estimation, Sangyé Gyatso exhibited skill in the five arts of craft, medicine, linguistics, logic, and Buddhism itself from a young age, and wondered if he might not be the reincarnation of some former scholar also skilled in the arts.[13] Between the ages of thirty and forty this early preference began to produce results. He boasts that he delighted in whatever textual traditions he encountered, and in addition to running the kingdom found the time to compose twenty volumes on linguistics, logic, practical arts, medicine—and even Buddhism.[14] Before this time he had memorized the three smaller of the *Four Tantras*, the *Root*, *Explanatory*, and *Subsequent*, and had already begun making his own contribution to medical literature. Sangyé Gyatso spent a good deal of time engaged in text-critical work on the *Four Tantras* themselves. Their textual history was of great concern for him, and he relates both his and his predecessor's efforts to improve the text. The print of the *Four Tantras* made at Dratang in 1546 by Zurkhar Lodrö Gyelpo[15] had been used by the court physician to the Dalai Lama, Jango Nangso Dargyé (Byang ngo Nang so dar rgyas), as the basis for new printing blocks in 1662. Nangso Dargyé felt that this Dratang print was an authoritative witness ideal for reproduction. Thus, according to Sangyé Gyatso at least, he made no effort to use other versions for his new print.

In 1670 Sangyé Gyatso began to look at various recensions of the *Four Tantras* himself, and decided that the Dratang print was not as reliable as his elders believed. He became convinced that his master and his court physician had made a mistake in relying exclusively on it.[16] He believed the version edited by Nangso Dargyé to be filled with gaps and confused sections. He therefore took a chance and told the Great Fifth that his colophon to Nangso Dargyé's 1662 print was inaccurate when it heaped praise only on the Dratang print. Because this most recent edition of the *Four Tantras* had been prepared under the auspices of the Fifth Dalai Lama, criticizing that text was tantamount to criticizing the Dalai Lama himself. Sangyé Gyatso seems acutely aware of this dilemma. He was, after all, saying that the bodhisattva Avalokiteśvara himself did not really know his scripture all that well.[17] His language in describing this situation is supremely deferential, yet the basic point is clear: "My master, the Great Fifth [Dalai Lama], who knows everything of ultimate meaning and who sees all and everywhere as if it were in the palm of his hand . . . manifested ignorance of the three [smaller] tantras, the outlines, and the tree diagrams for the sake of the lowly."[18] The Dalai Lama was pleased at his seventeen-year-old protégé's industry, and encouraged him to begin re-editing the *Four Tantras*.[19] This project was to last twenty-four years, ending in 1694 (twelve years after the death of the Fifth Dalai Lama) when Sangyé Gyatso had new blocks of the text carved.

Despite his studies and his extensive writing, Sangyé Gyatso admits to doubting his editorial abilities to the point of anxiety.[20] He was apparently able to overcome these feelings, however, and provides a detailed account of his efforts. The editorial process was a massive project, in which he consulted more than forty separate *sūtras*, tantras, Buddhist treatises, and medical works in order to arrive at good textual readings. In addition to the

Dratang print itself, he used at least four other prints of the *Four Tantras* and a number of old handwritten manuscripts. He specifically names editors and patrons of prints from Dzonga, Gampo, Takten, and Bodong, providing some insight into the complexity of the textual traditions he confronted. By comparing older manuscripts with the Dratang print he sought to restore older verses, fix topical headings and outlines, emend faulty readings, clarify archaic terminology, and eliminate changes in the text that he considered to be guesses by the uninformed.[21]

THE PHYSICIAN AS TEXTUAL SCHOLAR

Despite his critique of former scholars' efforts, it is clear that Sangyé Gyatso drew inspiration from his predecessors in the medical field. The *Four Tantras'* insistence that physicians be expert textual scholars is taken up frequently by writers over the centuries. Jangpa Namgyel Draksang's (1395–1475) letter advice to physicians of 1467 makes this plea concisely in relation to direct experience, the ethics of patient care, and the potentially drastic soteriological effects of forsaking scholarship in medicine:

> Not knowing the meaning of the texts at all,
> And knowing only a little advice,
> You who are intent only upon food and drink,
> Are like a fox searching for a meal.

> Though you know many words in the text,
> If you have not relied upon a skilled teacher,
> And have no practical procedure grounded in observation,
> You are like a talking parrot.

> If you err in diagnosing disease,
> And with uncaring bias,
> Knowingly prescribe incorrect medicine,
> You are like the Death Lord wielding a sword in his hand.

> Not giving the correct medicine when available
> To the patient afflicted with pain:
> Such a physician is greedy indeed, and
> Greed is a cause for rebirth as a hungry ghost.[22]

Such invective is not uncommon in medical literature, though among Sangyé Gyatso's forerunners in the critical tradition of medical scholarship Zurkhar Lodrö Gyelpo stands out; more than any other writer active prior to the seventeenth century, he writes of medical scholarship with a passion reminiscent of Sangyé Gyatso. Born in 1509, Lodrö Gyelpo lived until at least 1573, when at the age of sixty-four he composed a defense of the *Four Tantras* as the word of the Buddha.[23] He was the author of a popular set of commentaries on the *Four Tantras*, known as the *Ancestors' Instructions*, and, as we have seen, the editor of the 1546 Dratang print.

Lodrö Gyelpo adamantly insisted that those learning the medical arts must study each of the *Four Tantras* in a particular order. The introductory passages of his commentaries evoke the image of an emotional scholar distraught at the state of his field. In the opening lines of his 1542 commentary on the *Root Tantra*, he waxes poetic: "The *Four Tantras* pervade the circumference of the Himalayas with sweet-sounding letters," he eloquently begins, immediately emphasizing the importance of the text, as written word given voice. And it is these sweet-sounding letters that must form the basis for all medical learning. Given their exalted status, the *Four Tantras* mandate commentaries with authoritative lineages, uncorrupted by the claims of those pretending to be teachers, which refute doubt, misunderstanding, and incomprehension, for only such commentaries will provide a solid basis for the continued existence of the *Four Tantras*. It is, of course, Lodrö Gyelpo himself who will present such commentary.[24] But before he begins he offers an emotional critique of the faulty scholarship he perceives around him. "These days," he writes,

> *because the actions of scholars are few, pure traditions have not been maintained. These days the great textual traditions are like milk at the market; the meaningful and the meaningless have become mixed together. Those wanting to write commentaries make their explanations hastily, without consulting the text itself. Because of such explanations, words and meanings that are contradictory are placed side by side. Some [commentators] have made things up by themselves, and amazingly hold to this as their "special teaching." They perform mistaken practices of diagnosis . . . and treatment that stem only from observation. They then say*

*that physicians who explain [things] based upon texts are not
profound, while those that stem from oral instructions are, and
they go elsewhere for instruction. Seeing only such efforts to harm
themselves and others with scattered backward practices, my mind
reels. Thinking only of the teachings in the medical treatises, . . .
[and] clarifying every word and meaning, . . . I set about composing this large commentary, which sets things right!*[25]

This passage is noteworthy for a number of reasons, but perhaps most interesting is the insight it offers into debates about
the relation between medical scholarship and medical practice in
sixteenth-century Tibet. Lodrö Gyelpo appears to be responding
to very real criticisms about the value, or lack thereof, of studying
medical treatises. Reading between the lines of this passage, we
can posit that there were some who held such study to be simply
a waste of time, with no value to medical practice.

Lodrö Gyelpo reacted strongly to this state of affairs. In his
1545 commentary on the *Exegetical Tantra*, he offers a powerful defense of commentarial literature in the medical context.
He begins by putting words in the mouth of his opponent, the
physician critical of commentaries: "Others say: 'There are all
sorts of commentaries, big, little, and small, on the *Four Tantras* in general by earlier [writers], and on the *Exegetical Tantra*
in particular. It is enough. What need is there to write another?
This reasoning which proves what has already been proven
grows weary!'"[26] Frustrated with this attitude, Lodrö Gyelpo offers his own polemically charged views on the importance of a
scholarly approach to medicine. He admits that, although most
commentaries are largely accurate, a great many are filled with
half-truths and mistaken ideas. It has been left to him, apparently,
to set things straight. "Those so-called scholars understand [the
Four Tantras] narrowly," he chides, "using sophistry and hearsay
to create meanings that exist only on paper." This is not merely
an abstract complaint, but comes from his heart. "These days,"
he laments, "when all learned people consider the teachings of
the medical art, they feel like weeping." And how might one re-
vive the medical tradition? With textual scholarship, of course.
"For these reasons," Lodrö Gyelpo offers, "I have inspected and
analyzed each letter of the words in the text. With a view toward
establishing terminology, I have made an explanation that cleans
up the words of the precious teaching, and is a model that will be
impressive to scholars, fools, and those in between."[27]

Lodrö Gyelpo then focuses on the place of the *Explanatory Tantra* in particular within a curriculum of medical learning. Again, the following passage shows that there was no lack of debate over the proper direction of medical learning, or even the relative value of the different sections of the *Four Tantras* themselves. "These days," he writes in a scathing tone, "physicians generally think the following: 'By knowing this *Explanatory Tantra* one does no more than repeat words. It is of no benefit to the process of [medical] practice.' [Such physicians also think:] 'These people who are learned in explanation are deficient in the realm of practice.'" Of his imagined interlocutors he laments, "For this reason they study the *Subsequent Tantra* without studying the *Explanatory Tantra*. They look narrowly with just a few practical techniques from that [Tantra], and leave it at that. Later they express arrogance, [saying] that they do not need to look at the *Explanatory Tantra* or the *Instructional Tantra*." He concludes with exasperation, "these [physicians] who desire to understand the meaning without knowing the words, which teach the practice, are astonishing."[28]

This passage was integrated into later commentaries on the *Explanatory Tantra* such as the 1886 work of the court physician of Degé, Rinchen Özer (Sde dge Sman bla Rin chen 'od zer), suggesting that the sentiment expressed by Lodrö Gyelpo in the sixteenth century could still find sympathizers centuries later.[29] It is reminiscent of Jangpa Namgyel Draksang's (1395–1475) 1468 description of the second of four types of ordinary physicians, the "page-turning physicians" who simply glance through a few instructions, find something that looks useful, and proceed to diagnose with no real understanding.[30] To those who would ask what the value of the *Explanatory Tantra* is to medical practice (as opposed to medical learning conceived of as a theoretical endeavor), Lodrö Gyelpo offers the following step-by-step outline of the relation between the theoretically oriented second tantra and the practice of healing the sick. Taking the progression of topics in the *Explanatory Tantra* itself as his framework, he argues that "whoever does not know the *Explanatory Tantra* does not know the characteristics of the body. Whoever does not know the characteristics of the body does not know the nature of illness. Whoever does not know the nature of illness does not know how to do an examination or prescribe diet. Whoever does not know how to do an examination or prescribe diet does not know a thing about the medical arts!" "Therefore," he concludes,

"how can those who don't know the medical arts know the practice of medicine? It is like someone wandering about in a dark
room wanting to see something without their eyes!"[31]

Finally, Lodrö Gyelpo describes what he considers to be the
proper course of study: "First, [those learning the medical art]
should study only the *Root Tantra* and the *Explanatory Tantra*.
When they have learned [these] . . . by heart, they should be introduced to the *Instructional Tantra* and the *Subsequent Tantra*.
Gradually, they need to learn the practice according to the words
of the text."[32] He provides a clear rationale for the importance
of textual scholarship to medical learning and medical practice;
Sangyé Gyatso himself could not have done better: the only place
one can learn the medical arts is in texts such as the *Explanatory
Tantra*. Without an intimate understanding of these arts, effective practice is simply not possible.

In his incomplete commentary on the *Subsequent Tantra*,
Lodrö Gyelpo laments that most physicians rely only on this,
the last of the *Four Tantras*, and ignore the previous three. The
Subsequent Tantra is valuable, of course, for it "clearly teaches the
steps of practice according to the order of its chapters, without
mixing them all together, for physicians of inferior mental skill."[33]
Although he admits that it is possible to benefit others by bas-
ing one's practice only on this tantra, those who really wish to
aid living beings, and those who wish to comment upon the *Four
Tantras*, will study all four according to commentators of the
past. For Lodrö Gyelpo a firm grounding in theories of physiol-
ogy, epidemiology, and reasoned diagnosis—and thus textual
scholarship—must precede medical practice. This was not the
only vision of the healing arts in his time; others did not bother
with the musings of scholars.

THE DALAI LAMA'S PHYSICIAN

Darmo Menrampa Lobsang Chödrak, a senior contemporary
of Sangyé Gyatso and one of the physicians working under the
Fifth Dalai Lama, took up the task of completing Lodrö Gyelpo's
unfinished commentary on the *Four Tantras*. Lobsang Chödrak
was also concerned about the state of medical scholarship in his
day. In the introduction to his commentary on the *Instructional
Tantra*, he chastises those who scoff at textual learning in a manner reminiscent of Lodrö Gyelpo. Much like his predecessor on

the *Subsequent Tantra*, Lobsang Chödrak argues that reliance on the practical methods of the *Instructional Tantra* is not enough. "Even though the *Instructional Tantra* is a necessity for those physicians who would engage in the practice of healing the sick," he writes with some humor, "learned and insightful physicians do not [just] rely on dexterity. Even though some physicians do not understand [the *Four Tantras*], they rashly think that understanding is easy. Some [on the other hand], see the [medical treatises] as difficult to understand, while others become frightened by the mere sight of a book!"[34]

In the face of such cowardice, Lobsang Chödrak could not but do his part to uphold the textual tradition. He goes on to give his reasons for writing a commentary on the practical instructions of the third tantra: "Through the force of time the letters have been ruined, and thus even making an analysis [of the *Four Tantras*] is [a task] fraught with errors. There is no tradition that produces certainty in the minds of people through fixing [the text] by explaining and studying." And like Lodrö Gyelpo, Lobsang Chödrak was emotionally compelled to contribute to the revival of Tibetan medicine through writing. "This great text, a wish-fulfilling jewel, was declining, and the welfare of people was being harmed," he complains. "I could not bear to see the sick [try to] heal themselves, left uncared for by others, and so I composed this commentary."[35] Text-critical work and commentarial writing were not simply exercises in scholarly pyrotechnics; they were ethical acts, motivated (at least rhetorically) by the desire to heal the sick. When the text of the *Four Tantras* suffers the degeneration inherent in the passage of time, one might say, so do the people of Tibet.

Namling Panchen Könchok Chödrak was the editor of the printed editions of both the *Ancestor's Instructions* and Lobsang Chödrak's supplement. The printing of these works was sponsored by the Fifth Dalai Lama, and in part by Sangyé Gyatso himself. Könchok Chödrak reports a self-deprecating comment made to him by Lobsang Chödrak: "Edit [this commentary] again for an ignoramus like me!"[36] Heeding his master's request, in 1679 he set about editing not only the commentaries but also the *Four Tantras* themselves. In a tone we are by now familiar with, he writes disapprovingly of previous editors who have done more harm than good: "In the time that has passed this [medical] treatise has come under the influence of do-it-yourselfers who are afraid of the great books." And these upstarts have, for the most part, only a passing knowledge of the medical classics. "Except for the meaning of the words, they have given up examining the general meaning. In some cases they merely see something easy to understand every few chapters, and without looking at the authoritative scriptures, they simply erase archaic terminology, and thus different readings that are easier to understand have increased."[37]

Apparently unafraid of big books, Könchok Chödrak set about editing both commentary and basic text by assembling many manuscripts and prints. "Given this [textual situation], a reliable [editorial reading] cannot be made on the basis of a single manuscript," he writes of his own strict editorial practice. "[I] looked at each book [of various medical treatises]. [I] followed the finer orthographic points of the Yargya [that is, the Dratang] print. [I] used the [grammatical treatise] of Shalu Lotsawa Chökyong Zangpo [known as] the Casket [Za ma tog]. I carefully read the words, the meaning, and the outlines, and emended omissions and additions according to the [Dratang] text." Finally, he states, "in some chapters that explain the effects of medicines there were points of great disagreement, which I checked against the scattered annotations given by [Darmo] Menrampa Lobsang Chödrak."[38]

THE DALAI LAMA'S LEARNED GOVERNMENT

Aside from revealing several interesting details regarding his own editorial methods, Könchok Chödrak's comments help place the activities of Sangyé Gyatso in an intellectual context. Sangyé Gyatso has been credited with initiating the intense scrutiny of the textual history of the Four Tantras, and he himself characterized his work in this way when he criticized Jango Nangso Dargyé for relying too heavily on Lodrö Gyelpo's Dratang print. Yet we can see from Könchok Chödrak's description of his own editorial activities that in terms of both inspiration and methodological approach, Sangyé Gyatso was carrying on a critical tradition that dated back at least a hundred years to Lodrö Gyelpo and extended through both Lobsang Chödrak and Könchok Chödrak.

As the heir to these scholars' efforts, Sangyé Gyatso portrays himself as the medical scholar par excellence. Yet the value he places on the textual study of medical treatises comes directly from his conception of medicine in relation to the other classically defined arts and sciences, and in relation to the larger Mahāyāna Buddhist theme of the bodhisattva. Textual scholarship is important not merely because it produces soundly edited texts or technically correct commentaries; Sangyé Gyatso argues that it is an essential part of the Mahāyāna Buddhist path. In the introductory passage of the *Beryl Mirror*[39] he locates the study of medicine within the proper activity of a bodhisattva. Citing a host of *sūtra*s, tantras, and Indian and Tibetan *śāstra*s, he argues that the five arts are all essential components of the path toward enlightenment, for they each contribute to the welfare of sentient beings, and thus to the progress of the bodhisattva. The study of treatises on medical arts is important, a certain *sūtra* claims, for by this "humans will become free of the eighty-four diseases of nonvirtue." If the bodhisattva can heal beings with such love and kindness, it will cause them to have faith in the bodhisattva. With this peaceful attitude of faith beings will remember the Buddha, and thus be ready for the bodhisattva to lead them to the other shore, to enlightenment.[40] At the beginning of his history of medicine, then, Sangyé Gyatso makes a powerful claim: the study of medicine is directly linked to the highest soteriological goal of Buddhism, enlightenment itself, and therefore the study of even the minutiae of medical texts is imbued with a value far exceeding its most immediate goals, the mastery of a complex body of literature and its application toward improving human life.

Furthermore, the five arts form an essential part of the bodhisattva's progress toward omniscience, as the lines from the *Mahāyānasūtrālaṃkāra* cited by Sangyé Gyatso (and Yutok Yönten Gönpo in his own *Interior Analysis* long before) suggest: "If one is not diligent in the five arts, even the most noble will not become omniscient."[41] Sangyé Gyatso offers a *sūtra* quotation that makes the equation clear: "If the bodhisattva has not studied the five arts, there is no way he will attain the omniscient wisdom of complete enlightenment. Therefore, in order to attain unexcelled enlightenment, one must study the five arts."[42]

The other four arts are also essential. For Sangyé Gyatso the limbs of scholarship are incomplete if any of the five arts is neglected.[43] In an extended commentary on chapter 31 of the *Explanatory Tantra* toward the end of *Beryl Mirror*,[44] he argues in more detail that the well-rounded physician must be adept in all five. He must be skilled with his hands in order to prepare medicines or to make such medical implements as the *gce'u*—the long brass tube used to administer medicines. He must have a way with words and know how to act in order to put his patients at ease.[45] He must be skilled in reasoning, so as to approach diagnosis and medical analysis with a clear mind. The language arts are of particular importance for understanding word formation and word derivation in medical terminology.[46] Since medical texts contain many synonyms, the good physician must study such works as the *Amarakośa* in order to easily understand them.[47] For similar reasons the physician must study poetics, prosody, and even dramaturgy. Finally, astrology should be included in the well-rounded medical scholar's training.

In short, Sangyé Gyatso portrays the ideal physician as a renaissance scholar with a deep knowledge of all the major and minor arts.[48] One can see this quite well in a sort of scholarly joke he plays at the beginning of the *Beryl Mirror*. He immediately follows up his introductory verse with a quote, the first of hundreds in the work. Yet where one might expect a verse from the *Four Tantras* themselves or from some classic Indian medical treatise, there are four lines from Daṇḍin's *Mirror of Poetics* (*Kāvyādarśa*) (considered, incidentally, to be a Buddhist work by Tibetan scholars), which signals that in the *Beryl Mirror* medicine will not be treated in isolation from the other arts. This commentary, Sangyé Gyatso suggests by citing Daṇḍin, is written to impress the scholar among scholars. May those afraid of books beware!

Though Sangyé Gyatso may have made the most sustained effort to argue that the work of the physician is the work of the bodhisattva, he was certainly not the first to do so. Indeed, this was a pervasive theme in the "interior analysis" (*khog dbubs/dbug*) genre. In the earliest example presently known, Yutok Yonten Gönpo lists the development of the enlightened mind upon the bodhisattva path as the first of nine qualities for which physicians should be renowned.[49] Drangti Pelden Tshojé includes a command to produce the intention toward enlightenment as the last of seven decrees to physicians attributed to Trisong Detsen (in contrast to other versions of the seven decrees, which include no mention of the intention to become enlightened).[50] Finally, Zurkhar Lodrö Gyelpo styles his own *Interior Analysis* of medical traditions as "that of which physicians desiring to engage in the work of the bodhisattva must not be ignorant."[51] In the introduction to this work, he concedes that the teachings of the Buddha are sufficient in and of themselves for understanding all paths. Nevertheless, for the bodhisattva, or "one wishing to take responsibility for all beings," there is nothing that is not a valid area of study, even non-Buddhist and worldly subjects. A passage from the *Introduction to the Bodhisattva's Way,* to the effect that there is nothing without merit for sons of the Buddha, proves his point.[52] Like Sangyé Gyelpo would after him, Lodrö Gyelpo devotes a section of his work to commenting on the line from the *Exegetical Tantra,* "Learn writing and reading completely, for whether [you] are capable or incapable depends on these,"[53] offering a detailed presentation of Sanskrit, Tibetan, and the materials of writing: pen, ink, and paper.[54] In the final analysis, "one wishing to become a scholar without reading, writing, and grammar is a source of amazement, like someone who wants to make offerings to the gods without any money."[55]

This chapter has dealt principally with medical texts, but with specific questions in mind about the role of textual scholarship in Tibetan scholarly culture as a whole. The end of chapter 2 detailed the specific editorial and philological methods that went into gathering, editing, and preparing the collected works of a particular Buddhist writer active during Sangyé Gyatso's lifetime, Jamyang Shepé Dorjé. In the colophons to his writings, practically every aspect of the editorial process—and the process of textual production more broadly—was detailed, commented upon, and called into question. Clearly these were important matters of critical reflection for the editors. Even a brief look at Sangyé Gyatso and his predecessors shows that such textual issues were of no less importance in the medical traditions, and that the well-known voluminous printing of medical literature during the late seventeenth century developed amid a heated debate about the relation of philology to application. With the widespread use of block printing by the late seventeenth century, texts could be disseminated on a large scale. Those who controlled their creation, distribution, and use (that is, the institution of education) controlled—ideally, at any rate—the production of knowledge. Yet the extent to which the prescriptive writings of Sangyé Gyatso and others actually influenced the practice of medicine and medical learning is an important subject to which further research should be devoted, but which lies outside the scope of concern here.

These medical scholars used medical books and the areas of expertise associated with them were utilized as symbols in the construction and maintenance of authority. Their defense of textual scholarship strongly criticizes those physicians who do not have the "proper" training and seeks to determine precisely what

that is. When coupled with the rhetorical power of the bodhisattva ideal, such a critique denies the legitimacy of medical practice
traditions not sanctioned by Sangyé Gyatso, Lodrö Gyelpo, and
others—not merely on scholastic grounds, but by implying that
they are not properly Buddhist (ironic when one considers that
the principal Indian medical literature upon which the *Four Tantras* are based was not produced by Buddhist writers). If "religion
invest[s] specific human preferences with transcendent status by
misrepresenting them as revealed truths, primordial traditions,
[or] divine commandments and . . . insulates them against most
forms of debate and critique, assisting their transmission from
one generation to another as part of a sacred canon,"[56] then the
use of the bodhisattva ideal as a defense of a particular medical
tradition is a classic example of the function of religious rhetoric. Seen in this light, the connection among textual scholarship,
medical tradition, and Mahāyāna social/soteriological ideals becomes something more: a persuasive technique to argue for the
authority of certain groups and against the authority of others.
As the lines from the *Four Tantras* with which the chapter began state: "The physician without a lineage . . . deserves no one's
respect." "Like a fox that seizes the king's throne," the physician
without the proper credentials impersonates authority. And it
was up to the medical scholars themselves to determine the extent of such credentials, or that credentials existed in the first
place. They sought to define the parameters of lineage, to create a
tradition by delimiting the extent of propriety. One major factor
in this delimitation was textual scholarship: "The physician who
does not understand the texts . . . can discern neither the disease
nor the cure."

At the close of the *Beryl Mirror* Sangyé Gyatso prays that the
Ganden government will heal the ills that Tibet had incurred
through warfare and strife. He thus suggests that the most important healer is none other than the principal bodhisattva of
his era, the Fifth Dalai Lama (to whom Sangyé Gyatso, not sur-
prisingly, pays homage in the opening verse of the *Beryl Mirror*
as well),[57] and his government.[58] Sangyé Gyatso had spent much
of his life learning under the Fifth Dalai Lama, promoting and
subsequently leading the Ganden government, and there is every reason to believe that his efforts in medical scholarship were
an integral part of these efforts. The founding of an institution of
medical learning adjacent to the seat of government, the Potala,
can also be understood as part of an effort to control the pro-

duction of medical knowledge. Sangyé Gyatso was striving not merely to rule Tibet in a strictly political sense, but to create a cultural hegemony extending to a variety of areas, including time (astrology and astronomy), space (ritual), monastic curriculum, and medicine.[59] This insight provides a theory to explain the extraordinary range of subjects Sangyé Gyatso took up in his writing and their relation to his role as secular leader of Tibet. Just as he undertook to impress upon his subjects the veracity and authority of the Fifth Dalai Lama as the actual incarnation of Avalokiteśvara, the bodhisattva of compassion, through rituals and a series of written works, so he worked to establish his government through the promotion of the medical arts within the larger ideology of the bodhisattva.

The writers whose medical works are mentioned here were nothing if not passionate about what seem, on the surface at least, the most mundane philological details of the *Four Tantras*. For them the quality of the medical text was directly related to the quality of medical practice, the work of the textual critic intimately bound with the work of the physician, and the emotionally charged activities of the medical scholar classically dictated to be part and parcel of the bodhisattva's effort to alleviate the suffering of human beings. However, when considered in relation to Sangyé Gyatso's political undertakings, this passion had as much to do with authority as with words on the page, or even healing the sick. The authority of tradition (the medical lineage stemming from Yutok Yönten Gönpo to Sangyé Gyatso himself), the propriety of a privileged mode of learning (textual scholarship) and a privileged body of knowledge (scholarly medicine), and the authority of the government were all linked and maintained by a rhetoric that argued for the inseparability of philology and exegesis from altruism, enlightenment, and "healing" conceived in bodily, soteriological, and political terms. But if intimate ties could be claimed between textual scholarship and political rule in central Tibet, such was not always the case elsewhere, as a meeting between a scholar and his patron, the king of Degé, illustrates in the following chapter.

THE SCHOLAR AND THE KING

On a certain day in the late 1730s, within the halls of Lhündrupt-eng monastery in the eastern Tibetan region of Kham, Shuchen Tsültrim Rinchen, the "Great Editor" of Degé, stood in a banquet reception line waiting to be greeted by his king and patron, Kunga Trinlé Gyatso. When the King of Degé approached Shuchen, he asked the scholar, "What have you been editing these days?" Shuchen replied, "I have been editing the Sanskrit-language version of the *Avadānakalpalatā*." The king retorted, "This *Kalpalatā* has been edited over and over again! What reason is there to edit it now?" Shuchen was very disturbed by this censure, but had to acquiesce. "I had [already] edited part of the first section," he recounts in his autobiography, "yet the Sanskrit remained un-touched. Even though there were obvious scribal errors, I had to leave them be in accordance with the wishes of [my] patron. I thought, 'Future textual scholars will know [of my lapse] when they look at this.' And yet, *what* was I to do?"[1]

This autobiographical note by one of the most prominent editors of Buddhist texts in Tibetan history laments the precari-ous social position of the textual scholar. His work is valued by the king—but only up to a point. He is the recipient of royal patronage—yet the good will of his patron has its limits. And even though his reputation in the future may depend on the qual-ity of his work today, social exigency might require that he leave his project in an unfinished state. In this particular case, it appears as well that the king had a point. Kṣemendra's *Avadānakalpalatā*, or *Creeping Vine of Lives*, an elegant collection of hagiographies dedicated to the Buddha and his many rebirths, had indeed been worked and reworked by generations of Tibetan scholars, from the fourteenth to the seventeenth centuries; Shuchen's ef-forts in Degé during the 1730s were only the most recent.[2] It was Shuchen's opinion that there were many corrupt letters intro-duced into the Sanskrit by scribes, and he had collected some forty manuscripts to use as source material for creating a proper edition. But by the time he was prepared to complete the editing, his patron ordered him to stop. The king felt that since the original prints from the Potala were edited by many scholars, they were reliable; it was impossible for any errors to remain. Shuchen disagreed but left the text as it was, appending a plea for later scholars to finish his work: "Since [corruptions] were left as they were, if later intelligent people were to edit [the text] this would clean up the teaching, so I beg [you] to consider it."[3]

By the early 1740s Shuchen had edited literally thousands of Buddhist texts under the patronage of the Degé rulers Tenpa Tsering (1678–1738) and his son Püntsok Tenpa (alias Kunga Trinlé Gyatso), for he was the chief editor of a Tengyur that was carved into wood blocks and printed at Degé between 1737 and 1744. His contemporary Situ Panchen Chökyi Jungné (1700–74) worked a decade earlier as chief editor on the other half of the Tibetan Buddhist canon, the Kangyur, as it was carved into printing blocks between 1729 and 1733 under Tenpa Tsering.

This chapter sketches the labors of Shuchen and Situ during these few years as they produced the canons. Both scholars wrote autobiographies, and both wrote encyclopedic reference works to the Buddhist canon; their writings contain perhaps the richest reflections known in Tibetan literature on the textual scholar's work in editing Buddhist texts. In 1743 the leader of Degé asked Shuchen to compile an account of the Tengyur production, which was to include the origins of the Buddhist teachings as well as the ancestral and contemporary history of Degé. It took one year to complete this large work. Shuchen's catalog and omnibus for the Tengyur, the *New Moon*, contains a chapter devoted to the making of the canon, which includes among other things a detailed description of the process of textual editing.[4] Shuchen's life was intimately bound up with literary scholarship, and thus his autobiography, entitled *Leaves of Pleasure and Pain*, is also a valuable source for learning about the work of editing in eighteenth-century Degé.[5]

The intensive editorial efforts of Situ and Shuchen occurred during an era of massive increases in the production of block-printed books. The eighteenth century witnessed major growth in the production of Tibetan Buddhist (and Bönpo) canons, the zenith of the convergence between the technology of woodblock printing and the long-standing production of Buddhist canons in the form of handwritten manuscripts. In the more than

300 years between the first printing of the Kangyur in 1411 and the first blocks made in the eighteenth century, only one other new set of blocks was created, the Litang Kangyur of 1615. In the 42-year period from 1731 to 1773, by contrast, approximately six Kangyurs and Tengyurs were newly carved and printed in Tibetan cultural regions—in Degé to the southeast (Kangyur completed 1733, Tengyur 1744), Choné to the northeast (Kangyur 1731, Tengyur 1773), and Shekar (Kangyur 1732, Tengyur 1742) to the southwest. Just why this explosion of printing occurred during the eighteenth century and not earlier despite the fact that the technology had been available for centuries is a fascinating question yet to be explored in detail, though the concentrations of economic and human capital in the newly formed polities such as the Ganden government in Lhasa, the Degé kingdom, and the Qing government in Beijing certainly played a crucial role. Nevertheless, thenceforth the technology of wood-block printing had a tremendous effect on the development of the Tibetan canons. Although manuscripts continued to be produced, with the full-scale adoption of printing by major institutions, these large bodies of literature could be duplicated with relative ease, and redactions with a minimum of internal variation could be disseminated in quantities unheard of in previous centuries. The Degé Kangyur, for instance, is said by Shuchen to have been printed an incredible 1,500 times between its completion in 1733 and 1744 (the year in which the Tengyur was completed).[6] A calculation of the production levels provides some sense of the sheer mass of materials and labor represented by this number. At least certain editions of the Degé Kangyur consist of 1,109 works, and the Tengyur includes 3,358 works, totaling 4,469 works contained in 316 separate volumes. The total number of two-sided folios for both was 97,525,[7] the printing of which thus required nearly 200,000 individually carved wood-block sides. So at approximately 33,000 folios per Kangyur, 1,500 printings amounts to some 49,500,000 pieces of paper, and 99,000,000 individually imprinted folio sides (or pages). If the the Kangyur was indeed printed 1,500 times within this 12-year period, then it was printed an average of 125 times per year. In other words, according to Shuchen, a single Kangyur was printed approximately every three days (at a rate of approximately 11,000 folios per day). Nearly a million pages printed—this was a mass-production of religion the likes of which had not been seen prior to the 1720s, and the social and religious effects must have been great, espe-

cially on local traditions of literature and craftsmanship. To gain at least some gross historical perspective on how distant this is from the early production of canons in central Tibet, we might compare the output of this veritable factory of Buddhist scripture for slightly more than a decade to the mere nine handwritten copies said to be made throughout the entire fourteenth century from the old canonical collection of Nartang monastery in western-central Tibet.[8]

This massive carving and printing project could not have taken place without substantial patronage, in this case from the kings of Degé. The kingdom of Degé was a relatively independent area during the eighteenth century. It was free from the direct rule of the Dalai Lamas of central Tibet, yet benefited financially from the treasuries of the Qing Empire to the east, owing to newly forged relationships between Tenpa Tsering and the Manchu court.[9] Ruling over an area roughly the size of the state of Maine, the kings of Degé made their seat of power in the town from which the region derived its name, which also had the largest monastery and the great printery. Degé's ruling family had been involved in the patronage of Buddhist life and literature for several hundred years, though only since the preceding century had major institution-building initiatives taken place. During the middle decades of the seventeenth century, the thirty-seventh ruler from this family, Jampa Püntsok, completed the monastery of Lhündrupteng, otherwise known as the Great Monastery of Degé, and there established a continuous abbatial lineage. At the same time he considerably expanded the lands under his family's dominion. The founding of a monastery coupled with the acquisition of land—and by extension the acquisition of revenue in the form of taxes[10] from that land—laid the groundwork for the establishment of a printing house in 1721 by the third abbot of the Great Monastery, Sangyé Tenpa.

A decade later, under the most famous of the Degé kings, Tenpa Tsering, the printing of the Kangyur was begun. Like his ancestor Jampa Püntsok half a century before, Tenpa Tsering was able to amass more territory under the control of his family. More significantly, this territory was de facto under the control of the monastery as well, for Tenpa Tsering was simultaneously the fortieth secular head of the Degé ruling family and the fifth abbot of the monastery. This consolidation of political and religious authority resulted in a vibrant period of religious expression, which included the printing of the Buddhist canon and a host of other indigenous Tibetan works, the founding of new temples and monasteries throughout the kingdom, and considerable patronage for Buddhist arts, all under the guidance of a new generation of eastern Tibetan "renaissance scholars" such as Situ Panchen Chökyi Jungné.

In 1729, the renowned scholar and artist Situ Panchen—then only 30 years of age—began editing texts for the carving of the new Kangyur under Tenpa Tsering's patronage.[11] In 1733, he composed a catalog and encyclopedic companion to this collection entitled the *Young Creeping Vine*.[12] The *Young Creeping Vine* chronicles the printing of the canon itself, of which Situ was of course the editor-in-chief.[13] In this wide-ranging work he first presents a brief historical sketch of the editing (*zhus dag pa*) of the various Kangyurs, then goes on to describe in some detail the materials, the workforce, and the stages of production that went into making the more than 100 volumes of the word of the Buddha. He also provides a lengthy account of the advent of Buddhism in India and Tibet, the genealogy of the rulers of Degé, and the history of the Buddhist canon in Tibet. This work constitutes a rich and essential source,[14] and the following will concentrate only on the small part that deals with the actual production of the Kangyur.

THE KING'S EDITORS

Like their predecessors, the Degé editors Situ and Shuchen were both concerned to place their labors on the canons in an aesthetic, social, and political context. They also spent a great deal of space detailing the process of editing texts. As editors-in-chief of their respective projects, Situ and Shuchen managed editorial teams and were ultimately responsible for decisions regarding problematic passages.[15] Shuchen's staff in charge of the Tengyur consisted of nine scholars, who were in turn divided into three separate subgroups: one in charge of editing the original manuscripts, one checking the secondary manuscripts, and a third responsible for checking the final printed text.[16] Yet it was (by their own accounts at least) Situ and Shuchen who were concerned with developing the methodological principles upon which the work of the many scholars under them would be based and making sure that these methods were consistently performed.

The editors of Degé have much to say about the three main branches of editorial practice, namely recension—the critical appraisal and arrangement of sources, examination—the process of determining which readings are authentic and which are corrupt, and emendation—the changing of corrupt readings.[17] To begin, both Situ and Shuchen give an account of the primary sources upon which they based their work. Not only do they list which editions of canonical collections they employed, they also provide a qualitative assessment of the collections and arrange them in a hierarchy of importance defined in terms of editorial criteria. As is well known, the Degé Kangyur was based primarily upon the Jang Satam block-print Kangyur of 1609–11,[18] and secondarily upon the Lhodzong manuscript Kangyur. Situ relates that the editing of the Jang Satam Kangyur produced by the Sixth Shamarpa, Chökyi Wangchuk, was good, but by no means perfect. "In general," he writes, "the Jang Satam Kangyur provided a very clean foundation, because . . . the analysis [carried out upon it] by many holy people was complete. Still, during the block printing, the Omniscient [Karmapa] Chökyi Wanchuk was not able to edit all [the volumes]. There were misordered pages that were not caught by the supervisors, and some small errors of elision and insertion appeared."[19] It is doubtful Chökyi Wangchuk would have agreed, for in his catalog of the Kangyur he dutifully, if briefly, praises the workers.[20] That nothwithstanding, Situ saw fit to improve upon the Jang Satam Kangyur by supplementing his developing edition with readings from the Lhodzong manuscript Kangyur, as well as several unspecified *sūtras* and tantras that were not in it.[21] Noteworthy here in terms of editorial methodology is the fact that Situ used his sources according to his opinion of the editorial work performed on them. It seems that the antiquity of the textual witnesses at his disposal was not his primary criterion, for despite the fact that he had access to works as old as Ga Anyen Pakshi's[22] fourteenth-century Kangyur, he chose for his base text a seventeenth-century witness.[23]

In addition to Tibetan texts, Situ used Sanskrit manuscripts to edit no fewer than six major tantras, including the *Sarvadurgatipariśodhana*, the *Guhyasamāja*, the *Caṇḍamahāroṣaṇa*, the *Hevajra*, the *Laghusaṃvara*, and the *Saṃvarodaya* tantras. In a diary entry for 1731 he relates that he also had in his possession an Indic text of the *Kālacakratantra*, and mentions in a very interesting aside that he hoped soon to add further to the Kangyur by translating the *Nirvāṇasūtra* from Chinese.[24] Though he did use these Indic—and perhaps Chinese—texts to locate inconsistencies in the Tibetan translations, it does not seem that the former held primary authority for making emendations, as Situ's intellectual predecessor, Shalu Lotsawa, might have called for. Rather, Situ used Indic commentaries upon these tantras—though presumably in Tibetan translation—to resolve doubtful passages.[25]

Shuchen provides a more detailed assessment of the sources for the Tengyur. As is well known, he used four Tengyurs in the making of the Degé collection: the early manuscript of Ga Anyen Pakshi; the manuscript edition prepared by Situ on the basis of an edition housed at Chingwa Taktsé, the family estate of the Fifth Dalai Lama; a personal edition that had belonged to the Eleventh Karmapa, Yeshé Dorjé (1676–1702); and finally a manuscript penned in silver ink belonging to the king of Degé, Tenpa Tsering. Shuchen presents these Tengyurs in the order of their relative importance for his work, from least to greatest. Beginning with the Tengyur of Ga Anyen Pakshi, he tells us that "among the original treatises we had collected, some of the manuscript treatises from the *sūtra* and tantra commentary sections that came from Ga Anyen were quite clean and reliable." However, "The majority of the works from the tantra commentary section, the linguistics section, and the logic and epistemology section," he complains, "had become mixed up and damaged, and much of it was incomplete. Extra miscellaneous works had just been thrown into an appendix. Since the scribes were inexperienced, and there were many faulty elisions and insertions, many of [Ga Anyen Pakshi's treatises] were unreliable, and therefore did not offer more than a little assistance."[26]

Shuchen's opinion of the Eleventh Karmapa's edition is only slightly higher. He writes: "The collection of volumes ordered by the Karmapa was indeed a feast for the eye as an example of craftsmanship." Yet in this case, beauty was only cover-deep. "Since absolutely no proofreading was undertaken after [the manuscripts] had been written down by the scribes," Shuchen again complains, "there were many elisions and insertions. Since this was the product of inexperienced scribes, in some cases there was not inconsiderable difficulty in reading [the manuscript], and thus it was not reliable." Attention to this edition was not a total waste of time, however, for some of its textual readings proved useful. "At points where the order [of certain texts] was disturbed and we wondered whether [the text] was written down from a manuscript recension that descended from an early period, [this Tengyur] was of some assistance," he admits.[27] Tenpa Tsering's devotional silver Tengyur was thus the least valuable, for it was a direct copy of the Eleventh Karmapa's edition and thus was, as Shuchen puts it, "of no more benefit than pouring water from one vase to another."[28]

While Shuchen claims to hold the manuscript Tengyur prepared by his predecessor, Situ Panchen, in the highest regard, it too was not without problems: "In the case of the logic and epistemology section, there were great scribal errors, and there were many elisions, insertions, and textual corruptions that were quite difficult to analyze." Reservations aside, Shuchen felt compelled to make use of this edition, if only because it provided texts not available elsewhere. "Since we had no original manuscripts other than those that were just like this one, these did not provide more than a little assistance. Still, given that reliable originals that we might use for comparison and that were different from the [Tengyur of Situ] were extremely difficult to acquire in Kham, we left [passages in this Tengyur] as they were, even though there were some doubtful cases."[29] Like Situ, Shuchen thought the most important factor in organizing his sources into a scheme of editorial importance to be not their relative antiquity, but the perceived competence of the scribes and editors who had produced them. Shuchen held the work of his predecessor in high esteem, yet even Situ's manuscript, the best of Shuchen's sources, was not without major editorial problems. The most serious factor in his choice of source material revolved around three problematic moments in the editorial process, which apparently even Situ was not able to overcome to Shuchen's satisfaction: the elision of sound passages, the insertion of corrupt passages, and the faulty emendation of otherwise readable text.

It is with good reason then that Shuchen devotes the next section of the *New Moon* to a general discussion of just how such errors occurred and what measures he and his editorial team took to prevent them. But before turning to his comments on emendation it is instructive to consider how he takes up the topic of textual recension and its pitfalls in a lengthy discussion of an earlier project. Prior to working on the Tengyur, Shuchen completed the sixteen-volume collection of works of the five early masters of the Sakya school.[30] In 1734 a resident scholar of Degé, Dorjé Chang Tashi Lhündrup,[31] asked him to come to the monastery of Lhündrupteng and there put the project in context.

"The patron, Tenpa Tsering, through the force of his accumulated merit, had the Kangyur produced. Now there is a great need to make the commentaries on the word of the Buddha available." By this Tashi Lhündrup did not mean the Tengyur, but rather the commentaries of Tibetan writers, specifically the five great masters of the Sakyapa school. "Textual traditions for these are very rare," Tashi Lhündrup went on, "so hearing and seeing copies of their collected works is rare even for the people of the schools that follow them who strive to attain clear understanding. Therefore, efforts at oral teachings and reading are poor."[32] This was a dire situation, for the chance to simply pay one's respects to the founding works of the tradition, much less study them in any detail, is extremely rare. Out of blind faith, disciples seek instruction in the teachings of the Sakya masters, regardless of whether such teachings represent what Tashi Lhündrup calls "an unsullied and definitive instruction stemming from a complete lineage and concordant with scripture and reasoning." To counteract this, a well-edited edition of the works must be printed and disseminated. This is no easy task for, as Tashi Lhündrup laments, "even though collected works of the Sakyapa hierarchs have been produced, there is no history of them having been well edited, and thus clean block prints do not exist." To perpetuate such poorly edited block prints would be worse than nothing at all, for the evil effects of bad prints spreading throughout the country would be great.

With these grave warnings, Tashi Lhündrup encouraged Shuchen to join the editorial staff of the project. And it is perhaps understandable that the young scholar was reluctant. Shuchen felt unqualified; he had studied the order of the collected works of the five Sakya masters briefly when he had been given the ritual permission to read them, but had no experience editing the great scriptures of the past. He pleaded not to be assigned this task, but was ordered to do it. And thus he began working with three other "editorial companions" on collating the various editions that would form the basis of their work.

They used five extant collections of the Five Masters' writings hailing from various monasteries and temples, including one at Lhündrupteng itself. The well-known early block prints from Gongkar in central Tibet did not constitute a complete collection, and Shuchen and his team used what prints he could collect. The actual task of editing presented certain challenges. There were many cases in which Shuchen states that "the word and the meaning were different," by which he means that the orthography of any given manuscript often varied from the ideal intended meaning—at least as he, the editor, understood it. The writings of the first three masters, Kunga Nyingpo, Sönam Tsemo, and Drakpa Gyeltsen, came into being in stages. At first many of their teachings were set down by their disciples, who then took these records back to their individual homelands. Such manuscripts formed the basis of further copies, though in the process many changes were wrought, the most serious of which was the introduction of numerous compounded words, problematic for the ambiguity they add to the text. For Shuchen a text that was descended from a manuscript known to be reworked, edited, and fixed by the author himself was authoritative. He speaks more about editorial method elsewhere (as will be seen below), though he does claim to have been a cautious textual critic even in his early efforts. In the case of some tantric technical terminology, he analyzed the readings as best he could and emended only what was certain to him. In some commentaries on points that were difficult to emend, he compared the *sūtra* or treatise that was the subject of the commentary. In cases where these were different readings, he made strong editorial changes as far as he was able. When the editors had finished their work, 16 scribes created the fair copies that would form the basis of the carving, work that was in turn taken up by some 150 carvers. The entire project took almost three years. The printing was inaugurated in 1734 and continued through 1736. The scribes finished most of their work in 1735, and the project came to an end with the final editing of prints from the newly carved blocks in 1736. The Degé leader asked for a catalog of the new edition, which Tashi Lhündrup himself kindly provided. Shuchen had only a small break before he was assigned to the largest project yet undertaken by the rulers of Degé, the carving of a new Tengyur.

Given his now substantial acquaintance with recensional problems, Shuchen knew that it was important to have textual witnesses from more than one recensional line, for without these there was no basis for comparison and thus no way to easily discern the errors of earlier editors for the next step in the editorial process, emendation. "Some of the above-mentioned original [Tengyur texts]," he observes, "stem from a single textual recension. Some recensions with elisions and insertions proliferated because of lazy, dim-witted, and scatterbrained scribes and proofreaders who dealt with every text according to their own ideas, and nothing was correctly emended. Elisions remained the same, and insertions remained the same. In some cases there were obvious insertions that corrupted the word and the sense. Subsequent editors worked with their individual abilities, according to different methods of analysis, and corrupt emendations were introduced."[33]

Shuchen elaborates on such problems in his autobiography, *Leaves of Pleasure and Pain*. He laments that his predecessors had ventured so many ill-advised changes to the treatises, complaining that "[Past Tengyurs] were made by mediocre editors, and the work of each [successive] editor remained unseen because of their lazy and scattered minds. Some editors made all sorts of emendations even though they did not understand the text completely. Some compared the texts with others, but arrogantly proceeded to make all sorts of emendations based upon doubts that fell in line with their own ignorance."[34]

In addition to the unconscious mistakes of scribes, one of the greatest obstacles facing Shuchen's team was the deliberate but misguided editorial work of scholars before them. One of their primary tasks, then, was to discern and undo corrupt emendations. Shuchen refers to this process as an analysis (*dpyod pa*) in which the editor has three basic choices: to insert text, to remove text, or to leave the manuscript as it is. As a general rule, the editor was not to make decisions based upon his own sense of the meaning of the text, but to use comparison wherever possible. The editors constantly referred to *sūtras* and treatises upon which the text under scrutiny commented. If this method of comparison did not yield a satisfactory reading, the text would be set aside and subjected to a further round of editing.

Editors and scribes alike at Degé were encouraged to work in this fashion through strict managerial discipline. Individual attempts at emendation by divination—i.e., allowing the perceived meaning of the textual passage as a whole to dictate the particular reading—were not tolerated.[35] Although the goal was to remove old corruptions and create a readable text, Shuchen and his managers went to great lengths to assure that no new corruptions were introduced. Evoking images of a working environment that must have been very difficult at times, he describes the general procedures. "When indications of a [previous] emendation were noticed by . . . the editors, they had to emend it again if they knew it to be a faulty emendation. In these cases, the policy of the managers, Tsering Pel and Karma Peldrup, was very strict." Shuchen makes the practical implications clear: "If the scribes made a corrupt letter or the editors made a corrupt emendation just twice they would meet with a fine as punishment. For this reason, if the editors saw the sign of a corrupt emendation, they would only make an emendation on the basis of another original, for fear of being slapped with a fine."[36]

The threat of textual corruption increasing during the process of editing, copying, and printing was persistent. The editors thus sought to make their textual emendations as easy to read as possible for the scribes. Rather than making interlinear annotations above, below, or to the side of the corrupt text, they used a sharp knife to shave off a layer of paper containing the corruption and wrote the emendation right in the blank space.[37] This allowed the scribes to read edited texts with ease, without having to make out small annotations or make any editorial choices themselves. Passages that were so mixed up or so corrupt as to defy this method of cut-and-paste editing were passed up to Shuchen himself to be analyzed further.[38] Indeed, it appears that only he and perhaps a select few others among the editorial team were allowed to make emendations based upon divination.

Minor variation between textual witnesses was not in itself a negative phenomenon for Shuchen. He tells of passages in which the text was faded beyond recognition every ten to twenty words. In such cases, as he relates in his autobiography, his team would compare the patchy texts to various early and later translations of the same work in order to flesh out the missing parts. If words were seen to be in a slightly different order than in older translations, they would be left alone. It was only when words were found to be either repeated or missing that they would be emended.[39]

For both Situ and Shuchen, the foundations for such reasoned examination and impartiality were definitively laid down in the grammatical treatises of the early translators. Tönmi Sambhota's *Sum cu pa* and *Rtags kyi 'jug pa*, together with the *Mahāvyutpatti*, the *Sgra sbyor bam po gnyis pa*, and the *Vacanamukha* of Smṛtijñānakīrti, formed the core of their grammatical and stylistic manuals.[40] The editors working under Situ and Shuchen were all required to have a firm command of these works; indeed, Shuchen's lengthy praise of his team is primarily concerned with their grammatical brilliance.[41] And yet, despite the immense importance of the famous grammatical treatises, Situ admits that they did not cover everything an editor might encounter in a text, and for this reason scholars of the past had been obliged to create their own styles in some cases. This led to a certain stylistic variation throughout the Kangyur. According to Situ, the *vinaya*, *sūtra*, and tantra sections—that is, the better part of the canon—were all fairly consistent in terms of orthography. Nevertheless, from text to text and within different subsections minor variations were apparent. As with Shuchen's attitude toward word order, Situ allowed a certain amount of stylistic variance to be left in the edited version, editing for consistency within single texts, but leaving differences be throughout the various sections. He does mention, however, that he removed all Tibetan regionalisms, for scholars, he informs his readers, "do not like vulgar speech."[42]

Much may be discerned about the methods of the editors of the Kangyur and Tengyur from their discussion of the problems specifically associated with mantras. The editing of mantras proved to be one of the most difficult tasks to which Situ and Shuchen were put. The primary reason was not that the mantras were in Sanskrit—for both editors claimed competence in this language—but rather that they appeared in a variety of different Indic languages. Speaking in general methodological terms on his team's use and treatment of Indian-language materials, Situ comments that texts in central Indian languages were emended solely on the basis of Sanskrit. The several that were based on Apabhraṃśa, a medieval Prakrit dialect, were left alone. "Sanskrit names for regions, flora, and fauna were written by the translators of old in ways that would be easy for the Tibetans in [various] regions to read. [For example, we find] *gau ta ma* and *'go'u ta ma*. Those that seemed reasonably similar to Sanskrit were left alone, though we emended several that could not be left unchanged."[43] His policy regarding mantras is no different than his treatment of flora and fauna. He and his team were ready to emend Sanskrit mantras yet took a more hands-off approach to those in other languages. "Mantras," he explains, "were compared with [Indic] manuscripts when they were available. When [Indic texts] were not available, if [the mantras] were in a language we could not identify as Sanskrit, such as Dravidian, Paiśācī, Apabhraṃśa, or the arcane symbolic language, we principally chose the most prevalent from similar manuscripts." However, "if [the mantras] were actually in Sanskrit, we would compare them with a grammar textbook and work according to our own judgment. Those that we could not judge we left as they were."[44] As does Shuchen, here Situ emphasizes editorial caution, for the fear of making the text even more corrupt overshadowed the attempt to clean up mantras of the less well-known Indic dialects. For these editors the best course of action when unsure of a particularly problematic reading was to leave it well alone.

Language was not the only problem in editing mantras; script was also an issue. According to our editors, the cursive Tibetan script was also a major source of error and confusion. Shuchen describes the orthographic problems that arose from this "script without a head," noting with understatement that "mantras were not among the more quickly [edited] textual passages. Previously, there appears to have been less editing of block prints and words. Books were written primarily in the cursive script, and in the majority of manuscripts some letters were mixed up, such as *ta* and *da*, *pa* and *sa*, [aspirated] *dha* and *ha*, as well as the [retroflex] *ta* series and the [plain] *ta* series. Intermediate dots [punctuation marks] were lost as lines, and various graphic corruptions occurred."

Shuchen conjures an image of the process of textual deterioration as new errors are introduced while mantras are replicated throughout ever-widening lines of Tibetan manuscripts: "Just as a great forest blazes in fire from the igniting of a small spark, [the mantras] have come to be neither Tibetan nor Indic, and neither those skilled in writing nor [those skilled] in reading could make any improvement in their appearance." Amid such widespread corruption, the prospects of successfully editing a text were not good. "Since we could not weigh [these corrupt mantras] on the scale of reasoned examination," Shuchen despairs, "impartiality was lost. The rescensions that proliferated from these [corrupt cases] were extremely difficult to examine."[45]

FINANCING A CANON

We have begun with Situ's editorial work, but this is not where he begins his own account of the Kangyur's production; he begins by detailing the economic aspects of printing. "It is needless to say," Situ assures his readers, "that for all of the printing and writing materials, the paper, ink, wood for blocks and so forth, we neither extorted the peasants with force nor imposed any tax; a price exceeding the current rate was paid." This was—he seeks to persuade us—an endeavor of the highest ethical standards in which no worker was undervalued or underpaid, let alone mistreated. Here Situ touches on two related subjects—Buddhist sore points, if you will—the use of tax revenue to fund the production of the Kangyur and the use of force, either physical or institutional, as means to gather materials. Many writers of canonical catalogs engage in similar apologetics, presumably because the use of force and taxes vitiates the generosity evinced by the project's patron and thus potentially reduces the amount of merit he or she will accrue. Situ obviously felt a need to distinguish this sacred project from secular labors. Taxes imposed in the form of grains, goods, and labor were no small part of lay life in Tibet; they were no doubt a major source of revenue for the royal house of Degé, and by extension the monastery. Though Situ gives no explicit reason tax revenue was not considered an appropriate funding source for the printing, it is likely that since by definition such payment was mandatory, taxes could not be seen as donations—and thus as willing contributions to the dharma and therefore sources of merit for the giver or the recipient. The funding was to come solely from the treasuries of the Degé king, and though one might ask how riches came to be *there* in the first place, any assistance meted out by the king was considered a donation, a merit-making act of compassion.

To the extent that Situ Panchen's portrayal of the funding is accurate and not simply a rhetorical flourish meant to please his patron, Tenpa Tsering, it may explain how Situ and his staff were able to attract and train a great number of skilled artisans in times when few were available: "While there were few competent scribes indeed who could write the printed letters in Tibet in the past, no sooner than this magnificent work project began, there assembled many scribes who came without being invited with the best of tools and were our guests of great merit." These scribes were not all fully trained in the orthographic standards that he deemed necessary to print the words of the Buddha, and thus needed to undergo a training session before the work commenced. They studied orthography "with great assiduity," recounts Situ, "and after training just a short time became skilled."

In the end more than 60 master calligraphers formed the school of wood-block scribes in the great hall of Lhündrupteng monastery, but this was only a small part of the workforce. There were also 400 block carvers, a group of 10 proofreaders, woodworkers, paper workers, and ink workers. Situ portrays their efforts in grand terms, boasting that "through a process of uninterrupted dedication [on the part of these workers], the editing was completed and the texts for the wood blocks were scribed. When each text was complete the scribe would proofread it twice, and then the proofreaders would check it twice again, so that [each text] was proofread four times." "When this was complete," he continues, "the blocks were carved . . . [led by] the monk Karma Pedro . . . and the secretary Tsering Pel. With tremendous effort this was accomplished during the five years from 1729 to 1733." And of the production cost, he states: "The total expense for the remuneration for each work crew, including the food and drink which had to be continually prepared throughout this time, occasional feasts and countless extravagant tips, together with the wood blocks and other items, was roughly 7,622 [ingots of silver to produce] 103 volumes."[46] In all, Situ lists six classes of workers, including scribes, block carvers, proofreaders, woodworkers, and paper and ink workers, totaling upwards of 500 people. As related in other accounts of printing projects, the carving of blocks was the single most labor-intensive and costly part of the printing process, with some 400 carvers working for nearly five years to produce approximately 66,000 carved pages. Situ concludes by emphasizing that the labor force was well-fed, housed, entertained, and generally treated to the good life, a point strongly emphasized in most accounts of canon production.

Like his predecessor, Shuchen Tsültrim Rinchen writes at length on the quality of the craftsmen and the nature of labor conditions at Degé during the printing of the Tengyur. He provides a scriptural defense of the reverence due the laborers engaged in good Buddhist works, which translated economically into a great deal of revenue. "In general it is necessary to please the artisans, the craftspeople," he begins, for "in the *Consecration Tantra* it is said: 'With all manner of ornamentation, worship the artisans after [work is done]. Whatever courtesy is shown to the [deity] should be offered to [the artisans as well].' And in the *Wish-Fulfilling Jewel* chapter of the *Medicine Buddha* it is prescribed that 'with a sound mind and a clean body, wearing modest and humble attire, with reverence and a collection of valuable gifts, make offerings to the deity and the artisan without distinction.'" In accord with these traditional prescriptions, "those learned in the arts were worshipped by everyone, and according to what has been taught about showering them with abundant presents, throughout this project, food and drink were continu-

ally prepared for the artisans. At various times there were ban-
quets in which [the artisans] could eat whatever they wanted."

Shuchen demurs from going further, offering that "if I were
to give a detailed account of how they were showered with gifts
in gratitude for their work, I would have to write a great deal, and
since there is little need, I will not write at length. I will simply
give a summary here."[47] Yet Shuchen continues on a theme already touched upon by Situ—the importance of not using taxes
to pay for these good Buddhist works. "In general," Shuchen
claims, "most projects of kings and ministers call for taxes imposed upon others and conscripted labor, and given this custom
of working one might wonder whether the project here was so
accomplished."[48] This was most certainly not the case, he states,
and proceeds to give a cost account in order to settle any doubts.
"If you count the number of beautifully ornamented folios in the
200 precious volumes that collectively make up the commentaries on the [Buddha's] teachings," he begins, "there are 62,287 folios which have been block printed. [In order to fund this] the
long hand of [the King of Degé, Tenpa Tsering,] lord of beings
and protector of the vows was extended with great donations.
The treasure stores of this great and learned king, which leave
no desire unfulfilled, were opened like a cache of jewels opened
wide to his own son. Grain stores and cattle lands were generously opened, unbound by greed." This generosity included offerings of various sorts, which Shuchen goes on to list: "Precious
gold, silver, coral, pearls, shells, turquoise, fine clothing, many
types of silk, cotton, woolen goods, various types of dress and
jewelry, sundry necessities, . . . tobacco, horses and livestock—in
short, whatever item of wealth each [artisan] wanted or needed
they received in plenty."[49] Shuchen thus illustrates that the Degé
Tengyur was founded not on conscripted labor and taxes but
upon the generosity of its patron. And amid amid his very vivid
and suggestive description, what is perhaps most striking is the
lavishness of the gifts with which the craftspeople were showered. If Shuchen is to be taken at his word, whatever status the
woodcutter may have had when cutting firewood, while cutting
timber into the blocks onto which the block carvers would carve
the text he was an honored guest, eating the meat of the king's
cattle, smoking the king's tobacco, for he was at work on the
words of the Buddha.

Much the same story is told in an account of a related printing project undertaken between 1753 and 1773 at Choné, a pol-

ity located north of Degé. Decades earlier the Choné rulers had sponsored the printing of a Kangyur, which was completed in 1731.[50] It took another twenty-two years to organize the resources for a Tengyur. As in the Degé printing house, at Choné the life of an artisan was well rewarded, and taxation was crucially absent during the making of the Tengyur. Könchok Jikmé Wangpo's account is worth quoting in full, principally because it recounts the long process of canon production (two decades in this case) with relative brevity:

> Though the leaders (of Choné)—the mother and her son—had earlier hoped to block print the Tengyur, it was postponed slightly owing to various complications. Later, the elder and holder of vows, the religious lord Sangyé Pelzang, in whom the stars and planets of insight twinkled over the mountain peak of meditation born from the ocean of proper conduct, said, "If you were to publish a block-print Tengyur, the benefit to the teachings would be quite great." So we drank from the trough of the great and pure deeds of Rinchen Peldzom—the goddess Tārā in human form, whose eyes, as wide as the sky, perceive the two ethical codes [religious and secular], who defies even the God of Wealth with her hordes of wish-fulfilling riches—and the great Minister Tensung Tsering. Without extorting the peasants with force or imposing taxes, a price exceeding the current rate was paid for the printing materials such as paper, ink, and wood blocks. When everything was set, the chief printer, the astute monk Ngawang Dargyé, the manager Kadum Tsering—whose intelligent eyes were wide open to the ways of the world—[both of whom worked] with great precision and were close the minister, managed [the project]. Peljor Gyatso painted the frontispiece deities. There were many groups of craftsmen, including 10 editors, more than 300 block carvers, woodworkers, ink makers, papermakers. With great effort [the printing] was completed with no interruptions in 21 years, between 1753 and 1772.
>
> The scribes and the carvers were given gifts of great value, and were awarded the tax-exempt status of darhan. Each division of workers was made content with food, drink, and valuable gifts (list of donors not included). These were supplemented by offerings of sundry items from the faithful and led by my offering of 100 silver ingots (srang). Taking into account [these donations] and the items that came both before and after from the holy Landlord's treasury, the cost came to 13,937 ingots, 7 zho, and 7 karma.

Because the gates have been opened to a generosity that will never run dry, every [donor] who defended the good will experience the glory of an unprecedented happiness. After completing the printing a wonderful temple was constructed, and [the Tengyur] was placed there. The consecration was performed according to the tantric explanations with beginning, middle, and end complete. This king of power, the precious Tengyur that fulfills the wishes of infinite living beings, was well done.[51]

As in the case of the Kangyur and the Tengyur at Degé, this account of the Tengyur production at Choné explicitly states that no taxes were imposed to fund the printing project. This implies that the workers involved may well have paid little or no tax for just over twenty years—surely a major economic benefit. It is well known that the Choné Tengyur is based upon the Degé Tengyur, but what is most fascinating here is that the author of the Choné Tengyur chronicle quotes Situ's account of the Degé Kangyur almost word for word when discussing this very point. This direct connection suggests that perhaps, in addition to disseminating the words of the Buddha, the editors of Degé had a hand in prescribing and spreading guidelines for religious work. The queen and prince of Choné went one step further still than the King of Degé and granted tax exemption to all of the several hundred workers who participated.[52] This must surely have been among the most favored ways the Buddhist canon played a role in people's lives, for aside from any soteriological benefit to be derived from its blessing power, working on the project was of direct benefit to their economic lives.

Returning to Degé, Shuchen provides a more meticulous description of printing costs. He makes his cost assessment for the production of the Tengyur in terms of two commodities that function as ubiquitous economic yardsticks: barley and tea. Barley was a common commodity in Tibet and was used for trading, wages, taxes, and donations into the twentieth century. Shuchen's list is no mere accounting sheet, however, but a rare window into the workshop of the printing house, for here may be glimpsed both the variety of workers involved in the project and their relative importance (at least when measured in terms of their wages). Shuchen lists 10 types of scholars and artisans in hierarchical order, from the highest paid to the lowest: chief editors, junior editors, painters, carvers of deities, scribes, wood-block carvers, wood-block proofreaders, page liners, papermakers, and woodcutters. Passing over most of the financial details (see appendix 3 for a more detailed account), two comprehensive figures are worthy of note. The total cost of food and drink for these several hundred workers, figured for a period of four years, was 168,400 bushels of barley, and the cost of all wages and materials was 274,932 bushels (the vast majority of which went to wages for the woodblock carvers: 202,335 bushels, or over 73 percent), for a grand total of 443,332 bushels. We find similar numbers if we compare the cost of the Choné Tengyur, cited above at 13,937 ingots of silver. In 1680 the Fifth Dalai Lama's regent, Sangyé Gyatso, calculated the exchange rate in Lhasa between ingots (*srang*) of silver and bushels (*khal*) of barley to be 1 ingot per 18 bushels.[53] Using this figure it can be roughly estimated that the Choné leaders spent 250,866 bushels of barley on their Tengyur, or very close to the 274,932 spent on wages and materials at Degé.

Of course, these figures mean little unless they can be compared to the costs of other religious and secular endeavors. Very little has been written about the financial aspects of Tibetan monastic establishments, especially regarding monasteries prior to the twentieth century, and the comparative economy of monumental cultural projects in Tibet remains to be undertaken. Nevertheless, one example may help to form a rough notion of the relative expense of the canons produced at Degé. This comes from Dakpo Shedrup Ling monastery in the first half of this century. The total amount of barley needed to pay the stipends for Dakpo Shedrup Ling's 800 monks as well as all administrative costs was approximately 8,000 bushels per year.[54] In rough numbers, then, the cost of carving the blocks of the Tengyur at Degé was some 50 times greater than the annual operations budget of a single large monastery in central Tibet; with the budget of the Tengyur, Dakpo Shedrup Ling could have remained in operation for half a century. The great expense of printing is also attested to in the chronicle of the Nartang Tengyur at Shekar monastery, a project that employed more than 1,100 artisans for one and a half years; just the initial costs drained two full years of it's the monastery's annual budget, after which grants from the central government in Lhasa and numerous private donations funded the canon's completion.

The printing of the Buddha's word was indeed big business, and thus the patrons of such religious works were due great praise. Indeed, Shuchen's 900-page *New Moon* chronicle of the Tengyur and its social, cultural, and cosmological setting can be seen as an extended homage to his patron, his patron's kingdom, and its importance in the history of Buddhism. At the close of the passage examined here, Shuchen offers one of many praises to his benefactor, Kunga Trinlé Gyatso: "For causing the precious and powerful teachings to live long by opening wide his great three-storied treasury in order to fund the materials for producing the foundation [of the Buddha's word, and for his] sincerity, which brings together good friends in the world of living beings—for these outstanding deeds I believe that this excellent lord and up-holder of vows is without equal."[55]

THE KING'S CANONS

Shuchen's counterparts in central Tibet might not have agreed with his estimation of his ruler's unequaled status, considering it perhaps the hyperbole of a minor principality on the border-lands. Rather, they likely would have put the same rhetoric to use in praise of their own leaders in Lhasa. An early twentieth-century geographical report relates an anecdote about the canon-ical production at Degé and its repercussions in central Tibet: "The lamas claim that the blocks were cut by orders of the King of Degé some hundreds of years ago, and that it was the envy of a petty king having forestalled them that caused the lamas of cen-tral Tibet to set about making the Nartang edition now used at Lhasa."[56] Is there any truth to this tale of regional competition?[57]

According to the massive biography of a towering figure in eighteenth-century central Tibetan politics, Polané Miwang Sönam Tobgyé (1689–1747), there is. This well-known work by Tsering Wangyal offers a glimpse of the production of canonical volumes being carried out in central Tibet concurrently with the work at Degé. Polané was the administrator and de facto ruler of central Tibet from 1728/1729 until his death in 1747, and though the biography only covers his life until 1733,[58] this is enough to provide a voice from the patron's side of canonical production to contrast with the editors' perspectives. So the focus now turns to the King of Tibet and the patron of no fewer than four cen-tral Tibetan canons—two printed and two handwritten, the so-called Nartang Kangyur (1731–1732) and Tengyur (1741–1742), a gold Kangyur (circa 1732), and a gold Tengyur (1734). The two Kangyur projects are of concern here.[59]

Writing about Polané's activities circa 1730, Tsering Wang-yal portrays a wealthy leader turning his attention toward the dharma. The central issue motivating Polané's patronage and support of producing canons was how best to use the vast material resources at his disposal as leader of central Tibet. "Because the positive previous disposition awoke in him," Tsering Wangyal begins, "a benevolent attitude of virtue was born in him." "Alas," the great leader broods over the difficulty of meaningful patronage, "most of what exists in the world that is given is generally not holy; it is expended with no result. Even those actions that tire body and mind that are accomplished are of little value. Being involved only in the activities of this life is supreme madness!" He must make a change: "Now, taking the essence of wealth from wealth, I will begin to work to unwaveringly promote the precious teachings of the Buddha—the root and branch of all welfare and efficacious joy, and so that embodied beings now and henceforth will experience joy." And so Polané sets out to follow the Buddhist path, not through philosophical training or contemplative technologies but through the creation of a Buddhist canon.

"The first indispensable door for those claiming to be Buddhists is taking the undeceiving holy refuge in the three jewels," he instructs readers on the Buddha, dharma, and sangha, having been transformed (in the biographer's portrayal, that is) from political leader to devout aspirant. "By remembering the mass of good qualities of the [three jewels], faith is purified and one trains perfectly in the [the three jewels]. . . . Just so I will give up all faults and perfect all good qualities." And the supreme jewel, according to Polané, is the dharma, for if there are no Buddhist teachings then there is no opportunity for a Buddhist community to develop and thus no chance for anyone to seek enlightenment. Now, dharma exists primarily within texts, and in the sponsorship of scripture Polané finds he has a host of illustrious forbearers: "The holy leaders of old and the great dharma kings bequeathed inexhaustible, limitless volumes of the Buddha's word translated into Tibetan with gold, silver, and vermillion drawings upon them." Yet, he complains, "the great technology of printing [these volumes] has not appeared in the regions of U and Tsang up to the present. Even with the great offering by the Sixth Dalai Lama toward [making] twenty-eight volumes of primarily the *Perfection of Wisdom*, for seven years the craftsmen and people experienced fatigue, the goods of the great treasury were exhausted, and thus there was no chance to complete it and it was left unfinished." After that, Lhazang Khan, the ruler of Tak Nampar Tsewa, and powerful Daiching Batur (Kang chen nas Bsod nams rgyal po, governor of Mnga' ris skor gsum) and others made vows to complete what they could of the remainder. "Nevertheless," he continues, "lazy thieves stole the wealth of virtue and thus not even a single volume was obtained." This is all the more tragic because economic prosperity was high, "Tibet was not fragmented, and thus rulers' holdings were vast, and even the subjects were not very destitute and obtained the opportunity to do as they liked." If in good times such as those central Tibet could not print a canon, what hope has he after the war-torn early eighteenth century? For, he continues, "the subjects of old, the major and minor forts along with their subjects have suffered misfortune. Even the remainder, subject to continuous weariness of war, have become destitute from the unending outflow of tribute. The great internal and external treasuries have been emptied. The power to accomplish these actions of mine is very small indeed." Polané, in other words, is claiming bankruptcy, which makes it all the more wondrous in Tsering Wangyal's telling that he turned his attention toward the dharma when this was economically difficult. Thus Polané concludes with a vow: "There is no doubt that effort on the virtuous path will be only accomplished by the compassion of the precious three jewels. This goal I must quickly accomplish without doubt."

Despite his vow, his advisors ("ignorant and weak-willed people" according to Tsering Wangyal) counsel him against such a heavy outlay. "Alas, Lord of Men," they compliment him, "this great deed that has arisen in your mind is good; it is beyond the thoughts and words of ordinary people." But even one such as Polané would have difficulty with the task, for "earlier even when the Ganden government—the singular pinnacle of the white umbrella of religious and worldly teachings—covered the whole country, it could not complete a print of the precious Kangyur." The requisite government funds were lacking, say the advisors, and willing subjects were absent. And even though a succession of Tibetan leaders have vowed to complete what remained, obstacles of a more ethereal yet still serious nature have barred them from success, and even proven harmful. In Kham, for instance, the Karmapa printed the Kangyur, and thus the life of the reincarnation was shortened. "Now," claim Polané's advisors, "the Karmapa teaching crashes down like an avalanche!"

Against this counsel Polané decided to carry out his plans, for the Kangyur was nothing less than "the single light of the world, the holy root and branch of welfare and joy." And since the Kangyur contained the words of the Buddha, producing it would be tantamount to inviting Shakyamuni himself to visit Tibet. In short, he considered that "the faultless origin of all virtuous activity [directed] in this world toward enlightenment relies upon the precious Kangyur residing without fail in the worldly realm." His ministers might be right, but if by printing the Buddha's word he "were able to pervade all the regions of the world with the holy appearance of the holy dharma," he would do so. "Though it be easy for demons to obstruct me and take my life," he vowed, "though it be easy for all my wealth and power to be lost and I to become a beggar, I will never abandon this good thought that has arisen."

After so declaring his intentions, Polané began a lengthy series of prayers in temples around Lhasa. He offered veneration to the many monastic populations engaged in reciting the Kangyur. He propitiated wrathful deities, "the demon-garbed sentinels with adamantine power and the wisdom eye shining in the ten directions who defend the teaching of Victor," to ensure that his project would suffer no setbacks. After these ritual preliminaries, preparations of a more tangible sort began. One of his aides, Ngadak Drakpa, traveled to Shekar monastery in the southeast to make preparations for the production of the blocks. He related his success to Polané by post, and when the favorable conditions were confirmed to the Tibetan leader in a dream, the project finally began. On the twenty-fourth day of the eighth month of the Iron Male Dog Year (1730) work was initiated at the Shekar printing house. The natural and supernatural surroundings gave their approval with wondrous apparitions, for "the sky was spotless, shining bright blue light like an Indranila flower. The sun blazed brightly with a beautiful rainbow surrounding it, and not even a slight breeze arose. Experiencing these omens of virtue caused everyone to take in the festival with unending happiness. Such was the significance of everything," concludes Tsering Wangyal. "A meaningful task had been initiated."

Nevertheless, no more than a hundred artisans had been assembled, and Ngadak Drakpa knew from previous failures that it would be difficult to complete the task even in the space of twenty years with this small workforce. He "wore this heavy on his neck" and traveled to meet his ruler to explain the situation.

Polané considered the matter "with the treasury of his intellect open wide." "My establishment of the root of virtue through producing the prints of the Kangyur—which will serve as an inexhaustible gift of dharma—is not only for today," he reasoned, for henceforth all the major and minor lands would be filled with artisans skilled in block carving, and the dharma in the Kangyur and Tengyur "shall fall like rain." In other words, for Polané the project was certainly about the promotion of dharma, but it was also about the state sponsorship of skilled craftsmen. He therefore issued a letter of command to all district headmen stating that those among their subjects who knew block carving were to be sent to work exclusively on the Kangyur project. Furthermore, anyone who appeared to possess the aptitude for such work must also enter the Kangyur workforce at Shekar.

Not long after, nearly one thousand artisans skilled in block carving from all regions were assembled—ten times more than Ngadak Drakpa had initially been able to muster. There were clear differences in quality between individual craftsmen, and this was acknowledged in the form of both wages and punitive measures. "Those who had good orthographic form, who understood differences in quality, who worked quickly and accurately," relates Tsering Wangyal, "were provided with much fine silk clothing and silver coins." Those who made no effort, "or whose orthographic form was bad, or who loitered, were encouraged through many means such as being whipped a bit on the cheek with a hand whip, scolded with harsh words or accused." Given such measures, even those artisans who initially only "worked for their own benefit eventually moved beyond this, and subsequently came to spend the time in supreme effort, needing no encouragement from others," and "not even thinking of food and drink." Regardless of what one makes of Tsering Wangyal's psychological portrait of the artisans, by all accounts they worked with great efficiency. "Previously," he recounts, "the best of those who produced the precious printed word of the Buddha would complete five or six boards for block printing each month, middling three or four, and the rest not more than one or two." At Shekar, by contrast, "the best artisans produce between sixteen and twenty-three per month, the middling between fifteen and ten, and some between twelve and eight, while most produced between seven and five, and even the lesser produced three." This is why, Tsering Wangyal concludes, "in only a year and a half beginning in 1730 we were able to complete" the project—no mean feat; recall that the Tengyur produced at Choné required two decades.

Up to this point the project materials had come in small part from the items collected in the annual tribute from the subjects of Shekar, and in large part from Polané's own financial resources. "So other than encouraging the subjects of Shekar to work," Tsering Wangyal boasts, "there was no need to levy a tax upon other districts." Furthermore, when it became widely known that Polané was having the Kangyur printed at Shekar, the news spread by word of mouth that "however much is produced will suffice," in other words, that people were free to donate what they could to the project. Funding did come from a host of patrons, and Tsering Wangyal directs his reader's attention to the catalog of this canon authored by Shepé Dorjé for a more detailed account of its benefactors.[60]

After extolling the benefits of reproducing volumes containing the word of the Buddha, Tsering Wangyal concludes his account by suggesting that there is a qualitative difference between scribal production and printing. "If it is taught that even by handwriting volumes one becomes endowed with so much benefit," he writes, "what need is there even to speak of the [the benefits] of printing, which offers forth the dharma without end?" He does not elaborate upon the specifics of this difference, though it certainly must have to do with the "rain of dharma" that the printed work promises to shower down upon Tibet. With the blessing of the Seventh Dalai Lama, Kelsang Gyatso, the blocks of the Kangyur were moved to Nartang monastery (from which this Kangyur takes its name in contemporary usage), where Polané established a printery in order to carry out his vow "to fill all the regions that had not obtained their share of the dharma with hundreds of prints of the precious Kangyur." "He had many printed," Tsering Wangyal states without providing a specific number, "and the gift of dharma increased to fill the sky." This was only partly poetic license, for almost two centuries later the canonical production set in motion at Nartang by Polané and the Dalai Lama was still active: on a diplomatic visit to the Panchen Lama in 1906 at nearby Tashilhunpo monastery, British liaison Charles Bell stoped at Nartang (his "Na-tang") to see the publishing house for himself. "Thirty-three monks are employed in the printing establishment," Bell recounts, "which is said to be the largest in Tibet. The letters are carved on heavy rectangular blocks of wood, which are arranged on high racks in the rooms assigned to them, and numbered alphabetically." Bell took an interest in the process, relating that the paper was imported from Bhutan, and that "the printing is done rapidly. Three monks work together, one taking the impressions, another handling the paper, and the third looking after the blocks." Polané's "gift of dharma" was still giving in Bell's time; fully three copies of the Tengyur were in production as he beheld the activity at Nartang.[61]

According to his biographer, Polané also assembled the printers from the Kangyur project at Shekar to produce a new printed edition of Tsongkhapa's *Great Stages of the Path* to replace an older worn edition. He also had textbooks for Ganden, Drepung, and Sera monasteries printed, "for novice monks spent too much effort copying books and it was difficult for monks of little means to acquire copies." Here the "rain of dharma" assumed a more pragmatic form, as printing was also a way to assure "that the good explanations of the great scholars would continue without fail" through state sponsorship.

Yet regardless of the difference between them, scribal production did not cease with the widespread adoption of printing, and Polané himself sponsored a scribally produced canon immediately after his printed edition was completed. This handwritten canon was an intensely personal affair, for it was dedicated to the memory of his mother, who passed away in the early 1730s. She was cremated and her remains were purified and mixed with medicine, and incorporated into holy items such as clay figurines, images of the Buddha and the Sixteen Arhats, and Padmasambhava. Her remains were also mixed with ink used to produce the volumes of Polané's Kangyur.[62] "Now," Tsering Wangyal begins, Polané "had opened wide the doors of the gift of dharma through printing, and thereby had provided unequaled sustenance for the welfare and joy of the Teaching and living beings." He also understood that "all good qualities of existence and quiescence in this life and the next arise from the precious Kangyur of the Victor." And—most interestingly for the present narrative of book making—Polané was certain that a canon produced from the finest materials "would be the best for completing the accumulations of wisdom and merit" so important for personal liberation. In other words, the physical characteristics of the book were directly related to its soteriological effectiveness: more gold meant more wisdom, more jewels meant more merit. "The *sūtras* say that jewels are the best," Polané mused. If produced from fine materials, "supports for worship" such as canons would serve as effective motivators for those seeking enlightenment, for they would harness "essence of material items" in order to "renew the undivided faith in the word of the Victor." "Volumes written in ink from refined gold upon paper that was as if made from the Indranila flower would," he thought, "become a holy lamp for the world."

With this rationale in mind, Polané first assembled all those from the É and Nyemo regions who were skilled in painting to begin illustrating his memorial Kangyur. He selected from among them those who were skilled in writing with good form, and those who did not have sufficient skills he sent to restore the scattered volumes from the Kangyur and Tengyur that were housed in a certain temple in Lhasa. Even though he was busy with all the affairs of his kingdom, Tsering Wangyal writes that he constantly managed this project himself. "This making of the precious Kangyur, the single lamp of welfare and joy for the world, has been an unexcelled great goal for me," Polané reflected, "yet most others who are concerned with the affairs of the kingdom are like children making sand castles." So each day Polané personally inspected the work of every scribe. "This is good form," he would compliment them. "Write the gold thickly and you will be given good gifts." "This is not good scribal form," he would scold, "the gold ink is written thinly, so you should be humbled!" "This writing has nothing missing and nothing duplicated," he might say, "so give good wages." "This has missing and duplicated passages, and the writing is obliterated and hazy," he might censure them, "so you will be reprimanded!" In Tsering Wangyal's telling, Polané carefully examined all of the work to ensure quality and uniformity, acting as king, patron, and editorial overseer, as if embodying the personas of both Butön and the lord of the Shalu manor.

Tsering Wangyal waxes long on the most precious and costly substance being poured into the project—gold. The gold ink "was used in a manner unlike the scribal styles of earlier generations"— that is, a great deal was used—and in order to attain the quantity necessary to write like this, the liquid gold was depleted again and again. This caused consternation for the treasurers and those in charge of producing other holy objects for the temples of Lhasa. At one point when the gold came near to running out, the treasurers became afraid and beseeched Polané: "Lord, if the gold runs out now, what should we do?" Polané commanded,

"With the remaining gold, pray to the two Jowo statues, the Avalokiteśvara, and the other gods of the temples for liquid gold." The treasurers responded, "If the gold for producing the Kangyur comes close to running out, how will the liquid gold for the temples be made?" Polané said, "Ignorant fools, do as I instruct!" So despite their misgivings the treasurers praised what he said and gave whatever was left of the gold to the canon. And when the gold was about to run out they made an offering of whatever was left to the images of the Buddha and his spiritual sons in the temples. But Polané was not as confident in private and, in addition to making prayers for more gold, he acknowledged that the work was in danger and sought to borrow one hundred measures of gold from Tashilunpo monastery. "But in the end," Tsering Wangyal states, "the loan from Tashilhunpo was not required, and the Lhasa project was completed in style." "The letters on the first page of those volumes were a full hand span high," the biographer writes, "and on either side were buddhas, bodhisattvas, peaceful and wrathful deities, and lineages of masters raised and leafed with gold." Other features of Polané's volumes merit mention in his biography as well. The covering was made of various types of Mongolian and Chinese satin, and only of the finest gold color. The book boards were covered in gold as well, so that gold suffused the volumes from the inside out. The titles on the sides of the book boards were inset within a beautiful decorative floral pattern crafted of iron and covered with gold. The gold-covered book buckles were made by Chinese artisans, and, finally, the title tags were made of fine silk.

Tsering Wangyal concludes with a final note on the social location of these books in central Tibet. Polané's volumes (each, it must be remembered, containing a piece of his mother within its golden letters) are quite simply without equal, "for [this edition] is even finer than the Kangyur known as the 'World Revolver' that is located at Drepung and was famous throughout Tibet in previous generations." That canon was, the biographer relates in a incidental note, based upon a set of volumes "praised by Chökyi Gyeltsen," likely referring to the past abbot of Tashilhunpo, Sera Jetsün Chökyi Gyeltsen (1469–1544). These were brought to Drepung from Tashilhunpo to be duplicated, and the artisans who worked on it were paid and entertained. Likewise, Tsering Wangyal says, Polané treated his workers well, and worked to benefit one of central Tibet's famous monasteries rather than himself. For rather than placing his manuscript Kangyur in his own residence, as would presumably have been his prerogative, Polané bequeathed it to Ganden monastery and had it placed in a temple that he had renovated for just this purpose. There also were laid to rest a portion of his mother's remains, transformed into the golden letters of the dharma, reembodied in the form of the king's finely crafted volumes of scripture.

*T*he studies undertaken here are not primarily a history of the Tibetan book in its material existence. Rather, they constitute a history of people talking about books, of the book as a significant object through which to describe, prescribe, and contest culture. Here Polané's golden Kangyur is as much a rhetorical tool employed by his biographer as it is a finely crafted object. This concluding chapter renders this discussion more explicit by considering the book as a symbolic object, first looking at a single work of history, the *Blue Annals*, for what it may reveal about the range of discourse about books. With several hundred references to books, their materials, and the practices associated with them scattered throughout its relentless listings of Buddhist saints, scholars, teachings, and traditions in early Tibet, the *Blue Annals* is ideally suited to such thematic mining. The chapter then moves to more vivid and detailed discussions that treat the book as an object at once physical, social, and symbolic. Finally, it returns to the central characters of the previous chapter, Situ and Shuchen, the editors of eighteenth-century Degé, to ask what value the canons may have had for both their patrons and themselves. In so doing, I hope to sketch a plausible vision of the social and cultural landscape upon which the traditions of textual scholarship explored in previous chapters flourished.

Works such as Gö Lotsawa's *Blue Annals*, a veritable microcosm of Buddhist culture through the late fifteenth century, offer a wider perspective on the culture of the book in Tibet. The book is the crafted object most frequently mentioned in the *Blue Annals*, not surprising after one considers the vast outpouring of human and material resources in the production of books in the centuries before and up to Gö Lotsawa's time. One example from another source will help us imagine the possible context of its evidence. During the production of a manuscript Tengyur at Shalu monastery in 1362, thirteen types of skilled craftsmen and scholars were employed, including directors, scribal managers, proofreaders, chief scribes, papermakers, engravers, goldsmiths who worked on the book covers, page numberers, collators, book-strap makers, and finally blacksmiths who made the buckles for the straps.[1] Wood, fiber, paper, ink, and metal were utilized to produce finely crafted volumes, all under strict supervision of a management team.[2] This project followed upon four decades of canonical production in which—estimated conservatively solely from the evidence of the *Blue Annals*—several thousand volumes and over one million pages were produced at a handful of institutions in central Tibet. By the early fifteenth century, on the eve of Gö Lotsawa's history, the leaders of nearby Gyantsé alone sponsored the production of hundreds of canonical volumes every single year.

This chapter focuses on only two of many possible aspects of book culture that are suggested by a reading of the *Blue Annals*: the book as an object of offering and exchange—in other words, as a part of economic life; and the book as a symbolic object, at once depending on and extending beyond its material aspects. The reconciliation of these two visions poses a problem that lies at the heart of the culture of the book in Tibet. These two facets of the book, economic and symbolic, have more in common than it might at first seem, and an attempt to understand their interrelations will be productive for further studies of the book and its place in the social, cultural, and religious history of Tibet.

THE BOOK AS PROPERTY

Unlike the sources touched upon in previous chapters, the *Blue Annals* does not make prescriptive statements about the material aspects of the book, but it does have something to say about book materials. Scriptures are routinely said to be written in gold or silver ink, paper is mentioned frequently, and dye for the edges of book pages is mentioned. The Kangyur and Tengyur at Nartang in the early fourteenth century were, according to Gö Lotsawa, made possible in part by gifts of ink sent by a Tibetan living in the Yuan court in China. Golden Kangyurs and Tengyurs are said to have been produced by priests with royal patronage in the early fourteenth century, only decades after the two collections achieved their name and form. These continued to be produced throughout central Tibet into Gö Lotsawa's time and beyond.[3] Other books were also commissioned to be produced in gold, including even indigenous works such as a collection of Kagyu teachings written in gold and likened in size to the sprawling *Avataṃsaka Sūtra*.[4] Yet when the raw materials of books are mentioned in the *Blue Annals*, it is almost always in an economic context, in passages dealing with property, wealth, exchange, and donation. In other words, in the *Blue Annals* the book is most often already treated as a social object involved in relationships between people and institutions. It is therefore useful to discuss the book in Gö Lotsawa's history from three perspectives: as personal property, as institutional property, and as an item of exchange.

Books were personal property in the centuries before Gö Lotsawa. Though monks and religious leaders are most often mentioned as the owners of books, artisans such as painters might also own some.[5] Very often books were passed on from master to disciple,[6] as when an elderly dying leader urged his disciples to look after the books in the bookcase.[7] As personal property, books could also be used to establish the succession of reincarnate masters, as in the case of the Fifth Karmapa, who is stated to have warned his attendants not to disperse his books and images, for the owner would return.[8] Books were important family property as well. A family living near Shekar Dzong during the twelfth century, for instance, counted *sūtra*s among their valuables.[9] As significant property, books could be passed on from generation to generation either at death[10] or between living family members,[11] and ancestral books could become the focus of devotional rituals.[12] The ability to actually produce books might even be a reason to forge familial ties. One early Nyingmapa disciple could not afford to continue his studies in tantra or to make copies of the requisite books for such practice. His master induced him to marry the daughter of wealthy patrons, thereby producing merit for the patrons and allowing the disciple to use his newfound wealth and property to obtain tantric initiations and to copy books.[13]

If books as personal property are clearly in evidence, how many people actually owned them? How many people might one find in a single location in the possession of private copies of any one book? The *Blue Annals* provides some figures. By the end of the eleventh century large numbers of students are said to possess personal texts, as in the case of one teacher, who in the 1090s taught more than 23,000 students, each with their own copy of the text.[14] In another, perhaps more realistic teaching scene from the eleventh century, 300 students who personally owned texts assembled before a Buddhist teacher.[15] In the early thirteenth century a teacher taught 100 monks, all of whom possessed a personal copy of the book under discussion.[16] A Sakyapa scholar taught the *Kālacakra Tantra* to more than 500 scholars who owned the text.[17] And 500 copies of the *Pradīpodyotananāmaṭīkā*, the famous commentary on the *Guhyasamāja Tantra*, are said to be housed in the hermitage of one of its lineage holders.[18] From this it may be surmised that, from the eleventh century onward, in any given educational setting there could be hundreds of people with private copies of classical Buddhist texts.

Books were also an important feature of institutional wealth. Monastic and temple libraries might develop in a variety of ways, one of which was the passing of books from private collections to institutional collections. An influential teacher amassing wealth might bequeath his books to the monastery, as when the Kagyupa scholar Ling Repa sent all books he received to Phakmodrü monastery.[19] On other occasions a leader's books might fall to his institution upon his death. After Sönam Gyatso's death in 1482, two things happened. First his own collected works were edited as part of funeral proceedings, indicating that the collected works of revered writers were assembled at such times for memorialization. Second, his disciples kept his books at the monastery, suggesting that privately owned books could become the property of institutions associated with that person.[20] Abbots were often in charge of such libraries, and the *Blue Annals* explicitly links the assumption of the abbatial throne to the assumption of authority over books. Chak Lotsawa, for instance, as an elder monk of some renown and authority in the late thirteenth century, "received the keys of 80 monasteries . . . and 300 volumes of sacred scriptures."[21] And upon installation as abbot of Nyedo at the age of 22, Mawé Sengé was entrusted with two items meant to symbolize his authority, the religious conch and the books of the monastery. Shortly after this, a promise was made to erect a new temple on site and to fill it with books.[22]

Once books were housed in institutional libraries, access to them was subject to the rule of the institution's leaders. Books deemed unsuitable for teaching could be kept under lock and key. A library might thus contain books to which no one save abbots and librarians had access. As the first abbot of Taklung drew near to death, he entrusted the library keys to his student and successor, revealing that in the library "there are aspects of doctrine that are not publicly known." "I did not show avarice in matters pertaining to this doctrine," he confides, "but I hid it because of some omens on advice from Phakmodrüpa. But you," he grants to his student, "can reveal it and bestow it on those who ask."[23] Books sealed in monastic libraries could also be unsealed by leaders who might hold different views than their predecessors regarding the accessibility of such knowledge.

Like smaller private collections, institutional libraries belonging to monasteries and temples could be moved or even disbanded. Moving collections between institutions must have required significant effort. In cases where there were disagreements, such events could be a cause of conflict between religious leaders over resources and authority, as scenes from the history of Taklung and Phakmodrü monasteries vividly testify. In Gö Lotsawa's telling, during the expansion of Taklung under its second abbot, it became apparent that its builders had amassed too many books and images to fit in the existing temple. This was no small problem. The *Blue Annals* provides an anecdotal, yet nonetheless impressive sense of Taklung monastery's library holdings when it relates that while one Taklung leader was ill, he ordered all the books in the library to be recited as they were dusted. With this added labor, it took three years for a team of 250 monks to dust those books.[24] At any rate, this crisis of plenty sparked a debate about the character and direction of the institution, and the abbot thus asked the advice of various leaders on the building of a larger temple. Some argued fervently against the continued expansion of the library. "Any kind of temple will do!" said one master: "We should practice meditation and the exposition of the doctrine. A single hermit is better than a hundred *Perfection of Wisdom* (books) written in gold!" Others spoke in favor of building a new chapel in which to "meditate *and* expound the doctrine," an opinion that apparently won the day, for the new large temple at Taklung was constructed over a six-year period, between 1224 and 1228.[25]

The first Taklung abbot was also instrumental in building a temple stocked with books at Phagmodrü, the seat of his master. In this he was aided by the Drikung Kagyu founder, Jikten Gönpo, though their cooperation ended when Jikten Gönpo had the library of Phakmodrü moved to Gampo monastery without the Taklung abbot's consent, "filling one side of the Temple of Gampo" with them. This caused great displeasure among the laymen of the Phakmodrü area, who accused Jikten Gönpo of destroying his teacher's monastery. The Taklung abbot was also disappointed and questioned the Drikung hierarch's decision. Gö Lotsawa relates a fascinating bit of hearsay that, owing to the breakup of the library at Phakmodrü, the Taklung abbot died of a broken heart.[26]

THE BOOK AS EXCHANGE ITEM

Some perspective on the first Taklung abbot's distress may be gained by looking at the role books played in economic relations between both individuals and institutions. Books were important objects of exchange and often figure prominently among lists of donations and offerings in the *Blue Annals*. The *Perfection of Wisdom sūtras* in their varying lengths are most frequently mentioned as offerings and objects of exchange: the famed translator of the eleventh and twelfth centuries, Ra Lotsawa, offered six golden copies of the *Perfection of Wisdom* in 100,000 lines, among other provisions, to a certain monastery in Tsang, along with 100 volumes each to 2 monasteries, 50 to another, and a full copy of the 100,000-line *Perfection of Wisdom* to another translator, Ngok Lotsawa, his gifts totaling almost 300 volumes.[27] The First Karmapa offered presents from central Tibet to Gampo monastery, including 4 golden copies of the 100,000, a copy of the *Collected Sūtras*, and 108 other volumes (as well as 10 pieces of turquoise and 50 horses and yaks). He also offered 100 volumes written in gold to Daklha Gampo.[28] In instances such as these the object or service for which the book was exchanged is, as in most cases, left unstated. We might expect the notion of merit to figure prominently in these scenes of books offered, but it is all but absent in the *Blue Annals*. Yet there is explicit evidence of exchange. Books might be offered as repayment for teachings, as when the fortunes of one disciple increased and he thereupon offered more than 100 volumes to his teacher.[29] Another student presented to his teacher 17 gold copies of the large *Perfection of Wisdom Sūtras* in exchange for teachings leading to insight.[30] In another case the *Perfection of Wisdom in Eight Thousand Lines*, written in gold ink, is offered along with 10 measures of gold in exchange for teachings on the *Guhyasamāja Tantra*.[31] Books were commonly bestowed as gifts from wealthy leaders to their disciples, well-wishers, and supportive institutions.

Both Tibetan and Indic books were also exchanged across cultural boundaries. When Tropu Lotsawa wished to invite the Indian master Buddhaśrī to Tibet in the mid-thirteenth century, he sent a letter composed in Sanskrit to the monastic unviersity of Jaggadala in Bengal, along with a copy of the *Heart Sūtra* written in gold and other presents.[32] The well-known legions of Sanskrit manuscripts that formed the basis of Tibetan translations very often traveled through the Kathmandu Valley, and not always in the hands of scholars. Other social groups transmitted books as well, as in the case of a copy of the *Kriyasammucaya*, which was obtained by a Tibetan from a Nepalese merchant. It may be wondered if this book of esoteric practice was in fact a part of the merchant's wares, one product among others.[33] In terms of both their materials and the high degree of craft represented by their ornate features, books were a significant form of wealth that could be readily exchanged for other goods and services.

The first Taklung abbot had received numerous books amid other sorts of offerings, including a great deal of gold and silver, and during his return visits to the seat of his old master, Phakmodrüpa, he in turn donated volumes to the temple that he and the Drikung abbot had built in their master's honor. In one list of offerings the books figure prominently among a host of items: 550 books on blue and ordinary paper, 40 bars of gold and pieces of turquoise, 60 bricks of tea, 3000 ceremonial silk scarves, 100 head of cattle and horses, votive lamps made of more than 100 gold ingots, many robes, and armor plates. As he drew near to death he again offered 700 books on blue paper and uncounted volumes on ordinary paper, 50 gold bars, 50 pieces of turquoise, 2,500 silk scarves, and other items. Given his vast material efforts dedicated to Phakmodrü, is it any wonder that when in 1209 he heard that the books had been removed to another institution without his consent, his health suffered?[34]

If books themselves were items of exchange, it follows that practices of book production were also part of an economy. Gö Lotsawa directs readers' attention to three forms of such labor: scribal work, recitation, and translation. First, a student might serve as scribe to a teacher as payment for instruction, as when a student copied 40 folios of the *Kālacakra Tantra* to pay for his initiation into the same tantric teachings.[35] More frequently mentioned is recitation, which seems to have been a significant form of employment. Trying to escape a famine in his homeland, one twelfth-century figure moved to a different region and recited texts for the wealthy in exchange for food. With the money he obtained he was able to support both himself and a group of people back home.[36] Milarepa's great disciple, Rechungpa, worked as a reciter in his village and gave his earnings to his uncle.[37] Reciters were also employed as house priests, as in the case of Machik Labdrön, who was hired to recite *Perfection of Wisdom* texts as the house priestess of Drapa Ngonshé.[38] A grand scale is alluded to in a passage on the origins of continuous canon recitation. The benefactor of this practice was a lama of means, having more than a thousand shepherds, "each carrying their own quiver," at his disposal, and thus he became the wealthiest man around. Here the very possibility of reciting the Kangyur is premised upon wealth created through amassing what appears to be a large mercenary army.[39]

The most explicit statements about the economy of book production in the *Blue Annals* have to do with the prices for translation and translated teachings. It was expensive to have works translated from Sanskrit into Tibetan, so finances could be a barrier to success. For example, the Kashmirian scholar Somanātha wished to spread the Kālacakra teachings in Tibet but had trouble finding a benefactor, so he asked a certain Tibetan scholar if he might be able to translate the work into Tibetan. The Tibetan replied, "I am unable to translate it, but there is a way out of this. I shall send a message to the son of the virtuous friend Chepa of Zangyul in Yorpo; he will be able to assist you with finances." Chepa and his son offered Somanātha three measures of gold as well as clothing and a mantle, and beseeched him to stay with them for a time. When he departed toward Chushül they offered thirty loads of wine for the journey. After this Somanātha met a Tibetan translator by the name of Azha Gyagartsek, whom he hired to translate for an entire year. He paid Azha thirty measures of gold initially (perhaps he gained this from selling the wine given to him earlier?), as well as subsidizing the living expenses of thirty men and horses, all of whom were apparently part of Azha's retinue. In the end he paid a total of sixty measures of gold to have Azha translate the *Kālacakra Tantra*.[40]

Some, it appears, sought to recoup expenditures by fixing prices for translated texts. In the biographical note on the eleventh/twelfth-century translator Ra Lotsawa, Gö Lotsawa states that he set prices for some 20 tantric teachings, mostly small texts. A copy of the *Vajrabhairava Tantra* cost one gold ingot. Other teachings cost one gold *zho* each, or one tenth that price. These teachings were known as "golden dharma," a term not apparently used as a metaphorical description but precisely because gold was required to purchase them. To these fixed-price works Gö Lotsawa contrasts other offerings received by Ra Lotsawa, referred to as unregulated offerings. It is unfortunately not clear from the passage if these prices were for the initiation, the reading transmission, or the material text, though given the context it appears that the latter (at least) was likely. Ra Lotsawa turned some of his profits back into work with texts, sending 100 measures of gold as far as Eastern India, to the monastic university of Vikramaśila, to fund the recitation of gold and silver *Perfection of Wisdom* texts.[41]

THE BOOK AS SYMBOL

In addition to playing a major role in the Tibetan economy, the book also served as a symbol—as an object representing something beyond itself. One may wonder if there is ever a time when a book is *not* doing this, but in order to narrow the discussion to a manageable size the following will focus on a single area in which the book symbolizes important cultural values and practices: scholastic expertise. The book is the symbol par excellence of the authority gained from a reputation for learning. In order to be influential, in order to wield authority, leaders are all but required to be skilled in reading, writing, and scholarly pursuits. This is illustrated powerfully in a negative image by the case of the leader who founded a monastery and gathered some hundred monks around him, only to find himself severely handicapped in his ability to work for the benefit of others by his illiteracy.[42] Reading and writing are skills that an effective leader must possess. This subject has been treated in chapter 3 in some detail in the case of Shalu Lotsawa, and the *Blue Annals* adds numerous vignettes to the portrayal of the translator from Tsang.

The vast majority of instances of the book as symbol of scholarly prowess stress the close link between religious experts and the book in positive terms, equating minute details of scholarly quirkiness with vast erudition. One leader is described as never without a copy of the *Kālacakra Tantra*, and as studying diligently even when touring the countryside.[43] Another made a vow from the ages of seventeen through forty-five to never be without pen and ink.[44] The scholar would own working copies of the great tantras that could be written upon for study and teaching. One early student of the *Kālacakra Tantra* marked his copy with white to indicate passages he did not understand.[45] Gö Lotsawa relates in an aside that he had seen one such text of the *Hevajra Tantra* with 182 marks used in teaching sessions, a sign of the manuscript owner's great intelligence.[46] For Gö Lotsawa, the good scholar should be someone for whom books are even the stuff of dreams. Such was the case for the abbot who dreamed that five women led him to a temple, inside which he found many unpainted doors, each leading to large rooms filled with books. The women handed him a large bundle of keys and ordered him to take charge of the books "for the good" they urged him, "of the dharma."[47]

Reading and writing abilities were often signs of extraordinary intelligence in the very young. One young prodigy was able to recite the *Perfection of Wisdom Sūtra* in 25,000 lines at the age of 7. His father was dubious and made his son recite the work again in his presence. When the boy finished, his father knelt before him in praise.[48] As a precocious young child, Aro Yeshé Jungné told a group of monks that he would recite prayers with them. They handed him the *Guide to the Bodhisattva's Way*, thinking that he would not know what to do with the classic text. To their chagrin he recited perfectly.[49] A young Phakmodrüpa Dorjé Gyelpo knew how to write without studying and was able to assist his abbot in preparing a 100,000-line *Perfection of Wisdom Sūtra* in silver.[50] And when learning the fundamental texts of logic and epistemology, one thirteenth-century student knew the entire first page after his master had recited the first line of verse.[51]

The long biography of Gö Lotsawa's contemporary Sönam Gyatso (1424–84) contained in book 10 of the *Blue Annals* (the longest single biography in that work) offers a detailed portrayal of the scholar and his involvement in book culture. As a youth he became expert in the recitation of sacred texts and was able, like a brahmin student learning the Veda, to perform each sentence backward as well as forward. Each day as his teacher preached a variety of texts, Sönam Gyatso memorized twenty pages, each the length of an arrow. He memorized Nagarjuna's *Letter to a Friend* while riding a horse, completing it in only a single stage of his journey.[52] An entire chapter of his biography is dedicated to his gargantuan efforts at studying and reading and offers an impressive ideal: "He studied all the sacred texts contained in the Kangyur and elsewhere, and acquired a deep understanding of the essence of the meaning of each word in these texts . . . [he read] twice [each] the Tengyur, the *Collected Works of Butön*, the *Collected Topics* [a massive work by Bodong Panchen, on whom more will be said below], and other texts, everything that was to be found in the Tibetan language. In short, wherever he went, he used to read all available sacred texts, large or short. Every day he used to expand the ocean of his mind, completely filled with the games of knowledge."[53]

Books were also prominent symbols of esoteric knowledge. Here the book achieves its greatest level of abstraction, for as it becomes a metaphor for esoteric learning it often changes into or comes out of other material items. One yogin had a dream that he had prepared one tantric text as parched barley, another as vegetables, and eaten them. His master concluded that this was a sign he should compose a commentary.[54] Another tantric adept transformed his consort into a book and then hid it (her) around his waist before traveling.[55] As another yogin practiced in mountain retreat, a red woman placed a book into his mouth, and thus "there was not a single doctrine translated into Tibetan that he did not understand."[56] A blue woman placed a volume in the mouth of yet another adept, and he thus understood the meaning of all books. Based upon this revelation he wrote several commentaries on the tantras, though some accused him of fabricating the instructions therein himself.[57] Even specific parts of a book could be used to make philosophical points, as when we are told that the absolute pervades the entire world and all beings in it just like the dye covers the entire edge of a book.[58] In several instances Gö Lotsawa also attributes esoteric power to books themselves, as when a volume of *Perfection of Wisdom* literature is placed upon an abbatial throne in order to counteract black magic against the institution[59] or when reading or learning the *Perfection of Wisdom Sūtras* is said to aid in healing the body, especially in the prevention of headaches.[60]

Finally, if books symbolized both scholarly and esoteric authority, they could also signal failed aspirations and lost authority. Books could be a cause of suffering, as when a traveler encounters a pitiful figure "carrying with him many books and beating his chest with his hand, expressing disappointment with his studies," and is filled with sadness.[61] Another student was disappointed when he did not receive new teachings from his master, and in effect resigned from his tutelage by giving back his books and sacred images to the master.[62] Here the transfer of books from one party to another implies no sense of reverence or holds any promise of gaining merit. It is an insult, an act signaling the end of a relationship between master and disciple, a break in the structure of authority, a harsh reversal of the book's symbolic power against those who rely upon it for their scholarly identities.

The *Blue Annals* offers a convenient anthology of disparate images of the book as symbol, but it was not the first work to wax long on the symbolic richness of scriptural volumes. An early source for the book as symbol is the collection authored by the famous Chögyal Pakpa Lodrö Gyeltsen. During the period 1273 to 1278 Pakpa composed no fewer than nine short works commemorating the production of fine volumes of Buddhist scripture for the Mongol Khan, the queen, the princes, and important religious leaders such as Töntsul Rinchenpel.[63] In addition to being crucial sources for understanding the formation of the Buddhist canons in Tibet, Pakpa's brief verse works are among the most vivid evocations of books as both material and symbolic objects.[64] In 1275 Pakpa journeyed back from China to Sakya monastery, and the Mongol prince Jingim (Chinese: Zhenjin, 1243–86), Qubilai's second son, made part of the trek with him. It was around this time that Jingim and others sponsored a number of book projects that were to lead to a major scriptural collection at Sakya. Pakpa wrote in praise of this collection in 1278 while staying there. His poetic ode to scriptural volumes patronized by the Mongol leaders develops a most elaborate correlation between the materials of the books and the enlightened body of the Buddha:[65]

> *Blue paper, surface, a blue-black volume*
> *With the best river gold dust,*
> *Fashioned by the current scribes of miraculous script,*
> *Like a golden necklace, steals one's thoughts away.*
>
> *Groups of artisans skilled in a variety of arts,*
> *Covers and book boards, book straps, and wraps*
> *Made complete and beautiful*
> *To perfect the human mind.*

Such voluptuous volumes required a monastic community of the highest standards to put them to best use. He addresses not just any community of monks but a community of scholars who will appreciate his verses of praise:

A sangha assembled like an ocean
Performed well the consecration as if with the voice of the
Buddha.
A basis for increasing happiness and wealth,
The books have become a receptacle for offering from all beings.

These books are the object of practice for many exalted people,
They captivate the minds of all wonderful people.
A magical manifestation engaged by nobles,
They entice living beings in the three worlds.

Seeing the ways of scholars in this method
Spread through the grace of poets,
Those learned in the traditions of poetry
Should listen to this, and heed well.

Here Pakpa begins an unrelenting series of equations between each feature of the ideal scriptural volume and natural or supernatural phenomena. The sun, the stars, the sky are likened to letters of gold upon blue-black paper. The graphs on the page become buddhas and gods, the decorative motifs on the book boards become the major and minor marks of the Buddha's body, and the silk book covers become the robes of the Buddha as monk:

Blue-black paper, with the radiance of a great sapphire,
Embellished with strings of golden letters—
It is as if its light outshines
The brightness of the sun.

Or else, the blue-black paper, with the radiance of the tingka bird,
Is like the color of the clear blue sky.
The golden letters arrayed
Are like the stars and planets arranged in a line.

Or else, as if upon a clear field,
A ground of beryl,
Are arranged emanated bodies of the Sage,
Who display all manner of magical appearances.

Bedecked with ornaments,
Letters, with limbs bent over,

Are like hosts of celestial beings and nobles,
Going to pay homage to him.

The melody of recitation brought forth
By reciters reading the strings of letters
Is like scripture spoken
By the sixty aspects of the Lord of Sages.

The minds of the ocean of people assembled,
Made calm and placid
By the zither melody of recitation,
Are like the disciples made so by turning the wheel of
dharma.

The books have the radiance of the smile of
That beautiful Buddha body with ten powers.
The books have a light that is the light of the Sugata.
The decorated book boards have the ornaments of the major and
minor marks of the Buddha.

The fabric covers so beautiful,
The book boards quite ornamented,
The "robe and garments," the labels, are all arranged,
Like the decorated body of the Sage.

Out of the great spring—the merit acquired with effort—
Grows the wish-fulfilling tree with the fruit of perfect wealth
Endowed with the shade of beneficence, leaves—blue-black
paper—and fragrant beautiful flowers—strings of letters—,
The source of all desires for celestials, noncelestials, and serpents
alike.

Here is the poetry of the culture of the book. Here is the book
in its most evocative form, transformed so thoroughly into metaphor as to be all but intangible and yet, precisely because of this
metamorphosis, charged with gripping emotional resonance
usually found only in tales of the Buddha himself. But how can
this poetry be linked with another aspect of the culture of the
book—the economic realities of book production, in which the
actual producers of those blue-black volumes filled with gold
lettering prosaically toil in the scriptorium under the manager's
watchful eye?

The challenge presented by the passages evoked here—from the *Blue Annals* to Pakpa's ode to books as the body of the Buddha—is how to understand them in a unified fashion. How can one study, describe, and explain the book as both a preeminent symbol of Buddhist soteriology and as something with a material reality so thoroughly enmeshed in economic life? Because books are among the most discursively charged crafted objects, they offer a good opportunity to consider the symbolic richness of material goods. To do this it will be helpful to juxtapose three passages from other sources, so as to bring the evidence of the *Blue Annals*, Pakpa, and the rest into greater relief. The first two passages portray in bold terms the issues of book as symbol and book as economic object that have been raised here. The third provides a tactful bridge between the first two. The first is by Tsongkhapa, that wellspring of the Geluk tradition; the second is from a Dunhuang manuscript; and the third is from a fifteenth-century scholar, Bodong Panchen, who was perhaps the most prodigious writer in the history of western Tibet.

Tsongkhapa gives a fairly typical injunction to treat the words of the Buddha with respect, though it does appear to cast aspersions on the numerous examples of exchange and sale of books in the *Blue Annals*. "Never show disrespect for writings on the Buddhist teachings," he proscribes, "even those composed of as little as four words. . . . You should not pawn volumes of scriptures (or) treat them as merchandise. . . . Treat them with respect, as though they were the jewel of the teaching itself."[66] To this can be contrasted a document from Dunhuang detailing the duties of managers in a scriptorium producing *Perfection of Wisdom* volumes. A manager

> *should be required to overbear opposition: if supplies of paper should be available, he should collect it at once; if supplies of paper should not be available, or if any persons should demand their own price, he should arrest one of their kin, senior or junior, and send him to prison, and he should be imprisoned in the presence of the donor. The scribes must complete at once the supplies of paper entrusted to them: until completion has been made, their cattle, property, and so on of twice the value should be taken as*

security. . . . If the person in charge be not equal to opposition or
should not have collected the allotments, (he should be punished)
by whipping at the rate of ten lashes per roll of paper.[67]

(Similar tales of the travails of life in the scriptorium may be
found in twentieth-century accounts as well).[68]

If the passage from Tsongkhapa at first seems naïve, given the
economy of books evinced in the *Blue Annals*, the passage from
Dunhuang is troubling, for it makes it difficult to explain how the
book can be a symbol having anything to do with the Buddha's
benevolent grace in a social world where its production is based
upon such strict punitive measures. And if the first passage seems
to forbid all economic activity, the second reduces our vision
of book production purely to economics. Tsongkapa was likely
aware of this conundrum, and his injunction is more astute than
it first appears. But it is fruitfully read through a third passage, the
instruction to producers of books by Bodong Panchen. Bodong
Panchen suggests a way to negotiate (at least in part) the gap between the pious proscriptions of Tsongkhapa and the stark view
of life in a Buddhist scriptorium. This remarkable scholar from
western Tibet was among the most prolific scholars in all of Tibetan history. The works of Bodong Panchen were produced by
one of the most fascinating women in Tibetan history, the royal
nun Chökyi Drönma (circa 1422–55).[69] The daughter of rulers in
the Gungtang royal line, Chökyi Drönma played an important
role in the development of the Bodong tradition of Tibetan Buddhism in western Tibet, and to a lesser extent in the development
of the tradition of the great saint and bridge builder, Tangtong
Gyelpo (1361–1485). Chökyi Drönma is also reckoned as the first
of the most prominent line of female incarnations in Tibet, the
Dorjé Phakmo line—a tradition that continues today under the
twelfth incarnation, Dechen Chökyi Drönma (b. 1938).

Chökyi Drönma's father was a patron of several Buddhist
masters, among whom Bodong Panchen stood out. This fact
goes a long way to explain why, when Chökyi Drönma eventually
took vows, she did so under Bodong Panchen. The relationship
between secular rulers of Gungtang and religious leaders of the
Bodong tradition was a multigenerational affair, for Lhawang Gyeltsen's father was tutored by Bodong Panchen's maternal uncle,
Drakpa Gyeltsen (1352–1405), who in turn founded the monastery of Dzongkha in Gungtang. Chökyi Drönma took ordination

as a novice nun from Bodong Panchen at his western Tibetan hermitage of Chöding. Sometime between 1444 and 1450, or between the ages of twenty and twenty-six, Chökyi Drönma became one of the few women in Tibetan history to take vows as a fully ordained nun. Bodong Panchen stood as her preceptor, and another male leader at Chöding served as the master of ceremonies. The *Life of Chökyi Drönma* is succinct in its description, stating: "in the midst of a large and very distinguished sangha she became an actual *bhikṣuṇī*."

Chökyi Drönma's master died in 1451 at his longtime hermitage of Chöding. She was a principal actor in the funeral ceremonies, offering the last memorial verses to Bodong Panchen. More lasting perhaps were her efforts in the production of a complete manuscript set of his assemblage of Buddhist knowledge, the *Collected Topics*. Bodong Panchen's reputation for prolific scholarship verges on the miraculous, though this reputation is likely the result of Chökyi Drönma's labors as much as his own. A popular image of the scholar at work finds him dictating 20 different teachings to 20 scribes simultaneously.[70] The *Collected Topics* bears this reputation out, for it is a massive work running between 110 and 140 volumes. It might be considered an alternative Tengyur, containing much of the same material found in the "orthodox" Tibetan canons yet organized into a coherent course of education, one that was to become the basis of both the Bodong and the Dorjé Phakmo traditions.[71]

Much like Polané centuries later in Lhasa, Chökyi Drönma appears to have acted as a sort of executive producer in the project of crafting the fine volumes in her homeland monastery at Gungtang. Like the Tengyur, Bodong Panchen's *Collected Topics* was part of the widespread cult of the book in Tibet, for the volumes could work miracles—and often of a very practical sort. The *Life of Chökyi Drönma* gives two vivid examples: as this great work was in process, a virulent epidemic developed in the region, and everyone was overcome with fear. Chökyi Drönma sent a letter to all the surrounding areas informing people of the creation of the holy volumes, thus relieving public anxiety. Thanks to the efficacious power of Bodong Panchen's books, all disease was eradicated and the people were able to rest at ease. On another occasion news came to Gungtang that the army of Latö Jang was approaching, and people were again filled with fear. Chökyi Drönma placated them with assurances that while the volumes were being created there would be no trouble from the enemy.

The saving grace attributed to these books is no doubt due in part to the way their material form was, one might say, "energized," for the ink with which they were penned was mixed with blood from the nose of Bodong Panchen himself,[72] just as the ink for Polané's Kangyur was mixed with his mother's blood.

By bringing into being her master's books, Chökyi Drönma was in fact following well in his footsteps, for his *Collected Topics* contains explicit advice to book producers. "If one wishes to produce supports for the dharma," Bodong Panchen writes, "acquire good bases such as paper, stiff and with clear complexion, of even thickness. Use ink of the best minerals, or silver or gold—whatever contrasts in color with the background (of the paper). The scribe should be very learned in the composition of letters. . . . If he copies well, it will be very meaningful to see the writing or to read it, and the benefit will be unfathomable. The craftsmanship, the color of the paper, and the color of the ink must be equally superb." Up to this point Bodong Panchen has not said much more than has been stated in previous chapters. Yet he concludes his prescriptions with an important injunction: "Copy so that one is filled with faith by the mere sight of it." He elaborates, "If false *sūtras* and tantras made by foolish Tibetans acting as scholars, or treatises that teach heretical ideas were to increase and spread, the work of the precious Buddhist teaching would diminish, so do not write down such texts. Write without mixing up bad or unedited letters with pretty form for the sake of pretense and desire. Make the writing complete and well edited . . . and the book boards ornamented. Perform well the consecration. . . . Have common books work for the benefit of beings in ordinary ways. Hide uncommon books from the unfortunate and work for the benefit of the fortunate."[73]

Tsongkhapa exemplifies the ideology of the book drawn from *Perfection of Wisdom* literature, even going so far as to forbid the economic exchange of books, a practice for which there is clear evidence in the *Blue Annals* (the mere fact that Tsongkhapa felt compelled to mention this might be taken as a sign of its presence in his day). The Dunhuang manuscript suggests that the realities of scribal production could have little to do with the bodhisattva ideology of the sort promoted by Tsongkhapa, even when the products are the very texts promoting that ideology. Bodong Panchen's words (put into practice by his disciple, the nun Chökyi Drönma) are more subtle: they provide a glimpse of the application of this ideology to the material production of books, the product of scriptoria with strict rules and also finely crafted physical instantiations of the word of the Buddha, which can serve well as objects of reverence. Bodong Panchen reveals what the Dunhuang manuscript cares not to and what Tsong-khapa dares not to—that the ideology of reverence toward scriptural volumes (and thus toward all those individuals and institutions whose authority derives from those volumes) rests on a material base that is constructed, not eternal, that is social and contingent, not soteriological. Perhaps Bodong Panchen said more than Tsongkhapa would have liked him to (for it seems as if Bodong Panchen pulls the curtain back from the machinery of reverence a bit too far). But he is not simply teaching his readers how to practice religion; he is providing them the methods and theories necessary to *construct* a religion. He is providing the material and rhetorical tools with which to create a faith that seems to spontaneously erupt, as if from the depths of reverence, toward the Buddha himself upon sight of a single highly crafted object, the book. "Copy so that one is filled with faith by the mere sight of it." Here the technology of scribal production is employed directly to the production of a psychological disposition; here the material book becomes the symbolic book.

If Bodong Panchen bridges the two competing perspectives of book culture in the first two passages, he also provides the means to join them: "Copy so that one is filled with faith by the mere sight of it." It is not the words within the book that should produce a response; it is the volume itself. The book is not a container of Buddhist teaching; it is a Buddhist injunction—but only if properly produced by trained and managed craftsmen. In Bodong Panchen's phrase, as an early master of cultural studies famously stated, "the medium is the message." Form takes precedence completely over content; here the book is pure symbol. It is the mere appearance of the book, the paper, ink, and pen stroke, that does the work of instilling faith, inspiring patrons, motivating the economies that in turn fuel the culture of the book in Tibet.

Extrapolating from Bodong Panchen's directions to scribal overseers, it may be posited that if the scriptorium is not run efficiently, then books are not produced efficiently and with care. If that is the case, they will not inspire faith. And if the books are not capable of inspiring faith, which might be interpreted as the production of authority through appeal to a shared set of assumptions about the significance of books, then they are less valuable both as crafted objects of exchange and as symbols of authority, personal, institutional, scholarly, or otherwise. If the books produced are not impressive looking, then what value do they have lining the walls of the temple? Here, from the perspective of its producers, the book cannot *but* be judged by its cover.

Aside from Bodong Panchen's astute remarks, his important relation between the production of the book and its social value is most succinctly stated in the letter from Butön Rinchendrup to the managers of the scriptorium at Shalu monastery in the middle decades of the fourteenth century. Butön encourages these managers to ensure, under threat of fines, efficiency and high-quality work by all, from the lowliest scribe to highly trained editors, not because they are creating holy books containing the Buddha's word but because they are producing finely crafted volumes for their patron, their source of funding, the secular leader of Shalu. In these instructions, all aspects of book production, from making paper to editing difficult passages of philosophy, are geared toward the creation of an object of significant social and economic value.

In light of this reading of the *Blue Annals* and with the aid of Bodong Panchen, Butön, and Tsongkhapa, a few general conclusions may be offered. Tsongkhapa's injunction that the book be treated as part of a devotional practice and not as part of economic practice notwithstanding, the book would not be a valuable symbol if it were *not* part of an economy, not used and valued in situations such as offering and exchange. Yet its social or economic importance as a crafted object would not exist without a communal sense of the book as symbolic of shared (or at least uncontested) values. By forbidding the pawning and sale of books, Tsongkhapa makes a move that is crucial to their value: he distinguishes the book from other objects that might be economic goods. Because the point of these shared values is that the book is a physical instantiation of the Buddha's voice, we must agree that the book of scripture by definition cannot be considered part of an economy or it would be just one among many commodities, and thus not worthy of reverence. To retain its potency as symbol, it must be kept separate from other objects that are clearly not symbols (in another idiom, the book is sacred only to the extent that it can be successfully separated from other objects considered profane). Tsongkhapa removes the book from the reality of the scriptorium precisely in order that it might retain its symbolic value, and thereby retain any economic value exceeding the costs of reproduction.

Given this reading of the injunction it is possible to understand Bodong Panchen to be working in much the same way as Tsongkhapa. He distinguishes the book as an object of faith, or as a symbol of practices and discourses extending far beyond its material form, from the discursive meaning of its words. Both writers want to distinguish the book as having unlimited value—Tsongkhapa by rhetorically sequestering it from the economy in which it is materially enmeshed, Bodong Panchen by separating it from the discursive significance that it so often is considered to contain—and thereby maintain it as a symbol of all that is worthy of the reverence of faithful Buddhists, regardless of whether it is ever read. This, in turn, sustains the value of books in the economy of religion glimpsed in the anecdotes of the *Blue Annals*. The words of Tsongkhapa, Bodong Panchen, and others suggest that the culture of the book in Tibet is a good place to address questions about possible relationships between symbols and economies, a place where dreams are full of libraries, libraries are never separate from the prestige of scholars and kings, and the scribe may come under the influence of the workshop manager's whip as much as the merit accrued from putting the Buddha's works on paper. A return to eighteenth-century Degé will illustrate this relationship one last time, and bring it to bear upon the very identities of the scholars whose stories have pervaded the latter half of the present narrative, Situ Panchen and Shuchen Tsültrim Rinchen.

AN ECONOMY OF SIGNIFICANCE

In the printing house of Degé the discourses and practices of religion were inseparable from economic practice as well. Economic boons to laborers, such as tax exemption and release from forced labor, were to be motivated by a conviction that the teachings of the Buddha must rest on a foundation of compassionately motivated craftsmanship. This conviction in turn should provide the religious motivation for the kings of Degé to open up their treasuries to pay for the work and, in a further entwinement, this financial generosity provided a chance to accrue religious merit. Yet the importance of economic issues for the production of the canon is founded upon certain rhetorical moves that turn this importance on its head. It is precisely because the teachings of the Buddha are priceless that they deserve to fetch such a high price. "The only door through which people can attain peace and happiness," Shuchen urges, "is the precious teaching of the Omniscient Victor." Therefore, he continues, "The essence of these teachings is of limitless value."[74] Here he uses the same term for "value" or "price" that he did in his more mundane account of prices for goods and services. A spiritual economy, if you will, subsumes and interpenetrates the finances of printing the Buddha's word; a symbolic value at once infinitely exceeds the costs of printing and provides the very reason for spending so much money, so much barley, on books.

In order to illustrate the invaluable nature of the teachings and the consequent value of printing them, Shuchen devotes some words to the Buddhist philosophical underpinnings of three activities closely bound with the book that have been constantly present in this study: patronage, study, and worship. Viewed from the perspective of these three ubiquitous elements of Buddhist practice, the printing projects of eighteenth-century Tibet become become the continuation of traditions spanning almost two millennia. The patronage, study, and worship of the written word are promoted at length by the scriptures themselves—by the *sūtras*, tantras, narratives, and doctrinal treatises that make up the Buddhist literary imagination and into which so many resources, more or less tangible, have been poured. By extension, the relatively recent technology of wood-block printing participates in this economy of significance.

The patron of religious works is allied to none other than that arch-hero of Mahāyāna Buddhism, the bodhisattva. Here Shuchen argues on several levels, at once describing the great deeds of his patron the King of Degé, Kunga Trinlé Gyatso, while prescribing a vision of patronage that is at once beneficial for the king—he acquires merit; the Buddha's teachings; and the continued vitality of the sangha, or in this particular case the religious community at Degé. "The patron of the Buddhist religion is one who facilitates the work of the bodhisattva in the spiritual development of other people."[75] To be sure, this includes the donation of material goods, but the most precious type of donation—what Shuchen eloquently describes as "the very heart of patronage"— is the gift of religion. In a somewhat apocalyptic passage the great editor of Degé begins to describe the good works of his patron, now identified with the bodhisattva (as stated in *sūtras* Shuchen has quoted prior to this). "The people of this degenerate time are quite troubled," he laments, "for desire, hatred, and stupefication are rampant. There is no respect, no veneration for the holy religious teachings spoken by the Lord Buddha." In this dismal epoch, there is nevertheless a ray of hope: none other than the ruler of Degé. "Like the ascension of the sun over the western peaks," Shuchen writes, "the bodhisattvas Tenpa Tsering and his son, the third Degé Leader [Kunga Trinlé Gyatso]—gods in the midst of humanity who have completely captivated our hearts—have promoted the holy teachings, the texts, the books, the instructions, the learning, the reading and reciting by block printing the original teachings of the Tathāgata in the language of the land of snows. The incredible and wondrous benefit to others of this is inconceivable."[76]

Shuchen's effusive praise for his patrons is perhaps outdone only by his praise of the Buddhist teachings, and in particular of the written forms upon which, in his estimation, Buddhist religious life is based (here he differs from Bodong Panchen's emphasis on the external features of the scriptural volume, focusing instead upon the more traditional concern of scholars, intellectual content). At the beginning of a lengthy passage on the virtues of writing books he lists a set of ten scholarly practices that, as he says, "constitute the heart of the practice." As Shuchen himself relates, the following list is based upon the well-known work by Maitreya, the *Madhyāntavibhāga*. These practices are: 1) writing down texts of the holy teachings; 2) making offerings to books; 3) giving them to others; 4) hearing them being read by others; 5) reading them for oneself; 6) acquiring books; 7) explaining both the words and the meaning without error; 8) reciting them; 9) contemplating their meaning; and finally 10) meditating in accordance with what is explained in books. In contrast with the importance placed on orally transmitted teachings, often held in Tibetan literature to be integral to the authoritative transmission of Buddhist teachings, Shuchen uses this scripturally sanctioned outline for religious scholarly method as a support for the enterprise of printing. Books are to him essential for Buddhist practice. "If you do not base yourself on books in which are written the stainless teachings," he warns, "from the beginning to the conclusion of these very beneficial stages of religious practice, your self-indulgent efforts will be devoid of any heart!"

The stress on the importance of study is part of a larger rhetoric of veneration for books, and from the above warning our author develops a defense of the crucial centrality of books as the very foundation of Buddhist religiosity. Here he cites a dizzying array of scriptural passages, including the *Prajñāpāramitā in Eight Thousand Lines,* the *Lotus Sūtra,* the *Ratnakūṭa,* and the *Diamond Cutter Sūtra* (this section of his canonical omnibus constitutes a veritable sourcebook for Mahāyāna ideologies of the book). One of several passages from *Prajñāpāramitā* works reads like an instruction manual for the worship of books: "Through the grace of the Tathāgata, the [teachings of the *Perfection of Wisdom*] should be written down in a great book with extremely clear letters, and should be worshipped and revered with flowers, incense, perfumes, garlands, essential oils, music, cloth, parasols, banners, bells, flags, and rows of butter lamps all around."[77]

And this is indeed the scene described by Shuchen in his discussion of the consecration of the newly printed Tengyur and the temple in which it was housed. The worship of books and their benefits also extended to the places where books were created, read, or even merely thought about. The practical benefits are made explicit in a well-known passage from the *Amṛtavyāharaṇa Sūtra*[78]: "The land in which *sūtras* are embraced, in which dharma is taught, or in which Buddhist teachings are written in books, will be completely free of epidemics, injury, infection, or disturbance."[79] Elsewhere Shuchen cites a scriptural passage (by now familiar to many students of Buddhism in one form or another) that links such places with the very moment of the Buddha's enlightenment: "Sons of good families on which plot of earth a dharma teaching is read, taught, explained or written down, thought of, declared, recited, or made into a book, whether it be it a grove, a temple, a house, or some place, under a tree, a building, a place of rest, or in a cave—on that plot of earth a *stūpa* for the Tathāgata should be built." Why is this, the *sūtra* asks rhetorically? Well, it replies with far-reaching implications, "That plot of earth should be known as the heart of enlightenment of all Tathāgatas. It should be known that on that plot of earth all Tathāgatas, Arhats, as well as perfect and completely enlightened ones have achieved buddhahood, complete, perfect, and unexcelled enlightenment. It should be known that on that plot of earth all Tathāgatas have turned the wheel of dharma, and on that plot of earth all Tathāgatas have been totally liberated from suffering."[80]

This is of course the formula found in a number of *sūtras* that has been isolated as the crucial rallying call for a cult of the book in Indian Mahāyāna Buddhism. Shuchen was quite aware of the canonical sources for making such a concrete connection among book, place, and the power of the Buddha's teaching, and it is clear that, at least in rhetorical terms, for him Degé was just such a place. Time and again Shuchen refers to the heart of the teachings, the heart of study, the heart of enlightenment, and in this passage from the *Lotus Sūtra* the same symbol of life-giving force is used to describe the words of the Buddha given physical form in writing, in books. If Shuchen's evocation of the *Lotus Sūtra* is taken seriously, for him the printing house of Degé *is* where the enlightenment of the Tathāgatas is taking place. Printing the *Lotus Sūtra* (and the several thousand works that had accreted around it in the form of the Kangyur and Tengyur) was for Shuchen a sacralizing act made possible through the grace of the Buddha. Arguing according to classical Buddhist doctrine, Shuchen assures his patrons and other readers that printing the Buddha's word does nothing less than bring buddhas to life at Degé. For the contemporary reader, what is so exhilarating about Shuchen's long survey of the Tengyur and its many contexts is that he allows, even encourages one to see the Buddhist cult of the book as but one aspect of a Tibetan culture of the book.

It is time to return to the scene with which Shuchen's narrative began in chapter 5, the reception-line conversation concerning editing between the scholar and the king. Situ and Shuchen (and their forbearers) put great stock in their editorial efforts and took pains to leave a record of their activities. Both wrote large accounts of their projects, Situ of the Kangyur and Shuchen of the Tengyur. Both also wrote extensively about the editing of the canons—and their lives as textual scholars more generally—in their autobiographies. In these writings they portray their editorial work as integral to their identities as scholars and, more than that, to their identities as men of religion. They write emotionally, passionately about working with texts, about working with and reworking the words of the Buddha. Far from being a dry intellectual pursuit, divorced from other concerns of religious life, editing was for these two men a source of personal pride. It was also, at times, an occasion for spiritual self-doubt. In their writings, textual scholarship bears a complex relationship to the machinations of monastic political life and to the development of an interior spiritual life.

Situ, for one, was clearly proud of the work he had overseen and considered his team to have produced a Kangyur of lasting value. And his work was a source of regional pride with which the kingdom of Degé could vie with even the likes of the Chinese imperial past. He concludes his tale of editing with a statement of personal satisfaction: "The scriptural collections are vast, and the editors of low acumen were not intelligent [enough for the work], for they were like butterflies searching for the end of the sky." Situ writes ardently that he and his team had achieved such heavenly heights; his final appraisal of the Degé Kangyur is nothing short of superlative: "Though I cannot say that the [editors of old] were totally wrong and without intelligence," he admits, "I believe that [*our* Kangyur] will prove to be most reliable to those who inspect it.[81] [I believe] that it is much better than both the old Kangyur produced by the great Yongle Ming Emperor in China,[82] and the Kangyur produced by the King of Jang Satam, which was the exemplar for this, [our Kangyur]."[83]

Less interested in the political implications of the Degé Tengyur, Shuchen evinces in his autobiography a more complex personal relationship to his work. In a poignant moment, he reveals the difficulties he had experienced in his meditation practice, informing the reader that such literary endeavors as editing the life of the Buddha were directly responsible. Writing of a period in his early thirties, he confesses: "I had not been able to devote the effort needed for meditative experience and realization to arise in my mind. I was intimate with laziness; I had been waylaid by its power. I had been overpowered by the roving tempest of such work as editing, and thus I did not attain a high degree of realization."[84] So great was his interest in books (perhaps morbid interest, given the troubles he blames on these objects of intellectual obsession) that he took to dreaming of libraries and their forbidden volumes. One night in late 1755 or early 1756 he dreamed that he met the Sakya masters Sakya Pandita and Sönam Tsemo. They set a volume of treatises on linguistics in his hand and gave him the key to the library at Degé. Shuchen took these dreams to be good omens,[85] and with this visionary encouragement he continued to work on canonical literature in the decades after the printing of the Tengyur. In an autobiographical entry from 1757, for instance, Shuchen relates something of his efforts to acquire canonical material from central Tibet. Sangyé Gyatso had in the late seventeenth century produced an expanded Tengyur as a gift for the Fifth Dalai Lama, for which he had scoured the institutions of central Tibet in search of additional texts. These supplementary works were, according to Shuchen, for the most part included in the Degé Tengyur—but not all were. The editor from Degé made requests for originals, but received only several volumes of central Tibetan print copies, not the originals. "The printing was poor quality, the paper was rough, and they were thus not clear and the letters were difficult to recognize. Unless the originals that are not printed are found, there is little benefit to printing these, and we left them be."[86] Thus did competition between central and eastern Tibet continue, mitigated through the culture of the book.

And so Shuchen continued his career as an editor, a textual scholar dedicated to the culture of the book (as was the institution of Degé after his time, for many thousands of volumes were printed in addition to the canons of Situ and Shuchen[87]). Rather than acquiescing to his fate as a failed contemplative, he relates in his autobiography that he decided to take advantage of his proclivities and devote himself to scholarly pursuits. Inspired by Vasubandhu's encouraging words in the *Madhyāntavibhāga* regarding the merits of literary scholarship,[88] he gave renewed vigor to the work of editing and went on to produce and refine some of the most important monuments of Tibetan Buddhist literature. Yet the title of Shuchen, "Great Editor," came at a price; though he was to leave a profound literary legacy, he was in his own opinion a spiritual failure—at least in this life. He would not be known as a Great Adept, a Mahāsiddha, but merely as a man of the world and the book, a "defender of the text."[89] No wonder, then, that when the king chided Shuchen for spending *too much time editing*, Shuchen was uncertain about his fate, standing in the hall of the great monastery on a certain day in Degé.

*O*nce, in a land called Yawa, a householder had a son who was quite sharp. The householder and his wife sent this son out to learn his letters and numbers, and they sent their other son out to be a servant. When the elder son would study his letters and numbers, the servant boy would also learn all about writing and reading. The elder son became a teacher, and the servant boy became a shepherd.

Once in the big field outside the fort there were a lot of shepherds gathered around. The shepherd had faith in writing the *Diamond Cutter Sūtra*, for he had heard of its benefits when studying writing under a scribe along with the elder son. He thought to buy ink and pen, so he reduced the food he consumed and [saved money], becoming weak during his shepherd's work. Yet he still could not afford paper. So he borrowed a copy of his object of devotion. He mixed the ink in a jar and took up the pen. Upon a level spot of the pasturelands, he cut a reed, made measurements with it, and formed an outline equal to the size of the drawing. *Taking all the letters in a row*, he thought, *I will write this object of devotion, the* Diamond Cutter.

Yet even as he was considering this another thought struck him: *If I write this holy teaching upon the ground, many people and animals will step on it and crush it, and will thus all be reborn among the evil lower classes.* So with reverence he made an offering to the four directions, and considered, *I wish to write the* Diamond Cutter, *but there is not sufficient paper, for I am poor. I will write it out just as it is upon the sky.*

Well, that shepherd dipped his pen in the ink, looked at each and every letter in the text of his devotions, and wrote them upon the sky. Then the shepherd offered incense and prayed, "If the power of this holy object is true as in the scripture, may I attain good signs and great merit as did Buddha who spoke this holy object." Then, in the space of the outline that he had fashioned, the rough grass became soft, the flowers had a sweet fragrance, and in neither day nor night was there frost, hail, wind, or rain—all through the blessing power of writing the holy object.

Homage to the Virtuous Friends of All People.

An appeal to the ear of virtuous friends, the religious stewards and distinguished scholars who are producing the great treatises, and a request that you work in accordance with the instructions I have given: through looking them over sufficiently, the guidelines of my advice will come fully to distinguished scholars. Take them to heart; it is extremely important that those distinguished scholars listen. Have [the scribes] insert missing words to be added in [their] original place; affix a paper patch right upon that [spot] on the thin paper [of the original manuscript, and] write upon those [patches]. Do not write contractions; even those [contractions] present in the original [manuscript] should be expanded. In spots where insertions of missing words are needed, repeatedly look over each small passage [of text] previous [to those spots] when you proofread. See whether or not the small marginal numbers and notations are legible, and have [the workers] insert [them] so as to make those that are illegible or unintelligible, intelligible. See whether or not the size of the letters and the slash and dot [punctuation marks] are consistently spaced, and whether or not each line contains 115 to 120 letters. Please instruct [the scribes] that incomplete [lines] must be written out completely. Please instruct the writers of printing-style letters to make [them] small, complete, joined, and firmly printed, and [instruct] the writers of cursive letters to make [them] such that they do not exceed proper orthographic dimensions, [to make them] smooth, generally even, and correctly spelled. During proofreading, [the text] should be read out loud slowly and with clarity by the recitator, and the scribes should certify that reading with the certifier in between work [periods]. At the end of completed texts [the scribes] should write a full [record of certification]. Please instruct [the workers] to make no omissions or additions. [The text division called] *bam po* marks the beginning [of a section], and the [text division called] *le'u* marks the end [of a section], and therefore [these cases] require a blank space. Please instruct [the workers] to make a detailed analysis of the [punctuation marks:] the single slash, double slash, quadruple slash, and dot-and-slash. Add a double slash after such phrases as "In the *sūtra* . . ." and after the completion of root verses [within a commentary]. Add them in between commentary and a second [quote from the root verses], [after] phrases such as 'So it is said . . ', [and after] reduplicated letters. Add a dot-and-slash in between commentarial words following those [root verses]. Since an understanding of the word and the meaning are dependent upon each other, when some doubt arises, understand the meaning from the word by looking at [the word] analytically, and the [correct] graph will be understood from the meaning. Separate [Sanskrit] mantra graphs and Tibetan graphs. Also, write the long and short [vowels] and the aspirated and unaspirated [consonants] in mantras with no mistakes, according to the claims of each individual *sādhana* evocation ritual. Do not make the mistake of patterning your hat after your boot! Since there are many different manuals on spelling, for those clear cases I have mentioned, work according [to my instructions], and for other cases follow the *Imperial Decrees* and *Gyelzang* spellers. Though there are correct [instructions] in all manuals, since there is the possibility for incorrect [points] in even the best spellers, [they] are not reliable. Again, for every single letter have [the workers] make a detailed inspection. Please instruct [them] to write new writer's colophons and not rewrite the old [colophons], even if they were written by patrons. If [the scribes] are not producing letters both distinct and complete, or if they are not listening to instructions, the religious steward must have a word [with them]. Kindly inform the scribes and proofreaders of the scriptorium that the fine will be half a pound of tea if [they] do not come in when the break-time bell has sounded. In short: this is not just writing down some village family's small *sūtra*. These are the manuscripts of the Nobleman [of Shalu], and therefore care is vital for everyone. Great efforts should go into attaining provisions [for the workers]. Since we will handsomely provide wages and bonuses afterward as befits the qualifications [of the different workers], care is vital for everyone, so very vital. Be well.[1]

The Tibetan Buddhist canon produced at the Degé printing house in Kham contains approximately 4,570 individual works in 316 volumes (the total folios amount to more than 97,500, or more than 195,000 printed sides). Taken as a whole, the Degé Kangyurs and Tengyurs—and the canons of Tibetan Buddhism more generally—present by virtue of their arrangement a sort of literary history of Indian Buddhism, beginning with the "words of the Buddha" in the form of manuals of monastic conduct, *sūtras*, and tantras, moving through the commentarial literature and independent treatises of exoteric and esoteric writers, and concluding with a structured presentation of the major fields of learning that would have been shared by any intellectual community in India regardless of religious affiliation. As might be expected in a two-part collection that boasts anywhere between 4,500 and 5,200 titles and has developed over a millennium, the Kangyur and Tengyur as a whole were never permanently fixed, though of course some sections remained more stable than others. Considered in this light, the Tibetan collection might be thought of as a "canon" not in the sense of the biblical canon (with its relatively small number of approved works) but rather like a literary canon, a collection of "great books," the authority of which may be agreed upon by a large majority of concerned intellectuals, yet details of which are the subject of constant debate as the collection is reproduced.

The most basic division made within this collection is between the Kangyur, or "The Word in Translation," and the Tengyur, or "The Treatises in Translation," a distinction made by the thirteenth century at the latest. Every work contained in the Kangyur is in principle the word of the Buddha—although both traditional and contemporary scholarship cast a critical eye upon the literary history of the *sūtras* and tantras. The assignation of the term "Word" (*bka'*) to a particular work in the Tibetan canons might better be understood as an attribution of authority rather than a statement about its historical provenance, and tra-

APPENDIX 2:
THE
CONTENTS
OF THE
BUDDHIST
CANONS

ditional bibliographers were well aware that this was a fluid category open to criticism and debate. The works contained in the Tengyur are treatises composed by Buddhist writers flourishing in the long millennium that constituted Buddhism's florescence in India—from the second century until the twelfth century— though there are even works composed as late as the seventeenth century included in later sections of the Tengyur, as well as translations made in the eighteenth century included in later editions. The Kangyur is further divided into nine sections according to the section titles contained within the volumes themselves, though there are numerous and varied ways to group the more than 1,100 texts that make up this first half of the canon, as will shortly become apparent.

Situ Chökyi Jungné, editor-in-chief of the Degé Kangyur and author of the principal history and catalog of the collection, states that the canon as a whole is organized in the order in which the Buddha taught the scriptures contained within it. The editors therefore chose to begin with what tradition considers to be the earliest works compiled by the Buddha's immediate disciples, namely *vinaya* literature treating monastic conduct and institutional life. These seven works $(D_{1}-7)^{1}$ fill thirteen volumes and are arranged according to a system known as the Four Classes of Vinaya Scripture: *The Foundations of Monastic Conduct (Vinayavastu)* (D1); the *Analysis of Monastic Conduct*, which in turn comprises four separate works that present rules for monks and nuns and offer explanatory case studies for those rules (D2–5); the *Ancillary Foundations of Monastic Conduct* (D6); and finally the *Appendix to Monastic Conduct* (D7).

The next section contains thirty-six works classified as *Perfection of Wisdom* literature (D8–43), which are according to tradition the second of the three "turnings of the wheel of dharma." These are arranged first by size, from the *100,000-Line Perfection of Wisdom* in twelve volumes (the largest single work in the Kangyur) to the *Diamond Banner Sūtra* of only one-half folio (D29). These are followed by thirteen works (D31–43) grouped not by topic or size but rather by translator. These were all translated by the Sri Lankan scholar Ānandaśrī and his Tibetan partner Nyima Gyeltsen in the first half of the fourteenth century. They are styled by canonical catalogers from the mid-fourteenth century onward as "new translations,"[2] and they are indeed among the latest translations of *sūtra*s into Tibetan. Their place in the *Perfection of Wisdom* section is not an easy fit, and scholars such as Butön Rinchendrup wondered whether they were properly classified as Mahāyāna (as the inclusion in the *Perfection of Wisdom* section suggests) or Theravāda literature (as contemporary scholarship has shown them to be).

Two unique *sūtra* collections make up the next two sections of the Degé Kangyur. The *Flower Ornament Sūtra (Avataṃsaka)* (D44) chronicling the epic journey of Sudhana throughout various celestial realms in search of teachings has its own section in four volumes, as does the *Jewel Heap (Ratnakūṭa)* collection (D45–93). A large and varied group of more than 250 *sūtras* constitute the next section, known simply as the "*Sūtra* Section" (D94–359). These are organized by several principles, the first of which is tradition-based: Mahāyāna *sūtras* (D94–287) have pride of first place, followed by Hīnayāna *sūtras* (D287–359), and finally a handful of narratives of the Buddha's lives (D343–349) followed by *sūtras* translated from Chinese (D350–359). Within the two major sections works are again organized largely by size in descending order—with the two-volume Buddha biography entitled *Fortunate Eon* (*Bhadrakalpika*, D94) beginning the Mahāyāna section and the four-volume *Application of Mindfulness in the Good Dharma* (*Saddharmasmṛtyupasthāna*, D287) leading off the Hīnayāna section—with translator and, it seems, notions of importance for the tradition also serving as organizational factors.

The second largest section of the Kangyur contains more than 460 works classified as tantra (D360–827). The main tantra section comprises 20 volumes, though this section is followed (in at least some Degé editions) by three related sections that can be considered an extension of the Tantra collection, namely the *Ancient Tantras* (D828–844) (only in a late edition), the *Stainless Light* commentary on the *Wheel of Time Tantra* (D845), and the *Collected Spells* (D846–1107). The tantra section proper is organized first by the hierarchical scheme of topical classification formalized for the Tibetan tradition by Butön Rinchendrup, commonly known as the Four Classes of Tantra. The Degé Kangyur orders these from highest to lowest, beginning with the Highest Yoga class in seven volumes (D360–478), the Meditation class in two and a half volumes (D479–493), the Practice class in one volume (D494–501), and finally the Ritual class in 10 volumes (D502–773). The most prominent tantras in the Tibetan tradition begin each of these sections, such as the *Chanting the Names of Mañjuśrī* (D360), the *Compendium of Topics* (D479, beginning

APPENDIX 2:
THE
CONTENTS
OF THE
BUDDHIST
CANONS

the Yoga Class), the *Enlightenment of Mahāvairocana* (D494, beginning the Practice Class), and the *Three Commitments* (D502, beginning the Ritual Class), and ancillary works follow each of these major tantras. These sections are followed by a group of "difficult-to-classify works," including very old tantric scriptures such as the *Questions of Subāhu* (D805), and a host of small verse works that Situ Chökyi Jungné does not even bother to list in his catalog. Many of the latter works in the tantra section are not strictly tantras, but rather *dhāraṇī*s, or ritual spells (D687–804).

The structure of the Degé Tengyur may perhaps be thought of as a mirror image of the Degé Kangyur; the basic arrangement is tantra, *sūtra*, and *vinaya* as opposed to the Kangyur's *vinaya*, *sūtra*, and tantra. The principal editor of the collection, Shuchen Tsültrim Rinchen, notes this difference by referring to the arrangement of the Kangyur as a low-to-high structure (conceived presumably in terms of soteriological authority) and the arrangement of his Tengyur as a high-to-low structure. Shuchen's discussion of the various structures (contained in his catalog of the Degé Tengyur, about which more will be said later) illustrates that traditional bibliographers were actively involved in debates about the ordering of canonical literature: "In general," he writes, "the order in which the scriptures are placed may be as follows. In accord with how they are studied by those who wish to enter the sanctuary of thinking people and scholars, the treatises may be arranged with the fine arts first, then medicine, grammar, logic, and the inner arts [of Buddhism]." But there are other options as well: "Alternatively," he continues, "they may be arranged in accord with how they are taken into one's experience: monastic conduct, *sūtra*, and higher dharma (*abhidharma*). Or they may be arranged from low to high: worldly treatises, external arts, internal arts, the lesser way, and the common and uncommon greater ways." "None of these is wrong," Shuchen relates, "but here [in the Tengyur] they will be arranged from high to low." He thus lays out the basic structure of his Tengyur: uncommon great way (i.e., works relating to tantra); common great way (that is, works relating to *sūtra*); treatises of the lesser way; and then logic, grammar, medicine, and finally arts and crafts.[3]

Yet even within this basic difference between the low-to-high arrangement of the Degé Kangyur and the high-to-low arrangement of the Degé Tengyur there are significant variations that stem principally from the immense variety of types of literature included under what is, it must be admitted, the rather vague title of "Treatises in Translation," or "Tengyur." The first section of the

Tengyur is entitled Collected Hymns (D1109–1179). A single volume holds 170 short poems of praise to the Buddha, his disciples, Buddhist deities, and the famous author-saints of the classical Buddhist past. These brief epideictic pieces are arranged first by author chronology, then by translator chronology. As in other sections, very late translations such as those of Shalu Lotsawa (D1178–1179) conclude the section.

The tantra section (D1180–3785) makes up the bulk of the Tengyur, its 2,700 titles in 78 volumes comprising more than a third of the Tengyur's total 210 volumes. As in the Kangyur, the tantra section is arranged according to the Four Classes of Tantra, from "highest" to "lowest": 4) Supreme Meditation (D1180–2500); 3) Yoga Tantra (D2501–2531); 2) Practice (D2662–2669); and 1) Ritual (D2670–3139). Yet this tidy structure is able to accommodate barely two thirds of the works in the Tantra section, and another 700 words are loosely grouped within the General and Miscellaneous section (D3140–3755). Within that the organizational hierarchy is generally as follows: author chronology, genre (commentary [line-by-line, commentary on difficult points, commentary on the "intention"], ritual instruction, poetry), minor canons (such as Advayavajra's collected works, Padampa Sangyé's poetry anthologies), and finally late and difficult-to-classify works at the end.

Exoteric treatises make up the remaining 132 volumes. Whereas the fabricators of the Kangyur had only to create a scheme for the works attributed to the Buddha, those who worked with Buddhist treatises faced the much more difficult task of developing a classificatory architecture able to hold a far greater variety of works, and it is in the exoteric sections that this may be discerned most clearly. The 16-volume *Perfection of Wisdom* section (D3786–3823) follows immediately upon the Tantra section, yet where one might expect the *Sūtra* section to follow based upon the logic of the Kangyur, one finds instead the Central Way philosophy (Dbu ma/Madhyamaka: 157 works in 17 volumes, D3824–3980) inserted between *Perfection of Wisdom* and the 39 *sūtra* commentaries (16 volumes: D3981–4019). The Central Way section likely holds pride of place here at the beginning due to its broad preeminence in Tibetan philosophy. Following the *sūtra* commentaries are the Mind Only treatises of the Cittamatra/Yogācara tradition (D4020–4085: 66 titles in 16 volumes), *Abhidharma* commentaries (D4086–4103: 18 titles in 11 volumes), *Vinaya* commentaries (D4104–4149: 46 works in 18 volumes), and letters from famous scholars to kings, rulers,

Sections of the Degé (Sde dge) wood-block prints of the Kangyur (Bka' 'gyur, completed 1733) and Tengyur (Bstan 'gyur, completed 1744) in the Kham region of Eastern Tibet. D = number in Hakuji Ui, et al., *A Complete Catalog of the Tibetan Buddhist Canons (Bka' 'gyur and Bstan 'gyur)* (Sendai: Tōhoku Imperial University, 1934).

SECTION TITLE (ACCORDING TO UI, ET AL.)	# WKS	# VOLS	RUNNING # S D	ORGANIZATIONAL SCHEMES AND/OR SUBDIVISIONS
KANGYUR				
Monastic conduct ('Dul ba: Vinaya)	7	13	1–7	Size [large narrative collections, shorter lists of rules]
Perfection of Wisdom (Shes phyin: Prajñāpāramitā)	36	21	8–43	Size [measured in number of verses, then short works]
Great Host *Sūtra* (Phal po che: Avataṃsaka)	1	4	44	Old narrative anthology: a "mini-canon"
Jewel Heap *Sūtra* (Dkon brtsegs: Ratnakūṭa)	49	6	45–93	Old anthology of small *sūtras*: a "mini-canon"
Sūtras (Mdo sde: *Sūtra*)	267	32	94–359	1. Mahāyāna *Sūtras* [by subgenre, then size] ; 2. Hīnayāna (D287–359), Narrative Lives (Avadāna, D343–349)
Tantras (Rgyud 'bum: Tantra)	468	20	360–827	Class of Tantra: 4. Supreme Meditation (annutarayoga, D360–478), 3. Yoga Tantra (rnal 'byor, yoga, D479–493), 2. Behavioral Practice (spyod pa, caryā, D494–501); 1. Ritual action (bya ba, kriyā, D502–773); Prayers of Blessing (D774–808); Difficult to classify (D809–827) [Note: up to here (along with select comms.) represents early ninth-century catalogs]
Ancient Tantras (Rnying rgyud)	17	3	828–844	17 "Ancient Tantras." Not included in Situ's 1733 catalog of the Degé Kangyur.
Stainless Light [commentary on the Wheel of Time Tantra] Dus 'khor 'grel bshad: Vimalaprabhā	1	1	845	Included in the Kangyur because is "like the word of the Buddha" despite being a treatise and not strictly a *sūtra*.
Collected Spells (Gzungs 'dus: Dhāraṇī-saṅgraha	263	2	846–1107	Loosely grouped by translator; contains many duplicates already found in the Tantra section.
Kangyur Total	1109	102	1–1108	
TENGYUR				
Collected Hymns (Bstod tshogs: Stotra-gaṇa)	71	1	1109–1179	Author chronology (Nāgārjuna, etc.), then translator, then late translations, i.e, Shalu Lotsawa (D1178–1179)
Tantric Commentary (Rgyud: Tantra)	2608	78	1180–3785	Class of Tantra (same as Kangyur): 4. Supreme Meditation (annutarayoga, D1180–2500), 3. Yoga Tantra (rnal 'byor, yoga, D2501–2531), 2. Behavioral Practice (spyod pa, caryā, D2662–2669); 1. Ritual action (bya ba, kriyā, D2670–3139); General and Miscellaneous (D3140–3755). Within that: author chronology; genre (commentary

[line-by-line, commentary on difficult points, commentary on the "intention"], ritual instruction, poetry, minor canons [Advayavajra's collected works, Padampa's poetry anthologies]. Then late works at end.

Category	Texts	Volumes	D range	Description
Perfection of Wisdom Commentary (Shes phyin: Prajñāpāramitā)	38	16	3786–3823	Size, translator
Central Way Philosophy (Dbu ma: Madhyamaka)	157	17	3824–3980	Author chronology/importance [Nāgārjuna, Candrakīrti, Śāntideva, Atiśa, etc.], topic [tenets, ethics, meditation], translator
Sūtra Commentary (Mdo grel: Sūtra)	39	10	3981–4019	Author chronology, topic, translator, source language
Mind Only Philosophy (Sems tsam: Cittamātra)	66	16	4020–4085	Author chronology, topic, translator
Higher Learning Commentary (Mngon pa: Abhidharma)	18	11	4086–4103	Author chronology, topic, translator
Monastic Conduct Commentary ('Dul ba: Vinaya)	46	18	4104–4149	Author chronology, topic, translator
Rebirth Tales (Skyes rabs: Jātaka)	7	5	4150–5147	Author chronology, genre [rebirth tale anthology, drama, poetry]
Letters (Spring yig: Lekha)	31	1	4158–4202	Author chronology, topic, translator
Logic and Epistemology (Tshad ma: Pramāṇa)	65	20	4203–4268	Author chronology, topic, translator, Shalu Lotsawa at end [fifteenth/sixteenth century]
Language Arts (Sgra mdo: Śabda-vidyā)	37	4	4269–4305	Topic [grammar, poetics/aesthetics, metrics], translator, author chronology. Eighteenth-century translations at end.
Medicine (Gso rig pa: Cikitsā-vidyā)	7	5	4306–4312	Author, topic
Arts and Crafts (Bzo rig pa)	25	1/2	4313–4327	Topic [alchemy, iconometry, incense, astrology and divination]
Secular Treatises (Thun mong ba lugs kyi bstan bcos)	18	1/2	4328–4345	Topic [secular ethics, narrative, horse medicine]
Miscellaneous (Sna tshogs)	119	9	4346–4464	Tibetan works [grammar, catalogs, philosophy], seventeenth-century translations and works [grammar D4420–4433, medicine D4434–4443], late misc. works
Catalog of the Kangyur and Tengyur (Dkar chag)	2	2	4568, 4569	Composed by the editors [Situ on Kangyur, Shuchen on Tengyur]
TENGYUR TOTAL	3358	212		
KANGYUR AND TENGYUR TOTAL	4469	316	1109–4464	

APPENDIX 2:
THE
CONTENTS
OF THE
BUDDHIST
CANONS

and nobles (D4158–4202: 31 titles in a single volume). At this point the Tengyur moves from properly Buddhist writings to works often classified under the fivefold rubric of the domains of knowledge (*rig gnas*), or what might loosely be called the arts and sciences. The five arts and sciences are typically presented in the following order: 1) fine arts (*bzo rig*); 2) medicine (*gso rig*); 3) language arts (*sgra rig*); 4) logic and epistemology (*tshad ma*); 5) Buddhism, or the Interior Arts (*nang rig*). The Degé Tengyur presents these in reverse order, with the Logic and Epistemology section following directly after the Epistles (D4203–4268: 65 titles in 20 volumes). In most of these sections, from Central Way philosophy to Logic and Epistemology, the internal organization has largely followed author chronology, with topics the second most important rubric and translators the third. Thus, for instance, Nāgārjuna holds pride of place in the Central Way section, with 17 works (D3824–3840) beginning the section and Āryadeva (D3844–3851), Bhavaviveka (D3854–3956), and Candrakīrti (D3860–3868) following him. Nāgārjuna's famous *Verses on the Central Way* begins the section, and commentaries upon this work by the above-mentioned authors and others follow shortly upon Nāgārjuna's works (D3842, 3853, 3854, etc.). Subsequent works by minor writers and commentaries are grouped by topic, except in the case of major late writers such as the tenth/eleventh-century scholar Atiśa with 16 works (D3946–3961). A minor work by the twelfth-century figure Śākyaśībhadra (D3980) concludes the section.

The final section of the Degé Tengyur is appropriately entitled the Miscellaneous Section (D4346–4464). This collection of 121 works in nine volumes ranges wide over topic and temporal range, including indigenous Tibetan works from the imperial period of the eighth and ninth centuries (D4346–4364) to late works translated in the seventeenth century under the Fifth Dalai Lama (D4441, 4443, etc.). Small collections of aspiration prayers (D4377–4397) and dedicatory verses (D4398–4419) from a variety of translators follow, after which come 14 works of grammatical literature filling three and a half volumes, and 11 works of medical lore (D4433–4443), most of which are late translations from the fifteenth through seventeenth centuries (D4420–4433). The final volume of the Degé Tengyur (volume *Po*, D4452–4464) contains 13 works, most of which are either grammatical or divinatory treatises, and six of which are translated by Shalu Lotsawa Chökyong Zangpo.

APPENDIX 3

THE COST OF THE CANON AT DEGÉ

These accounting figures for the cost of producing the Tengyur at Degé from 1738 through 1744 are taken from Shuchen Tsultrim Rinchen's catalog and history of the Degé Tengyur, the *New Moon*: Zhu chen Tshul khrims rin chen (1697–1769), *Kun mkhyen nyi ma'i gnyen gyi bka' lung gi dgongs don rnam par 'grel pa'i bstan bcos gangs can pa'i skad du 'gyur ro 'tshal gyi chos sbyin rgyun mi 'chad pa'i ngo mtshar 'phrul gyi phyi mo rdzogs ldan bskal pa'i bsod nams kyi sprin phung rgyas par dkrigs pa'i tshul las brtsams pa'i gtam ngo mtshar chu gter 'phel ba'i zla ba gsar pa* (Lhasa: Bod ljongs mi dmangs dpe skrun khang, 1985), 577.21–578.20.

LABORER	PRODUCT AMOUNT OR UNIT OF TIME	PAYMENT PER PRODUCT AMOUNT OR UNIT OF TIME IN CYLINDERS (*'DONG*) OF BARLEY (*NAS*) (EXCEPT WHERE NOTED)	TOTAL COST IN BUSHELS (*KHAL*) OF BARLEY (EXCEPT WHERE NOTED)
Chief editor (*zhus dag pa rnams kyi zhus dpon*) (*full capacity*)	1 written piece per day (*bris pa rab cig*)	22	see next
Chief editor (below full capacity)	Less than one written piece per day	14	see next
Editor (*zhus dag pa*)	Per day	13	6,960
Painter of deities (*lha ris pa*)	2 frontispiece deities	25	835
Carver of deities (*lhas brkos pa*)	2 images	3 bushels (*khal*) of barley	640
Scribe (*yi ge ba*)	1 folio	22 (rate averaged over three wage rates)	34,261
Wood-block carver (*par brkos pa*)	1 carved wood block	3 bushels and 60 *zho* (rate averaged over three wage rates)	202,335
Wood-block proofreader	Per day	13	2600
Plumb-line makers	Per day	10	500
Paper workers	Per day	10	2720
Woodcutters	140 (blank) blocks	5 bushels	2,223

**** (Materials cost only)	40 square bundles of paper	1 brick of tea	3,123
**** (Materials cost only)	16 blocks	1 brick of tea	19,455
**** (Materials cost only)	Food and drink	****	168,400

TOTAL COST FOR THE TENGYUR IN BUSHELS OF BARLEY	Shuchen's figure: 274,932 (Actual total from above: 275,652)

NOTES

PREFACE

1. The literature on book history has grown tremendously in the past several decades. A useful overview is provided in Leslie Howsam, *Old Books and New Histories: An Orientation to Studies in Book and Print Culture* (Toronto: University of Toronto Press, 2007). Joseph P. McDermott, *A Social History of the Chinese Book: Books and Literati Culture in Late Imperial China* (Hong Kong: Hong Kong University Press, 2006), offers a readable and engaging survey of Chinese book history from 1000 to 1800, as well as a useful bibliographic essay at 263–278. György Kara, *Books of the Mongolian Nomads: More Than Eight Centuries of Writing Mongolian* (Bloomington: Research Institute for Inner Asian Studies, 2005), surveys a broad range of topics in the written culture of Mongolia, and should prove inspirational to students of book culture in Tibet. More narrow in focus, Glen Dudbridge's *Lost Books of Medieval China* (London: The British Library, 2000) has nevertheless inspired this project through its sensitive attention to the working methods of medieval Chinese textual scholars and their self-reports. Note that the epigraph from Valéry is taken from Terry Eagleton, *Criticism and Ideology: A Study in Marxist Literary Theory* (London: NLB, 1976).

2. D. F. McKenzie, *Bibliography and the Sociology of Texts* (London: The British Library, 1986), 20.

3. Roger Chartier, *Forms and Meanings: Texts, Performances, and Audiences from Codex to Computer* (Philadelphia: University of Pennsylvania Press, 1995), 89.

4. Armando Petrucci, *Writers and Readers in Medieval Italy: Studies in the History of Written Culture* (New Haven: Yale University Press, 1995), 145.

1. THE STUFF OF BOOKS

1. Bu ston Rin chen grub (1290–1364), *Dpal gsang ba 'dus pa'i rdzogs rim rim lnga'i dmar khrid kyi man ngag yid bzhin nor bu rin po che'i za ma tog*, in *The Collected Works of Bu-ston* (New Delhi: International Academy of Indian Culture, 1971), 10:31–70 (21 folios) at fol. 21a.2. George N. Roerich, trans., *The Blue Annals* (New Delhi: Motilal Banarsidass, 1976), 424–425.

2. Roerich, *Blue Annals*, 732.

3. Roerich, *Blue Annals*, 733.

4. Roerich, *Blue Annals*, 187.

5. Roerich, *Blue Annals*, 951.

6. Roerich, *Blue Annals*, 1001.

7. Roerich, *Blue Annals*, 998–999.

8. See the biography of Chos kyi rgyal mtshan of Ding ri (1897–1959): Anonymous, *La stod shel dkar rdzong 'og ding ri ba chos rgyan nas rgyal ba'i gsung rab zab mo par bskrun zhus pa'i dkar chag dad ldan thar lam 'dren pa'i shing rta*, in *Dge slong ngag dbang blo bzang bstan 'dzin tshul khrims rgyal mtshan gyi spyod tshul drang por brjod pa myong snang 'khrul pa'i zlos gar gyi kha skong: A Continuation of the Autobiography of Shel dkar bka' 'gyur bla ma*, Edited by Chu bzang sprul sku blo bzang sangs rgyas bstan pa'i sgron me, Together with *La stod shel dkar rdzong 'og ding ri ba chos kyi rgyal mtshan nas rgyal ba'i gsung rab zab mo par bskrun zhus pa'i dkar chag dad ldan thar lam 'dren pa'i shing rta: An Account of the Career of a Tibetan Master Block Carver Ding ri ba chos kyi rgyal mtshan* (New Delhi: B.N. Sopa, 1975), 45 folios. [comp. 1956].

9. Sba Gsal snang, *Sba bzhed ces bya ba las sba gsal snang gi bzhed pa*, ed. Mgon po rgyal mtshan (Beijing: Mi rigs dpe skrun khang, 1982), 77.3.

10. McComas Taylor and Lama Choedak Yuthok, trans., *The Clear Mirror: A Traditional Account of Tibet's Golden Age, Sakyapa Sönam Gyaltsen's Clear Mirror on Royal Genealogy* (Ithaca, N.Y.: Snow Lion, 1996), 87.

11. Tsuguhito Takeuchi, *Old Tibetan Contracts from Central Asia* (Tokyo: Daizo Shuppan, 1995), esp. 57–58.

12. Leon Hurvitz, trans., *Scripture of the Lotus Blossom of the Fine Dharma (The Lotus Sūtra)* (New York: Columbia University Press, 1976), 175.

13. In this book the notion of merit is not a primary focus, though its role in canonical production certainly deserves full treatment. Provocative starting points might be John Kieschnick, *The Impact of Buddhism on Chinese Material Culture* (Princeton, N.J.: Princeton University Press, 2003), 164–185, and the comments thereupon in Henrik Sorensen, "Buddhism and Material Culture in China," *Acta Orientalia* 68 (2007): 247–280, at 266–274.

14. Roerich, *Blue Annals*, 79.

15. Roerich, *Blue Annals*, 585.

16. Roerich, *Blue Annals*, 448.

17. Roerich, *Blue Annals*, 691.

18. Roerich, *Blue Annals*, 949, 959.

19. Roerich, *Blue Annals*, 712.

20. Roerich, *Blue Annals*, 726. Yangwenpa, the reincarnation of Gotsangpa, mastered reading after a brief introduction: Roerich, *Blue Annals*, 237.

21. Roerich, *Blue Annals*, 537.

22. Roerich, *Blue Annals*, 582. See also 699.

23. Roerich, *Blue Annals*, 499.

24. Roerich, *Blue Annals*, 689.

25. Roerich, *Blue Annals*, 728.

26. Roerich, *Blue Annals*, 971.

27. Roerich, *Blue Annals*, 712, 758, 900.

28. Roerich, *Blue Annals*, 660.

29. Roerich, *Blue Annals*, 749.

30. Roerich, *Blue Annals*, 1010.

31. Roerich, *Blue Annals*, 294.

32. Roerich, *Blue Annals*, 55.

33. Roerich, *Blue Annals*, 604. One yogin could copy a life story from the author's original in a single day: Roerich, *Blue Annals*, 604.

34. Roerich, *Blue Annals*, 414.

35. Roerich, *Blue Annals*, 666

36. Roerich, *Blue Annals*, 667.

37. Toward the end of his life Pha Dam pa Sangs rgyas asked his congregation if anyone possessed a copy of the *Perfection of Wisdom Sūtra in Eight Thousand Lines*. The chaplain offered to prepare one for him, to which Pha Dam pa replied, "Copy it in printed or cursive script, and bring it here in one month." The chaplain was not able to finish the volume within the month, to the great displeasure of Pha Dam pa: Roerich, *Blue Annals*, 903.

38. Roerich, *Blue Annals*, 641.

39. Steng pa Lo tsa'a ba Tshul khrims 'byung gnas copied twenty volumes of *Perfection of Wisdom* literature begun by his father and collected many man-loads of Indian books, but cut short translating some when his Indian colleagues passed away: Roerich, *Blue Annals*, 1053–1054.

40. The five-volume collection of Padampa Sangyé's Pacification teachings produced in Dranang, situated south of Lhasa along the Tsangpo, is one of the few examples available. These are presented in Dan Martin, "Padampa Sangye: A History of Representation of a South Indian Siddha in Tibet," in *Holy Madness: Portraits of Tantric Siddhas* (New York: Rubin Museum of Art, 2006), 108–123. The manuscript library at Tabo monastery may contain exemplars dating to as far back as the eleventh century; See Paul Harrison, "Philology in the Field: Some Comments on Selected Mdo Mang texts in the Tabo Collection," in *Tabo Studies II: Manuscripts, Texts, Inscriptions, and the Arts*, ed. C.A. Scherrer-Schaub and E. Steinkellner (Rome: Istituto Italiano per l'Africa e l'Orient, 1999), 37–54, at 41; and Christina A. Scherrer-Schaub, "Was Byaṇ chub sems dpa' a Posthumous Title of King Ye śes 'od?" in ibid., 207–226, at 222, as well as other contributions to *Tabo Studies II*.

41. There are a number of works on forms of artistic knowledge that include brief descriptions of writing and book production: Anonymous, *Bzo rig kha shas kyi pa tra lag len ma*, in *Bzo rig kha shas kyi pa tra lag len ma and Other Texts on the Minor Sciences of the Tibetan Scholastic Tradition* (Dharamsala: Library of Tibetan Works and Archives, 1981), 1–20, at 10.1–11.7 and 16.2–.7 discusses the production of black paper and gold and silver lettering. See also *Bzo rig pa tra: A Revealed Work on the Methods of Indo-Tibetan Silpasastra by an as yet Unknown Gter-ston, with Other Rare Texts from the Library of Tibet House* (New Delhi: Tibet House, 1985). Dus 'khor zhabs drung (17ᵀᴴ century), *Rig gnas lnga'i rnam dbye cung zad bshad pa legs bshad nor bu'i phreng ba blo gsal mgul rgyan*, in *Rig gnas phyogs bsdebs: A Collection of Miscellaneous Works on Tibetan Minor Sciences* (Dharamsala: Library of Tibetan Works and Archives, 1981), 1–105, at 21.4–22.6 mentions select aspects of producing the verbal supports (*gsung rten*) for worship of the Buddha.

42. 'Brug chen IV Padma dkar po (1527–1592), *Li ma brtag pa'i rab byed smra 'dod pa'i kha rgyan*, in *The Collected Works (gsuṇ 'bum) of Kun-mkhyen Padma-dkar-po* (Darjeeling: Kargyud Sungrab Nyamso Khang, 1973), 1:293–305, at 305–306. Compare the nearly identical lines in Anonymous, *'Jig rten lugs kyi bstan bcos las dpyad don gsal ba'i sgron me* (Thimphu: Kun bzang stobs rgyal, 1975), 17.3–.6. William Woodville Rockhill, *Notes on the Ethnology of Tibet* (Washington: Government Printing Office, 1895), 719, states "when printing the Tibetans use paper made in Nepaul and Bhutan from the bark of various species of Daphnae, and especially of Edgeworthia gardneri, which has been previously washed with a little milk and watter, so that it may not blot. They also manufacture themselves a paper from the root of a small shrub, which is of a much thicker texture and more durable than Daphne paper. In western Tibet this paper is manufactured with a species of Astragalus, the whole shrub being reduced to pulp." An interesting diagram of an inkwell is found in P. H. Pott, *Introduction to the Tibetan Collection of the National Museum of Ethnology, Leiden* (Leiden: E. J. Brill, 1951), 125. R. O. Meisezahl, "Über den Degé Tanjur der ehemaligen Preussischen Staatsbibliothek," *Libri* 10, no. 4 (1960): 292–306, at 300–301, reports on a chemical analysis of paper in a Degé print.

43. See Lucette Boulnois, *Poudre d'Or et Monnaies d'Argent au Tibet* (Paris: Éditions du Centre National de la Recherche Scientifique, 1983), 128, and Rato Khyongla Nawang Losang, *My Life and Lives: The Story of a Tibetan Incarnation* (New York: E. P. Dutton, 1977), 11.

44. Samuel Turner, *An Account of an Embassy to the Court of the Teshoo Lama, in Tibet; Containing a Narrative of a Journey Through Bootan, and Part of Tibet* (London: W. Bulmer, 1800), 99–100. Fascinating research on the history of Tibetan paper is being undertaken by Agnieszka Helman-

Wazny; see her "Tibetan Manuscripts: Scientific Examination and Conservation Approaches," in *Edinburgh Conference Papers 2006: Proceedings from the Fifth International Conference of the Institute of Paper Conservation and First International Conference of the Institute of Conservation, Book and Paper Group,* ed. Jaques Shulla (London: Institute of Conservation [ICON], 2007), 247–256.

45. This is related by William Woodville Rockhill, "Tibet: A Geographical, Ethnographical, and Historical Sketch, Derived from Chinese Sources," *The Journal of the Royal Asiatic Society of Great Britain and Ireland* (1891):1–133 and 185–292, at 122, summarizing a Chinese source of 1702: "Well-educated persons carry in their belts a small iron case in which are bamboo pens; it is connected with a small copper or lacquered box for liquid ink. When they want to write, they dip their pen in the ink, then take a piece of skin or paper which they put on the ground and line by making folds in it. Then they put it on their knee and write in horizontal lines from left to right."

46. See David L. Snellgrove, *The Hevajra Tantra: A Critical Study* (Oxford: Oxford University Press, 1959), 1:115, or G. W. Farrow and I. Menon, *The Concealed Essence of the Hevajra Tantra* (Delhi: Motilal Banarsidass, 1992), which reads (267–268): "The book should be written on birchbark twelve finger-widths long by one who keeps the Observance of the Vow. Collyrium should be used as ink and human bone for the pen. If an unworthy person sees either the book or the picture, there is no accomplishment in this or the next life [for the one who shows them]. They may be seen at any time by a follower of the tradition. Whilst on the road the book should be concealed either in the hair or under the armpit."

47. Stag tshang Lo tsa'a ba Shes rab rin chen (born 1405), *Rten gsum bzhengs tshul dpal 'byor rgya mtsho,* in *Stag tshang lo tsa'a ba shes rab rin chen gyi gsung skor* (Kathmandu: Sa skya rgyal yongs gsung rab slob gnyer khang, n.d.), 1:449–540, at 509.7–511.2. A detailed technical discussion of nine methods of making ink by Mi pham rgya mtsho (1846–1911), *Bzo gnas nyer mkho'i za ma tog,* in *Collected Writings* (Gangtok: Sonam Topbay Kazi, 1972), 10:71–138 (in a recent edition: Mi pham rgya mtsho, *Bzo gnas nyer mkho'i za ma tog* [Xining: Mtsho sngon mi rigs dpe skrun khang, 1993] at 4–8) is translated in Christoph Cüppers, "On the Manufacture of Ink," *Ancient Nepal* 113 (1989): 1–7. The contents of this important work on arts and crafts are listed in Dieter Schuh, *Tibetische Handschriften und Blockdrucke (Teil 5)* (Wiesbaden: Franz Steiner Verlag, 1973), 64–66, and David P. Jackson and Janice Jackson, *Tibetan Thangka Painting: Methods and Materials* (Ithaca: Snow Lion, 1988), 7–8.

48. Shen Weirong, "Kh. Tib. 67: A Preliminary Survey of a Tibetan Manuscript of the 12th Century from Khara Khoto in the St. Petersburg Col-

lection," paper delivered at the Centre National de la Recherche Scientifique, Paris, May 29, 2008.

49. The attempt in Robert Shafer, "Words for 'Printing Block' and the Origin of Printing," *Journal of the American Oriental Society* 80, no. 4 (1960): 328–329, to place the origins of printing in Asia in Tibetan cultural regions on etymological grounds has not been borne out by further research (see the criticism of Walter Simon, "Tibetan 'par, dpar, spar', and Cognate Words," *Bulletin of the School of Oriental and African Studies* 25, no. 1–3 (1962): 72–80). The statement in David Snellgrove and Hugh Richardson, *A Cultural History of Tibet* (London: George Weidenfeld and Nicolson, 1968), 160, that there is not evidence of Tibetan-language printing before the Ming Bka' 'gyur of 1411, has long since been superseded, and recent works such as Evelyn S. Rawski, "Qing Publishing in Non-Han Languages," in *Printing and Book Culture in Late Imperial China*, ed. Cynthia Brokaw and Kai-wing Chow (Berkeley: University of California Press, 2005), 304–321, which cites Snellgrove and Richardson as current research at 327, n. 25, should be updated to account for the four decades of research undertaken since Snellgrove and Richardson's overview of Tibetan history.

50. See Luciano Petech, *Central Tibet and the Mongols: The Yüan–Sa-skya Period of Tibetan History* (Rome: Istituto Italiano per il Medio ed Estremo Oriente, 1990), esp. 5–33, for a survey of the rise of the Mongol imperial family in China and its impact on Tibetan Buddhist institutions. Information on the life of Pakpa gleaned from his collected writings is assembled in four essays by Jânos Szerb: "Glosses on the Oeuvre of bla-ma 'Phags-pa: On the Activity of Sa-skya Pandita," in *Tibetan Studies in Honour of Hugh Richardson: Proceedings of the International Seminar on Tibetan Studies, Oxford, 1979*, ed. Michael Aris and Aung San Suu Kyi (New Delhi: Vikas, 1980), 290–300; "Glosses on the Oeuvre of bla-ma 'Phags-pa: II. Some Notes on the Events of the Years 1251–1254," *Acta Orientalia* 34 (1980): 263–285; "Glosses on the Oeuvre of Bla-ma 'Phags-pa: III. The 'Patron–Patronized' Relationship," in *Soundings in Tibetan Civilization: Proceedings of the 1982 Seminar of the International Association for Tibetan Studies Held at Columbia University*, ed. Barbara Nimri Aziz and Matthew Kapstein (Delhi: Manohar), 165–173; "Glosses on the Oeuvre of bla ma 'Phags pa: 4. A Propos of Tolui," in *Religious and Lay Symbolism in the Altaic World and Other Papers: Proceedings of the 27th Meeting of the Permanent International Altaistic Conference, Walberberg, Federal Republic of Germany, June 12th to 17th, 1984*, ed. Klaus Sagaster and Helmut Eimer (Wiesbaden: Otto Harrasowitz, 1989), 365–378.

51. Petech, *Central Tibet and the Mongols*, 22.

52. On whom see Petech, *Central Tibet and the Mongols*, 26.

53. 'Phags pa Blo gros rgyal mtshan, *Kye'i rdo rje zhes bya ba'i rgyud kyi rgyal po*, in *Sa skya bka' 'bum ma phyi gsar rnyed phyogs bsgrigs* (Lhasa: n.p., 199?), 3:529–707, colophon at 707.2–.6. See Leonard W. J. van der Kuijp, "Two Mongol Xylographs (Hor Par Ma) of the Tibetan Text of Sa skya Paṇḍita's Work on Buddhist Logic and Epistemology," *Journal of the International Association of Buddhist Studies* 16, no. 2 (1993): 279–298, as well as the corrections to this article in Leonard W. J. van der Kuijp, "Apropos of Some Recently Recovered Manuscripts Anent Sa skya Paṇḍita's Tshad ma rigs pa'i gter and Autocommentary," *Berliner Indologische Studien* 7 (1993): 149–162, at 150, n. 4, and especially Leonard [W. J.] van der Kuijp, *The Kālacakra and the Patronage of Tibetan Buddhism by the Mongol Imperial Family* (Indiana University: Department of Central Eurasian Studies, 2004), at 8–11, 20–31, for a discussion of early dated xylographs.

54. Note also that only a decade later, from 1285 to 1287, the Mongol emperor Qubilai Khan had a catalog of Buddhist scripture prepared in which Tibetan texts were compared to Chinese texts. On this canonical project undertaken in the Yüan capital of Dadu, see Herbert Franke, "Der Kanonkatalog der Chih-yüan-Zeit und seine Kompilatoren," in *Chinesischer und Tibetischer Buddhismus im China der Yüanzeit: Drei Studien* (München: Kommission für Zentralasiatische Studien, Bayerische Akademie der Wissenschaften, 1996), 67–124.

55. On which see Leonard W. J. van der Kuijp, "A Treatise on Buddhist Epistemology and Logic Attributed to Klong chen Rab 'byams pa (1308–1364) and Its Place in Indo-Tibetan Intellectal History," *Journal of Indian Philosophy* 31 (2003): 381–437, at 391, 424, n. 30.

56. On early central Tibetan printing projects, see David P. Jackson, "The Earliest Printings of Tsong-kha-pa's Works: The Old Dga'-ldan Editions," in *Reflections on Tibetan Culture: Essays in Memory of Turrell V. Wylie*, ed. Lawrence Epstein and Richard F. Sherburne (Lewiston: The Edwin Mellen Press, 1990), 107–116; David P. Jackson, "More on the Old dGa'-ldan and Gong-dkar-ba Xylographic Editions," *Studies in Central and East Asian Religions* 2 (1989): 1–18. Work on early printings of the collected works of the Sakya masters has been undertaking by David P. Jackson, "Notes on Two Early Printed Editions of Sa-skya-pa Works," *The Tibet Journal* 8, no. 2 (1983): 3–24, and continued by Hidetoshi Fushimi, "Recent Finds from the Old Sa-skya Xylographic Edition," *Wiener Zeitschrift für die Kunde Südasiens und Archiv für Indische Philosophie* 43 (1999): 95–108.

57. Anonymous, *Gangs can gyi ljongs su bka' dang bstan bcos sogs kyi glegs bam spar gzhi ji ltar yod pa rnams nas dkar chag spar thog phyogs tsam du bkod pa phan bde'i pad tshal 'byed pa'i nyin byed*, in *Three Dkar Chag's* (New Delhi: Ngawang Gelek Demo, 1970), 169–243. See E. Gene Smith, "Banned Books in the Tibetan Speaking Lands," in *21st Century Tibet*

Issue: Symposium on Contemporary Tibetan Studies, Collected Papers (Taipei: Mongolian and Tibetan Affairs Commission, 2004), 368–381, for comments on this work in the context of book banning.

58. Heinrich Harrer offers an informative, if diminutive account of the Zhöl printing houses and their labors in *Seven Years in Tibet* (New York: E. P. Dutton, 1954), 264–265: "Shö, which stands at the foot of the Potala, is the home of the state printing press—a high, dark building from which never a sound issues into the outer world. There is no humming of machines and only the voices of the monks echo through the halls. Wooden blocks lie piled on long shelves. They are used only when a new book is printed. The preparation of a new book entails endless work. The monks must first cut out small wooden boards by hand, as there are no sawmills here, and then carve the squiggly letters one by one in the birchwood boards. When they are ready the tablets are carefully placed in order. Instead of printer's ink they use a mixture of soot, which the monks make by burning yak dung. Most of them get black from head to foot during their work. At last the separate pages are printed off on handmade Tibetan paper. . . . One can either order books in the printing press or buy them from one of the booksellers in the Parkhor."

59. See the biography of Chos kyi rgyal mtshan of Ding ri (1897–1959): Anonymous, *La stod shel dkar rdzong 'og ding ri ba chos rgyan nas rgyal ba'i gsung rab zab mo par bskrun zhus pa'i dkar chag dad ldan thar lam 'dren pa'i shing rta.*

60. Corneille Jest, "A Technical Note on the Tibetan Method of Block-Carving," *Man* 61 (1961): 83–85, introduces the tools used by Himalayan block carvers. A brief description of the printing process may be found in Josef Kolmaš, *The Iconography of the Degé Kanjur and Tanjur: Facsimile Reproductions of the 648 Illustrations in the Degé Edition of the Tibetan Tripitaka Housed in the Library of the Oriental Institute in Prague* (New Delhi: Sharada Rani, 1978), 17–18. Tibetan moveable-type printing appears to have originated with the Capuchin missions. According to J. M. Lenhart, "Capuchins Introduce Printing into Tibet in 1741," *Franciscan Studies* 10 (1950): 62–72, at 68, the type was created in Rome in 1738 and transported to Lhasa in 1741. For the context of this apparently short-lived transfer of technology, see Isrun Engelhardt, "Between Tolerance and Dogmatism: Tibetan Reactions to the Capuchin Missionaries in Lhasa, 1707–1745," *Zentralasiatische Studien* 34 (2005): 55–98, especially 62 and further references at n. 98.

61. See Loden Sherap Dagyab, *Tibetan Religious Art,* 2 vols. (Wiesbaden: Otto Harrassowitz, 1977), 1:58–59, for a descriptive account of woodblock carving, and 2:58, for an especially clear and instructive photograph of wood-block printing. A general description of printing at Degé may be

found in André Migot, *Tibetan Marches*, trans. Peter Fleming (London: Rupert Hart-Davis, 1955), 163–164.

62. Gö Lotsawa explicitly mentions some twenty manuscript copies of the Kangyur proliferating from Nartang monastery throughout central and eastern Tibet. Roerich, *Blue Annals*, 390.

63. Paul Harrison, "Preliminary Notes on a gZungs 'dus Manuscript from Tabo," in *Suhṛllekhāḥ: Festgabe für Helmut Eimer*, ed. Michael Hahn, Jens-Uwe Hartmann, and Roland Steiner (Swisttal-Odendorf: IeT Verlag. 1996), 49–68, at 51, n. 7.

64. See Paul Harrison, "A Brief History of the Tibetan Kangyur," in *Tibetan Literature: Studies in Genre*, ed. José Ignacio Cabezón and Roger R. Jackson (Ithaca: Snow Lion Publications, 1996), 70–94, as well as the other works listed in his bibliography. More recently, see Peter Skilling, "From bKa' bstan bcos to bKa' 'gyur and bsTan 'gyur," in *Transmission of the Tibetan Canon: Proceedings of the 7th Seminar of the International Association for Tibetan Studies, Graz 1995*, ed. Helmut Eimer et al. (Wien: Verlag der Österreichischen Akademie der Wissenschaften, 1997), 3:87–111. The essays collected in Helmut Eimer, *Ein Jahrzehnt Studien zur Überlieferung des tibetischen Kangyur* (Wien: Arbeitskreis für tibetische und buddhistische Studien Universität Wien, 1992), are foundational for the modern study of the Tibetan Buddhist canons.

65. Paul Harrison, "In Search of the Tibetan Bka' 'gyur,: A Reconnaissance Report," in *Tibetan Studies: Proceedings of the 6th Seminar of the International Association for Tibetan Studies*, ed. Per Kvaerne (Oslo: The Institute of Comparative Research in Human Culture, 1994), 1:309.

66. See Kurtis R. Schaeffer and Leonard W.J. van der Kuijp, *An Early Tibetan Catalogue of Buddhist Literature: The Bstan pa rgyas pa nyi ma'i 'od zer of Bcom ldan ral gri*. Cambridge, Mass.: Harvard Oriental Series, 2009.

67. New catalogs are becoming increasingly available, which will aid greatly in understanding the early fourteenth-century state of the canons. See for instance Rang byung rdo rje, *Chos rje rang byung rdo rje'i thugs dam bstan 'gyur gyi dkar chag*, in *Karma pa rang byung rdo rje'i gsung 'bum* (Zi ling: Mtshur phu mkhan po lo yag bkra shis, 2006), 4:415–594, which unfortunately for present purposes contains neither introductions nor colophons of any great length; Rang byung rdo rje, *Bstan bcos 'gyur ro 'tshal gyi dkar chag*, in *Karma pa rang byung rdo rje'i gsung 'bum* (Zi ling: Mtshur phu mkhan po lo yag bkra shis, 2006), 4:595–717 (introductory verses are found at 596.1–597.1).

68. Peter Skilling has summarized this state of affairs by stating, "There is not one Kangyur, there are only Kangyurs. It follows that we should avoid speaking of 'editions' or 'recensions' of '*the* Kangyur' where we may sim-

ply say Kangyurs." Skilling's call has provided the impetus to look more closely at Kangyurs and Tengyurs on the local level. Skilling, "From bKa' bstan bcos to bKa' 'gyur and bsTan 'gyur," 101.

69. D. C. Greetham, *Textual Scholarship: An Introduction* (New York: Garland, 1994), 296. This sentiment is echoed in Dung dkar Blo bzang 'phrin las, "Bod kyi dpe rnying par skrun dang 'brel ba'i gnad don 'ga' zhig skor gleng ba," in *Dung dkar blo bzang 'phrin las kyi gsung rtsom phyogs bgrigs* (Beijing: Krung go'i bod kyi shes rig dpe skrun khang, 1997), 406–451, at 406–407, an important article also to be found collected with the author's informative studies of traditional cataloging (*dkar chag rig pa*) as well as several other articles on printing in Dung dkar Blo bzang 'phrin las, *Bod kyi dkar chag rig pa* (Beijing: Mi rigs dpe skrun khang, 2004).

70. On this last question see, in addition to subsequent chapters, Jampa S. Samten, "Notes on the Lithang Edition of the Tibetan bKa'-'gyur," *Tibet Journal* 12, no. 3 (1987): 17–40, esp. 20–36, for passages describing the methods of the scribes and editors of the Tshal pa Kangyur of 1347–49.

71. See David Seyfort Ruegg, *The Life of Bu ston Rin po che* (Roma: Is.M.E.O., 1966), 123, and Sgra tshad pa Rin chen rnam rgyal (1318–1388), *Chos rje thams cad mkhyen pa bu ston lo tsā ba'i rnam par thar pa snyim pa'i me tog*, in *Bde bar gshegs pa'i bstan pa'i gsal byed chos kyi 'byung gnas gsung rab rin po che'i mdzod* (Beijing: Krung go'i bod kyi shes rig dpe skrun khang, 1981), 318–374, at 348.3–.4. These activities are also mentioned in the biographical summary of Butön in Bkra shis don grub's mid-sixteenth century history of Shalu. See Bkra shis don grub (16th century), *Chos grwa chen po dpal zha lu gser khang gi bdag po jo bo lce'i gdung rabs* (Tibetan Buddhist Resource Center: manuscript, 55 folios), 31a.4–.5. See Dan Martin, *Tibetan Histories: A Bibliography of Tibetan-Language Historical Works* (London: Serindia Publications, 1997), entry 171, for more information on this work. See also the history of the Myang valley, which recapitulates much of the phrasing of Sgra tshad pa's biography of Butön: Tāranātha (1575–1634) [authorship uncertain], *Myang yul stod smad bar gsum gyi ngo mtshar gtam legs bshad mkhas pa'i 'jug ngogs* (Lhasa: Bod ljongs mi dmangs dpe skrun khang, 1983), 176–177.

72. Among the most comprehensive studies by a contemporary Tibetan scholar of the methods and materials of textual scholarship is Klu Tshang Rdo rje rin Chen, *Bod kyi rtsom rigs rnam bzhag* (Beijing: Mi rigs dpe skrun khang, 1992). This useful work is divided into the following chapters: 1. Orthography (*yi ge'i rnam bzhag bshad pa*); 2. Block Printing (*par skrun gyi rnam bzhag bshad pa*); 3. Style of Print Media (*par gzhi'i rnam bzhag bshad pa*); 4. Editing (*zhu dag gi rnam bzhag bshad pa*); 5. Annotated Commentary (*mchan 'grel gyi rnam bzhag bshad pa*); 6. Catalogs (*dkar*

chag gi rnam bzhag bshad pa). Guenther Grönbold, "Die Schrift- und Buchkultur Tibets," in *Der Weg zum Dach der Welt,* ed. C. C. Müller and W. Raunig (Innsbruck: Pinguin-Verlag, 1982), 363–380, provides a useful summary of the physical aspects of book production in Tibet (and see the more general remarks in Guenther Grönbold, "Tibet: Literature und Buchkunst," in *Das Buch im Orient: Handschriften und Kostbare Drucke aus Zwei Jahrtausenden* [Wiesbaden: Dr. Ludwig Reichert Verlag, 1982], 253–264), to which may be added Cristina A. Scherrer-Schaub, "Towards a Methodology for the Study of Old Tibetan Manuscripts: Dunhuang and Tabo," in *Tabo Studies II,* ed. Scherrer-Schaub and Steinkellner, 3–35. Charles Briggs, "Historiographical Essay: Literacy, Reading, and Writing in the Medieval West," *Journal of Medieval History* 26, no. 4 (2000): 397–420, surveys recent work on European literacy, reading, writing, and book production more generally in a manner suggestive for the study of Tibetan intellectual history.

73. Arjun Appuradai, ed., *The Social Life of Things: Commodities in Cultural Perspective* (Cambridge: Cambridge University Press, 1986).

74. See Bruce Lincoln, "Culture," in *Guide to the Study of Religion,* ed. Willi Braun and Russell T. McCutcheon (London: Cassell, 2000), 416.

75. Edward Conze, *The Perfection of Wisdom in Eight Thousand Lines and Its Verse Summary* (San Francisco: Four Seasons Foundation, 1973), 299–300.

2. THE EDITOR'S TEXTS

1. Rin chen rnam rgyal, *Chos rje thams cad mkhyen pa bu ston lo tsā ba'i rnam par thar pa,* 370, in David Seyfort Ruegg, *The Life of Bu ston Rin po che* (Roma: Is.M.E.O., 1966), 164–165. Two beautiful images of Butön holding a manuscript can be found in Amy Heller, *Tibetan Art: Tracing the Development of Spiritual Ideals and Art in Tibet 600–2000 A.D.* (Milan: Jaca Book, 1999), pls. 63 and 64.

2. See Ruegg, *The Life of Bu ston,* 118, where it is stated that Butön collected the majority of the works in the Kangyur. See Rin chen rnam rgyal, *Chos rje thams cad mkhyen pa bu ston lo tsā ba'i rnam par thar pa,* 345.7–346.1. See Paul Harrison, "In Search of the Tibetan Bka' 'gyur: A Reconnaissance Report," in *Tibetan Studies: Proceedings of the 6th Seminar of the International Association for Tibetan Studies,* ed. Per Kvaerne (Oslo: The Institute of Comparative Research in Human Culture, 1994), 1:295–317, at 302–306, on the problem of the Kangyur at Shalu.

3. *Phags pa 'da' ka ye shes shes bya ba theg pa chen po'i mdo*: Hakuji Ui, et al., *A Complete Catalog of the Tibetan Buddhist Canons* (Sendai: Tōhuko Imperial University, 1934), no. 122.

4. See Ruegg, *The Life of Bu ston,* 66.

5. Rin chen rnam rgyal, *Chos rje thams cad mkhyen pa bu ston lo tsā ba'i rnam par thar pa*, 348.5–.7. See Ruegg, *The Life of Bu ston*, 123.

6. Rin chen rnam rgyal, *Chos rje thams cad mkhyen pa bu ston lo tsā ba'i rnam par thar pa*, 343.19–.22. See Ruegg, *The Life of Bu ston*, 112.

7. See Ruegg, *The Life of Bu ston*, 118 and elsewhere. This image is also evoked in Tāranātha (1575–1634) [Authorship uncertain], *Myang yul stod smad bar gsum gyi ngo mtshar gtam legs bshad mkhas pa'i 'jug ngogs* (Lhasa: Bod ljongs mi dmangs dpe skrun khang, 1983), 176.

8. Gser mdog Paṇ chen Śākya mchog ldan (1428–1507), *Dpal ldan a ti sha sras dang brgyud bar bcas pa'i ngo mtshar mdzad pa'i phreng ba spel legs*, in *The Complete Works (gsuṅ 'bum) of Gser-mdog Paṇ-chen Śākya-mchog-ldan* (Thimphu: Kunzang Tobgey, 1975), 16:538.3–550.2, at 548.1–.3.

9. Rin chen rnam rgyal, *Chos rje thams cad mkhyen pa bu ston lo tsā ba'i rnam par thar pa*, 367 (Ruegg's edition: fol. 37a.7–37b.1). See Ruegg, *The Life of Bu ston*, 159–160 for a paraphrase of this difficult passage. Writing in 1779, the Dge lugs pa scholar Ye shes rgyal mtshan (1713–93) concluded his summary of Butön's life with a paraphrased version of this scene. See Tshe mchog gling Yongs 'dzin Ye shes rgyal mtshan (1713–1793), *Thams cad mkhyen pa bu ston rin chen grub kyi gsung 'bum gyi dkar chag bstan pa rin po che'i mdzes rgyan phul byung gser gyi phreng ba* (comp. 1779), in *The Collected Works (Gsuṅ-'bum) of Tshe-mchog-gliṅ yoṅs-'dzin ye-śes-rgyal-mtshan* (New Delhi: Tibet House, 1975), 5:261–375, at 354.

10. See Roberto Vitali, *Early Temples of Central Tibet* (London: Serendia, 1990), 89–122 for a detailed discussion of the early history of Shalu, and 98–103 for the Sku zhang rulers in particular.

11. Bu ston Rin chen grub, *Bstan 'gyur gyi dkar chag yin bzhin nor bu dbang gi rgyal po'i phreng ba*, in *The Collected Works of Bu-ston* (New Delhi: International Academy of Indian Culture, 1971), 26:401–644, at 637.6–638.1. See Ruegg, *The Life of Bu ston*, 32–33.

12. It is certainly possible that this letter was sent to some other editors; perhaps to those in charge of the production of a Kangyur at Tsel Gungtang, the consecration of which Butön had overseen at Gungtang in 1351 at the invitation of Tselpa Kunga Dorjé (alias Gewé Lodrö, 1309–64): see Zahirrudin Ahmad, *A History of Tibet by Ṅag-dBaṅ Blo-bZaṅ rGya-mTSHo, Fifth Dalai Lama of Tibet* (Bloomington: Indiana University Research Institute for Inner Asian Studies, 1995), 109; Ruegg, *The Life of Bu ston*, 134. It is more likely, however, that Butön was writing to the scholars working on the Tengyur at his home institution of Shalu. First of all, arguing from negative evidence, we have no definite statement at our disposal that Butön actually played a role in the making of the Kangyur of 1347–49 at Tsel Gungtang; the scribal colophons of the Tselpa Kangyur preserved in the Litang block-print Kangyur list the names of many scholars, and

Butön is not among them. See Jampa S. Samten, "Notes on the Lithang Edition of the Tibetan bKa'-'gyur," *Tibet Journal* 12, no. 3 (1987): 20–36. Paul Harrison, "In Search of the Tibetan Bka' 'gyur," 315, n. 70, cautiously suggests only that "the Tshal pa Rgyud may have been influenced by Bu ston's work to some extent." Second, Butön employs similar terms for his scholarly audience in both his letter to editors and his Tengyur catalog, including "distinguished scholar" (*yon tan mkhan po*) (Bu ston Rin chen grub, *Bstan 'gyur gyi dkar chag*, 638.3) and "virtuous friend (*dge ba'i bshes gnyen*) (Bu ston Rin chen grub, *Bstan 'gyur gyi dkar chag*, 637.7). These scholars are also said to have received gifts in both the letter and the Tengyur catalog (Bu ston Rin chen grub, *Bstan 'gyur gyi dkar chag*, 638.3). Finally, passages in the letter itself referring to common phrases in *sūtras* make it clear that Butön was giving instructions for canonical literature. It is with guarded confidence, then, that the letter can be read as directed toward a particular workshop at Shalu monastery.

13. Rin chen grub, "Directions to the editors and publishers of the Buddhist Scriptures," in *The Collected Works of Bu-ston* (New Delhi: International Academy of Indian Culture, 1971), 26:345.

14. Compare Si tu Paṇ chen Chos kyi 'byung gnas, *Thon mi'i legs bshad sum cu pa'i snying po ljon pa'i dbang po*, in *Sum rtags rtsa ba dang de'i 'grel pa si tu'i zhal lung* (Beijing: Mi rigs dpe skrun khang, 1994), 74–78.

15. See Bu ston Rin chen grub, *The Collected Works of Bu-ston* (New Delhi: International Academy of Indian Culture, 1971), vol. 16.

16. Dpa' ris sangs rgyas, *Dpe chos rna ba'i bdud rtsi* (Xining: Mtsho sngon mi rigs dpe skrun khang, 1985), 323–324, glosses the term *zhwa dpe lham bkab* as follows: *zhwa gang zhes dris pa la lham 'di zhes ston pa ste / gzhug bya dang 'jug byed nor bu'i dpe'o /.* See also Acharya Sangyé T. Naga and Tsepak Rigzin, *Bod dbyin shan sbyar gyi tshig tshogs dang gtam dpe: Tibetan Quadrisyllabics, Phrases and Idioms* (Dharmsala: Library of Tibetan Works and Archives, 1994), 205.

17. The text clearly reads *rgyab bzang*, but I am provisionally emending this to *rgyal bzang* with the thought that this refers to a text of that name, and that *rgyal bzang* may well be short for *rgyal ba bzang po*. Perhaps this refers to the thirteenth-century medical scholar Brang ti Rgyal ba bzang po, on whom see Bla ma skyabs, *Bod kyi mkhas pa rim byon gyi gso rig gsung 'bum dkar chag mu tig phreng ba* (Lanzhou: Kan su'u mi rigs dpe skrun khang, 1997), 181–182. This member of the famous Brang ti medical family was active at Sa skya and thus well within the intellectual sphere of Shalu.

18. The term *bkas bcad* occurs in the introduction and conclusion of *Sgra sbyor bam po gnyis pa* (completed 814/815), where it denotes the edicts of Trisong Detsen ordering the translation and revision of *sūtras* and

*śāstra*s. For further information on *bkas bcad* in the context of the *Sgra sbyor bam po gnyis pa* see especially Géza Uray, "Contributions to the Date of the Vyutpatti-Treatises," *Acta Orientalia Academiae Scientarium Hungaricae* 43, no. 1 (1989): 3–21. See also Mie Ishikawa, *A Critical Edition of the Sgra sbyor bam po gnyis pa: An Old and Basic Commentary on the Mahāvyutpatti* (Tokyo: The Toyo Bunko, 1990), 2, 4; Pieter C. Verhagen, "Tibetan Expertise in Sanskrit Grammar: Ideology, Status, and Other Extra-Linguistic Factors," in *Ideology and Status of Sanskrit: Contributions to the History of the Sanskrit Language*, ed. Jan E.M. Houben (Leiden: Brill, 1996), 275–287, at 282–286; David Snellgrove, *Indo-Tibetan Buddhism: Indian Buddhists and Their Tibetan Successors* (Boston: Shambhala, 1987), 2:442–443; Nils Simonsson, *Indo-Tibetische Studien: Die Methoden der Tibetischen Übersetzer, untersucht im Hinblink auf die Bedeutung ihrer Übersetzungen für die Sanskritphilologie* (Uppsala: Almqvist & Wiksells Boktryckeri AB, 1957), 238–280, and in particular 246, 259, and 263. For recent Tibetan scholarship on this topic, see Gsang bdag, "Skad gsar bcad rnam pa gsum gyi dus rim gyi dbye ba dang de'i dgos don skor bshad pa," *Krung go'i bod kyi shes rig* 2 (1993): 33–40. For a detailed survey of the lexicographic and grammatical entries of the *Sgra sbyor bam po gnyis pa*, see Pieter C. Verhagen, *A History of Sanskrit Grammatical Literature in Tibet: Volume One, Transmission of the Canonical Literature* (Leiden: Brill, 1994), 15–45. Butön quotes from the *Sgra sbyor* in his *History of Buddhism* in reference to the *bkas bcad* issued by Ral pa can. Compare Bu ston Rin chen grub, *Bde bar gshegs pa'i bstan pa'i gsal byed chos kyi 'byung gnas gsung rab rin po che'i mdzod* (Beijing: Krung go'i bod kyi shes rig dpe skrun khang, 1981), 1–317, at 190.25 through 191.4, with Simonsson, *Indo-Tibetische Studien*, 241–242, sections 2 and 3. See also Eugene Obermiller, trans., *The History of Buddhism in India and Tibet by Bu-Ston* (Heidelberg: Harrassowitz, 1932), 196–197. See Uray, "Contributions to the Date of the Vyutpatti-Treatises," for an exhaustive discussion of the confusion between Khri lde srong btsan and Ral pa can in Tibetan historiography dealing with the translation and revision. He also lists three *bkas bcad* works in the catalog of scripture and treatises in chapter 4 of the *History of Buddhism*. See Bu ston Rin chen grub, *Bde bar gshegs pa'i bstan pa'i gsal byed chos kyi 'byung gnas*, 310.21–22, and Nishioka Soshū, "Index to the Catalog Section of Bu-ston's 'History of Buddhism,'" in *Annual Report of the Institute for the Study of Cultural Exchange, The University of Tokyo*, 4 (1980): 61–92 [part I]; 5 (1981) 43–94 [part II]; 6 (1983), 47–200 [part III]; part III, 116.

19. See Simonsson, *Indo-Tibetische Studien*, 218 and R.A. Stein, "Tibetica Antiqua I," *Bulletin de l'École Francaise d'Extreme-Orient* 72 (1983): 149–236, at 151–152.

20. See Verhagen, "Tibetan Expertise in Sanskrit Grammar," on this figure.

21. Skyogs ston Lo tsā ba Rin chen bkra shis (16th century), *Bod kyi skad las gsar rnying gi brda'i khyad par ston pa legs par bshad pa li shi'i gur khang*, in *Dag yig skor gyi dpe rgyun dkon po 'ga' phyogs gcig tu bsgrigs pa mu tig tshom bu* (Xining: Mtsho sngon mi rigs dpe skrun khang, 1998), 397–424, at 398–399.

22. Compare Rin chen bkra shis, *Bod kyi skad las gsar rnying gi brda'i khyad par ston pa legs par bshad pa li shi'i gur khang*, 398–399, with Bcom ldan ral gri (1227–1305), *Sgra'i bstan bcos smra ba rgyan gyi me tog* (Beijing: CPN manuscript, 22 folios), 4b.6–5b. 7. Note that Bcom ldan ral gri's dates have been determined from the biography written at the request of his uncle by Bsam gtan bzang po: Bsam gtan bzang po, *Bcom ldan ral gri'i rnam thar ldad pa'i ljong shing* (Beijing: CPN manuscript, 26 folios), fols. 19a.5–19b.2, 20a.5.

23. Zhwa lu Lo tsā ba Chos skyong bzang po, *Bod kyi brda'i bstan bcos legs par bshad pa rin po che'i za ma tog bkod pa*, in *Dag yig skor gyi dpe rgyun dkon po 'ga' phyogs gcig tu bsgrigs pa mu tig tshom bu* (Xining: Mtsho sngon mi rigs dpe skrun khang, 1998), 89.

24. Klong rdol Bla ma Ngag dbang blo bzang (1719–1794), *Rig gnas che ba sgra rig pa / snyan ngag [/] sdeb sbyor / zlos gar / mngon brjod / brda gsar rnying gi khyad par rnams las byung ba'i ming gi grangs*, in *Klong rdol ngag dbang blo bzang gi gsung 'bum* (Lhasa: Bod ljongs bod yig dpe rnying dpe skrun khang, 1991), 1:657–686, at 684.

25. Franz-Karl Ehrhard, *The Oldest Block Print of Klong-chen Rab-'byams-pa's Theg mchog mdzod: Facsimile Edition of Early Tibetan Block Prints* (Lumbini: Lumbini International Research Institute, 2000), xix, translates an account of a printing project of 1533, in which the craftsmen were said to be compensated well. The scribes who worked on the Kangyur at 'Bri gung were also treated well, at least according to 'Bri gung Che tshang IV Bstan 'dzin padma'i rgyal mtshan (1770–1826), *Nges don bstan pa'i snying po mgon po 'bri gung pa chen po'i gdan rabs chos kyi byung tshul gser gyi phreng ba* (Lhasa: Bod ljongs bod yig dpe rnying dpe skrun khang, 1989), 134.

26. Bsod nams dpal bzang po, Śākya 'od, and Byang chub rgyal mtshan [Incorrectly attributed to Sgra tshad pa Rin chen rnam rgyal], *Bstan bcos 'gyur ro 'tshal gyi dkar chag yid bzhin nor bu rin po che'i za ma tog*, in *The Collected Works of Bu-ston* (New Delhi: International Academy of Indian Culture, 1971), 28:343–574, at 568. I have been unable to determine the meanings of *kag ta pa* and *gdong kag pa*. On the historical background of this project see Leonard W. J. van der Kuijp, "Fourteenth-Century Tibetan Cultural History I: Ta'i-si-tu Byang-chub rgyal-mtshan as a Man of Religion," *Indo-Iranian Journal* 37 (1994): 139–149, at 140–142.

27. See 'Bri gung Che tshang IV Bstan 'dzin padma'i rgyal mtshan, *Nges don bstan pa'i snying po mgon po 'bri gung pa chen po'i gdan rabs*, 134.

28. See Ruegg, *The Life of Bu ston*, 318.

29. Tshal pa Kun dga' rdo rje (1309–1364), *Deb ther dmar po rnams kyi dang po hu lan deb ther* (Beijing: Mi rigs dpe skrun khang, 1981), 103.13.

30. 'Bri gung Che tshang IV Bstan 'dzin padma'i rgyal mtshan, *Nges don bstan pa'i snying po mgon po 'bri gung pa chen po'i gdan rabs*, 130.1–.3. A century later, between 1435 and 1468, the thirteenth abbot of 'Bri gung mthil, Rin chen dpal bzang (1421–69), commissioned a gold-on-black Kangyur, which was completed in three months. See 'Bri gung Che tshang IV Bstan 'dzin padma'i rgyal mtshan, *Nges don bstan pa'i snying po mgon po 'bri gung pa chen po'i gdan rabs*, 150.10–.14.

31. See 'Bri gung Che tshang IV Bstan 'dzin padma'i rgyal mtshan, *Nges don bstan pa'i snying po mgon po 'bri gung pa chen po'i gdan rabs*, 135–136.

32. See Samten, "Notes on the Lithang Edition of the Tibetan bKa'-'gyur," 30.

33. See 'Jigs med grags pa (15th century), *Rgyal rtse chos rgyal gyi rnam par thar pa dad pa'i lo thog dngos grub kyi char 'bebs* (1479–81) (Lhasa: Bod ljongs mi dmangs dpe skrun khang, 1987), 169, 181. This biographical work on the rulers of Rgyal rtse is rich with details on the making of manuscripts during the fifteenth century, and deserves further study.

34. 'Jigs med 'bangs (15th century), *Dpal ldan bla ma dam pa thams cad mkhyen pa phyogs thams cad las rnam par rgyal ba'i zhabs kyi rnam par thar pa ngo mtshar kyi dga' ston* (Lhasa: Bod ljongs bod yig dpe rnying dpe skrun khang, 1991), 223.

35. See Bo dong Paṇ chen Phyogs las rnam rgyal (1375–1451), *Byis pa 'jug pa'i sgo*, in *Encyclopedia Tibetica: The Collected Works of Bo-dong paṇ-chen phyogs-las-rnam-rgyal* (New Delhi: Tibet House, 1969), 9:12–188, at 128.5–132.7, and Bo dong Paṇ chen Phyogs las rnam rgyal, *Rten gsum bzhengs tshul bstan bcos lugs bshad pa*, in *Encyclopedia Tibetica: The Collected Works of Bo-dong paṇ-chen phyogs-las-rnam-rgyal* (New Delhi: Tibet House, 1969), 2:265–342, at 333.3–342.6. I think that the *Rten gsum bzhengs tshul bstan bcos lugs bshad pa* can be placed within Bo dong Paṇ chen's *Introduction for Scholars* (*Mkhas pa 'jug pa'i sgo*). According to his biographer, 'Jigs med 'bangs (15th century), the *De kho na nyid 'dus pa* was divided into four parts, or "introductions" ('*jug pa'i sgo*): 1) *Byis pa 'jug pa'i sgo*; 2) *Mkhas pa 'jug pa'i sgo*; 3) *Mdo la 'jug pa'i sgo*; 4) *Sngags la 'jug pa'i sgo*. Reading and writing are included by 'Jigs med 'bangs in the *Byis pa 'jug pa'i sgo*, and practical arts (*bzo rig pa*) in the *Mkhas pa 'jug pa'i sgo*. The *Rten gsum bzhengs tshul bstan bcos lugs bshad pa* certainly fits within this category. See 'Jigs med 'bangs (15th century), *Dpal ldan bla ma dam pa thams cad mkhyen pa phyogs thams cad las rnam par rgyal ba'i zhabs kyi rnam par thar pa*, 227.10–228.13.

36. See Skyogs ston Lo tsā ba Rin chen bkra shis (16th century), *Rje btsun zhwa lu lo tsā ba'i rnam par thar pa brjed byang nor bu'i khri shing* [comp. 1517] (Beijing: CPN manuscript, 42 folios), fol. 32a.2. See also Zhwa lu Ri phug Sprul sku Blo gsal bstan skyong (1804–c. 1874), *Dpal ldan zhwa lu pa'i bstan pa la bka' drin che ba'i skyes bu dam pa rnams kyi rnam thar lo rgyus ngo mtshar dad pa'i 'jug ngogs*, in *On the History of the the Monastery of Zhwa-lu* (Leh: Tashi Yangphel Tashigang, 1971), 1–471, at 236.2–.3. Blo gsal bstan skyong uses Rin chen bkra shis' biography of Zha lu Lo tsā ba in his work, as he tells us at *Dpal ldan zhwa lu pa'i bstan pa la bka' drin che ba'i skyes bu dam pa rnams kyi rnam thar*, 241.1.

37. Skyogs ston Lo tsā ba Rin chen bkra shis, *Rje btsun zhwa lu lo tsā ba'i rnam par thar pa*, fol. 32b.4–.6.

38. See E. Gene Smith, *Among Tibetan Texts: History and Literature of the Himalayan Plateau*, ed. Kurtis R. Schaeffer (Boston: Wisdom, 2001), 171–176, for more on this important eighteenth-century scholar.

39. See Tshe mchog gling Yongs 'dzin Ye shes rgyal mtshan, *Thams cad mkhyen pa bu ston rin chen grub kyi gsung 'bum gyi dkar chag*, 367.5, where the letter is refered to as *yig mkhan rnams la gdams pa*, "instruction to scribes," and is listed in volume *Za* (22) of the twenty-two-volume edition of Bu ston's works located at Bkra shis bsam gtan gling.

40. See Sgra tshad pa Rin chen rnam rgyal, *Kun mkhyen bu ston gyi bka' 'bum dkar chag*, in *The Collected Works of Bu-ston* (New Delhi: International Academy of Indian Culture, 1971), 28:333–342, at 341.5–.6; Sgra tshad pa Rin chen rnam rgyal, *Bka' 'bum gyi dkar chag rin chen lde mig*, in *The Collected Works of Bu-ston* (New Delhi: International Academy of Indian Culture, 1971), 28:319–332, at 331–332; Bu ston Rin chen grub, *Bu ston rin po che'i bka' 'bum gyi dkar chas chos rje nyid kyis mdzad pa*, in *The Collected Works of Bu-ston* (New Delhi: International Academy of Indian Culture, 1971), 26:645–656, at 654.

41. I paraphrase from Ta'a la'i Bla ma VIII 'Jam dpal rgya mtsho (1758–1804), *Dpal ldang bla ma dam pa rigs dang dkyil 'khor rgya mtsho'i mnga' bdag bka' drin gsum ldan yongs 'dzin paṇḍi ta chen po rje btsun ye shes rgyal mtshan dpal bzang po'i sku gsung thugs kyi rtogs pa brjod pa thub btsan padmo 'byed pa'i nyin byed*, in *Biography of Tshe-gling Yongs-'dzin Ye-shes-rgyal-mtshan by Dalai Lama VIII* (New Delhi: Ngawang Gelek Demo, 1969), 298.3–300.1.

42. See among other places Ensho Kanakura, ed., *A Catalog of the Tohoku University Collection of Tibetan Works on Buddhism* (Sendai: Seminary of Indology, Tohoku University, 1953), no. 5282, where we are informed of the *Rgyud thams cad kyi rgyal po dpal gsang ba 'dus pa'i rgya cher bshad pa sgron ma gsal ba'i tshig don ji bzhin 'byed pa'i mchan gyi yang 'grel*, 476 fols. in vol. *nga* of the eighteen-volume New Zhol Par khang edition of the collected works of Tsong kha pa.

43. Ensho Kanakura, ed., *A Catalog of the Tohoku University Collection of Tibetan Works on Buddhism*, no. 5077: *Sgron ma gsal bar byed pa'i bshad sbyar mtha' drug rab tu gsal bar byed pa*, 271 fols. in vol. 9 of the Lha sa Zhol Gsar print of Bu ston's *gsung 'bum*.

44. Ensho Kanakura, ed., *A Catalog of the Tohoku University Collection of Tibetan Works on Buddhism*, no. 5284: *Rgyud kyi rgyal po dpal gsang ba 'dus pa'i rgya cher bshad pa sgron ma gsal ba'i dka' ba'i gnas kyi mtha' gcod rin po che'i myu gu*, 138 fols. in vol. *ca* of the New Zhol Par khang edition.

45. See David P. Jackson, "The Earliest Printings of Tsong-kha-pa's Works: The Old Dga'-ldan Editions," in *Reflections on Tibetan Culture: Essays in Memory of Turrell V. Wylie*, ed. Lawrence Epstein and Richard F. Sherburne (Lewiston: The Edwin Mellen Press, 1990), 106, 114, n. 2.

46. See chapter 7 of Sde srid Sangs rgyas rgya mtsho (1653–1705), *Blang dor gsal bar ston pa'i drang thig dwangs shel me long nyer gcig pa* [comp. 1681], in *Blaṅ dor gsal bar ston pa'i draṅ thig dwaṅs śel me loṅ: A Treatise on the Sixteen Fundamental Principles of Tibetan Administrative Law* (Dolanji: Tibetan Bonpo Monastic Center, 1979), 1–83, at 37.6–40.2.

47. See 'Bri gung Che tshang IV Bstan 'dzin padma'i rgyal mtshan, *Nges don bstan pa'i snying po mgon po 'bri gung pa chen po'i gdan rabs chos kyi byung tshul gser gyi phreng ba*, 257–289 for a biography of Chos kyi grags pa, and 279.16–.22 for a brief account of this Kangyur production.

48. Chos kyi grags pa (1595–1659), *Bka' 'gyur gyi dkar chag gsal bar bkos pa chos kyi rnam grangs legs par rtogs byed*, in *The Collected Works (gsuṅ 'bum) of Kun-mkhyen Rig-pa 'dzin-pa Chen-po Chos-kyi-grags-pa* (Dehradun: Drikung Kagyu Institute, 1999), 2:11–174, at 165.4–166.1.

49. The following is based upon Chos kyi grags pa, *Bka' 'gyur bzhengs dus dpon yig rnams kyi bca' yig*, in *The Collected Works (gsuṅ 'bum) of Kun-mkhyen Rig-pa 'dzin-pa Chen-po Chos-kyi-grags-pa* (Dehradun: Drikung Kagyu Institute, 1999), 2:175–180. Chos kyi grags pa also briefly mentions the editorial guidelines employed by scribes at *Bka' 'gyur gyi dkar chag*, 166.6–167.4.

50. Chökyi Drakpa writes: "At the end and the breaks in *sūtras* and tantras, make a quadruple punctuation line of a full *mtho*. At the *bam po*, the *le'u*, the *skabs*, and the *brtag pa*. Place a single half-breadth punctuation line at intervals within many topics, at dividing points in mid-sized topics, at the end of short topics, and after words ending in *ga*. Despite the fact that it is said that at the close of prose passages and after words with an *o* one must place a double punctuation line, after words with an *o* such as *dbang po, dags po, kha mdogs dkar po*, there is no double punctuation line. Except after *nga*, there is no puncutation dot at the above punctuation lines. Use *'ang* and *yang* when the verse line is complete or incomplete. At the end of *ga, da, ba, sa*, and the *da drag* . . . and if those need to complete the

verse, write *yang*." (There follows a short passage on rules of euphonic combination of final letters and particles.)

51. There follows rules for editing archaic orthography: "Even though there is some difficulty reciting the *mya* (the letter *ma* letter with a subfixed *ya*) and the *da drag*, a thorough analysis of archaic translations reveals a *da drag* (a post-postfix letter *da*) every ten pages of scripture. The *mya* is not very necessary and dificult to recite, so dispense with it. Do not put the *da drag* after eleven pages. Now this is straight."

52. See David P. Jackson, *A History of Tibetan Painting: The Great Tibetan Painters and Their Traditions* (Wien: Verlag der Österreichischen Akademie der Wissenschaften, 1996), 76, 86, and notes 169–170, for a clarification of Bu ston's role as a planner in the production of maṇḍalas at Shalu.

53. Quoted in David Ganz, "Book Production in the Carolingian Empire and the Spread of the Caroline Minuscule," in *The New Cambridge Medieval History: Volume II c. 700–c. 900*, ed. Rosamond McKitterick (Cambridge, UK: Cambridge University Press, 1995), 786–807, at 791.

54. Matthew T. Kapstein, *The Tibetan Assimilation of Buddhism: Conversion, Contestation, and Memory* (New York and Oxford: Oxford University Press, 2000), 56. See Rosamond McKitterick, *The Carolingians and the Written Word* (Cambridge, UK: Cambridge University Press, 1989), 157–164 for a suggestive discussion of book ownership in Carolingian Europe.

55. Paul Harrison, "A Brief History of the Tibetan Kangyur," in *Tibetan Literature: Studies in Genre*, ed. José Ignacio Cabezón and Roger R. Jackson (Ithaca: Snow Lion, 1996), 85–86 touches on this issue.

56. The few studies of the life and works of the first 'Jam dbyangs bzhad pa'i rdo rje include Lokesh Chandra, "The Life and Works of 'Jam-dbyaṅs-bzhad-pa," *Central Asiatic Journal* 7, no. 4 (1962): 264–269; Jeffrey Hopkins, *Meditation on Emptiness* (London: Wisdom, 1983), 563–578; S. K. Sadhukhan, "Biography of the Eminent Tibetan Scholar 'Jam-dbyaṅs bshad-pa [*sic*] ṅag-dbaṅ brtson-'grus (A.D. 1648–1722)," *Tibet Journal* 16, no. 2 (1991): 19–33; Chizuko Yoshimizu, *Die Erkenntnislehre des Prāsaṅgika-Madhyamaka nach Dem Tshig gsal stoṅ thun gyi tshad ma'i rnam bśad des 'Jam dbyaṅs bźad pa'i rdo rje* (Wien: Arbeitskreis für Tibetische und Buddhistische Studien Universität Wien, 1996), 1–6. See Lokesh Chandra, *Materials for a History of Tibetan Literature* (New Delhi: Sharada Rani, 1963) for a brief summary of his *Collected Works*. On the monastery of Bla brang Bkra shis 'kyil, see Yonten Gyatso, "Le monastère de Bla-braṅ bkra-Śis 'khyil," in *Tibetan Studies: Proceedings of the 4th Seminar of the International Association for Tibetan Studies, Schloss Hohenkammer, Munich 1985*, ed. H. Uebach and J. L. Panglung (München: Kommission für Zentralasiatische Studien, Bayerische Akademie der Wissenschaften, 1988), 559–566.

57. Efforts to come to a greater precision regarding editorial terms—part of the motivation behind this chapter—may be found in A. Róna-Tas, "Some Notes on the Terminology of Mongolian Writing," *Acta Orientalia* 18 (1965): 119–147; Henry Serruys, "On Some 'Editorial' Terms in the Mongol Ganjur," *Bulletin of the School of Oriental and African Studies* 43, no. 3 (1980): 520–531; Friedrich A. Bischoff, "A Tibetan Glossary of Mongol 'Editorial' Terms," in *Suhṛllekhāḥ: Festgabe für Helmut Eimer*, ed. Michael Hahn, Jens-Uwe Hartmann, and Roland Steiner (Swisttal-Odendorf: IeT Verlag. 1996), 22–27.

58. Vladimir L. Uspensky, "The Life and Works of Ngag-dbang bkra-shis (1678–1738), the Second Abbot of the Bla-brang bkras-shis-'khyil Monastery," in *Proceedings of the 7th Seminar of the International Association for Tibetan Studies, Graz 1995*, ed. Helmut Eimer (Wien: Verlag der Österreichischen Akademie der Wissenschaften, 1997), 2:1005–1010 provides a very helpful biographical sketch of Ngag dbang bkra shis. See Leonard W. J. van der Kuijp, *An Introduction to Gtsang-nag-pa's Tshad-ma rnam-par nges-pa'i ṭi-ka legs-bshad bsdus-pa* (Kyoto: Rinsen Book Co., 1989), 17 for a brief discussion of this scholar's *bsdus grwa* work.

59. See 'Jam dbyangs bzhad pa'i rdo rje I Ngag dbang brtson 'grus (1648–1721), *'Phrin yig gi rnam par bzhag pa blo gsal rna rgyan sindhu wa'a ra'i phreng mdzes*, in *The Collected Works of 'Jam-dbyaṇs-bźad-pa'i-rdo-rje* (New Delhi: Ngawang Gelek Demo, 1974), 1:301–367.

60. A lag sha Ngag dbang bstan dar lha rams pa (1759–c. 1839), *Yi ge'i bshad pa mkhas pa'i kha rgyan*, in *Collected Gsung 'Bum of Bstan-dar lha-ram of A-lag-sha* (New Delhi: Lama Guru Deva, 1971), 2:215–266, at 226.1–.2. A brief biography of this scholar can be found in Ko zhul Grangs pa 'byung gnas and Rgya ba blo bzang mkhas grub, *Gangs can mkhas 'grub rim 'byon ming mdzod*, 1914–1916, though the authors give no year of death for him. The colophon to A lag sha Ngag dbang bstan dar lha rams pa, *Blo sbyong don bdun ma'i nyer mkho ba'i gtam theg mchog nye lam*, in *Collected Gsung 'Bum of Bstan-dar lha-ram of A-lag-sha* (New Delhi: Lama Guru Deva, 1971), 2:60–114, at 114 informs us that he composed the work in 1839 at the age of 81, thus suggesting that A lag sha lived until at least 1839.

61. 'Jam dbyangs bzhad pa'i rdo rje II Dkon mchog 'jigs med dbang po (1725–91), *Mkhas shing grub pa'i dbang phyug kun mkhyen 'jam dbyangs bzhad pa'i rdo rje'i rnam par thar pa ngo mtshar skal bzang 'jug ngogs*, in *The Collected Works of Dkon-mchog-'jigs-med-dbaṅ-po* (New Delhi: Ngawang Gelek Demo, 1971), 2:75–319, at 85.3–.5.

62. The centrality of the written word in the formation of this scholar's works stands in stark contrast to other collections in Tibetan literature that were created through the integration of spoken and written communication. As a rather arbitrary example one might cite the various redactions of the

Collected Works of Dagpo Lhajé Gampopa Sönam Rinchen (1079–1159), in which it is made clear that the actual writing down and, more importantly, the very arrangement of short spoken teachings into larger coherent works was undertaken by his disciples on the basis of his oral instruction. At the close of his *Teaching at an Assembly,* for instance, we read; "The holy religious teachings that were spoken to assembled clerics by the defender of the world, the glorious Gampopa, were noted down and anthologized by myself, the secretary Shogom Jangchub Yeshé" (Sgam po pa Bsod nams rin chen [1079–1159], *Tshogs chos yon tan phun tshogs,* in *Selected Writings of Sgam-po-pa Bsod-nams-rin-chen [Dwags-po lha-rje]* [Dolanji: Topden Tshering, 1974], 298–333, at 333).This difference has far-reaching implications for how the currently extant texts are treated. For instance, in the case of Gampopa we have no access to his teachings before they were written down by his students; whatever transformations occurred in the temporal and conceptual space between the words issuing from his mouth and the laying of pen to paper by his students or others are lost to us. In the case of Jamyang Shepé Dorjé this is not so; the block prints themselves are likely quite faithful reproductions of works written by the master himself, and it is quite possible that the autographs used by the editors some 200 years ago may come into the hands of present-day scholars.

63. 'Jam dbyangs bzhad pa'i rdo rje I Ngag dbang brtson 'grus, *Grub mtha'i rnam par bzhag pa 'khrul spong gdong lnga'i sgra dbyangs kun mkhyen lam bźang gsal ba'i rin chen sgron me.* in *The Collected Works of 'Jam-dbyaṅs-bźad-pa'i-rdo-rje* (New Delhi: Ngawang Gelek Demo, 1974), 1:221–257. Also *Collected Works,* 1:750–802;3:807–852; 15:1–31.

64. 'Jam dbyangs bzhad pa'i rdo rje I Ngag dbang brtson 'grus, *Skabs brgyad pa'i mtha' dpyod 'khrul sel gangga'a'i chu rgyun ma pham zhal lung,* in *The Collected Works of 'Jam-dbyaṅs-bźad-pa'i-rdo-rje* (New Delhi: Ngawang Gelek Demo, 1974), 8:335–537; *Phar phyin skabs brgyad pa'i mtha' dpyod bsam 'phel yid bzhin nor bu'i phreng mdzes skal bzang mig 'byed,* in *Collected Works,* 8:539–673.

65. See José Ignacio Cabezón, "Authorship and Literary Production in Classical Buddhist Tibet," in *Changing Minds: Contributions to the Study of Buddhism and Tibet in Honor of Jeffrey Hopkins,* ed. Guy Newland (Ithaca: Snow Lion, 2001), 233–264, for a discussion of the semantic range of *bris pa,* and more generally for a survey of information to be found in the colophons of Tibetan texts.

66. *myur bar sug bris su byas pa*: 'Jam dbyangs bzhad pa'i rdo rje I Ngag dbang brtson 'grus, *Kun mkhyen 'jam dbyangs bzhad pa'i rdo rje'i gsung 'bum thor bum khrig chags su bsdebs pa las smon la gyi skor,* in *The Collected Works of 'Jam-dbyaṅs-bźad-pa'i-rdo-rje* (New Delhi: Ngawang Gelek Demo, 1974), 1:735–749, at 749.

67. *'phral mar sug bris su byas pa*: 'Jam dbyangs bzhad pa'i rdo rje I Ngag
dbang brtson 'grus, *Chos kyi rje thams can mkhyen pa 'jam dbyangs bzhad
pa'i rdo rje'i gsung 'bum thor bu rnams khrigs chags su bsdebs pa las yi dam
sgrub skor*, in *The Collected Works of 'Jam-dbyaṅs-bźad-pa'i-rdo-rje* (New
Delhi: Ngawang Gelek Demo, 1974), 4:681–853, at 853.

68. *mtshams kyi thun mtshams zhig la bris pa*: 'Jam dbyangs bzhad pa'i rdo rje
I Ngag dbang brtson 'grus, *Kun mkhyen 'jam dbyangs bzhad pa'i rdo rje'i
gsung 'bum thor bum khrig chags su bsdebs pa las zhal gdams mgur ma'i skor*,
in *The Collected Works of 'Jam-dbyaṅs-bźad-pa'i-rdo-rje* (New Delhi: Ngawang Gelek Demo, 1974), 4:511–536, at 536.

69. 'Jam dbyangs bzhad pa'i rdo rje I Ngag dbang brtson 'grus, *Gzungs 'bul
gyi lhan thabs gnod sbyin dang tshogs bdag gi 'khor lo'i sgrub thabs*, in *The
Collected Works of 'Jam-dbyaṅs-bźad-pa'i-rdo-rje* (New Delhi: Ngawang
Gelek Demo, 1974), 1:510–522, at 522.

70. 'Jam dbyangs bzhad pa'i rdo rje I Ngag dbang brtson 'grus, *Kun mkhyen
'jam dbyangs bzhad pa'i rdo rje'i gsung 'bum thor bum khrig chags su bsdebs pa las 'pho ba'i bshad pa sogs*, in *The Collected Works of 'Jam-dbyaṅs-
bźad-pa'i-rdo-rje* (New Delhi: Ngawang Gelek Demo, 1974), 3:593–605,
at 604–605.

71. 'Jam dbyangs bzhad pa'i rdo rje I Ngag dbang brtson 'grus, *Bar ri brgya
rtsa'i rjes gnang gi lhan thabs dngos grub rin chen 'dren pa'i gru chen klag pas
don grub*, in *The Collected Works of 'Jam-dbyaṅs-bźad-pa'i-rdo-rje* (New
Delhi: Ngawang Gelek Demo, 1974), 3:289–359, at 358–359.

72. 'Jam dbyangs bzhad pa'i rdo rje I Ngag dbang brtson 'grus, *Rtags rigs kyi
rnam bzhag nyung gsal legs bshad*, in *The Collected Works of 'Jam-dbyaṅs-bźad-
pa'i-rdo-rje* (New Delhi: Ngawang Gelek Demo, 1974), 15:177–301, at 301.

73. 'Jam dbyangs bzhad pa'i rdo rje I Ngag dbang brtson 'grus, *Rje btsun bla
ma'i 'jam dbyangs bzhad pa'i gsung 'bum thor bu las sa chog*, in *The Collected Works of 'Jam-dbyaṅs-bźad-pa'i-rdo-rje* (New Delhi: Ngawang Gelek
Demo, 1974), 1:447–472, at 472.

74. Their names are: Dka' bcu Dkon mchog rgya mtsho and Dka' bcu Rab
brtan rgya mtsho, the supervisors Jo rigs thu Rab 'byams pa Blo bzang
bstan 'phel and Rab 'byams pa Kun dga' bstan 'dzin, the scribe Ngag
dbang chos 'byor, and the carver Kun dga' bstan 'dzin.

75. 'Jam dbyangs bzhad pa'i rdo rje I Ngag dbang brtson 'grus, *Bden bzhi'i
rnam bshad 'khrul bral lung rigs kyi nyi ma chen po*, in *The Collected Works
of 'Jam-dbyaṅs-bźad-pa'i-rdo-rje* (New Delhi: Ngawang Gelek Demo,
1974), 11:660–691, at 691.

76. 'Jam dbyangs bzhad pa'i rdo rje I Ngag dbang brtson 'grus, *Kun mkhyen
chen po 'jam dbyangs bzhad pa'i rdo rje'i gsung 'bum thor bum khrig chags
su bsdebs pa las do ha mdzod gyi mchan 'grel*, in *The Collected Works of
'Jam-dbyaṅs-bźad-pa'i-rdo-rje* (New Delhi: Ngawang Gelek Demo, 1974),
4:639–665, at 665.

77. 'Jam dbyangs bzhad pa'i rdo rje I Ngag dbang brtson 'grus, *Chos kyi rje thams can mkhyen pa 'jam dbyangs bzhad pa'i rdo rje'i gsung 'bum thor bu rnams khrigs chags su bsdebs pa las sna tshogs kyi skor,* in *The Collected Works of 'Jam-dbyaṅs-bźad-pa'i-rdo-rje* (New Delhi: Ngawang Gelek Demo, 1974), 4:479–510, at 506 (interlinear note).

78. *rje nyid kyi phyag bris ngo ma las bshus:* 'Jam dbyangs bzhad pa'i rdo rje I Ngag dbang brtson 'grus, *Rigs dang dkyil 'khor kun gyi bdag po khyab bdag bla ma dkon mchog mtshan can gyi bstod pa rig 'dzin grub pa'i sgra dbyangs,* in *The Collected Works of 'Jam-dbyaṅs-bźad-pa'i-rdo-rje* (New Delhi: Ngawang Gelek Demo, 1974), 15:63–71, at 70–71.

79. 'Jam dbyangs bzhad pa'i rdo rje I Ngag dbang brtson 'grus, *Bde mchog bskyed rim gyi bzhad pa'i zin bris,* in *The Collected Works of 'Jam-dbyaṅs-bźad-pa'i-rdo-rje* (New Delhi: Ngawang Gelek Demo, 1974), 2:325–345, at 345.

80. 'Jam dbyangs bzhad pa'i rdo rje I Ngag dbang brtson 'grus, *Darpa ?a a tsaryas mdzad pa'i gshin rje gshed dmar po'i 'tsho ba'i de kho na nyid la kun mkhyen 'jam dbyangs bzhad pas mchan 'god gnang ba,* in *The Collected Works of 'Jam-dbyaṅs-bźad-pa'i-rdo-rje* (New Delhi: Ngawang Gelek Demo, 1974), 4:629–638, at 638.

81. 'Jam dbyangs bzhad pa'i rdo rje I Ngag dbang brtson 'grus, *Rje red mda' ba'i dris lan gyi ṭikka rtsom 'phro,* in *The Collected Works of 'Jam-dbyaṅs-bźad-pa'i-rdo-rje* (New Delhi: Ngawang Gelek Demo, 1974), 3:543–571, at 571.

82. 'Jam dbyangs bzhad pa'i rdo rje I Ngag dbang brtson 'grus, *Chos kyi rje thams can mkhyen pa 'jam dbyangs bzhad pa'i rdo rje'i gsan yig thor bu gang rnyed phyogs gcig tu bsgrigs pa la tshan pa dang po,* in *The Collected Works of 'Jam-dbyaṅs-bźad-pa'i-rdo-rje* (New Delhi: Ngawang Gelek Demo, 1974), 4:5–124, at 124.

83. 'Jam dbyangs bzhad pa'i rdo rje I Ngag dbang brtson 'grus, *Kun mkhyen 'jam dbyangs bzhad pa'i rdo rje'i gsung 'bum las byang chub lam rim gyi rnams bshad lung rigs gter mdzod,* in *The Collected Works of 'Jam-dbyaṅs-bźad-pa'i-rdo-rje* (New Delhi: Ngawang Gelek Demo, 1974), 4:337–477, at 477.

84. 'Jam dbyangs bzhad pa'i rdo rje I Ngag dbang brtson 'grus, *Bstan bcos mngon par rtogs pa'i rgyan gyi mtha' dpyod shes rab kyi pha rol tu phyin pa'i don kun gsal ba'i rin chen sgron me,* in *The Collected Works of 'Jam-dbyaṅs-bźad-pa'i-rdo-rje* (New Delhi: Ngawang Gelek Demo, 1974), vols. 7–8.

85. Dbal mang Dkon mchog rgyal mtshan (1764–1853), *Mdo smad bstan pa'i 'byung gnas dpal ldan bkra shis dkyil gyi gdan rabs rang bzhin dbyangs su brjod pa'i lha'i rnga bo che,* in *The Collected Works of Dbal-maṅ Dkon-mchog-rgyal-mtshan* (New Delhi: Gyaltsan Gelek Namgyal, 1974), 1:1–613, at 329.1–2. A useful summary of the contents of Dbal mang Dkon mchog rgyal mtshan's chronicle of Labrang Tashikyil Monastery can be found

in A. I. Vostrikov, *Tibetan Historical Literature* (Surrey, England: Curzon Press, 1994), 89, n. 291.

86. This passage likely refers to the rebellion against China by the Kokonor ruler Bstan 'dzin Ching wang in 1723 and the subsequent retribution by the Chinese troops in 1724. See for instance Ho-chin Yang, *The Annals of Kokonor* (Bloomington: Indiana University, 1970), 49–50, and Smith, *Among Tibetan Texts*, 136.

87. One Lha dbang Pi chi ji: *Pi chi ji* is perhaps a Tibetan phonetic rendering of the Mongolian term *bichigechi*. See A. Róna-Tas, "Some Notes on the Terminology of Mongolian Writing," *Acta Orientalia Hungarica* 18 (1965): 119–147, at 127.

88. His biography can be found in Dbal mang Dkon mchog rgyal mtshan, *Mdo smad bstan pa'i 'byung gnas dpal ldan bkra shis dkyil gyi gdan rabs*, 448.4–457.2.

89. Dbal mang Dkon mchog rgyal mtshan, *Mdo smad bstan pa'i 'byung gnas dpal ldan bkra shis dkyil gyi gdan rabs*, 329.2–3. Vladimir Uspensky writes in "The Life and Works of Ngag-dbang bkra-shis, the Second Abbot of the Bla-brang bkras-shis-'khyil Monastery," 1007, that "Ngag-dbang bkra-shis had hidden the authentic writings of his late teacher." This may be implied, but it is not precisely what Dbal mang Dkon mchog rgyal mtshan has written.

90. Dkon mchog rgyal mtshan, *Mdo smad bstan pa'i 'byung gnas dpal ldan bkra shis dkyil gyi gdan rabs*, 344.2–3. According to Uspensky, "The Life and Works of Ngag-dbang bkra-shis," 1007, "The monastic chronicles say that Ngag-dbang-bkra-shis was the unrivalled progapator of the works of his teacher, 'Jam-dbyangs-bzhad-pa'i rdo-rje, whose works he printed in the new monastery." He gives no reference for this statement, and aside from the above passage, I have not been able to locate such a strong statement in Dbal mang Dkon mchog rgyal mtshan, *Mdo smad bstan pa'i 'byung gnas dpal ldan bkra shis dkyil gyi gdan rabs*.

91. 'Jam dbyangs bzhad pa'i rdo rje I Ngag dbang brtson 'grus, *Dbu ma 'jug pa'i mtha' dpyod lung rigs gter mdzod zab don kun gsal bzang 'jug ngogs*, in *The Collected Works of 'Jam-dbyaṅs-bźad-pa'i-rdo-rje* (New Delhi: Ngawang Gelek Demo, 1974), 9:3–885.

92. 'Jam dbyangs bzhad pa'i rdo rje I Ngag dbang brtson 'grus, *Bstan bcos mngon par rtogs pa'i rgyan gyi mtha' dpyod shes rab kyi pha rol tu phyin pa'i don kun gsal ba'i rin chen sgron me*.

93. 'Jam dbyangs bzhad pa'i rdo rje I Ngag dbang brtson 'grus, *'Dul ba'i dka' gnas rnam par dpyad pa 'khrul spong blo gsal mgul rgyan tsinta ma ni'i phreng mdzes skal bzang re ba kun skong las gzhi stod* and *gzhi smad*, in *The Collected Works of 'Jam-dbyaṅs-bźad-pa'i-rdo-rje* (New Delhi: Ngawang Gelek Demo, 1974), 6:3–633, 635–959.

94. See Hopkins, *Meditation on Emptiness*, 564.

95. The earth-tiger year (*sa stag*). See 'Jam dbyangs bzhad pa'i rdo rje II Dkon mchog 'jigs med dbang po, *Mkhas shing grub pa'i dbang phyug kun mkhyen 'jam dbyangs bzhad pa'i rdo rje'i rnam par thar pa*, 319.1.

96. 'Jam dbyangs bzhad pa'i rdo rje I Ngag dbang brtson 'grus, *Kun mkhyen 'jams dbyangs bzhad pas mdzad pa'i thal 'gyur che ba'i rnam bzhag mdor bsdus*, in *The Collected Works of 'Jam-dbyaṅs-bźad-pa'i-rdo-rje* (New Delhi: Ngawang Gelek Demo, 1974), 3:775–793, at 793.

97. A Har chin Ching wang Ratnasiddhi patronized the long biography of Lcang skya II Rol pa'i rdo rje (1717–86), which was composed sometime between 1792 and 1794; see Smith, *Among Tibetan Texts*, 133.

98. 'Jam dbyangs bzhad pa'i rdo rje I Ngag dbang brtson 'grus, *Dpal rdo rje 'jigs byed kyi chos 'byung khams gsum las rnam par rgyal ba dngos grub kyi gter mdzod*, in *The Collected Works of 'Jam-dbyaṅs-bźad-pa'i-rdo-rje* (New Delhi: Ngawang Gelek Demo, 1974), 5:3–835, at 834–835.

99. See Lokesh Chandra, ed., *The Amarakoṣa in Tibet* (New Delhi: International Academy of Indian Culture, 1965).

100. See 'Jam dbyangs bzhad pa'i rdo rje II Dkon mchog 'jigs med dbang po, *Mkhas shing grub pa'i dbang phyug kun mkhyen 'jam dbyangs bzhad pa'i rdo rje'i rnam par thar pa*, 270.6–271.1.

101. The following is taken from 'Jam dbyangs bzhad pa'i rdo rje I Ngag dbang brtson 'grus, *Mngon brjod kyi bstan bcos 'chi ba med pa'i mdzod*, in *The Collected Works of 'Jam-dbyaṅs-bźad-pa'i-rdo-rje* (New Delhi: Ngawang Gelek Demo, 1974), 15:567–791, at 790–791.

102. Anonymous, *Sgron ma gsal bar byed pa zhes bya ba'i rgya cher bshad pa*: Hakuji Ui, et al., *A Complete Catalog of the Tibetan Buddhist Canons*, no. 1785. I have been unable to locate an overt reference to the *Amarakoṣa* in the *Pradīpodyotana*.

103. Dbal mang Dkon mchog rgyal mtshan, *Mdo smad bstan pa'i 'byung gnas dpal ldan bkra shis dkyil gyi gdan rabs*, 329.4.

104. See Brag dgon Dkon mchog bstan pa rab rgyas (1800/1–66), *Yul mdo smad kyi ljongs su thub bstan rin po che ji ltar dar ba'i tshul gsal bar brjod pa deb ther rgya mtsho* (Lanzhou: Kan su'u mi rigs dpe skrun khang, 1982), 368.12–.19.

3. THE SCHOLAR'S DREAM

1. Skyogs ston Lo tsā ba Rin chen bkra shis, *Rje btsun zhwa lu lo tsā ba'i rnam par thar pa brjed byang nor bu'i khri shing* [comp. 1517] (Beijing: CPN manuscript, 42 folios), fol. 32b.4–.6.

2. Mang thos Klu sgrub rgya mtsho (1523–1596), *Bstan rtsis gsal ba'i nyin byed lhag bsam rab dkar*, in *Bstan rstis gsal ba'i nyin byed* (Lhasa: Bod ljongs mi dmangs dpe skrun khang, 1987), 1–251, at 233–236. Composed during Shalu Lotsawa's life, Rinchen Tashi's 1517 biography is likely drawn in great part from an earlier work by the Sakyapa scholar Bum-

trag Sumpa (1433–1504), a student of the first abbot of Ngor monastery, Kunga Zangpo (1382–1465). Essentially the same work is also included in Ngawang Kunga Sönam's 1636 history of the *Kālacakra Tantra*, which is explicitly based primarily on Rinchen Tashi's earlier work. See 'Jam mgon A myes zhabs Ngag dbang kun dga' bsod nams (1597–1662), *Dpal dus kyi 'khor lo'i zab pa dang rgya che ba'i dam pa'i chos 'byung ba'i tshul legs par bshad pa ngo mtshar dad pa'i shing rta* (TBRC: manuscript, 282 folios), at fols. 126a.6–170a.3. Ngawang Kunga Sönam's work fortunately picks up where Rinchen Tashi's leaves off, taking us from 1517 to Shalu Lotsawa's death in 1528.

3. Franco Ricca and Erberto Lo bue, *The Great Stūpa of Gyantse: A Complete Tibetan Pantheon of the Fifteenth Century* (London: Serindia Publications, 1993), 18–28.

4. Pieter C. Verhagen, "'Royal' Patronage of Sanskrit Grammatical Studies in Tibet," in *Ritual, State, and History in South Asia: Essays in Honour of J. C. Heesterman*, ed. A W. van den Hoek, D. H. A. Kolff, and M. S. Oort (Leiden: Brill, 1992), 374–392, has stressed the importance of the relationship between patronage and textual scholarship.

5. Skyogs ston Lo tsā ba Rin chen bkra shis, *Rje btsun zhwa lu lo tsā ba'i rnam par thar pa*, fol. 26a.4.

6. Skyogs ston Lo tsā ba Rin chen bkra shis, *Rje btsun zhwa lu lo tsā ba'i rnam par thar pa*, fol. 27a.5

7. Skyogs ston Lo tsā ba Rin chen bkra shis, *Rje btsun zhwa lu lo tsā ba'i rnam par thar pa*, fol. 27b.3.

8. Skyogs ston Lo tsā ba Rin chen bkra shis, *Rje btsun zhwa lu lo tsā ba'i rnam par thar pa*, fol. 27b.5.

9. Skyogs ston Lo tsā ba Rin chen bkra shis, *Rje btsun zhwa lu lo tsā ba'i rnam par thar pa*, fol. 28a.6. There also appear to have been Indian *bhikṣus* among the Karmapa's entourage, for Shalu Lotsawa gave teachings to one.

10. Zhwa lu Ri phug Sprul sku Blo gsal bstan skyong (1804–c. 1874), *Dpal ldan zhwa lu pa'i bstan pa la bka' drin che ba'i skyes bu dam pa rnams kyi rnam thar lo rgyus ngo mtshar dad pa'i 'jug ngogs*, in *On the History of the the Monastery of Zhwa-lu* (Leh: Tashi Yangphel Tashigang, 1971), 384.1.

11. Skyogs ston Lo tsā ba Rin chen bkra shis, *Rje btsun zhwa lu lo tsā ba'i rnam par thar pa*, fol. 31a.5.

12. Skyogs ston Lo tsā ba Rin chen bkra shis, *Rje btsun zhwa lu lo tsā ba'i rnam par thar pa*, fol. 32a.4.

13. Skyogs ston Lo tsā ba Rin chen bkra shis, *Rje btsun zhwa lu lo tsā ba'i rnam par thar pa*, fol. 22b.

14. Skyogs ston Lo tsā ba Rin chen bkra shis, *Rje btsun zhwa lu lo tsā ba'i rnam par thar pa*, fol. 24a.3.

15. Skyogs ston Lo tsā ba Rin chen bkra shis, *Rje btsun zhwa lu lo tsā ba'i rnam par thar pa*, fol. 39b.4.

16. Skyogs ston Lo tsā ba Rin chen bkra shis, *Rje btsun zhwa lu lo tsā ba'i rnam par thar pa*, fol. 25a.6.

17. Skyogs ston Lo tsā ba Rin chen bkra shis, *Rje btsun zhwa lu lo tsā ba'i rnam par thar pa*, fol. 29b.5.

18. Portions of the following draw from Kurtis R. Schaeffer, "Dying Like Milarepa: Death Accounts in a Tibetan Hagiographic Tradition," in *The Buddhist Dead: Practices, Discourses, Representations*, ed. Bryan J. Cuevas and Jaqueline I. Stone (Honolulu: University of Hawaii Press), 208–233.

19. Author unknown, *Rnal 'byor dbang phyug lha btsun chos kyi rgyal po'i rnam thar gyi smad cha* (Kathmandu: NGMPP L456/7. 32 folios), 22b.4.

20. This version of the story is based upon Lha btsun pa Rin chen rnam rgyal (1473–1557), *Grub thob gtsang smyon pa'i rnam thar dad pa'i spu slong g.yo ba*, in *Bde mchog mkha' 'gro snyan rgyud (ras chung snyan rgyuad), Two Manuscript Collections of Texts from the Yig-cha of Gtsang-smyong He-ru-ka* (Leh: S. W. Tashigangpa, 1971), 1:1–129 (folios 1–65), fols. 48b.3–50a.3.

21. Andrew H. Quintman, *Mi la ras pa's Many Lives: Anatomy of a Tibetan Biographical Corpus* (Ph.D. diss., University of Michigan, 2006), details the history of the Milarepa poetic corpus up to Tsangnyön Heruka.

22. George N. Roerich, trans., *The Blue Annals* (New Delhi: Motilal Banarsidass, 1976), 707; 'Gos Lo tsā ba Gzhon nu dpal (1392–1481), *Deb ther sngon po* (New Delhi: International Academy of Indian Culture, 1974), 618.3.

23. Tshal pa Kun dga' rdo rje (1309–64), *Deb ther dmar po rnams kyi dang po hu lan deb ther* (Beijing: Mi rigs dpe skrun khang, 1981), 79.21.

24. Stag lung Ngag dbang rnam rgyal (1571–1626), *Brgyud pa yid bzhin nor bu'i rtogs pa brjod pa ngo mtshar rgya mtsho* (Lhasa: Bod yig dpe rnying dpe skrun khang, 1992), 470. Mention of this occurs in the story of the twelfth Abbot of Stag lung, Ngag dbang grags pa dpal bzang (1418–96).

25. Karma pa III Rang byung rdo rje (1284–1339), *Rnal 'byor gyi dbang phyug mi la bzhad pa rdo rje'i gsung mgur mdzod nag ma zhes pa karma pa rang byung rdo rjes phyogs gcig tu bkod pa* (Dalhousie: Damchoe Sangpo, 1978), 2:553.6. The attribution of this work to Rang byung rdo rje requires inquiry: the colophon at vol. 2, 553.2–554.1 does not state that the work was composed by Rang byung rdo rje, but rather that it was compiled based upon his work.

26. E. Gene Smith, *Among Tibetan Texts: History and Literature of the Himalayan Plateau*, ed. Kurtis R. Schaeffer (Boston: Wisdom, 2001), 70–73; Helmut Eimer and Pema Tsering, "Blockprints and Manuscripts of Mi la ras pa's *Mgur 'bum* Accessible to Frank-Richard Hamm," in *Frank-Richard Hamm Memorial Volume*, ed. Helmut Eimer (Bonn: Indica et Tibetica

Verlag, 1990), 59–88. Note that Eimer and Tsering's edition "J" of the *Mi la'i mgur 'bum*, a "Xylograph in the British Library, formerly belonging to Heinrich August Jäschke (1817–1883)" (71–72), appears to be a print of the blocks carved by Gtsang smyon's student Lha btsun pa Rin chen rnam rgyal in the 1550s.

27. Thu'u bkwan Blo bzang chos kyi nyi ma (1737–1802), *Khyab bdag rdo rje sems dpa'i ngo bo dpal ldan bla ma dam pa ye shes bstan pa'i sgron me dpal bzang po'i rnam par thar pa mdo tsam brjod pa dge ldan bstan pa'i mdzes rgyan* (Lanzhou: Kan su'u mi rigs dpe skrun khang, 1989), 43–44. The story of Gtsang smyon is located at 38–45. Blo bzang chos kyi nyi ma used Rgod tshang ras pa's *rnam thar* to write this summary; see Thu'u bkwan Blo bzang chos kyi nyi ma, *Khyab bdag rdo rje sems dpa'i ngo bo dpal ldan bla ma dam pa ye shes bstan pa'i sgron me dpal bzang po'i rnam par thar pa*, 45.9–.11. See Smith, *Among Tibetan Texts*, chapter 11, for more on this *rnam thar*.

28. Smith, *Among Tibetan Texts*, 60, 285, n. 141.

29. Rgod tshang ras pa Sna tshogs rang grol (1494–1570), *Gtsang smyon he ru ka phyogs thams cad las rnam par rgyal ba'i rnam thar rdo rje theb pa'i gsal byed nyi ma'i snying po*, in *The Life of the Saint of Gtsaṅ* (New Delhi: Sharada Rani, 1969), 8.1.

30. Rgod tshang ras pa Sna tshogs rang grol, *Gtsang smyon he ru ka phyogs thams cad las rnam par rgyal ba'i rnam thar*, 4.5.

31. These dates are taken from Ko shul Grags pa 'byung gnas and Rgyal ba Blo bzang mkhas grub, *Gangs can mkhas grub rim byon ming mdzod* (Lanzhou: Kan su'u mi rigs dpe skrun khang, 1992), 1613–1614.

32. For instance, Tsangnyön styles Milarepa's final opponent as a Buddhist scholar critical of Milarepa's antischolastic ways rather than the Bonpo priest of Rgyal thang pa's thirteenth-century account. See Francis V. Tiso, "The Death of Milarepa: Towards a *Redaktionsgeschichte* of the *Mila rnam thar* Traditions," in *Tibetan Studies: Proceedings of the 7th Seminar of the International Association of Tibetan Studies, Graz 1995*, ed. Helmut Krasser et al. (Wien: Verlag der Österreichischen Akademie der Wissenschaften, 1997), 2:987–995, at 994.

33. The twelve acts of the Buddha: 1. Descent into the world from Dga' ldan; 2. Entry into the womb; 3. Birth; 4. Miracles; 5. Delights with a wife; 6. Departure; 7. Ascetic practice; 8. Going to the heart of enlightenment; 9. Becoming Buddha; 10. Turning the wheel of dharma; 11. Magical apparitions; 12. Death. There are variations on this list.

34. Rgod tshang ras pa Sna tshogs rang grol, *Gtsang smyon he ru ka phyogs thams cad las rnam par rgyal ba'i rnam thar*, 72.6–73.2.

35. Rgod tshang ras pa Sna tshogs rang grol, *Gtsang smyon he ru ka phyogs thams cad las rnam par rgyal ba'i rnam thar*, 137.7–138.7. See Quintman, *Mi la ras pa's Many Lives*, 199–200, for another translation of this passage.

36. Rgod tshang ras pa Sna tshogs rang grol, *Gtsang smyon he ru ka phyogs thams cad las rnam par rgyal ba'i rnam thar*, 161.6.

37. In the late 1960s E. Gene Smith was able to provide details on some twenty-two works published in wood-block print by Tsangnyön and his disciples; see Smith, *Among Tibetan Texts*, chapter 5. Today we have access to more than fifty extant prints from the same group of scholars and crafstmen; see Kurtis R. Schaeffer, "The Printing Projects of Tsangnyön Heruka and His Disciples," paper presented at the eleventh seminar of the International Association for Tibetan Studies, 2006.

38. The works produced by Gotsang Repa are nearly all undated. Most were printed at the hermitage of Rechungpuk during Gotsang Repa's lifetime, so the terminus ante quem for his corpus is 1570.

39. Of these, fourteen have publishing dates, ranging from 1538 to 1563, though this latter date is problematic because Rinchen Namgyel is believed to have died in 1557.

40. See Author Unknown, *Rnal 'byor dbang phyug lha btsun chos kyi rgyal po'i rnam thar gyi smad cha*, 8a.1. See also a reference to printing of Ras chung's *Rnam thar* and *Mgur 'bum* at 12a.1 and 22a.6.

41. Brag dkar rta so Sprul sku Chos kyi dbang phyug (1775–1837), *Grub pa'i gnas chen brag dkar rta so'i gnas dang gdan rabs bla ma brgyud pa'i lo rgyus mdo tsam brjod pa mos ldan dad pa'i gdung sel drang srong dga' ba'i dal gtam* [comp. 1816] (Kathmandu: NGMPP 940/8, 52 folios), 22b.4–23b.1. See also 29b.2, at which Rin chen rnam rgyal establishes a printing house at Brag dkar rta so, and 34a.5, at which Karma blo bzang renovates the printing house.

42. Wood blocks were carved for major works in Mangyul Gungtang as early as the late fifteenth century. See Franz-Karl Ehrhard, *Early Buddhist Block Prints from Mang-yul Gung-thang* (Lumbini: Lumbini International Research Institute, 2000), esp. 13–18; Franz-Karl Ehrhard, *Four Unknown Mahāmudrā Works of the Bo-dong-pa School* (Lumbini: Lumbini International Research Institute, 2000), xiv. Such major works as Longchenpa's 500-folio *Treasury of the Supreme Way* were printed in the early 1530s; see Franz-Karl Ehrhard, *The Oldest Block Print of Klong-chen Rab-'byams-pa's Theg mchog mdzod* (Lumbini: Lumbini International Research Institute, 2000), xvi. A book of spells had been printed at the monastery of Pelkor Chodé in Gyantsé in 1539, and Sakya Pandita's famouse *Analysis of the Three Vows* was printed near Sakya in the 1540s; see Hidetoshi Fushimi, "Recent Finds from the Old Sa-skya Xylographic Edition," *Wiener Zeitschrift für die Kunde Südasiens und Archiv für Indische Philosophie* 43 (1999): 97–98.

43. Gtsang smyon He ru ka (1452–1507), *Rnal 'byor gyi dbang phyug dam pa rje btsun mi la ras pa'i rnam par thar pa dang thams cad mkhyen pa'i*

lam ston (Kathmandu: NGMPP L250/7, 115 folios), print colophon at 111a.6–115a.5.

44. Mentioned in Kaḥ thog Tshe dbang nor bu (1698–1755), *Bod rje lha bt-sad po'i gdung rabs mnga' ris smad gung thang du ji ltar byung ba'i tshul deb ther dwangs shel 'phrul gyi me long*, in *Bod kyi lo rgyus deb ther khag lnga* (Lhasa: Bod ljongs bod yig dpe rnying dpe skrun khang, 1990), 87–150, at 135.10.

45. Bya bral pa Tshul khrims dpal ldan (circa 16th century), *Mkhas grub rdo rje 'chang bsod nams blo gros kyi rnam thar yon tan gyi sbrang rtsi la dad pa'i bung ba rnam par rol pa* (Kathmandu: NGMPP L833/3), f. 53b. This biography was composed in Nyi shar in 1544.

46. Bya bral pa Tshul khrims dpal ldan, *Mkhas grub rdo rje 'chang bsod nams blo gros kyi rnam thar*, fols. 42b.2–43a.6.

47. The following is taken from Rgod tshang ras pa Sna tshogs rang grol, *Gt-sang smyon he ru ka phyogs thams cad las rnam par rgyal ba'i rnam thar*, 104b–113b. The second of Tsangnyön's three journeys to Kathmandu is detailed in Todd T. Lewis and Lozang Jamspal, "Newars and Tibetan in the Kathmandu Valley: Three New Translations from Tibetan Sources," *Journal of Asian and African Studies* 36 (1988): 187–211. See also Kurtis R. Schaeffer, *Himalayan Hermitess: The Life of a Tibetan Buddhist Nun* (Oxford and New York: Oxford University Press, 2005), 112 for Lhatsün Rinchen Namgyel's journey to the valley in the 1530s.

48. Rgod tshang ras pa Sna tshogs rang grol (1494–1570), *Rje btsun ras chung rdo rje grags kyi rnam thar rnam mkhyen thar lam rin po che gsal ba'i me long ye shes snang ba* (Kathmandu: NGMPP E2080/2), f. 240b.1.

49. On which see Kurtis R. Schaeffer, "Tibetan Narratives on Buddha's Acts at Vajrasana: Putting Hagiography in Place," in *Life of the Buddha: New Perspectives and Discoveries*, ed. Sonya Quintanilla (Leiden and New York: Brill, forthcoming).

4. THE PHYSICIAN'S LAMENT

1. G.yu thog Yon tan mgon po (1126–1202), *Bdud rtsi snying po yan lag brgyad pa gsang ba man ngag gi rgyud* (Lhasa: Bod ljongs mi dmangs dpe skrun khang, 1992), 99.8–.10.

2. The Fifth Dalai Lama's activities in this area were largely restricted to patronizing court physicians and their work editing and printing important medical works and composing new commentaries upon them. See Sde srid Sangs rgyas rgya mtsho, *Dpal mnyam med ri bo dga' ldan pa'i bstan pa zhwa ser cod pan 'chang ba'i ring lugs chos thams cad kyi rtsa ba gsal bar byed pa'i baiḍū rya ser po'i me long* (Beijing: Krung go bod kyi shes rig dpe skrun khang, 1991), 364–372.

3. For summaries of Sangs rgyas rgya mtsho's medical activities, see Fernand Meyer, "Introduction: The Medical Paintings of Tibet," in *Tibetan Medical Paintings: Illustrations to the Blue Beryl Treatise of Sangye Gyamtso (1653–1705)*, ed. Yuri Parfionovitch, Gyurme Dorjé, and Fernand Meyer (New York: Abrams, 1992), 1:2–13, at 6–7; Fernand Meyer, "Theory and Practice of Tibetan Medicine," in *Oriental Medicine: An Illustrated Guide to the Asian Arts of Healing*, ed. Jan van Alphen and Anthony Aris (Boston: Shambala, 1995), 109–141, at 116–118; Fernand Meyer, "The History and Foundations of Tibetan Medicine," in *The Buddha's Art of Healing: Tibetan Paintings Rediscovered*, ed. John fol. Avedon (New York: Rizzoli, 1998), 21–31, at 29–30; Rechung Rinpoche, *Tibetan Medicine: Illustrated in Original Texts* (Berkeley: University of California Press, 1976), 21–22; Pasang Yonten, "A History of the Tibetan Medical System," *Tibetan Medicine (gSo-rig)* 12 (1989): 32–51, esp. 45–47. Modern Tibetan studies include Dkon mchog rin chen, *Bod kyi gso rig dar tshul rgyas bsdus 'tsham par bkod pa bai ḍurya'i 'phreng ba* (Lanzhou: Kan su'u mi rigs dpe skrun khang, 1992), 115–121; Sman rams pa Pa sangs yon tan, *Bod kyi gso ba rig pa'i lo rgyus kyi bang mdzod g.yu thog bla ma dran pa'i pho nya* (Leh: Yuthok Institute of Tibetan Medicine, 1988), 136–143; Byams pa 'phrin las (1928–), *Gangs ljongs gso rig bstan pa'i nyin byed rim byon gyi rnam thar phyogs bsgrigs* (Beijing: Mi rigs dpe skrun khang, 1990), 313–317; and especially Byams pa 'phrin las, *Sde srid sangs rgyas rgya mtsho'i 'khrungs rabs dang mdzad rjes dad brgya'i padma rnam par bzhad pa'i phreng ba*, in *Byams pa 'phrin las kyi gsung rtsom phyogs bsgrigs* (Beijing: Krung go'i bod kyi shes rig dpe skrun khang, 1996), 402–442. See also Kristina Lange, *Die Werke des Regenten Saṅs rgyas rgya mc'o (1653–1705): Eine philologisch-historische Studie zum tibetischsprachigen Schriftum* (Berlin: Akademie-Verlag, 1976) for a comparative list of his writings. Wang Lei, *The Medical History of Tibet* (Hong Kong: Shanghai Foreign Language Education Press, 1994) is a rough paraphrase of Sangyé Gyatso's *Beryl Mirror*.

4. Sde srid Sangs rgyas rgya mtsho, *Dpal ldan gso ba rig pa'i khog 'bugs legs bshad ba'i ḍūrya'i me long drang srong dgyes pa'i dga' ston* (Lanzhou: Kan su'u mi rigs dpe skrun khang, 1982). See Dan Martin, *Tibetan Histories: A Bibliography of Tibetan-Language Historical Works* (London: Serindia Publications, 1997), entry 259, for further bibliographic information.

5. See Gyurme Dorjé, "The Structure and Contents of the Four Tantras and Sangyé Gyamtso's Commentary, the Blue Beryl," in *Tibetan Medical Paintings: Illustrations to the Blue Beryl Treatise of Sangye Gyamtso (1653–1705)*, ed. Yuri Parfionovitch, Gyurme Dorjé, and Fernand Meyer (New York: Abrams, 1992), 1:14–15, for a helpful outline of the contents of the *Four Tantras*.

6. Chapter 31 of the *Explanatory Tantra* is represented in plate 37 of Sangyé Gyatso's medical paintings. See Yuri Parfionovitch, Gyurme Dorjé, and Fernand Meyer, *Tibetan Medical Paintings: Illustrations to the Blue Beryl Treatise of Sangye Gyamtso (1653–1705)* (New York: Abrams, 1992), 1:89–90; 2:245–246.

7. Gyu thog Yon tan mgon po, *Bdud rtsi snying po yan lag brgyad pa gsang ba man ngag gi rgyud*, 96.2–.3. See also Barry Clark, trans., *The Quintessence Tantras of Tibetan Medicine* (Ithaca: Snow Lion, 1995), 223 for an alternative translation.

8. G.yu thog Yon tan mgon po, *Bdud rtsi snying po yan lag brgyad pa gsang ba man ngag gi rgyud*, 98.1–.2. Quoted in Sde srid Sangs rgyas rgya mtsho, *Dpal ldan gso ba rig pa'i khog 'bugs legs bshad ba'i ḍūrya'i me long*, 517.7–.8. See Clark, *The Quintessence Tantras of Tibetan Medicine*, 226. See also the twelfth-century commentary on these lines, which employs the same examples; Sum ston pa Ye shes gzungs (12th century), *'Grel pa 'bum chung gsal sgron nor bu'i 'phreng mdzes*, in *Gyu thog cha lag bco brgyad: A Corpus of Tibetan Medical Teachings Attributed to Gyu-thog the Physician Reproduced from a Set of Prints from the 17th Century Lhasa Żol Blocks* (Dolanji: Tibetan Bonpo Monastic Center, 1976), vol. 1, fols. 157–301, at fol. 57a.5.

9. Sde srid Sangs rgyas rgya mtsho, *Gso ba rig pa'i bstan bcos sman bla'i dgongs rgyan rgyud bzhi'i gsal byed bai ḍūr sngon po'i ma lli ka*, 4 vols. (Leh: D. L. Tashigang, 1981) [comp. 1688: Sde dge blockprint, 1748], 2:494.3–.5.

10. In the opening verses of the *Beryl Mirror* Sangs rgyas rgya mtsho elaborates on the title of his work, describing it as an exposition (*legs bshad*) that penetrates (*'bugs*) the interior (*khog*) of the medical tradition. See Sde srid Sangs rgyas rgya mtsho, *Dpal ldan gso ba rig pa'i khog 'bugs legs bshad ba'i ḍūrya'i me long*, 7–8. Although the implications of the Tibetan term *khog 'bugs/dbug*, the name of the genre of writing in which Sangs rgyas rgya mtsho places his work, have not been explored fully, it seems to refer primarily to the historical study of the lineages and texts of the medical tradition as well as the presentation of the ideal physician's education and qualities. Indeed, these subjects make up almost the whole of Sangs rgyas rgya mtsho's *Beryl Mirror*. G.yu thog Yon tan mgon po, *Khog dbug khyung chen lding ba*, in *Gyu thog cha lag bco brgyad: A Corpus of Tibetan Medical Teachings Attributed to Gyu-thog the Physician Reproduced from a Set of Prints from the 17th Century Lhasa Żol Blocks* (Dolanji: Tibetan Bonpo Monastic Center, 1976), vol. 1, fols. 1–16, at fols. 3a.5–8a.4 offers an early analysis of the term. The parameters of the genre as delineated by Tibetan scholars deserve separate study.

11. Brang ti Dpal ldan 'tsho byed (early 14th century.), *Bdud rtsi snying po yan lag brgyad gsang ba man ngag gi rgyud kyi spyi don shes bya rab gsas rgyas pa* (CPN manuscript, 48 fols.). Although this work does not contain the

word '*khog 'bugs* in its title, and Sangs rgyas rgya mtsho does not cite it
as such, it is structured in much the same way as both the *Beryl Mirror*
and Zur mkhar Blo gros rgyal po's *Khog dbub*: Zur mkhar Blo gros rgyal po (1509–c. 1573), *Gang dag byang chub sems dpa'i spyad pa spyod par
'dod pa'i sman pa rnams kyis mi shes mi rung ba'i phyi nang gzhan gsum gyis
rnam bzhag shes bya spyi khog dbub pa gtan pa med pa'i mchod sbyin gyi sgo
'phar yangs po* (Chengdu: Si khron mi rigs dpe skrun khang, 2001). The
death date of Blo gros rgyal po is not known, though he lived until at least
1573, as this is when he composed a short defense of the *Four Tantras* as
the Word (*bka'*) of the Buddha: Zur mkhar Blo gros rgyal po, *Rgyud bzhi
bka' dang bstan bcos rnam par dbye ba mun sel sgrom mes*, in *Bod kyi sman
rtsis ched rtsom phyogs bsdus* (Lhasa: Bod ljongs mi dmangs dpe skrun
khang, 1986), 64–71, at 71.

12. This is no more than a rough impression. The *Beryl Mirror* does not have
the highly structured nature of works such as the *Yellow Beryl*, the *White
Beryl*, or the *Blue Beryl*. There are no chapter headings, and though the
progress of the work does have a general coherence, certain subjects
receive scant attention in comparison with others.

13. Sde srid Sangs rgyas rgya mtsho, *Dpal ldan gso ba rig pa'i khog 'bugs legs
bshad ba'i ḍūrya'i me long*, 372.4–.5.

14. Sde srid Sangs rgyas rgya mtsho, *Dpal ldan gso ba rig pa'i khog 'bugs legs
bshad ba'i ḍūrya'i me long*, 376.2–.7.

15. Now available in G.yu thog Yon tan mgon po, *Grwa thang rgyud bzhi*.
(Beijing: Mi rigs dpe skrun khang, 2005), in which see the colophon by
Zur mkhar ba at 700–705, and especially 700.8–701.11 and 702.12–703.8
for caustic criticism of his editorial predecessors. This is part (volume 20)
of the series of rare and important medical literature published in the
Bod kyi gso ba rig pa'i gna' dpe phyogs bsgrigs dpe tshogs series under
the direction of Khro ru rtse rnam.

16. According to Sangs rgyas rgya mtsho, Nang so dar rgyas and the lesser
physicians were convinced that the Byang and Zur traditions were quite
different. But Sangs rgyas rgya mtsho felt that the two differed only in minor points, and therefore textual witnesses from both traditions should
be used in establishing an improved text of the *Four Tantras*.

17. On the development of the idea that the Dalai Lama was a reincarnation
of this bodhisattva, see Yumiko Ishihama, "On the Dissemination of the
Belief in the Dalai Lama as a Manifestation of the Bodhisattva Avalokitesvara," *Acta Asiatica* 64 (1993): 38–56.

18. Sde srid Sangs rgyas rgya mtsho, *Dpal ldan gso ba rig pa'i khog 'bugs legs
bshad ba'i ḍūrya'i me long*, 381.6–.11.

19. This episode has been related previously in Meyer, "Introduction: The
Medical Paintings of Tibet," 6.

20. Sde srid Sangs rgyas rgya mtsho, *Dpal ldan gso ba rig pa'i khog 'bugs legs bshad ba'i ḍūrya'i me long,* 383.4–.7.

21. Sde srid Sangs rgyas rgya mtsho, *Dpal ldan gso ba rig pa'i khog 'bugs legs bshad ba'i ḍūrya'i me long,* 385.9–.16.

22. Byang pa Rnam rgyal grags bzang (1395–1475), *'Tsho byed rnams la snying nas brtse ba'i man ngag 'phrul gyi yig chung,* in *Bod kyi sman rtsis ched rtsom phyogs bsdus* (Lhasa: Bod ljongs mi dmangs dpe skrun khang, 1986), 117–120, at 117–118.

23. Zur mkhar, *Rgyud bzhi bka' dang bstan bcos rnam par dbye ba,* 71.

24. Zur mkhar Blo gros rgyal po, *Bdud rtsi snying po yan lag brgyad pa gsang ba man ngag gi rgyud kyi tshig don phyin ci ma log par 'grel ba mes po'i zhal lung zhes bya ba las dum bu dang po rtsa ba'i rgyud kyi rnam bshad,* in *Rgyud bzhi'i 'grel pa mes po'i zhal lung* (Beijing: Krung go'i bod kyi shes rig dpe skrun khang, 1989), 1:1–88, at 2.

25. Blo gros rgyal po, *Bdud rtsi snying po yan lag brgyad pa gsang ba man ngag gi rgyud kyi tshig don phyin ci ma log par 'grel ba mes po'i zhal lung zhes bya ba las dum bu dang po rtsa ba'i rgyud kyi rnam bshad,* 2–3.

26. Criticism of the value of scholarly commentary for medical practice is found in the medieval Islamic world as well, to cite but one comparative example. The Iraqi physician Ibn Butlan (d. 1063), for instance, makes the following comment in his practical medical manual: "People are dissatisfied at the length to which the learned pursue their discussions and prolixity encountered when these are set down in writing in books; what [laymen] need from the sciences is that which will benefit them, not proofs for these things or their definitions." See Lawrence I. Conrad, "The Arab-Islamic Medical Tradition," in *The Western Medical Tradition: 800 BC to AD 1800,* ed. Lawrence I. Conrad et al. (Cambridge: Cambridge University Press, 1995), 93–138, at 122.

27. Zur mkhar Blo gros rgyal po, *Bdud rtsi snying po yan lag brgyad pa gsang ba man ngag gi rgyud kyi tshig don phyin ci ma log par 'grel ba mes po'i zhal lung zhes bya ba las dum bu gnyis pa bshad pa'i rgyud kyi rnam bshad,* in *Rgyud bzhi'i 'grel pa mes po'i zhal lung* (Beijing: Krung go'i bod kyi shes rig dpe skrun khang, 1989), 1:89–668, at 93.9–.16.

28. Zur mkhar Blo gros rgyal po, *Bdud rtsi snying po yan lag brgyad pa gsang ba man ngag gi rgyud kyi tshig don phyin ci ma log par 'grel ba mes po'i zhal lung zhes bya ba las dum bu gnyis pa bshad pa'i rgyud kyi rnam bshad,* 95.13–.19.

29. Sde dge Bla sman Rin chen 'od zer (19th century), *Bdud rtsi rnying po yan lab brgyad pa gsang ba man ngag gi rgyud las dum bu gnyis pa bshad pa'i rgyud kyi 'bru 'grel don gsal rab tu snang ba'i nyin byed,* in *Bdud rtsi snying po yan lag brgyad pa gsang ba man ngag gi rgyud las rtsa rgyud dang bshad rgyud kyi 'grel pa* (Chengdu: Si khron mi rigs dpe skrun khang,

2001), 139–554, at 146.6–.13. Little is known of this author. The dating of this work to 1886 (*me khyi*) is based upon the apparent mention of two figures, Situ Paṇ chen Chos kyi 'byung gnas (1699/1700–44) and 'Jam dbyangs mkhyen brtse dbang po (1820–1892), in the introductory verses at Sde dge Bla sman Rin chen 'od zer (19th century), *Bdud rtsi rnying po yan lab brgyad pa gsang ba man ngag gi rgyud las dum bu gnyis pa bshad pa'i rgyud kyi 'bru 'grel*, 4.

30. Byang pa Rnam rgyal grags bzang (1395–1475), *Bshad pa'i rgyud kyi rgya cher 'grel pa bdud rtsi'i chu rgyun* (Chengdu: Si khron mi rigs dpe skrun khang, 2001) [comp. 1463], 691.17. See before him Sum ston pa Ye shes gzungs, '*Grel pa 'bum chung gsal sgron nor bu'i 'phreng mdzes*, fol. 63a.1.

31. Zur mkhar Blo gros rgyal po, *Bdud rtsi snying po yan lag brgyad pa gsang ba man ngag gi rgyud kyi tshig don phyin ci ma log par 'grel ba mes po'i zhal lung zhes bya ba las dum bu gnyis pa bshad pa'i rgyud kyi rnam bshad*, 95.19–.24.

32. Zur mkhar Blo gros rgyal po, *Bdud rtsi snying po yan lag brgyad pa gsang ba man ngag gi rgyud kyi tshig don phyin ci ma log par 'grel ba mes po'i zhal lung zhes bya ba las dum bu gnyis pa bshad pa'i rgyud kyi rnam bshad*, 95.25–96.3.

33. Zur mkhar Blo gros rgyal po, *Bdud rtsi snying po yan lag brgyad pa gsang ba man ngag gi rgyud kyi tshig don phyin ci ma log par 'grel ba mes po'i zhal lung zhes bya ba las dum bu bzhi pa phyi ma 'phrin las rgyud kyi rnam bshad*, in *Rgyud bzhi'i 'grel pa mes po'i zhal lung* (Beijing: Krung go'i bod kyi shes rig dpe skrun khang, 1989), 1:669–728, at 669.16–.18.

34. Dar mo Blo bzang chos grags (1638–97/1700), *Bdud rtsi snying po yan lag brgyad pa gsang ba man ngag gi rgyud dum bu gsum pa man ngag rgyud kyi dka' 'grel legs bshad gser rgyan*, in *Rgyud bzhi'i 'grel pa mes po'i zhal lung* (Beijing: Krung go'i bod kyi shes rig dpe skrun khang, 1989), 2:1–527, at 524.10–.14.

35. Dar mo Blo bzang chos grags, *Bdud rtsi snying po yan lag brgyad pa gsang ba man ngag gi rgyud dum bu gsum pa man ngag rgyud kyi dka' 'grel*, 524.15–.22.

36. Zur mkhar Blo gros rgyal po, *Bdud rtsi snying po yan lag brgyad pa gsang ba man ngag gi rgyud kyi tshig don phyin ci ma log par 'grel ba mes po'i zhal lung zhes bya ba las dum bu gnyis pa bshad pa'i rgyud kyi rnam bshad*, 664.20–.21.

37. Zur mkhar Blo gros rgyal po, *Bdud rtsi snying po yan lag brgyad pa gsang ba man ngag gi rgyud kyi tshig don phyin ci ma log par 'grel ba mes po'i zhal lung zhes bya ba las dum bu gnyis pa bshad pa'i rgyud kyi rnam bshad*, 664.21–.25. Blo gros rgyal po speaks here of what is referred to in Latin text-critical traditions as *difficilior lectio*; see M. L. West, *Textual Criticism and Editorial Technique* (Stuttgart: B. G. Teubner, 1973), 51.

38. Zur mkhar Blo gros rgyal po, *Bdud rtsi snying po yan lag brgyad pa gsang ba man ngag gi rgyud kyi tshig don phyin ci ma log par 'grel ba mes po'i zhal lung zhes bya ba las dum bu gnyis pa bshad pa'i rgyud kyi rnam bshad*, 664.25–665.12.

39. Sde srid Sangs rgyas rgya mtsho, *Dpal ldan gso ba rig pa'i khog 'bugs legs bshad ba'i ḍūrya'i me long*, 8–20.

40. Sde srid Sangs rgyas rgya mtsho, *Dpal ldan gso ba rig pa'i khog 'bugs legs bshad ba'i ḍūrya'i me long*, 16.10–17.3, citing Anonymous, *Thabs mkhas pa chen po sangs rgyas drin lan bsab pa't mdo*, in *Sde dge bka' 'gyur, Mdo sde*, vol. A, fols. 86a–198b (Hakuji Ui et al., *A Complete Catalog of the Tibetan Buddhist Canons* [Sendai: Tōhuko Imperial University, 1934], no. 353).

41. Byams pa, *Theg pa chen po mdo sde'i rgyan shes bya ba'i tshig le'ur byas pa*, in *Sde dge Bstan 'gyur, Sems tsam*, vol. *Phi*, fols. 1–39 (Ui et al., *A Complete Cataglog*, no. 4020), fol. 15b.3–.4; Sde srid Sangs rgyas rgya mtsho, *Dpal ldan gso ba rig pa'i khog 'bugs legs bshad ba'i ḍūrya'i me long*, 9.13–.17. See also Sde dge Bla sman Rin chen 'od zer, *Bdud rtsi rnying po yan lab brgyad pa gsang ba man ngag gi rgyud las dum bu gnyis pa bshad pa'i rgyud kyi 'bru 'grel*, 139.4–.7.

42. Sde srid Sangs rgyas rgya mtsho, *Dpal ldan gso ba rig pa'i khog 'bugs legs bshad ba'i ḍūrya'i me long*, 9.4–.8, citing Anonymous, *Thabs mkhas pa chen po sangs rgyas drin lan bsab pa'i mdo*.

43. Sde srid Sangs rgyas rgya mtsho, *Dpal ldan gso ba rig pa'i khog 'bugs legs bshad ba'i ḍūrya'i me long*, 515.16–516.1.

44. Sde srid Sangs rgyas rgya mtsho, *Dpal ldan gso ba rig pa'i khog 'bugs legs bshad ba'i ḍūrya'i me long*, 508–547.

45. See Kurtis R. Schaeffer, "Death, Prognosis, and the Physician's Reputation in Tibet," in *Heroes and Saints: The Moment of Death in Cross-Cultural Perspectives*, ed. Phyllis Granoff and Koichi Shinohara (Newcastle: Cambridge Scholars Publishing, 2007), 159–172.

46. Sde srid Sangs rgyas rgya mtsho, *Dpal ldan gso ba rig pa'i khog 'bugs legs bshad ba'i ḍūrya'i me long*, 515.

47. Sde srid Sangs rgyas rgya mtsho, *Dpal ldan gso ba rig pa'i khog 'bugs legs bshad ba'i ḍūrya'i me long*, 518.17–519.1.

48. The call to integrate the study of medicine with other arts and sciences was heard in medieval Europe as well, as in for instance the following passage from Isidore of Seville (570–636): "The physician ought to know literature, 'grammatica,' to be able to understand or to explain what he reads. Likewise also rhetoric, that he may delineate in true arguments the things which he discusses; dialectic also so that he may study the causes and cures of infirmities in the light of reason." See Danielle Jacquart, "Medical Scholasticism," in *Western Medical Thought from Antiquity to the*

Middle Ages, ed. Mirko D. Grmek (Cambridge, Mass.: Harvard University Press, 1998), 197–240, 380–387, at 199.

49. G.yu thog Yon tan mgon po, *Khog dbug khyung chen lding ba*, 12a.2.

50. See Christopher I. Beckwith, "The Introduction of Greek Medicine Into Tibet in the Seventh and Eighth Centuries," *Journal of the American Oriental Society* 99 (1979): 297–313, at 304. Other versions of this decree have become available since the publication of Beckwith's essay.

51. Zur mkhar Blo gros rgyal po, *Gang dag byang chub sems dpa'i spyad pa spyod par 'dod pa'i sman pa rnams kyis mi shes mi rung ba'i phyi nang gzhan gsum gyis rnam bzhag shes bya spyi khog dbub pa*, 29–31.

52. Zur mkhar Blo gros rgyal po, *Gang dag byang chub sems dpa'i spyad pa spyod par 'dod pa'i sman pa rnams kyis mi shes mi rung ba'i phyi nang gzhan gsum gyis rnam bzhag shes bya spyi khog dbub pa*, 5.1–.13. Blo gros rgyal po cites Zhi ba lha/Śāntideva, *Byang chub sems dpa'i spyod pa la 'jug pa. Bodhisattvacaryāvatāra*, in *Sde dge Bstan 'gyur, Dbu ma*, vol. *La*, fols. 1–40 (Ui et al., *A Complete Catalog*, no. 3871), fol. 14a.3.

53. G.yu thog Yon tan mgon po, *Bdud rtsi snying po yan lag brgyad pa gsang ba man ngag gi rgyud*, 98.1–.2.

54. Zur mkhar Blo gros rgyal po, *Gang dag byang chub sems dpa'i spyad pa spyod par 'dod pa'i sman pa rnams kyis mi shes mi rung ba'i phyi nang gzhan gsum gyis rnam bzhag shes bya spyi khog dbub pa*, 361.4–373.12.

55. Zur mkhar Blo gros rgyal po, *Gang dag byang chub sems dpa'i spyad pa spyod par 'dod pa'i sman pa rnams kyis mi shes mi rung ba'i phyi nang gzhan gsum gyis rnam bzhag shes bya spyi khog dbub pa*, 373.7–.9.

56. Bruce Lincoln, "Culture," in *Guide to the Study of Religion*, ed. Willi Braun and Russell T. McCutcheon (London: Cassell, 2000), 409–422, at 416.

57. Sangs rgyas rgya mtsho, *Dpal ldan gso ba rig pa'i khog 'bugs legs bshad ba'i ḍūrya'i me long*, 1.9.

58. Sangs rgyas rgya mtsho, *Dpal ldan gso ba rig pa'i khog 'bugs legs bshad ba'i ḍūrya'i me long*, 560.5–.11.

59. This was suggested to me by E. Gene Smith, personal communication, May 2001.

5. THE KING'S CANONS

1. Zhu chen Tshul khrims rin chen (1697–1769), *Chos smra ba'i bande tshul khrims rin chen du bod pa'i skye ba phal pa'i rkang 'thung dge sdig 'dres ma'i las kyi yal ga phan tshun du 'dzings par bde sdug gi lo 'dab dus kyi rgyal mos re mos su bsgyur ba*, in *The Autobiography of Tshul-khrims-rin-chen of Sde-dge and Other Selected Writings* (Delhi: N. Lungtok and N. Gyaltsan, 1971), 494.2–.6.

2. The *Byang chub sems dpa'i rtogs pa brjod pa dpag bsam gyi 'khri shing*, in Dge ba'i dbang po, *Rtogs brjod dpal bsam 'khri shing gi rtsa 'grel*, ed. Mkha'

'gro tshe ring (Xining: Mtsho sngon mi rigs dpe skrun khang, 1997). See the colophons on 426–326 and 644–647. The work was first translated in the late 1260s at Mangyul by the Indian scholar Laksmikara and the Tibetan Shong ston Lo tsa'a ba Rdo rje rgyal mtshan. See Leonard W. J. van der Kuijp, "Tibetan Belles-Lettres: The Influence of Daṇḍin and Ksemendra," in *Tibetan Literature: Studies in Genre*, ed. José Ignacio Cabezón and Roger R. Jackson (Ithaca, N.Y.: Snow Lion, 1996), 393–410, esp. 401–402.

3. Dge ba'i dbang po, *Rtogs brjod dpal bsam 'khri shing gi rtsa 'grel*, 436.18.

4. Zhu chen Tshul khrims rin chen, *Kun mkhyen nyi ma'i gnyen gyi bka' lung gi dgongs don rnam par 'grel pa'i bstan bcos gangs can pa'i skad du 'gyur ro 'tshal gyi chos sbyin rgyun mi 'chad pa'i ngo mtshar 'phrul gyi phyi mo rdzogs ldan bskal pa'i bsod nams kyi sprin phung rgyas par dkrigs pa'i tshul las brtsams pa'i gtam ngo mtshar chu gter 'phel ba'i zla ba gsar pa* (Lhasa: Bod ljongs mi dmangs dpe skrun khang, 1985). Much of the following is based upon chapter 6, entitled *Ji ltar bskul ba bzhin dgongs 'grel par du sgrub pa*, "How the Commentaries on the Intention [of the Buddha's Word] Were Block Printed Just as Requested," at 479–601.

5. See Zhu chen Tshul khrims rin chen, *Chos smra ba'i bande tshul khrims rin chen du bod pa'i skye ba*, 507–509.

6. Zhu chen Tshul khrims rin chen, *Kun mkhyen nyi ma'i gnyen gyi bka' lung gi dgongs don rnam par 'grel pa'i bstan bcos*, 448.

7. Figures taken from Josef Kolmaš, *The Iconography of the Degé Kanjur and Tanjur: Facsimile Reproductions of the 648 Illustrations in the Degé Edition of the Tibetan Tripitaka Housed in the Library of the Oriental Insitute in Prague* (New Delhi: Sharada Rani, 1978), 51–54.

8. Paul Harrison, "A Brief History of the Tibetan Bka' 'gyur," in *Tibetan Literature: Studies in Genre*, ed. José Ignacio Cabezón and Roger R. Jackson (Ithaca, N.Y.: Snow Lion, 1996), 75.

9. Josef Kolmaš, *A Genealogy of the Kings of Derge: Sde-dge'i rgyal rabs: Tibetan Text Edited with Historical Introduction* (Prague: Oriental Institute, 1968), 38. See Tshe dbang rdo rje rig 'dzin (b. 1786), *Dpal sa skyong sde dge chos kyi rgyal po rim byon gyi rnam thar dge legs nor bu'i phreng ba 'dod dgu rab 'phel* (Lhasa: Bod ljongs mi dmangs dpe skrun khang, 1989), 42. See Joseph Scheir-Dolberg, *Treasure House of Tibetan Culture: Canonization, Printing, and Power in the Derge Printing House* (M.A. thesis, Harvard University, 2005), 74 and 97 for discussions of Bstan pa tshe ring's investiture from the Qing court.

10. Studies of taxation in Tibet include Melvyn Goldstein, "Taxation and the Structure of a Tibetan Village," *Central Asiatic Journal* 15, no. 1 (1971): 1–27; Surkhang W. Gelek, "Tax Measurement and Lag 'don Tax in Tibet," *Tibet Journal* 9, no. 1 (1984): 20–30; Surkhang W. Gelek, "Government,

Monastic and Private Taxation in Tibet," *Tibet Journal* 11, no. 1 (1986):
21–40.

11. Situ's diaries are also an important source for information regarding his
editorial efforts: Si tu Paṇ chen Bstan pa'i nyin byed, *Tā'i Si tur 'bod pa
karma bstan pa'i nyin byed kyi rang tshul drangs por brjod pa dri bral shel gyi
me long*, in *Tā'i Situ pa kun mkhyen chos kyi 'byung gnas bstan pa'i nyin byed
kyi bka' 'bum* (Kangra: Sherab Gyaltsen, 1990), 14:7–748, at 151.5.

12. Si tu Paṇ chen Bstan pa'i nyin byed, *Bde bar gshegs pa'i bka' gangs can gyi
brdas drangs pa'i phyi mo'i tshogs ji snyed pa par du bsgrubs pa'i tshul la nye
bar brtsams pa'i gtam bzang po blo ldan mos pa'i kunda yongs su kha byed
pa'i zla 'od gzhon nu'i 'khri shing*, in *Tā'i Situ pa kun mkhyen chos kyi 'byung
gnas bstan pa'i nyin byed kyi bka' 'bum* (Kangra: Sherab Gyaltsen, 1990),
9:9–500. Also published as: *Sde dge'i bka' 'gyur dkar chag* (Chengdu: Si
khron mi rigs dpe skrun khang, 1988).

13. "Rgyal ba'i gsung rab gangs ri'i khrod deng sang ji tsam snang ba par du
bsgrubs pa'i byung ba dngos legs par bshad pa," chapter 6 in Si tu Paṇ
chen Bstan pa'i nyin byed, *Bde bar gshegs pa'i bka' gangs can gyi brdas
drangs pa'i phyi mo'i tshogs ji snyed pa par du bsgrubs pa'i tshul*, 195–207.
The divisions of the initial chapters are different in the 1988 Chengdu
edition, and thus the chapter on printing is chapter 3, 275–318. See Pieter C. Verhagen, "Notes Apropos the Oeuvre of Si-tu Paṇ-chen Chos-kyi
'byuṇ-gnas (1699?–1774) (2): Dkar-chag Materials," in *Gedenkschrift J. W.
de Jong*, ed. H. W. Bodewitz and Minoru Hara (Tokyo: The International
Insitute for Buddhist Studies, 2004), 207–237, on the different editions of
Situ's canonical catalogs.

14. See Verhagen, "Notes Apropos the Oeuvre of Si-tu Paṇ-chen Chos-kyi
'byuṇ-gnas (1699?–1774) (2): Dkar-chag Materials," 207–237, as well as
Helmut Eimer, *Some Results of Recent Kanjur Research* (Sankt Augustin:
VGH Wissenschaftsverlag, 1983), 18–20.

15. In 1771 the famed Nyingma master Jigmé Lingpa began to produce another Buddhist canon under the sponsorship of the Degé kings, namely
the Collected Tantras of the Early Translation (the Snga 'gyur rgyud
'bum, otherwise known as the Rnying ma rgyud 'bum). See Janet Gyatso,
Apparitions of the Self: The Secret Autobiographies of a Tibetan Visionary
(Princeton: Princeton University Press, 1998), 141–142, for a brief account. Like his editorial predecessors Shuchen and Situ, Jigmé Lingpa
also offered advice on editing, which bears comparison with earlier works
on the subject: 'Jigs med gling pa Mkhyen brtse 'od zer (1729/30–1798),
*Sa skyong sde dge'i rgyal khab tu snga 'gyur rgyud 'bum rin po che par du
bzhengs pa'i dus zhu chen rnam gnyis la skabs dbye ba'i gtam*, in *'Jigs med
gling pa'i gtam tshogs* (Lhasa: Bod ljongs bod yig dpe rnying dpe skrun
khang, 1991), 390–394. See also 'Jigs med gling pa Mkhyen brtse 'od zer,

*Yul lho rgyud byung ba'i rdzogs chen pa rang byung rdo rje mkhyen brtse'i
'od zer gyi rnam par thar pa legs byas yongs 'du'i snye ma*, in *'Jigs med gling
pa'i rnam thar* (Chengdu: Si khron mi rigs dpe skrun khang, 1998), 1–461,
at 382.

16. Zhu chen Tshul khrims rin chen, *Kun mkhyen nyi ma'i gnyen gyi bka' lung
gi dgongs don rnam par 'grel pa'i bstan bcos*, 553.8–.14.

17. For a summary of this tripartite scheme of the editorial process from the
perspective of classical philology, see L. D. Reynolds and N. G. Wilson,
*Scribes and Scholars: A Guide to the Transmission of Greek and Latin Litera-
ture* (London: Oxford University Press, 1992), esp. 207–224. See also for
comparative purposes Gérard Colas, "The Criticism and Transmission of
Texts in Classical India," *Diogenes* 47, no. 2 (1999): 30–43.

18. On which see Yoshiro Imaeda, "L'Edition du Kanjur Tibétain de 'Jang
sa-tham," *Journal Asiatique* 270, no. 1–2 (1982): 173–189; Yoshiro Imaeda,
Catalog du Kanjur Tibétain de l'Edition de 'Jang sa-tham (Tokyo: Inter-
national Institute of Buddhist Studies, 1982, 1984); Helmut Eimer, "The
Position of the 'Jaṅ sa tham/Lithang Edition Within the Tradition of the
Tibetan Kanjur," *Acta Orientalia* 43, no. 2–3 (1989): 297–304; Jampa S.
Samten, "Notes on the Lithang Edition of the Tibetan bKa'-'gyur," *Tibet
Journal* 12, no. 3 (1987): 17–40.

19. Si tu Paṇ chen Bstan pa'i nyin byed, *Bde bar gshegs pa'i bka' gangs can
gyi brdas drangs pa'i phyi mo'i tshogs ji snyed pa par du bsgrubs pa'i tshul*,
412.1.

20. Zhwa dmar IV Chos kyi dbang phyug (1584–1630), *Chos kyi rgyal po chen
po karma mi pham tshe dbang bsod nams rab brtan zhes bya bas bde bar
gshegs pa'i bka' 'gyur ro 'tshal chos kyi phyi mo mi zad pa'i par du bzhengs
pa'i 'byung ba brjod pa* [Title from colophon; title page illegible] (Tibetan
Buddhist Resource Center W1CZ881), fol. 31a.8.

21. Si tu Paṇ chen Bstan pa'i nyin byed, *Bde bar gshegs pa'i bka' gangs can gyi
brdas drangs pa'i phyi mo'i tshogs ji snyed pa par du bsgrubs pa'i tshul*, 412.3.

22. Rga A gnyan pakshi died in 1303. Tshul khrims rin chen tells us that
before the time of Rga A gnyan pakshi there was not a strong scriptual
tradition in Khams. See Zhu chen Tshul khrims rin chen, *Kun mkhyen
nyi ma'i gnyen gyi bka' lung gi dgongs don rnam par 'grel pa'i bstan bcos*,
547.22–548.9, for a brief praise of him. See Eliot Sperling, "Some Remarks
on sGa A-gnyan dam-pa and the Origins of the Hor-pa Lineage of the
dKar-mdzes Region," in *Tibetan History and Language: Studies Dedicated
to Uray Géza on His Seventieth Birthday* (Wien: Arbeitskreis für Tibetische und Buddhistische Studien Universität Wien, 1991), 455–466, for a
translation of a Tibetan historical source dealing with Rga/Sga A gnyan
pakshi, alias A gnyan dam pa. Perhaps the arrival of the scriptural collections traced by our editors back to this influential statesman coincides

with his presence in Dkar mdzes during the years 1284/5–1289/90, on which see Sperling, "Some Remarks on sGa A-gnyan dam-pa," 463.

23. Contrast this basic methodological principle with the comments of Anthony Grafton, *Defenders of the Text: The Traditions of Scholarship in an Age of Science* (Cambridge, Mass.: Harvard University Press, 1991), 57–58, on the innovations of the fifteenth-century Italian scholar Angelo Poliziano, ancestor of modern Western notions of classical textual criticism: "He went back to the oldest sources—that is, to the oldest manuscripts. He recognized that they were not free from errors; but he insisted that they were the closest extant approximations to what the ancient authors had really written. The newer texts were removed by more stages of copying from antiquity, and any apparent correct readings they contained were merely the results of attempts at conjectural emendation."

24. Si tu Paṇ chen Bstan pa'i nyin byed, *Tā'i Si tur 'bod pa karma bstan pa'i nyin byed kyi rang tshul drangs por brjod pa*, 151.4.

25. One should compare the comments of Situ on the philology of the Kangyur with those of Anonymous, *Rgyal ba'i bka' 'gyur rin po che'i 'bri klog dang 'chad nyan byed mkhan rnams la nye bar mkho ba'i yi ge gzhan phan rnam dag gi gsal byed me long* (New Delhi: Tibet House, 1982), the 1918 work of a Mongolian scholar. This is the lengthiest work of comparative textual criticism of the Kangyurs in any language. See in relation to it Ts. Damdinsuren, "Corrections of Misprints and Errors in Tibetan Printings of Kanjur Made by Dandar Agramba," in *Documenta Barbarorum: Festschrift für Walther Heissig zum 70. Geburtstag* , ed. Klaus Sagaster and Michael Weiers (Wiesbaden: Otto Harrassowitz, 1983), 47–54.

26. Zhu chen Tshul khrims rin chen, *Kun mkhyen nyi ma'i gnyen gyi bka' lung gi dgongs don rnam par 'grel pa'i bstan bcos*, 549.6–.12. Zhu chen Tshul khrims rin chen, *Chos smra ba'i bande tshul khrims rin chen du bod pa'i skye ba*, 484.5–489.3 also provides a recension history of the canonical materials from which Zhu chen worked.

27. Zhu chen Tshul khrims rin chen, *Kun mkhyen nyi ma'i gnyen gyi bka' lung gi dgongs don rnam par 'grel pa'i bstan bcos*, 549.13–.19.

28. Zhu chen Tshul khrims rin chen, *Kun mkhyen nyi ma'i gnyen gyi bka' lung gi dgongs don rnam par 'grel pa'i bstan bcos*, 549.19–.21.

29. Zhu chen Tshul khrims rin chen, *Kun mkhyen nyi ma'i gnyen gyi bka' lung gi dgongs don rnam par 'grel pa'i bstan bcos*, 549.21–550.5.

30. The following is taken from Zhu chen Tshul khrims rin chen, *Chos smra ba'i bande tshul khrims rin chen du bod pa'i skye ba*, 472.2–476.5. Compare with Bkra shis lhun grub's catalog of the collection: Bkra shis lhun grub (17th/18th century), *Dpal ldan sa skya'i rje btsun gong ma lnga'i gsung rab rin po che'i par gyi sgo 'phar 'byed pa'i dkar chag 'phrul gyi lde'u mig*, in *Sa

*skya pa'i bka' 'bum: The Complete Works of the Great Masters of the Sa-skya
Sect of Tibetan Buddhism* (Tokyo: Tōyō Bunko, 1968), 15:819–950, at 941–
946. These events have been studied in David P. Jackson, *The Entrance
Gate for the Wise (Section III): Sa-skya Paṇḍita on Indian and Tibetan Traditions of Pramāṇa and Philosophical Debate* (Wien: Arbeitskreis für Tibetische und Buddhistische Studien Universität Wien, 1987), 1:232–236.

31. Tashi Lundrup was invited to Lhündrup Teng by Tenpa Tsering. See
Josef Kolmaš, "Dezhung Rinpoche's Summary and Continuation of the
Sde-dge'I rgyal rabs," *Acta Orientalia Hungarica* 42, no. 1 (1988): 119–152,
at 137.

32. This section follows Bkra shis lhun grub, *Dpal ldan sa skya'i rje btsun
gong ma lnga'i gsung rab rin po che'i par gyi sgo 'phar 'byed pa'i dkar chag,*
937.5–938.4.

33. Zhu chen Tshul khrims rin chen, *Kun mkhyen nyi ma'i gnyen gyi bka' lung
gi dgongs don rnam par 'grel pa'i bstan bcos,* 550.5–.12.

34. Zhu chen Tshul khrims rin chen, *Chos smra ba'i bande tshul khrims rin
chen du bod pa'i skye ba,* 490–491.

35. Divination (Latin: *divinatio*), also known as conjectural emendation, was
also a delicate matter in classical textual criticism. As R. J. Tarrant, "Classical Latin Literature," in *Scholarly Editing: A Guide to Research,* ed. D. C.
Greetham (New York: The Modern Language Association of America,
1995), 95–148, suggests at 118: "Of all the operations of classical editors,
conjectural emendation, the plainest exercise of editorial judgment, is
the most controversial; for the same reason, in the hagiography of textual
criticism skill at conjecture is usually portrayed as the essential mark of
real distinction. . . . The older synonym *divinatio* invests the process with
an aura of mantic revelation—though in classical Latin the word need
not imply more than guesswork."

36. Zhu chen Tshul khrims rin chen, *Chos smra ba'i bande tshul khrims rin
chen du bod pa'i skye ba,* 491.1–.4.

37. This method of scraping and rewriting upon the print is one of the primary ways to enter a change in the text in contemporary Tibet. I was able
to observe the editorial team of the new Lhasa Tengyur at work in Lhasa
in November 1998. Another method of emending the print was to change
the block itself, by carving out the offensive letters and gluing a "revision,"
that is a newly carved section, directly on the block. On this and other
methods of emending blocks and prints, see Helmut Eimer, "Hevajratantra II:v:1–2 and the History of the Tibetan Kanjur," *Berliner Indologische
Studien* 2 (1986): 3–12 (which follows upon the text critical remarks in
Leonard W. J. van der Kuijp, "A Text-Historical Note on *Hevajratantra* II:
v:1–2," *Journal of the International Association of Buddhist Studies* 8, no. 1
[1985]: 83–89), at 4.

38. Zhu chen Tshul khrims rin chen, *Chos smra ba'i bande tshul khrims rin chen du bod pa'i skye ba*, 491.4–.6.

39. Zhu chen Tshul khrims rin chen, *Chos smra ba'i bande tshul khrims rin chen du bod pa'i skye ba*, 491.6–492.4.

40. See Pieter C., Verhagen, *A History of Sanskrit Grammatical Literature in Tibet: Volume Two, Assimilation Into Indigeonous Scholarship* (Leiden: Brill, 2001), passim, for the discussions of the relationship between these works and knowledge of Indic grammatical theory in Tibet.

41. Zhu chen Tshul khrims rin chen, *Kun mkhyen nyi ma'i gnyen gyi bka' lung gi dgongs don rnam par 'grel pa'i bstan bcos*, 551.10–552.21.

42. Si tu Paṇ chen Bstan pa'i nyin byed, *Bde bar gshegs pa'i bka' gangs can gyi brdas drangs pa'i phyi mo'i tshogs ji snyed pa par du bsgrubs pa'i tshul*, 413.3.

43. Si tu Paṇ chen Bstan pa'i nyin byed, *Bde bar gshegs pa'i bka' gangs can gyi brdas drangs pa'i phyi mo'i tshogs ji snyed pa par du bsgrubs pa'i tshul*, 413.3.

44. Si tu Paṇ chen Bstan pa'i nyin byed, *Bde bar gshegs pa'i bka' gangs can gyi brdas drangs pa'i phyi mo'i tshogs ji snyed pa par du bsgrubs pa'i tshul*, 412.5.

45. Zhu chen Tshul khrims rin chen, *Kun mkhyen nyi ma'i gnyen gyi bka' lung gi dgongs don rnam par 'grel pa'i bstan bcos*, 550.17–551.4.

46. Si tu Paṇ chen Bstan pa'i nyin byed, *Bde bar gshegs pa'i bka' gangs can gyi brdas drangs pa'i phyi mo'i tshogs ji snyed pa par du bsgrubs pa'i tshul*, 414.

47. Zhu chen Tshul khrims rin chen, *Kun mkhyen nyi ma'i gnyen gyi bka' lung gi dgongs don rnam par 'grel pa'i bstan bcos*, 576–577.

48. Zhu chen Tshul khrims rin chen, *Kun mkhyen nyi ma'i gnyen gyi bka' lung gi dgongs don rnam par 'grel pa'i bstan bcos*, 577.

49. Zhu chen Tshul khrims rin chen, *Kun mkhyen nyi ma'i gnyen gyi bka' lung gi dgongs don rnam par 'grel pa'i bstan bcos*, 577.

50. See Co ne Grags pa bshad grub (1675–1748), *Co ne'i bka' 'gyur rin po che'i dkar chags gsal ba'i me long* (University of Washington: Tibetan microfilm collection, East Asia Library, Reel No. A3–7.2), 45 folios, at fols. 5a.7–5b.1 for dates.

51. 'Jam dbyangs bzhad pa'i rdo rje II Dkon mchog 'jigs med dbang po, *Bde bar gshegs pa'i bka'i dgongs 'grel bstan bcos 'gyur ro cog par du sgrub pa'i tshul las nye bar brtsams pa'i gtam yang dag par brjod pa dkar chag yid bzhin nor bu'i phreng ba* (Langzhou: Kan su'u mi rigs dpe skrun khang, 1986), 446.10–449.1.

52. 'Jam dbyangs bzhad pa'i rdo rje II Dkon mchog 'jigs med dbang po, *Bde bar gshegs pa'i bka'i dgongs 'grel bstan bcos 'gyur ro cog par du sgrub pa'i tshul*, 482.

53. Zahiruddin Ahmad, *Saṅs-rgyas rGya-mTSHO, Life of the Fifth Dalai Lama, Volume IV, Part I* (New Delhi: International Academy of Indian Culture, 1999), 307–308.

54. Ngawang L. Nornang, "The Monastic Organization and Economy of Dwags-po Bshad-grub-gling," in *Reflections on Tibetan Culture: Essays in Memory of Turrell V. Wylie*, ed. Lawrence Epstein and Richard F. Sherburne (Lewiston, N.Y.: The Edwin Mellen Press, 1990), 249–269, at 250, 265.

55. Zhu chen Tshul khrims rin chen, *Kun mkhyen nyi ma'i gnyen gyi bka' lung gi dgongs don rnam par 'grel pa'i bstan bcos*, 577–78.

56. Oliver Coales, "Eastern Tibet," *The Geographical Journal* 53, no. 4 (1919): 228–253, at 241.

57. Some two decades later the Degé Kangyur was one motivation for the Gyalrong rulers to begin a block-print edition of the Bönpo canon. This Tröchen canon was produced during a 16-year period from 1758 through 1774, during which 103 out of a proposed 113 volumes were completed: "Introduction," in *A Catalog of the Bon Kanjur*, ed. Dan Martin, Per Kvaerne, and Yasuhiko Nagano (Osaka: National Museum of Ethnology, 2003), 1–20, at 9. Samten G. Karmay, *Feast of the Morning Light: The Eighteenth-Century Wood-Engravings of Shenrab's Life-Stories and the Bon Canon from Gyalrong* (Osaka: National Museum of Ethnology, 2005), at 77–85, offers an account of the production of this canon. See also Tsering Thar, "The Bonpo Documents and Their Assembling," in *Theses on Tibetology in China*, ed. Liao Zugui and Zhang Zuji (Beijing: China Tibetology Publishing House, 1996), 325–365, especially 346–354. Kachu Yungdrung Püntsok, the author of an account of the project (and part of its editorial team) mentions Degé explicitly and compares the Bönpo canon's greater number of volumes to the hundred or so volumes of the Buddhist counterpart: Bka' bcu G.yung drung phun tshogs (18th century), *Ston pa thams cad mkhen pa'i gsung dbyangs mi mdzad chu bo gter ji snyed pa gangs can bod kyi tshig gis nye bar drangs pa dkar chags legs par bshad pa snang ba'i dga' ston las ci ltar par du sgrub tshul gyi le'u ste bzhi pa* (n.p., n.d., manuscript, 33 fols.), and *Ston pa thams cad mkhen pa'i gsung dbyangs mi mdzad chu bo gter ji snyed pa gangs can bod kyi tshig gis nye bar drangs pa dkar chags legs par bshad pa snang ba'i dga' ston las sngo smon gyi le'u ste lnga pa* (n.p., n.d., manuscript, 13 fols.). [comp. 1773]. Like Situ and Shuchen, Yungdrung Püntsok provides an account of the the patron and his region (3a.1–17b.1), the collection and editing of the works (17b.1–25a.2), the patronage of both the volumes of scripture and the temple in which they were housed (24a.2), sources for analyzing verb tense and archaic orthography (21b), the need to edit faulty archaic terminology employed by poor scholars with current usage, the issue of colloquial dialects (22a), the editing of mantras using *Kalāpa* and *Sarasvatī* grammars as well as mantra pronunciation manuals (22b), dealing with errors, doubtful readings, emendation, the grammatical treatises employed by

the editors (such as the *Sum rtags* and the works of Shalu Lotsawa) (23a),
and sources for the rules of gender and euphonic combination (23b).

58. Mdo mkhar zhabs drung Tshe ring dbang rgyal (1697–1763), *Dpal mi'i dbang po'i rtogs pa brjod pa 'jig rten kun tu dga' ba'i gtam* (Xining: Si khron mi rigs dpe skrun khang, 1981) relates the printing the Bka' 'gyur at Shel dkar at 734.2–748.17, as well as other book-production efforts of Pho lha nas at 818.9–828.20. Luciano Petech, *China and Tibet in the Early XVIIIth Century: History of the Establishment of Chinese Protectorate in Tibet, 2nd Rev. Ed.* (Leiden: E. J. Brill, 1972), 26–194 chronicles the career of Pho lha nas, based largely on Tshe ring dbang rgyal's biography.

59. On the gold Tengyur see Ngag dbang nor bu, *Gser bris bstan 'gyur gyi dkar chag* (Beijing: Mi ris dpe skrun khang, 2004), esp. 18–20; Peter Skilling, "A Brief Guide to the Golden Tanjur," *Journal of the Siam Society* 79, no. 2 (1991): 138–146; Shin'ichiro Miyake, "On the Date of the Original Manuscript of the Golden Manuscript Tenjur in Ganden Monastery," *Annual Memoirs of the Otani University Shin Buddhist Comprehensive Research Institute* 13 (1995): 13–16; Shin'ichiro Miyake, "Comparative Table of the Golden Manuscript Tenjur in dGa'-ldan Monastery with the Peking Edition of Tenjur," *Annual Memoirs of the Otani University Shin Buddhist Comprehensive Research Institute* 17 (2000): 1–65, where dates of 1733–40 are given for its production. On the printed Tengyur produced by Pho lha nas in 1742, see Phur bu lcog Ngag dbang byams pa (1682–1762), *Bstan bcos 'gyur ro cog gsung par du bsgrubs pa'i dkar chag tshangs pa'i dbyangs* (n.p., n.d., 144 folios. composed 1742). Ngag dbang byams pa details the workers involved (6a.5–7b.5), gives a general account of the project finances (7b.5–9a.7), and lists some 60 donors to the project, stipulating the name of the donor, the type and amount of the donation, and the specific recipients (9a.7–16a.1). See also Yeshe Gyaltsen's 1768 account of the Nartang prints of the Kangyur and Tengyur printed in 1760–61 for the monastery of Kyirong Tashi Samten Ling: Tshe mchog gling Yongs 'dzin Ye shes rgyal mtshan, *Bkra shis bsam gtan gling gi bka' bstan rin po che'i dkar chag thub bstan gsal byed*, in *The Collected Works (Gsuṇ-'bum) of Tshe-mchog-gliṇ yoṇ ṇs-'dzin ye-śes-rgyal-mtshan* (New Delhi: Tibet House, 1975), 16:421–553.

60. Tshe ring dbang rgyal refers to Sle lung Rje drung Bzhad pa'i rdo rje (b. 1697), *Bka' 'gyur rin po che'i gsung par srid gsum rgyan gcig rdzu 'phrul shing rta'i dkar chag ngo mtshar bkod pa rgya mtsho'i lde mig*, in in *Catalogue of the Narthang Kanjur* (New Delhi: International Academy of Indian Culture, 1983). See A. I. Vostrikov, *Tibetan Historical Literature*, trans. Harish Chandra Gupta (Surrey, England: Curzon Press, 1994), 212–213, for a brief brief summary and Dan Martin, *Tibetan Histories: A Bibliography of Tibetan-Language Historical Works* (London: Serindia Publications,

1997), entry 267, for more information. Bzhad pa'i rdo rje's expansive account of the finances and the labor force at 133–191 will repay attention. Note also that the production of the Bka' 'gyur at Shel dkar occasioned the writing of an ecclesiastical history of Shel dkar itself: Pasang Wangdu, Hildegard Diemberger, and Guntram Hazod, *Shel dkar chos 'byung, History of the White Crystal: Religion and Politics of Southern La stod* (Vienna: Verlag der Österreichischen Akademie der Wissenschaften, 1996), 108.

61. Charles Bell, *Tibet, Past and Present* (Oxford: Clarendon Press, 1924), 86. Alexandra David-Neel offers a more visceral account in *Magic and Mystery in Tibet* (New York: Claude Kendall, 1932), 87: "I went on to Narthang to visit the largest of the printing establishments in Tibet. The number of engraved wooden plates used for the printing of the various religious books was prodigious. Set up on shelves, in rows, they filled a huge building. The printers, spattered with ink up to their elbows, sat upon the floor as they worked, while in other rooms monks cut the paper according to the size required for each kind of book. There was no haste; chatting and drinking of buttered tea went on freely. What a contrast to the feverish agitation in our newspaper printing-rooms."

62. Mdo mkhar zhabs drung Tshe ring dbang rgyal, *Dpal mi'i dbang po'i rtogs pa brjod pa*, 818.9.

6. THE COST OF A PRICELESS BOOK

1. Bsod nams dpal bzang po, Śākya 'od, and Byang chub rgyal mtshan [incorrectly attributed to Sgra tshad pa Rin chen rnam rgyal], *Bstan bcos 'gyur ro 'tshal gyi dkar chag yid bzhin nor bu rin po che'i za ma tog*, in *The Collected Works of Bu-ston* (New Delhi: International Academy of Indian Culture, 1971), 28:343–574, at 568. The meanings of two terms in this list, *kag ta pa* and *gdong kag pa*, have eluded me. On this Tengyur, see Leonard W. J. van der Kuijp, "Fourteenth-Century Tibetan Cultural History I: Ta'i-si-tu Byang-chub rgyal-mtshan as a Man of Religion," *Indo-Iranian Journal* 37 (1994): 139–149.

2. For richer descriptions of the paper, ink, wood, silk, paint, gems, minerals, and metals that make up a book, one must look to treatises on the practical arts, which detail the methods and materials of various crafts. Most of these, however, are very late in terms of the period covered by the *Blue Annals* as well as the period of its composition.

3. A few examples drawn from the *Blue Annals* include: Rinchen Zangpo (1243–1319), a preacher at Yangon Gomdé of Tshalpa and priest of the royal household, prepared a copy of the Kangyur written in gold; George N. Roerich, trans., *Blue Annals* (New Delhi: Motilal Banarsidass, 1976), 408. Sometime around 1335 Rangjung Dorjé prepared a copy of the Kangyur and Tengyur at Samye Chimphu; Roerich, *Blue Annals*, 492.

A golden Kangyur was placed in Tsethang monastery in the 1440s; Roerich, *Blue Annals*, 1084. With the aid of various patrons, Sönam Gyatso
prepared gold copies of the commentaries and principal tantras, three
golden Kangyurs, and a Tengyur on regular paper; Roerich, *Blue Annals*,
823–824. A secular leader among the ancestry of the *Blue Annal*'s patrons
prepared a Kangyur in gold; Roerich, *Blue Annals*, 1088.

4. Roerich, *Blue Annals*, 953.

5. Roerich, *Blue Annals*, 932.

6. Roerich, *Blue Annals*, 446. The early twelfth-century translator Ma Lotsawa bequeathed his books and other things to his disciple Khonpuwa
   (d. 1144); Roerich, *Blue Annals*, 227.

7. Roerich, *Blue Annals*, 970.

8. Roerich, *Blue Annals*, 510. The Second Shamar sealed his books with his
   own seal in preparation for his next rebirth; Roerich, *Blue Annals*, 545.

9. Roerich, *Blue Annals*, 915.

10. Sixteen small volumes are given in a last will; Roerich, *Blue Annals*, 947.

11. In another case a father entrusts books to his twelve-year-old son and dis-
    ciple, who is also an incarnation; Roerich, *Blue Annals*, 973.

12. When Lama Zhang was a small boy his father encouraged him to spend
    several days meditating in front of a book formerly belonging to his an-
    cestors, in order to avoid being born in purgatory; Roerich, *Blue Annals*,
    711–712.

13. Roerich, *Blue Annals*, 114.

14. Roerich, *Blue Annals*, 73.

15. Roerich, *Blue Annals*, 115.

16. Roerich, *Blue Annals*, 1059.

17. Roerich, *Blue Annals*, 794.

18. Roerich, *Blue Annals*, 364.

19. Roerich, *Blue Annals*, 663.

20. Roerich, *Blue Annals*, 836–837.

21. Roerich, *Blue Annals*, 1058.

22. Roerich, *Blue Annals*, 956.

23. Roerich, *Blue Annals*, 623; Gzhon nu dpal, *Deb*, 543.5–.6. Lists of non-
    canonical blocks and block prints (often refered to as *dpar tho*, "print
    lists") owned by particular monasteries are extant from the late seven-
    teenth century. See Lokesh Chandra, "Tibetan Works Printed by the
    Shoparkhang of the Potala," in *Jñānamuktāvalī: Commemoration Volume
    in Honour of Johannes Nobel*, ed. Claus Vogel (New Delhi: International
    Academy of Indian Culture, 1959), 120–123; Lokesh Chandra, "Les Im-
    primeries Tibétains de Drepung, Degé, et Pepung," *Journal Asiatique* 249
    (1961): 503–517; Geza Bethlenfalvy, "A Tibetan Catalogue of the Blocks
    of the Lamaist Printing House in Aginsk," *Acta Orientalia* 25 (1972):

53–75; Lokesh Chandra, "Tibetan Buddhist Texts Printed by the Mdzod-dge-sgar-gsar Monastery," *Indo-Iranian Journal* 7 (1963–64): 298–306; R. O. Meisezahl, "Der Katalog der Klosterdruckerei A mčhog dga' ldan čhos 'khor gliṅ in Ch'ing-hai (Nordwest-China)," *Oriens* 29–30 (1986): 309–333; Helmut Eimer and Pema Tsering, "Die Liste der Druckplatten in Dga' ldan phun tshogs gling aus dem Jahre 1694," *Zentralasiatische Studien* 34 (2005): 29–54.

24. Roerich, *Blue Annals*, 643.

25. Roerich, *Blue Annals*, 624; Gzhon nu dpal, *Deb*, 544.5–.7.

26. Roerich, *Blue Annals*, 571; Gzhon nu dpal, *Deb*, 496.4–497.4. See also Roerich, *Blue Annals*, 620, and Gzhon nu dpal, *Deb*, 540.5 as well as Roerich, *Blue Annals*, 468, Gzhon nu dpal, *Deb*, 407.6.

27. Roerich, *Blue Annals*, 378–379. Rwa Ye shes seng ge, *Mthu stobs dbang phyug rje btsun dwa lo tsa'a ba'i rnam par thar pa kun khyab snyan pa'i rnga sgra* (Xining: Mtsho sngon mi rigs dpe skrun khang, 1989), contains numerous references to Ra Lotsawa's gifts of scripture: 139, 146, 161, 332, etc.

28. Roerich, *Blue Annals*, 479.

29. Roerich, *Blue Annals*, 296.

30. Roerich, *Blue Annals*, 139.

31. Roerich, *Blue Annals*, 364.

32. Roerich, *Blue Annals*, 1066.

33. Roerich, *Blue Annals*, 1045.

34. Roerich, *Blue Annals*, 620.

35. Roerich, *Blue Annals*, 784.

36. Roerich, *Blue Annals*, 596.

37. Roerich, *Blue Annals*, 436.

38. Roerich, *Blue Annals*, 97, 981.

39. Roerich, *Blue Annals*, 987.

40. Roerich, *Blue Annals*, 759.

41. Roerich, *Blue Annals*, 377.

42. Roerich, *Blue Annals*, 566.

43. Roerich, *Blue Annals*, 741.

44. Roerich, *Blue Annals*, 1057.

45. Roerich, *Blue Annals*, 761.

46. Roerich, *Blue Annals*, 412.

47. Roerich, *Blue Annals*, 723.

48. Roerich, *Blue Annals*, 940.

49. Roerich, *Blue Annals*, 1000.

50. Roerich, *Blue Annals*, 554.

51. Roerich, *Blue Annals*, 747.

52. Roerich, *Blue Annals*, 807–808.

53. Roerich, *Blue Annals*, 812.

54. Roerich, *Blue Annals*, 164.

55. Roerich, *Blue Annals*, 369.

56. Roerich, *Blue Annals*, 686, 700.

57. Roerich, *Blue Annals*, 663.

58. Roerich, *Blue Annals*, 723.

59. Roerich, *Blue Annals*, 577.

60. Roerich, *Blue Annals*, 899.

61. Roerich, *Blue Annals*, 734.

62. Roerich, *Blue Annals*, 989.

63. On whom see Luciano Petech, "Ston tshul: The Rise of Sa skya Para-mountcy in Khams," *Tibetan History and Language: Studies Dedicated to Uray Géza on His Seventieth Birthday*, ed. E. Steinkellner, Wiener Studien zur Tibetologie und Buddhismuskunde, Heft 26 (Wien: Arbeitskreis für Tibetische und Buddhistische Studien Universität Wien, 1991), 417–422.

64. The nine works are contained in *The Collected Works of the Founding Masters of the Sa-skya* (Dehra Dun: Sakya Center, 1992–93) [a reprint of the Sde dge Dgon chen edition of 1736], 15:599–637. The individual titles include: 1) *Bde bar gshegs pa'i gsung rab 'gyur ro 'tshal bzhengs pa'i bsal byed sdeb sbyor gyi rgyan rnam par bkra ba*, 599.1–610 [an account of the scriptural volumes produced at Markham Tsomdo (*smar khams tsom mdo*) and ultimately housed at Sakya monastery by 1278, sponsored by Jimgim, son of Qubilai Khan, composed at Sakya in 1278]; 2) *Chos rin po che nye bar bzhengs pa'i mtshon bye drab tu byed pa*, 610.2–615.1 [composed at Markham Gang (*smar khams sgang*) in 1276]; 3) *Dam chos rin po che shin tu rgyas pa'i sde snod bzhengs pa la bsngags pa*, 615.1–618.5 [composed 1277]; 4) *Manga la yab yum gyis rgyas 'bring bsdus gsum dang phal po che bzhengs pa'i mtshon byed*, 618.5–623.1 [composed at Tsomdo Nesar (*Tsom mdo gnas sar*) in 1275]; 5) *Ji big de mur gyis phal chen gser 'od stong phrag brgya pa rnams bzhengs pa'i mtshon byed*, 623.1–628.2 [composed in 1273 at Shinkun in Yarmotang (*G.yar mo thang gi sa cha shing kun*), regarding a book production project of 1272]; 6) *A rog ches 'bum bzhengs pa'i rab byed*, 628.2–630.2 [composed at Shingkun "on the border of China and Tibet (*rgya bod sa mtshams shing kun*)" in 1274]; 7) *Go pe las rgyas 'bring bsdus gsum bzhengs pa'i mtshon byed*, 630.2–633.2 [in praise of the *Perfection of Wisdom Sūtras* produced in 1274 at Markham Tsomdo Nesar (*smar khams tsom mdo gnas gsar*) and sponsored by Qubilai in 1274, composed at Tsomdo Nesar in 1275]; 8) *Dge 'dun bzang po sogs kyis sher phyin rgyas 'bring bsdus gsum bzhengs pa'i mtshon byed*, 633.2–635.3 [regarding *Perfection of Wisdom Sūtras* produced in 1271]; 9) *Rin chen dpal gyis 'bum bzhengs pa'i mtshon byed*, 635.3–637.3 [on the *Perfection of Wisdom in One Hundred Thousand Lines* sponsored by Tontsul Rinchenpel, the influential Mongolian-Tibetan speaking translator born in the Gangra region of

Domé (*mdo smad sgang ra*), produced in 1276 in order to carry out the last wishes of his teacher, for the long life of the king and his sons, and to answer the kindness of his mother and father].

65. The following is taken from 'Phags pa Blo gros rgyal mtshan (1235–80), *Bde bar gshegs pa'i gsung rab 'gyur ro 'tshal bzhengs pa'i bsal byed sdeb sbyor gyi rgyan rnam par bkra ba*, in *The Collected Works of the Founding Masters of the Sa-skya* (Dehra Dun: Sakya Center, 1992–93), 606.5–608.4.

66. Tsong kha pa Blo bzang grags pa (1357–1419), *Mnyam med tsong kha pa chen pos mdzad pa'i byang chub lam rim che ba* (Xining: Mtsho sngon mi rigs dpe skrun khang, 1985), 146.8; Tsong-kha-pa, *The Great Treatise on the Stages of the Path to Enlightenment* (Ithaca, N.Y.: Snow Lion, 2000), 1:195.

67. F. W. Thomas, *Tibetan Literary Texts and Documents Concerning Chinese Turkestan* (Londong: The Royal Asiatic Society, 1935), 2:82. On this passage see also Jean-Pierre Drège, *Les Bibliothèques en Chine au Temps des Manuscrits* (Jusqu'au Xᵉ Siècle) (Paris: École Française d'Extrême-Orient, 1991), 237. Tokio Takata, "Multilingualism in Tun-huang," *Acta Asiatica* 78 (2000): 49–70, at 60–62, offers a general overview of Tibetan scribal activity at Dunhuang during the imperial occupation, and at 61 mentions "coercive measures" used by the Tibetan imperial government to manage scriptoria, such as fines for tardiness.

68. See the edited version of the autobiography of Phun tshogs lung rtogs (1882–1926) in Peter Richardus, ed., *Tibetan Lives: Three Himalayan Autobiographies* (Surrey, England: Curzon Press, 1998), 1–68; he served as a minor scribe in the government of the Thirteenth Dalai Lama.

69. See Kurtis R. Schaeffer, "A Royal Nun in Fifteenth-Century Tibet: Notes on the Life of Chökyi Dronma (c. 1422–1455)," (paper presented at the 2004 annual meeting of the American Academy of Religion, Atlanta, Ga.), for more detailed comments on the life and biography of Chökyi Dronma, and especially her status as a fully ordained nun. Author unknown, *Ye shes mkha' 'gro bsod nams 'drin gyi sku skye gsum pa rje btsun ma chos kyi sgron ma'i rnam thar* (Beijing: CPN, 146 folios. Incomplete: ff. 145–146 missing), fol. 2b.2, gives her birth year as a *stag* year. According to the late 16th-century *Bo dong chos 'byung* of 'Chi med 'od zer (a copy of which is housed in the Tibetan Buddhist Resource Center, New York), translated in Hildegard Diemberger, Pasang Wangdu, Marlies Kornfield, and Christian Jahoda, *Feast of Miracles: The Life and Tradition of Bodong Chole Namgyal (1375/6–1451 A.D.) according to the Tibetan Texts "Feast of Miracles" and "The Lamp Illuminating the History of Bodong"* (n.p.: Porong Pema Choding Editions, 1997), 111, she died at age thirty-four. We know that she was present at the death of Bo dong Paṇ chen Phyogs las rnam rgyal (1375–1451), and thus the *stag* year is likely 1422. See Hildegard

Diemberger, *When a Woman Becomes a Religious Dynasty* (New York: Columbia University Press, 2008).

70. 'Jigs med 'bangs (15th century), *Dpal ldan bla ma dam pa thams cad mkhyen pa phyogs thams cad las rnam par rgyal ba'i zhabs kyi rnam par thar pa ngo mtshar gyi dga' ston* (Lhasa: Bod ljongs bod yig dpe rnying dpe skrun khang, 1991) [comp. 1453], at 225.15–226.2.

71. E. Gene Smith, *Among Tibetan Texts: History and Literature of the Himalayan Plateau*, ed. Kurtis R. Schaeffer (Boston: Wisdom, 2001), chapter 14.

72. Author unknown, *Ye shes mkha' 'gro bsod nams 'drin gyi sku skye gsum pa rje btsun ma chos kyi sgron ma'i rnam thar*, fols. 85a–96b, details the production of the *De nyid 'dus pa* and other holy objects after the death of Bo dong Paṇ chen.

73. Bo dong Paṇ chen Phyogs las rnam rgyal, *Rten gsum bzhengs tshul bstan bcos lugs bshad pa*, 339–341.

74. Zhu chen Tshul khrims rin chen (1697–1769), *Kun mkhyen nyi ma'i gnyen gyi bka' lung gi dgongs don rnam par 'grel pa'i bstan bcos gangs can pa'i skad du 'gyur ro 'tshal gyi chos sbyin rgyun mi 'chad pa'i ngo mtshar 'phrul gyi phyi mo rdzogs ldan bskal pa'i bsod nams kyi sprin phung rgyas par dkrigs pa'i tshul las brtsams pa'i gtam ngo mtshar chu gter 'phel ba'i zla ba gsar pa* (Lhasa: Bod ljongs mi dmangs dpe skrun khang, 1985), 470.

75. Zhu chen Tshul khrims rin chen, *Kun mkhyen nyi ma'i gnyen gyi bka' lung gi dgongs don rnam par 'grel pa'i bstan bcos*, 446.

76. Zhu chen Tshul khrims rin chen, *Kun mkhyen nyi ma'i gnyen gyi bka' lung gi dgongs don rnam par 'grel pa'i bstan bcos*, 447.

77. Zhu chen Tshul khrims rin chen, *Kun mkhyen nyi ma'i gnyen gyi bka' lung gi dgongs don rnam par 'grel pa'i bstan bcos*, 864. See also Edward Conze, *The Perfection of Wisdom in Eight Thousand Lines and Its Verse Summary* (San Francisco: Four Seasons Foundation, 1973), 299.

78. Anonymous, *'Phags pa bdud rtsi brjod pa zhes bya ba theg pa chen po'i mdo*, in *Sde dge bka' 'gyur, Mdo sde*, vol. A, fols. 271b.2–274b. 5 (Hakuji Ui, et al., *A Complete Catalog of the Tibetan Buddhist Canons* [Sendai: Tōhuko Imperial University, 1934], no. 197).

79. Cited here as it is presented in the catalog of the Tengyur printed in Choné: 'Jam dbyangs bzhad pa'i rdo rje II Dkon mchog 'jigs med dbang po, *Bde bar gshegs pa'i bka'i dgongs 'grel bstan bcos 'gyur ro cog par du sgrub pa'i tshul*, 501.

80. Zhu chen Tshul khrims rin chen, *Kun mkhyen nyi ma'i gnyen gyi bka' lung gi dgongs don rnam par 'grel pa'i bstan bcos*, 866–67. Compare Gregory Schopen, "The Phrase 'sa pṛtivīpradeśaś caityabhūto bhavet' in the Vajracchedikā: Notes on the Cult of the Book in Mahāyāna," *Indo-Iranian Journal* 17 (1975): 147–181, at 166.

81. Dr. Helmut Eimer (personal communication, August 16, 1998) suggested that Si tu Paṇ chen and Zhu chen were often attempting to justify their work to their sponsors. I take this passage to be a prime example of their efforts in this regard.

82. See Jonathan Silk, "Notes on the History of the Yongle Kangyur," in *Suhṛllekhāḥ: Festgabe für Helmut Eimer*, ed. Michael Hahn, Jens-Uwe Hartmann, and Roland Steiner (Swisttal-Odendorf: leT Verlag. 1996), 153–200, for a recent discussion of this early printed canon of 1410. Note that, contra Silk, 166, I have understood Situ to be saying here that the 'Jang sa tham Kangyur was the exemplar for Situ's new Kangyur—"this (*'di nyid*) [ie., our Kangyur]"—and not to the Yongle Kangyur, as this reading makes more sense in the context of Situ's previous discussion regarding his sources.

83. Si tu Paṇ chen Bstan pa'i nyin byed (1699/1700–74), *Bde bar gshegs pa'i bka' gangs can gyi brdas drangs pa'i phyi mo'i tshogs ji snyed pa par du bsgrubs pa'i tshul la nye bar brtsams pa'i gtam bzang po blo ldan mos pa'i kunda yongs su kha byed pa'i zla 'od gzhon nu'i 'khri shing,* in *Tā'i Situ pa kun mkhyen chos kyi 'byung gnas bstan pa'i nyin byed kyi bka' 'bum* (Kangra: Sherab Gyaltsen, 1990), 414.1.

84. Zhu chen Tshul khrims rin chen, *Chos smra ba'i bande tshul khrims rin chen du bod pa'i skye ba,* 471.2–.3.

85. Zhu chen Tshul khrims rin chen, *Chos smra ba'i bande tshul khrims rin chen du bod pa'i skye ba,* 521.3–.5.

86. Zhu chen Tshul khrims rin chen, *Chos smra ba'i bande tshul khrims rin chen du bod pa'i skye ba,* 523.4–524.3.

87. There have been several catalogs of the blocks preserved at Degé compiled in the last decade, including Karma rgyal mtshan, *Sde dge par khang gi par shing dkar chag bod rgya shan sbyar* (Chengdu: Si khron mi rigs dpe skrun khang, 2004), and Anonymous, *Sde dge par khang gi dkar chag zhib rgyas su bkod pa shes bya'i sgo byed* (Xining: Krung go'i bod kyi shes rig dpe skrun khang, 1994), 2 vols.: vol. 1, Gsung 'bum; vol. 2, Gter mdzod. For a summary of more recent history, see Anonymous, "Sde dge par khang gi lo rgyus in *Khams phyogs dkar mdzes khul gyi dgon sde so so'i lo rgyus gsal bar bshad pa nang bstan gsal ba'i me long* (Lhasa: Krung go'i bod kyi shes rig dpe skrun khang, 1995), 1:405–419.

88. Byams pa/Maitreya, *Dbus dang mtha' rnam par 'byed pa,* in *Sde dge Bstan 'gyur, Sems tsam,* vol. *Phi,* fols. 40b.–45a.6 (Ui et al., *A Complete Catalog,* no. 4021), at 44a.4–.5: "Writing books, offering, giving, rearning, reading, possessing, teaching, and reciting [them], reflecting and meditating [upon them]: these ten activities are of incomparable merit." See Zhu chen Tshul khrims rin chen, *Chos smra ba'i bande tshul khrims rin chen du bod pa'i skye ba,* 471.4–.5.

89. With inspiration from Anthony Grafton, *Defenders of the Text: The Traditions of Scholarship in an Age of Science* (Cambridge, Mass.: Harvard University Press, 1991).

EPILOGUE: THE BOY WHO WROTE *SŪTRAS* ON THE SKY

1. Phyugs rdzis rdo rje gcod pa nam mkha' la bris pa. This is the thirteenth of fifteen stories contained in Anonymous, *'Phags pa shes rab kyi pha rol tu phyin pa rdo rje gcod pa'i phan yon bshad pa'i mdo* (Sikkim: Sgang tog, 1972), fols. 34b–37b.

APPENDIX 1. BÜTON RINCHENDRUP'S LETTER TO EDITORS

1. Bu ston Rin chen grub, "Directions to the Editors and Publishers of the Buddhist Scriptures" [no Tibetan title], in *The Collected Works of Bu-ston* (New Delhi: International Academy of Indian Culture, 1971), 26:344–346, at 344–345.

APPENDIX 2. THE CONTENTS OF THE BUDDHIST CANONS

1. These "D" numbers refer to the catalog numbers assigned to each text in Hakuji Uï, et al., *A Complete Catalog of the Tibetan Buddhist Canons* (Sendai: Tōhuko Imperial University, 1934).

2. See Peter Skilling, "Theravādin Literature in Tibetan Translation," *Journal of the Pali Text Society* 19 (1993): 69–201, at 73–140.

3. Zhu chen Tshul khrims rin chen, *Kun mkhyen nyi ma'i gnyen gyi bka' lung gi dgongs don rnam par 'grel pa'i bstan bcos gangs can pa'i skad du 'gyur ro 'tshal gyi chos sbyin rgyun mi 'chad pa'i ngo mtshar 'phrul gyi phyi mo rdzogs ldan bskal pa'i bsod nams kyi sprin phung rgyas par dkrigs pa'i tshul las brtsams pa'i gtam ngo mtshar chu gter 'phel ba'i zla ba gsar pa* (Lhasa: Bod ljongs mi dmangs dpe skrun khang, 1985), 604.15–605.6.

REFERENCES

TIBETAN REFERENCES

Karma pa III Rang byung rdo rje (1284–1339). *Chos rje rang byung rdo rje'i thugs dam bstan 'gyur gyi dkar chag.* In *Karma pa rang byung rdo rje'i gsung 'bum,* vol. 4, 415–594. Zi ling: Mtshur phu mkhan po lo yag bkra shis, 2006.

———. *Bstan bcos 'gyur ro 'tshal gyi dkar chag.* In *Karma pa rang byung rdo rje'i gsung 'bum,* vol. 4, 595–717. Zi ling: Mtshur phu mkhan po lo yag bkra shis, 2006.

———. *Rnal 'byor gyi dbang phyug mi la bzhad pa rdo rje'i gsung mgur mdzod nag ma zhes pa karma pa rang byung rdo rjes phyogs gcig tu bkod pa.* 2 vols. Dalhousie: Damchoe Sangpo, 1978.

Kaḥthog Tshe dbang nor bu (1698–1755). *Bod rje lha btsad po'i gdung rabs mnga' ris smad gung thang du ji ltar byung ba'i tshul deb ther dwangs shel 'phrul gyi me long.* In *Bod kyi lo rgyus deb ther khag lnga,* 87–150. Lhasa: Bod ljongs bod yig dpe rnying dpe skrun khang, 1990.

Ko shul Grags pa 'byung gnas and Rgyal ba Blo bzang mkhas grub. *Gangs can mkhas grub rim byon ming mdzod.* Lanzhou: Kan su'u mi rigs dpe skrun khang, 1992.

Klu Tshang Rdo rje rin Chen. *Bod kyi rtsom rigs rnam bzhag.* Beijing: Mi rigs dpe skrun khang, 1992.

Klong rdol Bla ma Ngag dbang blo bzang (1719–94). *Rig gnas che ba sgra rig pa / snyan ngag [/] sdeb sbyor / zlos gar / mngon brjod / brda gsar rnying gi khyad par rnams las byung ba'i ming gi grangs.* In *Klong rdol ngag dbang blo bzang gi gsung 'bum,* vol. 1, 657–686. Lhasa: Bod ljongs bod yig dpe rnying dpe skrun khang, 1991.

Bka' bcu G.yung drung phun tshogs (eighteenth century). *Ston pa thams cad mkhen pa'i gsung dbyangs mi mdzad chu bo gter ji snyed pa gangs can bod kyi tshig gis nye bar drangs pa dkar chags legs par bshad pa snang ba'i dga' ston las ci ltar par du sgrub tshul gyi le'u ste bzhi pa.* Manuscript, 33 fols. N.p., n.d. [comp. 1773].

———. *Ston pa thams cad mkhen pa'i gsung dbyangs mi mdzad chu bo gter ji snyed pa gangs can bod kyi tshig gis nye bar drangs pa dkar chags legs par bshad pa snang ba'i dga' ston las sngo smon gyi le'u ste lnga pa.* Manuscript, 13 fols. N.p., n.d. [comp. 1773].

Bkra shis don grub (sixteenth century). *Chos grwa chen po dpal zha lu gser khang gi bdag po jo bo lce'i gdung rabs.* Manuscript, 55 fols. New York: Tibetan Buddhist Resource Center.

Bkra shis lhun grub (seventeenth/eighteenth century). *Dpal ldan sa skya'i rje bt-sun gong ma lnga'i gsung rab rin po che'i par gyi sgo 'phar 'byed pa'i dkar chag 'phrul gyi lde'u mig.* In *Sa skya pa'i bka' 'bum: The Complete Works of the Great Masters of the Sa-skya Sect of Tibetan Buddhism,* vol. 15, 819–950. Tokyo: Tōyō Bunko, 1968.

Dkon mchog rin chen. *Bod kyi gso rig dar tshul rgyas bsdus 'tsham par bkod pa bai ḍurya'i 'phreng ba.* Lanzhou: Kan su'u mi rigs dpe skrun khang, 1992.

Skyogs ston Lo tsā ba Rin chen bkra shis (sixteenth century). *Rje btsun zhwa lu lo tsā ba'i rnam par thar pa brjed byang nor bu'i khri shing.* Manuscript, 42 fols. Beijing: Cultural Palace of Nationalities [comp. 1517]. .

——. *Bod kyi skad las gsar rnying gi brda'i khyad par ston pa legs par bshad pa li shi'i gur khang,* in *Dag yig skor gyi dpe rgyun dkon po 'ga' phyogs gcig tu bsgrigs pa mu tig tshom bu,* 397–424. Xining: Mtsho sngon mi rigs dpe skrun khang, 1998.

Dge ba'i dbang po/Kṣemendra. *Byang chub sems dpa'i rtogs pa brjod pa dpag bsam gyi 'khri shing.* In *Rtogs brjod dpal bsam 'khri shing gi rtsa 'grel,* ed. Mkha' 'gro tshe ring. Xining: Mtsho sngon mi rigs dpe skrun khang, 1997.

'Gos Lo tsā ba Gzhon nu dpal (1392–1481). *Deb ther sngon po.* New Delhi: International Academy of Indian Culture, 1974.

Rgod tshang ras pa Sna tshogs rang grol (1494–1570). *Rje btsun ras chung rdo rje grags kyi rnam thar rnam mkhyen thar lam rin po che gsal ba'i me long ye shes snang ba.* 243 fols. Kathmandu: Nepal-German Manuscript Preparation Project E2080/2.

——. *Gtsang smyon he ru ka phyogs thams cad las rnam par rgyal ba'i rnam thar rdo rje theb pa'i gsal byed nyi ma'i snying po.* In *The Life of the Saint of Gtsaṇ.* New Delhi: Sharada Rani, 1969.

Sgam po pa Bsod nams rin chen (1079–1159). *Tshogs chos yon tan phun tshogs.* In *Selected Writings of Sgam-po-pa Bsod-nams-rin-chen (Dwags-po lha-rje),* 298–333. Dolanji: Topden Tshering, 1974.

Sgra tshad pa Rin chen rnam rgyal (1318–88). *Kun mkhyen bu ston gyi bka' 'bum dkar chag.* In *The Collected Works of Bu-ston,* vol. 28, 333–342. New Delhi: International Academy of Indian Culture, 1971.

——. *Bka' 'bum gyi dkar chag rin chen lde mig.* In *The Collected Works of Bu-ston,* vol. 28, 319–332. New Delhi: International Academy of Indian Culture, 1971.

——. *Chos rje thams cad mkhyen pa bu ston lo tsā ba'i rnam par thar pa snyim pa'i me tog.* In *Bde bar gshegs pa'i bstan pa'i gsal byed chos kyi 'byung gnas gsung rab rin po che'i mdzod,* 318–374. Beijing: Krung go'i bod kyi shes rig dpe skrun khang, 1981.

Ngag dbang nor bu. *Gser bris bstan 'gyur gyi dkar chag.* Beijing: Mi rigs dpe skrun khang, 2004.

Co ne Grags pa bshad grub (1675–1748). *Co ne'i bka' 'gyur rin po che'i dkar chags gsal ba'i me long.* 45 fols. University of Washington: Tibetan microfilm collection, East Asia Library, Reel No. A3–7.2.

Bcom ldan ral gri (1227–1305). *Sgra'i bstan bcos smra ba rgyan gyi me tog*. Manuscript, 22 fols. Beijing: CPN.

Chos kyi grags pa (1595–1659). *Bka' 'gyur gyi dkar chag gsal bar bkos pa chos kyi rnam grangs legs par rtogs byed*. In *The Collected Works (gsuṅ 'bum) of Kun-mkhyen Rig-pa 'dzin-pa Chen-po Chos-kyi-grags-pa*, vol. 2, 11–174. Dehradun: Drikung Kagyu Institute, 1999.

——. *Bka' 'gyur bzhengs dus dpon yig rnams kyi bca' yig*. In *The Collected Works (gsuṅ 'bum) of Kun-mkhyen Rig-pa 'dzin-pa Chen-po Chos-kyi-grags-pa*, vol. 2, 175–180. Dehradun: Drikung Kagyu Institute, 1999.

'Jam mgon A myes zhabs Ngag dbang kun dga' bsod nams (1597–1662). *Dpal dus kyi 'khor lo'i zab pa dang rgya che ba'i dam pa'i chos 'byung ba'i tshul legs par bshad pa ngo mtshar dad pa'i shing rta*. Manuscript, 282 fols. New York: Tibetan Buddhist Resource Center.

'Jam dbyangs bzhad pa'i rdo rje I Ngag dbang brtson 'grus (1648–1721). *Kun mkhyen 'jams dbyangs bzhad pas mdzad pa'i thal 'gyur che ba'i rnam bzhag mdor bsdus*. In *The Collected Works of 'Jam-dbyaṅs-bźad-pa'i-rdo-rje*, vol. 3, 775–793. New Delhi: Ngawang Gelek Demo, 1974.

——. *Kun mkhyen chen po 'jam dbyangs bzhad pa'i rdo rje'i gsung 'bum thor bum khrig chags su bsdebs pa las do ha mdzod gyi mchan 'grel*. In *The Collected Works of 'Jam-dbyaṅs-bźad-pa'i-rdo-rje*, vol. 4, 639–665. New Delhi: Ngawang Gelek Demo, 1974.

——. *Kun mkhyen 'jam dbyangs bzhad pa'i rdo rje'i gsung 'bum thor bum khrig chags su bsdebs pa las 'pho ba'i bshad pa sogs*. In *The Collected Works of 'Jam-dbyaṅs-bźad-pa'i-rdo-rje*, vol. 3, 593–605. New Delhi: Ngawang Gelek Demo, 1974.

——. *Kun mkhyen 'jam dbyangs bzhad pa'i rdo rje'i gsung 'bum thor bum khrig chags su bsdebs pa las smon la gyi skor*. In *The Collected Works of 'Jam-dbyaṅs-bźad-pa'i-rdo-rje*, vol. 1, 735–749. New Delhi: Ngawang Gelek Demo, 1974.

——. *Kun mkhyen 'jam dbyangs bzhad pa'i rdo rje'i gsung 'bum thor bum khrig chags su bsdebs pa las zhal gdams mgur ma'i skor*. In *The Collected Works of 'Jam-dbyaṅs-bźad-pa'i-rdo-rje*, vol. 4, 511–536. New Delhi: Ngawang Gelek Demo, 1974.

——. *Kun mkhyen 'jam dbyangs bzhad pa'i rdo rje'i gsung 'bum las byang chub lam rim gyi rnams bshad lung rigs gter mdzod*. In *The Collected Works of 'Jam-dbyaṅs-bźad-pa'i-rdo-rje*, vol. 4, 337–477. New Delhi: Ngawang Gelek Demo, 1974.

——. *Skabs brgyad pa'i mtha' dpyod 'khrul sel gangga'a'i chu rgyun ma pham zhal lung*. In *The Collected Works of 'Jam-dbyaṅs-bźad-pa'i-rdo-rje*, vol. 8, 335–537. New Delhi: Ngawang Gelek Demo, 1974.

——. *Grub mtha'i rnam par bzhag pa 'khrul spong gdong lnga'i sgra dbyangs kun mkhyen lam bzang gsal ba'i rin chen sgron me*. In *The Collected Works of 'Jam-dbyaṅs-bźad-pa'i-rdo-rje*, vol. 1, 750–802; see also vol. 3, 807–852 and vol. 15, 1–31. New Delhi: Ngawang Gelek Demo, 1974.

———. *Mngon brjod kyi bstan bcos 'chi ba med pa'i mdzod.* In *The Collected Works of 'Jam-dbyaṅs-bźad-pa'i-rdo-rje,* vol. 15, 567–791. New Delhi: Ngawang Gelek Demo, 1974.

———. *Chos kyi rje thams can mkhyen pa 'jam dbyangs bzhad pa'i rdo rje'i gsan yig thor bu gang rnyed phyogs gcig tu bsgrigs pa la tshan pa dang po.* In *The Collected Works of 'Jam-dbyaṅs-bźad-pa'i-rdo-rje,* vol. 4, 5–124. New Delhi: Ngawang Gelek Demo, 1974.

———. *Chos kyi rje thams can mkhyen pa 'jam dbyangs bzhad pa'i rdo rje'i gsung 'bum thor bu rnams khrigs chags su bsdebs pa las sna tshogs kyi skor.* In *The Collected Works of 'Jam-dbyaṅs-bźad-pa'i-rdo-rje,* vol. 4, 479–510. New Delhi: Ngawang Gelek Demo, 1974.

———. *Chos kyi rje thams can mkhyen pa 'jam dbyangs bzhad pa'i rdo rje'i gsung 'bum thor bu rnams khrigs chags su bsdebs pa las yi dam sgrub skor.* In *The Collected Works of 'Jam-dbyaṅs-bźad-pa'i-rdo-rje,* vol. 4, 681–853. New Delhi: Ngawang Gelek Demo, 1974.

———. *Rje btsun bla ma'i 'jam dbyangs bzhad pa'i gsung 'bum thor bu las sa chog.* In *The Collected Works of 'Jam-dbyaṅs-bźad-pa'i-rdo-rje,* vol. 1, 447–472. New Delhi: Ngawang Gelek Demo, 1974.

———. *Rje red mda' ba'i dris lan gyi ṭikka rtsom 'phro.* In *The Collected Works of 'Jam-dbyaṅs-bźad-pa'i-rdo-rje,* vol. 3, 543–571. New Delhi: Ngawang Gelek Demo, 1974.

———. *Rtags rigs kyi rnam bzhag nyung gsal legs bshad.* In *The Collected Works of 'Jam-dbyaṅs-bźad-pa'i-rdo-rje,* vol. 15, 177–301. New Delhi: Ngawang Gelek Demo, 1974.

———. *Bstan bcos mngon par rtogs pa'i rgyan gyi mtha' dpyod shes rab kyi pha rol tu phyin pa'i don kun gsal ba'i rin chen sgron me.* In *The Collected Works of 'Jam-dbyaṅs-bźad-pa'i-rdo-rje,* vols. 7–8. New Delhi: Ngawang Gelek Demo, 1974.

———. *Darpa ṇa a tsaryas mdzad pa'i gshin rje gshed dmar po'i 'tsho ba'i de kho na nyid la kun mkhyen 'jam dbyangs bzhad pas mchan 'god gnang ba.* In *The Collected Works of 'Jam-dbyaṅs-bźad-pa'i-rdo-rje,* vol. 4, 629–638. New Delhi: Ngawang Gelek Demo, 1974.

———. *Bde mchog bskyed rim gyi bzhad pa'i zin bris.* In *The Collected Works of 'Jam-dbyaṅs-bźad-pa'i-rdo-rje,* vol. 2, 325–345. New Delhi: Ngawang Gelek Demo, 1974.

———. *Bden bzhi'i rnam bshad 'khrul bral lung rigs kyi nyi ma chen po.* In *The Collected Works of 'Jam-dbyaṅs-bźad-pa'i-rdo-rje,* vol. 11, 660–691. New Delhi: Ngawang Gelek Demo, 1974.

———. *'Dul ba'i dka' gnas rnam par dpyad pa 'khrul spong blo gsal mgul rgyan tsinta ma ni'i phreng mdzes skal bzang re ba kun skong las gzhi stod and gzhi smad.* In *The Collected Works of 'Jam-dbyaṅs-bźad-pa'i-rdo-rje,* vol. 6, 3–633, 635–959. New Delhi: Ngawang Gelek Demo, 1974.

——. *Dpal rdo rje 'jigs byed kyi chos 'byung khams gsum las rnam par rgyal ba dngos grub kyi gter mdzod.* In *The Collected Works of 'Jam-dbyaṅs-bźad-pa'i-rdo-rje,* vol. 5, 3–835. New Delhi: Ngawang Gelek Demo, 1974.

——. *Phar phyin skabs brgyad pa'i mtha' dpyod bsam 'phel yid bzhin nor bu'i phreng mdzes skal bzang mig 'byed.* In *The Collected Works of 'Jam-dbyaṅs-bźad-pa'i-rdo-rje,* vol. 8, 539–673. New Delhi: Ngawang Gelek Demo, 1974.

——. *'Phrin yig gi rnam par bzhag pa blo gsal rna rgyan sindhu wa'a ra'i phreng mdzes.* In *The Collected Works of 'Jam-dbyaṅs-bźad-pa'i-rdo-rje,* vol. 1, 301–367. New Delhi: Ngawang Gelek Demo, 1974.

——. *Bar ri brgya rtsa'i rjes gnang gi lhan thabs dngos grub rin chen 'dren pa'i gru chen klag pas don grub.* In *The Collected Works of 'Jam-dbyaṅs-bźad-pa'i-rdo-rje,* vol. 3, 289–359. New Delhi: Ngawang Gelek Demo, 1974.

——. *Dbu ma 'jug pa'i mtha' dpyod lung rigs gter mdzod zab don kun gsal bzang 'jug ngogs.* In *The Collected Works of 'Jam-dbyaṅs-bźad-pa'i-rdo-rje,* vol. 9, 3–885. New Delhi: Ngawang Gelek Demo, 1974.

——. *Gzungs 'bul gyi lhan thabs gnod sbyin dang tshogs bdag gi 'khor lo'i sgrub thabs.* In *The Collected Works of 'Jam-dbyaṅs-bźad-pa'i-rdo-rje,* vol. 1, 510–522. New Delhi: Ngawang Gelek Demo, 1974.

——. *Rigs dang dkyil 'khor kun gyi bdag po khyab bdag bla ma dkon mchog mtshan can gyi bstod pa rig 'dzin grub pa'i sgra dbyangs.* In *The Collected Works of 'Jam-dbyaṅs-bźad-pa'i-rdo-rje,* vol. 15, 63–71. New Delhi: Ngawang Gelek Demo, 1974.

'Jam dbyangs bzhad pa'i rdo rje II Dkon mchog 'jigs med dbang po (1725–91). *Mkhas shing grub pa'i dbang phyug kun mkhyen 'jam dbyangs bzhad pa'i rdo rje'i rnam par thar pa ngo mtshar skal bzang 'jug ngogs.* In *The Collected Works of Dkon-mchog-'jigs-med-dbaṅ-po,* vol. 2, 75–319. New Delhi: Ngawang Gelek Demo, 1971.

——. *Bde bar gshegs pa'i bka'i dgongs 'grel bstan bcos 'gyur ro cog par du sgrub pa'i tshul las nye bar brtsams pa'i gtam yang dag par brjod pa dkar chag yid bzhin nor bu'i phreng ba.* Langzhou: Kan su'u mi rigs dpe skrun khang, 1986.

'Jigs med grags pa (fifteenth century). *Rgyal rtse chos rgyal gyi rnam par thar pa dad pa'i lo thog dngos grub kyi char 'bebs* [comp. 1479–81]. Lhasa: Bod ljongs mi dmangs dpe skrun khang, 1987.

'Jigs med gling pa Mkhyen brtse 'od zer (1729/30–98). *Yul lho rgyud byung ba'i rdzogs chen pa rang byung rdo rje mkhyen brtse'i 'od zer gyi rnam par thar pa legs byas yongs 'du'i snye ma.* In *'Jigs med gling pa'i rnam thar,* 1–461. Chengdu: Si khron mi rigs dpe skrun khang, 1998.

——. *Sa skyong sde dge'i rgyal khab tu snga 'gyur rgyud 'bum rin po che par du bzhengs pa'i dus zhu chen rnam gnyis la skabs dbye ba'i gtam.* In *'Jigs med gling pa'i gtam tshogs,* 390–394. Lhasa: Bod ljongs bod yig dpe rnying dpe skrun khang, 1991.

'Jigs med 'bangs (fifteenth century). *Dpal ldan bla ma dam pa thams cad mkhyen pa phyogs thams cad las rnam par rgyal ba'i zhabs kyi rnam par thar pa ngo mtshar kyi dga' ston.* Lhasa: Bod ljongs bod yig dpe rnying dpe skrun khang, 1991.

Tāranātha (1575–1634) [authorship uncertain]. *Myang yul stod smad bar gsum gyi ngo mtshar gtam legs bshad mkhas pa'i 'jug ngogs.* Lhasa: Bod ljongs mi dmangs dpe skrun khang, 1983.

Ta'a la'i Bla ma VIII 'Jam dpal rgya mtsho (1758–1804). *Dpal ldang bla ma dam pa rigs dang dkyil 'khor rgya mtsho'i mnga' bdag bka drin gsum ldan yongs 'dzin paṇḍi ta chen po rje btsun ye shes rgyal mtshan dpal bzang po'i sku gsung thugs kyi rtogs pa brjod pa thub btsan padmo 'byed pa'i nyin byed.* In *Biography of Tshe-gling Yongs-'dzin Ye-shes-rgyal-mtshan* by Dalai Lama VIII. New Delhi: Ngawang Gelek Demo, 1969.

Stag tshang Lo tsa'a ba Shes rab rin chen (b. 1405). *Rten gsum bzhengs tshul dpal 'byor rgya mtsho.* In *Stag tshang lo tsa'a ba shes rab rin chen gyi gsung skor,* vol. 1, 449–540. Kathmandu: Sa skya rgyal yongs gsung rab slob gnyer khang, n.d.

Stag lung Ngag dbang rnam rgyal (1571–1626). *Brgyud pa yid bzhin nor bu'i rtogs pa brjod pa ngo mtshar rgya mtsho.* Lhasa: Bod yig dpe rnying dpe skrun khang, 1992.

Thu'u bkwan Blo bzang chos kyi nyi ma (1737–1802). *Khyab bdag rdo rje sems dpa'i ngo bo dpal ldan bla ma dam pa ye shes bstan pa'i sgron me dpal bzang po'i rnam par thar pa mdo tsam brjod pa dge ldan bstan pa'i mdzes rgyan.* Lanzhou: Kan su'u mi rigs dpe skrun khang, 1989.

Dar mo Blo bzang chos grags (1638–1697/1700). *Bdud rtsi snying po yan lag brgyad pa gsang ba man ngag gi rgyud dum bu gsum pa man ngag rgyud kyi dka' 'grel legs bshad gser rgyan.* In *Rgyud bzhi'i 'grel pa mes po'i zhal lung,* vol. 2, 1–527. Beijing: Krung go'i bod kyi shes rig dpe skrun khang, 1989.

Dung dkar Blo bzang 'phrin las. "Bod kyi dpe rnying par skrun dang 'brel ba'i gnad don 'ga' zhig skor gleng ba,." In *Dung dkar blo bzang 'phrin las kyi gsung rtsom phyogs bgrigs,* 406–451. Beijing: Krung go'i bod kyi shes rig dpe skrun khang, 1997.

——. *Bod kyi dkar chag rig pa.* Beijing: Mi rigs dpe skrun khang, 2004.

Dus 'khor zhabs drung (seventeenth century). *Rig gnas lnga'i rnam dbye cung zad bshad pa legs bshad nor bu'i phreng ba blo gsal mgul rgyan.* In *Rig gnas phyogs bsdebs: A Collection of Miscellaneous Works on Tibetan Minor Sciences.* Dharamsala: Library of Tibetan Works and Archives, 1981.

Mdo mkhar zhabs drung Tshe ring dbang rgyal (1697–1763). *Dpal mi'i dbang po'i rtogs pa brjod pa 'jig rten kun tu dga' ba'i gtam.* Xining: Si khron mi rigs dpe skrun khang, 1981.

Sde dge Bla sman Rin chen 'od zer (nineteenth century). *Bdud rtsi rnying po yan lab brgyad pa gsang ba man ngag gi rgyud las dum bu gnyis pa bshad pa'i rgyud kyi 'bru 'grel don gsal rab tu snang ba'i nyin byed.* In *Bdud rtsi snying po yan lag brgyad pa gsang ba man ngag gi rgyud las rtsa rgyud dang bshad rgyud kyi 'grel pa,* 139–554. Chengdu: Si khron mi rigs dpe skrun khang, 2001.

Sde srid Sangs rgyas rgya mtsho (1653–1705). *Dpal mnyam med ri bo dga' ldan pa'i bstan pa zhwa ser cod pan 'chang ba'i ring lugs chos thams cad kyi rtsa ba gsal bar byed pa'i baiḍū rya ser po'i me long.* Beijing: Krung go bod kyi shes rig dpe skrun khang, 1991.

——. *Dpal ldan gso ba rig pa'i khog 'bugs legs bshad ba'i ḍūrya'i me long drang srong dgyes pa'i dga' ston.* Lanzhou: Kan su'u mi rigs dpe skrun khang, 1982.

——. *Blang dor gsal bar ston pa'i drang thig dwangs shel me long nyer gcig pa* [comp. 1681]. In *Blaṅ dor gsal bar ston pa'i draṅ thig dwaṅs śel me loṅ: A Treatise on the Sixteen Fundamental Principles of Tibetan Administrative Law*, 1–83. Dolanji: Tibetan Bonpo Monastic Center, 1979.

——. *Bod kyi dus rabs rims byung gi khrims yig phyogs bsdus dwangs byed ke ta ka.* Ed. Tshe ring bde skyid. Lhasa: Bod ljongs mi dmangs dpe skrun khang, 1987, 203–279.

——. *Bod kyi snga rabs khrims srol yig cha bdams bsgrigs.* Ed. Tshe ring dpal 'byor. Lhasa: Bod yig dpe rnying dpe skrun khang, 1989, 198–274.

——. Sde srid Sangs rgyas rgya mtsho. *Gso ba rig pa'i bstan bcos sman bla'i dgongs rgyan rgyud bzhi'i gsal byed bai ḍūr sngon po'i ma lli ka* [comp. 1688: Sde dge block print, 1748]. 4 vols. Leh: D. L. Tashigang, 1981.

Dpa' ris sangs rgyas. *Dpe chos rna ba'i bdud rtsi.* Xining: Mtsho sngon mi rigs dpe skrun khang, 1985.

Phur bu lcog Ngag dbang byams pa (1682–1762). *Bstan bcos 'gyur ro cog gsung par du bsgrubs pa'i dkar chag tshangs pa'i dbyangs.* 144 fols. N.p., n.d. [comp. 1742].

'Phags pa Blo gros rgyal mtshan (1235–80). *Go pe las rgyas 'bring bsdus gsum bzhengs pa'i mtshon byed.* In *The Collected Works of the Founding Masters of the Sa-skya*, vol. 15, 630.2–633.2 [comp. 1275]. Dehra Dun: Sakya Center, 1992–93.

——. *Bde bar gshegs pa'i gsung rab 'gyur ro 'tshal bzhengs pa'i bsal byed sdeb sbyor gyi rgyan rnam par bkra ba.* In *The Collected Works of the Founding Masters of the Sa-skya*, vol. 15, 599.1–610 [comp. 1278]. Dehra Dun: Sakya Center, 1992–93.

——. *Chos rin po che nye bar bzhengs pa'i mtshon bye drab tu byed pa.* In *The Collected Works of the Founding Masters of the Sa-skya*, vol. 15, 610.2–615.1 [comp. 1276]. Dehra Dun: Sakya Center, 1992–93.

——. *Dam chos rin po che shin tu rgyas pa'i sde snod bzhengs pa la bsngags pa.* In *The Collected Works of the Founding Masters of the Sa-skya*, vol. 15, 615.1–618.5 [comp. 1277]. Dehra Dun: Sakya Center, 1992–93.

——. *Manga la yab yum gyis rgyas 'bring bsdus gsum dang phal po che bzhengs pa'i mtshon byed.* In *The Collected Works of the Founding Masters of the Sa-skya*, vol. 15, 618.5–623.1 [comp. 1275]. Dehra Dun: Sakya Center, 1992–93.

——. *Ji big de mur gyis phal chen gser 'od stong phrag brgya pa rnams bzhengs pa'i mtshon byed.* In *The Collected Works of the Founding Masters of the Sa-skya*, vol. 15, 623.1–628.2 [comp. 1273]. Dehra Dun: Sakya Center, 1992–93.

221

——. *A rog ches 'bum bzhengs pa'i rab byed.* In *The Collected Works of the Founding Masters of the Sa-skya,* vol. 15, 628.2–630.2 [comp. 1274]. Dehra Dun: Sakya Center, 1992–93.

——. *Dge 'dun bzang po sogs kyis sher phyin rgyas 'bring bsdus gsum bzhengs pa'i mtshon byed.* In *The Collected Works of the Founding Masters of the Sa-skya,* vol. 15, 633.2–635.3. Dehra Dun: Sakya Center, 1992–93.

——. *Rin chen dpal gyis 'bum bzhengs pa'i mtshon byed.* In *The Collected Works of the Founding Masters of the Sa-skya,* vol. 15, 635.3–637.3. Dehra Dun: Sakya Center, 1992–93.

Bu ston Rin chen grub (1290–1364). *Bstan 'gyur gyi dkar chag yin bzhin nor bu dbang gi rgyal po'i phreng ba.* In *The Collected Works of Bu-ston,* vol. 26, 401–644. New Delhi: International Academy of Indian Culture, 1971.

——. "Directions to the Editors and Publishers of the Buddhist Scriptures" [no Tibetan title]. In *The Collected Works of Bu-ston,* vol. 26, 344–34. New Delhi: International Academy of Indian Culture, 1971.

——. *Bde bar gshegs pa'i bstan pa'i gsal byed chos kyi 'byung gnas gsung rab rin po che'i mdzod.* In *Bu ston chos 'byung,* 1–317. Beijing: Krung go'i bod kyi shes rig dpe skrun khang, 1981.

——. *Dpal gsang ba 'dus pa'i rdzogs rim rim lnga'i dmar khrid kyi man ngag yid bzhin nor bu rin po che'i za ma tog.* In *The Collected Works of Bu-ston,* vol. 10, 31–70. New Delhi: International Academy of Indian Culture, 1971.

——. *Bu ston rin po che'i bka' 'bum gyi dkar chas chos rje nyid kyis mdzad pa.* In *The Collected Works of Bu-ston,* vol. 26, 645–656. New Delhi: International Academy of Indian Culture, 1971.

Bo dong Paṇ chen Phyogs las rnam rgyal (1375–1451). *Rten gsum bzhengs tshul bstan bcos lugs bshad pa.* In *Encyclopedia Tibetica: The Collected Works of Bo-dong paṇ-chen phyogs-las-rnam-rgyal,* vol. 2, 265–342. New Delhi: Tibet House, 1969.

——. *Byis pa 'jug pa'i sgo.* In *Encyclopedia Tibetica: The Collected Works of Bo-dong paṇ-chen phyogs-las-rnam-rgyal,* vol. 9, 12–188. New Delhi: Tibet House, 1969.

Bya bral pa Tshul khrims dpal ldan (circa sixteenth century). *Mkhas grub rdo rje 'chang bsod nams blo gros kyi rnam thar yon tan gyi sbrang rtsi la dad pa'i bung ba rnam par rol pa.* Kathmandu: NGMPP L833/3 [comp. 1544].

Byang pa Rnam rgyal grags bzang (1395–1475). *'Tsho byed rnams la snying nas brtse ba'i man ngag 'phrul gyi yig chung.* In *Bod kyi sman rtsis ched rtsom phyogs bsdus,* 117–120. Lhasa: Bod ljongs mi dmangs dpe skrun khang, 1986.

——. *Bshad pa'i rgyud kyi rgya cher 'grel pa bdud rtsi'i chu rgyun.* Chengdu: Si khron mi rigs dpe skrun khang, 2001 [comp. 1463].

Byams pa/Maitreya. *Theg pa chen po mdo sde'i rgyan shes bya ba'i tshig le'ur byas pa.* In *Sde dge Bstan 'gyur, Sems tsam,* vol. Phi. fols. 1–39. In Hakuji Ui, et al., *A Complete Catalog of the Tibetan Buddhist Canons,* no. 4020. Sendai: Tōhuko Imperial University, 1934.

——. *Dbus dang mtha' rnam par 'byed pa*. In *Sde dge Bstan 'gyur, Sems tsam*, vol. Phi. fols. 40b.–45a.6. In Hakuji Ui, et al., *A Complete Catalog of the Tibetan Buddhist Canons*, no. 4021. Sendai: Tōhuko Imperial University, 1934.

Byams pa 'phrin las (b. 1928). *Gangs ljongs gso rig bstan pa'i nyin byed rim byon gyi rnam thar phyogs bsgrigs*. Beijing: Mi rigs dpe skrun khang, 1990.

——. *Sde srid sangs rgyas rgya mtsho'i 'khrungs rabs dang mdzad rjes dad brgya'i padma rnam par bzhad pa'i phreng ba*. In *Byams pa 'phrin las kyi gsung rtsom phyogs bsgrigs*, 402–442. Beijing: Krung go'i bod kyi shes rig dpe skrun khang, 1996.

Brag dkar rta so Sprul sku Chos kyi dbang phyug (1775–1837). *Grub pa'i gnas chen brag dkar rta so'i gnas dang gdan rabs bla ma brgyud pa'i lo rgyus mdo tsam brjod pa mos ldan dad pa'i gdung sel drang srong dga' ba'i dal gtam*. 52 fols. Kathmandu: NGMPP 940/8 [comp. 1816].

Brag dgon Dkon mchog bstan pa rab rgyas (1800/1–66). *Yul mdo smad kyi ljongs su thub bstan rin po che ji ltar dar ba'i tshul gsal bar brjod pa deb ther rgya mtsho*. Lanzhou: Kan su'u mi rigs dpe skrun khang, 1982.

Brang ti Dpal ldan 'tsho byed (early fourteenth century). *Bdud rtsi snying po yan lag brgyad gsang ba man ngag gi rgyud kyi spyi don shes bya rab gsas rgyas pa*. Manuscript, 48 fols. Beijing: CPN.

Bla ma skyabs. *Bod kyi mkhas pa rim byon gyi gso rig gsung 'bum dkar chag mu tig phreng ba*. Lanzhou: Kan su'u mi rigs dpe skrun khang, 1997.

Dbal mang Dkon mchog rgyal mtshan (1764–1853). *Mdo smad bstan pa'i 'byung gnas dpal ldan bkra shis dkyil gyi gdan rabs rang bzhin dbyangs su brjod pa'i lha'i rnga bo che*. In *The Collected Works of Dbal-maṅ Dkon-mchog-rgyal-mtshan*, vol. 1, 1–613. New Delhi: Gyaltsan Gelek Namgyal, 1974.

'Bri gung Che tshang IV Bstan 'dzin padma'i rgyal mtshan (1770–1826). *Nges don bstan pa'i snying po mgon po 'bri gung pa chen po'i gdan rabs chos kyi byung tshul gser gyi phreng ba*. Lhasa: Bod ljongs bod yig dpe rnying dpe skrun khang, 1989.

'Brug chen IV Padma dkar po (1527–92). *Li ma brtag pa'i rab byed smra 'dod pa'i kha rgyan*. In *The Collected Works (gsuṅ 'bum) of Kun-mkhyen Padma-dkar-po*, vol. 1, 293–305. Darjeeling: Kargyud Sungrab Nyamso Khang, 1973.

Sba Gsal snang. *Sba bzhed ces bya ba las sba gsal snang gi bzhed pa*. Ed. Mgon po rgyal mtshan. Beijing: Mi rigs dpe skrun khang, 1982.

Mang thos Klu sgrub rgya mtsho (1523–96). *Bstan rtsis gsal ba'i nyin byed lhag bsam rab dkar*. In *Bstan rstis gsal ba'i nyin byed*, 1–251. Lhasa: Bod ljongs mi dmangs dpe skrun khang, 1987.

Mi pham rgya mtsho (1846–1911). *Bzo gnas nyer mkho'i za ma tog*. In *Collected Writings*, vol. 10, 71–138. Gangtok: Sonam Topbay Kazi, 1972.

——. *Bzo gnas nyer mkho'i za ma tog*. Xining: Mtsho sngon mi rigs dpe skrun khang, 1993.

Sman rams pa Pa sangs yon tan. *Bod kyi gso ba rig pa'i lo rgyus kyi bang mdzod g.yu thog bla ma dran pa'i pho nya.* Leh: Yuthok Institute of Tibetan Medicine, 1988.

Gtsang smyon He ru ka (1452–1507). *Rnal 'byor gyi dbang phyug dam pa rje btsun mi la ras pa'i rnam par thar pa dang thams cad mkhyen pa'i lam ston.* 115 fols. Kathmandu: NGMPP L250/7.

Tshal pa Kun dga' rdo rje (1309–64). *Deb ther dmar po rnams kyi dang po hu lan deb ther.* Beijing: Mi rigs dpe skrun khang, 1981.

Tshe mchog gling Yongs 'dzin Ye shes rgyal mtshan (1713–93). *Bkra shis bsam gtan gling gi bka' bstan rin po che'i dkar chag thub bstan gsal byed.* In *The Collected Works (Gsuṅ-'bum) of Tshe-mchog-gliṅ yoṅs-'dzin ye-śes-rgyal-mtshan,* vol. 19, 421–553. New Delhi: Tibet House, 1975.

——. *Thams cad mkhyen pa bu ston rin chen grub kyi gsung 'bum gyi dkar chag bstan pa rin po che'i mdzes rgyan phul byung gser gyi phreng ba* [comp. 1779]. In *The Collected Works (Gsuṅ-'bum) of Tshe-mchog-gliṅ yoṅs-'dzin ye-śes-rgyal-mtshan,* vol. 5, 261–375. New Delhi: Tibet House, 1975.

Tsong kha pa Blo bzang grags pa (1357–1419). *Mnyam med tsong kha pa chen pos mdzad pa'i byang chub lam rim che ba.* Xining: Mtsho sngon mi rigs dpe skrun khang, 1985.

Tshe dbang rdo rje rig 'dzin (b. 1786). *Dpal sa skyong sde dge chos kyi rgyal po rim byon gyi rnam thar dge legs nor bu'i phreng ba 'dod dgu rab 'phel.* Lhasa: Bod ljongs mi dmangs dpe skrun khang, 1989.

Zhi ba lha/Śāntideva, *Byang chub sems dpa'i spyod pa la 'jug pa. Bodhisattvacaryāvatāra.* In *Sde dge Bstan 'gyur, Dbu ma,* vol. *La,* fols. 1–40. In Hakuji Ui, et al., *A Complete Catalog of the Tibetan Buddhist Canons,* no. 3871. Sendai: Tōhuko Imperial University, 1934.

Zhu chen Tshul khrims rin chen (1697–1774). *Kun mkhyen nyi ma'i gnyen gyi bka' lung gi dgongs don rnam par 'grel pa'i bstan bcos gangs can pa'i skad du 'gyur ro 'tshal gyi chos sbyin rgyun mi 'chad pa'i ngo mtshar 'phrul gyi phyi mo rdzogs ldan bskal pa'i bsod nams kyi sprin phung rgyas par dkrigs pa'i tshul las brtsams pa'i gtam ngo mtshar chu gter 'phel ba'i zla ba gsar pa.* Lhasa: Bod ljongs mi dmangs dpe skrun khang, 1985.

——. *Chos smra ba'i bande tshul khrims rin chen du bod pa'i skye ba phal pa'i rkang 'thung dge sdig 'dres ma'i las kyi yal ga phan tshun du 'dzings par bde sdug gi lo 'dab dus kyi rgyal mos re mos su bsgyur ba.* In *The Autobiography of Tshul-khrims-rin-chen of Sde-dge and Other Selected Writings,* 494.2–.6. Delhi: N. Lungtok and N. Gyaltsan, 1971.

——. *Bstan bcos 'gyur ro 'tshal gyi chos sbyin rgyun mi 'chad pa'i phyi mo rdzogs ldan bskal pa'i bsod nams kyi sprin phung rgyas par dkrigs pa'i bsngo ba smon lam gyi tshigs su bcad pa bde legs yid gtsugs mdza' na 'gugs pa'i rgyang glu.* In *Collected Writings on Buddhist Philosophy, Liturgy, and Ritual of Źu-chen Tshul-khrims-rin-chen,* vol. 7, 351–369. New Delhi: B. Jamyang Norbu, 1974. Also printed as *Thams cad mkhyen pa chen po nyi ma'i gnyen gyi bka' spyi dang bye brag gi dgongs pa ma lus pa rnam 'grel pa'i bstan bcos 'gyur ro 'tshal gyi chos sbyin rgyun mi chad pa'i phyi mo yongs su rdzogs par grub pa'i bsngo ba smon lam gyi tshigs su bcad pa gzhi lam 'bras bu'i dge legs yid bcugs mdza' bo 'gugs pa'i rgyang glu zhes bya ba par byang mdor bsdus tsam dang bcas pa* [title from colophon]. In *Sde dge bka' 'gyur, Sna tshogs*, vol. Nyo, fols. 354a–361a (not listed in In Hakuji Ui, et al., *A Complete Catalog of the Tibetan Buddhist Canons* [Sendai: Tōhuko Imperial University, 1934], but should follow no. 4419).

Zhwa dmar VI Chos kyi dbang phyug (1584–1630). *Chos kyi rgyal po chen po karma mi pham tshe dbang bsod nams rab brtan zhes bya bas bde bar gshegs pa'i bka' 'gyur ro 'tshal chos kyi phyi mo mi zad pa'i par du bzhengs pa'i 'byung ba brjod pa* [title from colophon; title page illegible]. New York: Tibetan Buddhist Resource Center, W1CZ881.

Zhwa lu Ri phug Sprul sku Blo gsal bstan skyong (1804–c. 1874). *Dpal ldan zhwa lu pa'i bstan pa la bka' drin che ba'i skyes bu dam pa rnams kyi rnam thar lo rgyus ngo mtshar dad pa'i 'jug ngogs*. In *On the History of the the Monastery of Zhwa-lu*. Leh: Tashi Yangphel Tashigang, 1971.

Zhwa lu Lo tsā ba Chos skyong bzang po (1441–1527). *Bod kyi brda'i bstan bcos legs par bshad pa rin po che'i za ma tog bkod pa* [comp. 1514]. In *Dag yig skor gyi dpe rgyun dkon po 'ga' phyogs gcig tu bsgrigs pa mu tig tshom bu*, 39–92. Xining: Mtsho sngon mi rigs dpe skrun khang, 1998.

Zur mkhar Blo gros rgyal po (1509–c. 1573). *Gang dag byang chub sems dpa'i spyad pa spyod par 'dod pa'i sman pa rnams kyis mi shes mi rung ba'i phyi nang gzhan gsum gyis rnam bzhag shes bya spyi khog dbub pa gtan pa med pa'i mchod sbyin gyi sgo 'phar yangs po*. Chengdu: Si khron mi rigs dpe skrun khang, 2001.

——. *Rgyud bzhi bka' dang bstan bcos rnam par dbye ba mun sel sgron me*. In *Bod kyi sman rtsis ched rtsom phyogs bsdus*, 64–71. Lhasa: Bod ljongs mi dmangs dpe skrun khang, 1986.

——. *Bdud rtsi snying po yan lag brgyad pa gsang ba man ngag gi rgyud kyi tshig don phyin ci ma log par 'grel ba mes po'i zhal lung zhes bya ba las dum bu gnyis pa bshad pa'i rgyud kyi rnam bshad*. In *Rgyud bzhi'i 'grel pa mes po'i zhal lung*, vol. 1, 89–668. Beijing: Krung go'i bod kyi shes rig dpe skrun khang, 1989.

——. *Bdud rtsi snying po yan lag brgyad pa gsang ba man ngag gi rgyud kyi tshig don phyin ci ma log par 'grel ba mes po'i zhal lung zhes bya ba las dum bu dang po rtsa ba'i rgyud kyi rnam bshad*. In *Rgyud bzhi'i 'grel pa mes po'i zhal lung*, vol. 1, 1–88. Beijing: Krung go'i bod kyi shes rig dpe skrun khang, 1989.

Ye shes mkha' 'gro bsod nams 'drin gyi sku skye gsum pa rje btsun ma chos kyi sgron ma'i rnam thar. 146 fols.; 145–146 missing. Beijing: Cultural Palace of Nationalities.

G.yu thog Yon tan mgon po (1126–1202). *Khog dbug khyung chen lding ba*. In *Gyu thog cha lag bco brgyad: A Corpus of Tibetan Medical Teachings Attributed to Gyu-thog the Physician Reproduced from a Set of Prints from the Seventeenth-*

Century Lhasa Źol Blocks, vol. 1, fols. 1–16. Dolanji: Tibetan Bonpo Monastic Center, 1976.

——. *Grwa thang rgyud bzhi*. Beijing: Mi rigs dpe skrun khang, 2005.

——. *Bdud rtsi snying po yan lag brgyad pa gsang ba man ngag gi rgyud*. Lhasa: Bod ljongs mi dmangs dpe skrun khang, 1992.

Rwa Ye shes seng ge. *Mthu stobs dbang phyug rje btsun dwa lo tsa'a ba'i rnam par thar pa kun khyab snyan pa'i rnga sgra*. Xining: Mtsho sngon mi rigs dpe skrun khang, 1989.

Si tu Paṇ chen Chos kyi 'byung gnas (1699/1700–74). *Tā'i Si tur 'bod pa karma bstan pa'i nyin byed kyi rang tshul drangs por brjod pa dri bral shel gyi me long*. In *Tā'i Situ pa kun mkhyen chos kyi 'byung gnas bstan pa'i nyin byed kyi bka' 'bum*, vol. 14, 7–748. Kangra: Sherab Gyaltsen, 1990.

——. *Thon mi'i legs bshad sum cu pa'i snying po ljon pa'i dbang po*, in *Sum rtags rtsa ba dang de'i 'grel pa si tu'i zhal lung*, 74–78. Beijing: Mi rigs dpe skrun khang, 1994.

——. *Bde bar gshegs pa'i bka' gangs can gyi brdas drangs pa'i phyi mo'i tshogs ji snyed pa par du bsgrubs pa'i tshul la nye bar brtsams pa'i gtam bzang po blo ldan mos pa'i kunda yongs su kha byed pa'i zla 'od gzhon nu'i 'khri shing*. In *Tā'i Situ pa kun mkhyen chos kyi 'byung gnas bstan pa'i nyin byed kyi bka' 'bum*, vol. 9, 9–500. Kangra: Sherab Gyaltsen, 1990. Also published as *Sde dge'i bka' 'gyur dkar chag*. Chengdu: Si khron mi rigs dpe skrun khang, 1988.

Sum ston pa Ye shes gzungs (twelfth century). *'Grel pa 'bum chung gsal sgron nor bu'i 'phreng mdzes*. In *Gyu thog cha lag bco brgyad: A Corpus of Tibetan Medical Teachings Attributed to Gyu-thog the Physician Reproduced from a Set of Prints from the Seventeenth-Century Lhasa Źol Blocks*. Dolanji: Tibetan Bonpo Monastic Center, 1976.

Sle lung Rje drung Bzhad pa'i rdo rje (b. 1697). *Bka' 'gyur rin po che'i gsung par srid gsum rgyan gcig rdzu 'phrul shing rta'i dkar chag ngo mtshar bkod pa rgya mtsho'i lde mig*. In *Catalogue of the Narthang Kanjur*. New Delhi: International Academy of Indian Culture, 1983.

Gsang bdag. "Skad gsar bcad rnam pa gsum gyi dus rim gyi dbye ba dang de'i dgos don skor bshad pa." *Krung go'i bod kyi shes rig* 2 (1993): 33–40.

Gser mdog Paṇ chen Śākya mchog ldan (1428–1507). *Dpal ldan a ti sha sras dang brgyud bar bcas pa'i ngo mtshar mdzad pa'i phreng ba spel legs*. In *The Complete Works (gsuṇ 'bum) of Gser-mdog Paṇ-chen Śākya-mchog-ldan*, vol. 16, 538.3–550.2. Thimphu: Kunzang Tobgey, 1975.

Bsam gtan bzang po. *Bcom ldan ral gri'i rnam thar ldad pa'i ljong shing*. Manuscript, 26 fols. Beijing: CPN.

Bsod nams dpal bzang po, Śākya 'od, and Byang chub rgyal mtshan [incorrectly attributed to Sgra tshad pa Rin chen rnam rgyal]. *Bstan bcos 'gyur ro 'tshal gyi dkar chag yid bzhin nor bu rin po che'i za ma tog*. In *The Collected Works of Bu-ston*, vol. 28, 343–574. New Delhi: International Academy of Indian Culture, 1971.

Lha btsun pa Rin chen rnam rgyal (1473–1557). *Grub thob gtsang smyon pa'i rnam thar dad pa'i spu slong g.yo ba*. In *Bde mchog mkha' 'gro snyan rgyud (ras chung snyan rgyuad), Two Manuscript Collections of Texts from the Yig-cha of Gtsang-smyong He-ru-ka*, vol. 1, 1–129 (fols. 1–65). Leh: S. W. Tashigangpa, 1971.

A lag sha Ngag dbang bstan dar lha rams pa (1759–circa 1838). *Blo sbyong don bdun ma'i nyer mkho ba'i gtam theg mchog nye lam*. In *Collected Gsung 'Bum of Bstan-dar lha-ram of A-lag-sha*, vol. 2, 60–114. New Delhi: Lama Guru Deva, 1971.

——. *Yi ge'i bshad pa mkhas pa'i kha rgyan*. In *Collected Gsung 'Bum of Bstan-dar lha-ram of A-lag-sha*, vol. 2, 215–266. New Delhi: Lama Guru Deva, 1971.

Anonymous. "Sde dge par khang gi lo rgyus in *Khams phyogs dkar mdzes khul gyi dgon sde so so'i lo rgyus gsal bar bshad pa nang bstan gsal ba'i me long*, vol. 1, 405–419. Lhasa: Krung go'i bod kyi shes rig dpe skrun khang, 1995.

——. *Rgyal ba'i bka' 'gyur rin po che'i 'bri klog dang 'chad nyan byed mkhan rnams la nye bar mkho ba'i yi ge gzhan phan rnam dag gi gsal byed me long* [comp. 1918]. New Delhi: Tibet House, 1982.

——. *'Jig rten lugs kyi bstan bcos las dpyad don gsal ba'i sgron me*. Thimphu: Kun bzang stobs rgyal, 1975.

——. *Thabs mkhas pa chen po sangs rgyas drin lan bsab pa'i mdo*. In *Sde dge bka' 'gyur, Mdo sde*, vol. A, fols. 86a–198b. In Hakuji Ui, et al., *A Complete Catalog of the Tibetan Buddhist Canons*, no. 353. Sendai: Tōhuko Imperial University, 1934.

——. *Rnal 'byor dbang phyug lha btsun chos kyi rgyal po'i rnam thar gyi smad cha*. 32 fols. (Kathmandu: NGMPP L456/7, n.d., n.p).

——. *'Phags pa bdud rtsi brjod pa zhes bya ba theg pa chen po'i mdo*. In *Sde dge bka' 'gyur, Mdo sde*, vol. A, fols. 271b.2–274b. 5. In Hakuji Ui, et al., *A Complete Catalog of the Tibetan Buddhist Canons*, no. 197. Sendai: Tōhuko Imperial University, 1934.

——. *'Phags pa 'da' ka ye shes shes bya ba theg pa chen po'i mdo*. In Hakuji Ui, et al., *A Complete Catalog of the Tibetan Buddhist Canons*, no. 122. Sendai: Tōhuko Imperial University, 1934.

——. *'Phags pa shes rab kyi pha rol tu phyin pa rdo rje gcod pa'i phan yon bshad pa'i mdo*. Sikkim: Sgang tog, 1972.

——. *Bzo rig kha shas kyi pa tra lag len ma*. In *Bzo rig kha shas kyi pa tra lag len ma and Other Texts on the Minor Sciences of the Tibetan Scholastic Tradition*. Dharamsala: Library of Tibetan Works and Archives, 1981.

——. *Bzo rig pa tra: A Revealed Work on the Methods of Indo-Tibetan Silpasastra by an as yet Unknown Gter-ston, with Other Rare Texts from the Library of Tibet House*. New Delhi: Tibet House, 1985.

Anonymous. *La stod shel dkar rdzong 'og ding ri ba chos rgyan nas rgyal ba'i gsung rab zab mo par bskrun zhus pa'i dkar chag dad ldan thar lam 'dren pa'i shing rta*.

Ur kho. "Rkyen gyi yi ge dang de'i 'jug tshul la rdo tsam dpyad pa." *Krung go'i bod kyi shes rig* 1 (1995): 136–141.

OTHER REFERENCES

Ahmad, Zahirrudin. *A History of Tibet by Ṅag-dBaṅ Blo-bZaṅ rGya-mTSHo, Fifth Dalai Lama of Tibet.* Bloomington: Indiana University Research Institute for Inner Asian Studies, 1995.

——. *Saṅs-rgyas rGya-mTSHO, Life of the Fifth Dalai Lama, Volume IV, Part I.* New Delhi: International Academy of Indian Culture, 1999.

Appuradai, Arjun, ed. *The Social Life of Things: Commodities in Cultural Perspective.* Cambridge: Cambridge University Press, 1986.

Beckwith, Christopher I. "The Introduction of Greek Medicine Into Tibet in the Seventh and Eighth Centuries." *Journal of the American Oriental Society* 99 (1979): 297–313.

Bell, Charles. *Tibet, Past and Present.* Oxford: Clarendon Press, 1924.

Bethlenfalvy, Geza. "A Tibetan Catalogue of the Blocks of the Lamaist Printing House in Aginsk." *Acta Orientalia* 25 (1972): 53–75.

Bischoff, Friedrich A. "A Tibetan Glossary of Mongol 'Editorial' Terms." In *Suhṛllekhāḥ: Festgabe für Helmut Eimer*, ed. Michael Hahn, Jens-Uwe Hartmann, and Roland Steiner, 22–27. Swisttal-Odendorf: leT Verlag, 1996.

Boulnois, Lucette. *Poudre d'Or et Monnaies d'Argent au Tibet.* Paris: Éditions du Centre National de la Recherche Scientifique, 1983.

Briggs, Charles. "Historiographical Essay: Literacy, Reading, and Writing in the Medieval West." *Journal of Medieval History* 26, no. 4 (2000): 397–420.

Cabezón, José Ignacio. "Authorship and Literary Production in Classical Buddhist Tibet." In *Changing Minds: Contributions to the Study of Buddhism and Tibet in Honor of Jeffrey Hopkins*, ed. Guy Newland, 233–264. Ithaca: Snow Lion, 2001.

Chandra, Lokesh. "Tibetan Works Printed by the Shoparkhang of the Potala." In *Jñānamuktāvalī: Commemoration Volume in Honour of Johannes Nobel*, ed. Claus Vogel, 120–123. New Delhi: International Academy of Indian Culture, 1959.

——. "Les Imprimeries Tibétains de Drepung, Degé, et Pepung." *Journal Asiatique* 249 (1961): 503–517.

——. "The Life and Works of 'Jam-dbyaṅs-bzhad-pa." *Central Asiatic Journal* 7, no. 4 (1962): 264–269.

——. "Tibetan Buddhist Texts Printed by the Mdzod-dge-sgar-gsar Monastery." *Indo-Iranian Journal* 7 (1963–64): 298–306.

——. *Materials for a History of Tibetan Literature.* New Delhi: Sharada Rani, 1963.

Chandra, Lokesh, ed. *The Amarakoṣa in Tibet.* New Delhi: International Academy of Indian Culture, 1965.

Chartier, Roger. *Forms and Meanings: Texts, Performances, and Audiences from Codex to Computer.* Philadelphia: University of Pennsylvania Press, 1995.

Clark, Barry, trans. *The Quintessence Tantras of Tibetan Medicine.* Ithaca: Snow Lion, 1995.

Coales, Oliver. "Eastern Tibet." *The Geographical Journal* 53, no. 4 (1919): 228–253.

Colas, Gérard. "The Criticism and Transmission of Texts in Classical India." *Diogenes* 47, no. 2 (1999): 30–43.

Conrad, Lawrence I. "The Arab-Islamic Medical Tradition." In *The Western Medical Tradition: 800 B.C. to A.D. 1800*, ed. Lawrence I. Conrad et al., 93–138. Cambridge: Cambridge University Press, 1995.

Conze, Edward. *The Perfection of Wisdom in Eight Thousand Lines and Its Verse Summary.* San Francisco: Four Seasons Foundation, 1973.

Cüppers, Christoph. "On the Manufacture of Ink." *Ancient Nepal* 113 (1989): 1–7.

Dagyab, Loden Sherap. *Tibetan Religious Art.* 2 vols. Wiesbaden: Otto Harrassowitz, 1977.

Damdinsuren, Ts. "Corrections of Misprints and Errors in Tibetan Printings of Kanjur Made by Dandar Agramba." In *Documenta Barbarorum: Festschrift für Walther Heissig zum 70. Geburtstag*, ed. Klaus Sagaster and Michael Weiers, 47–54. Wiesbaden: Otto Harrassowitz, 1983.

David-Neel, Alexandra. *Magic and Mystery in Tibet.* New York: Claude Kendall, 1932.

Diemberger, Hildegard. *When a Woman Becomes a Religious Dynasty: The Samding Dorje Phagmo of Tibet.* New York: Columbia University Press, 2008.

Diemberger, Hildegard, Pasang Wangdu, Marlies Kornfield, and Christian Jahoda. *Feast of Miracles: The Life and Tradition of Bodong Chole Namgyal (1375/6–1451 A.D.) According to the Tibetan Texts "Feast of Miracles" and "The Lamp Illuminating the History of Bodong."* N.p.: Porong Pema Choding Editions, 1997.

Dorjé, Gyurme. "The Structure and Contents of the Four Tantras and Sangyé Gyamtso's Commentary, the Blue Beryl." In *Tibetan Medical Paintings: Illustrations to the Blue Beryl Treatise of Sangye Gyamtso (1653–1705)*, ed. Yuri Parfionovitch, Gyurme Dorjé, and Fernand Meyer, vol. 1, 14–15. New York: Abrams, 1992.

Drège, Jean-Pierre. *Les Bibliothèques en Chine au Temps des Manuscrits (Jusqu'au Xe Siècle).* Paris: École Française d'Extrême-Orient, 1991.

Dudbridge, Glen. *Lost Books of Medieval China.* London: The British Library, 2000.

Eagleton, Terry. *Criticism and Ideology: A Study in Marxist Literary Theory.* London: NLB, 1976.

Ehrhard, Franz-Karl. *Early Buddhist Block Prints from Mang-yul Gung-thang.* Lumbini: Lumbini International Research Institute, 2000.

——. *Four Unknown Mahāmudrā Works of the Bo-dong-pa School.* Lumbini: Lumbini International Research Institute, 2000.

——. *The Oldest Block Print of Klong-chen Rab-'byams-pa's Theg mchog mdzod: Facsimile Edition of Early Tibetan Block Prints.* Lumbini: Lumbini International Research Institute, 2000.

Eimer, Helmut. *Some Results of Recent Kanjur Research.* Sankt Augustin: VGH Wissenschaftsverlag, 1983.

——. "Hevajratantra II:v:1–2 and the History of the Tibetan Kanjur." *Berliner Indologische Studien* 2 (1986): 3–12.

——. "The Position of the 'Jaṅ sa tham/Lithang Edition Within the Tradition of the Tibetan Kanjur." *Acta Orientalia* 43, no. 2–3 (1989): 297–304.

——. *Ein Jahrzehnt Studien zur Überlieferung des tibetischen Kangyur.* Wien: Arbeitskreis für tibetische und buddhistische Studien Universität Wien, 1992.

Eimer, Helmut and Pema Tsering. "Blockprints and Manuscripts of Mi la ras pa's *Mgur 'bum* Accessible to Frank-Richard Hamm." In *Frank-Richard Hamm Memorial Volume*, ed. Helmut Eimer, 59–88. Bonn: Indica et Tibetica Verlag, 1990.

——. "Die Liste der Druckplatten in Dga' ldan phun tshogs gling aus dem Jahre 1694." *Zentralasiatische Studien* 34 (2005): 29–54.

Engelhardt, Isrun. "Between Tolerance and Dogmatism: Tibetan Reactions to the Capuchin Missionaries in Lhasa, 1707–1745." *Zentralasiatische Studien* 34 (2005): 55–98.

Farrow, G. W. and I. Menon. *The Concealed Essence of the Hevajra Tantra.* Delhi: Motilal Banarsidass, 1992.

Franke, Herbert. "Der Kanonkatalog der Chih-yüan-Zeit und seine Kompilatoren." In *Chinesischer und Tibetischer Buddhismus im China der Yüanzeit: Drei Studien*, 67–124. München: Kommission für Zentralasiatische Studien, Bayerische Akademie der Wissenschaften, 1996.

Fushimi, Hidetoshi. "Recent Finds from the Old Sa-skya Xylographic Edition." *Wiener Zeitschrift für die Kunde Südasiens und Archiv für Indische Philosophie* 43 (1999): 95–108.

Ganz, David. "Book Production in the Carolingian Empire and the Spread of the Caroline Miniscule." In *The New Cambridge Medieval History: Volume II c. 700–c. 900*, ed. Rosamond McKitterick, 786–807. Cambridge, UK: Cambridge University Press, 1995.

Gelek, Surkhang W. "Tax Measurement and Lag 'don Tax in Tibet." *Tibet Journal* 9, no. 1 (1984): 20–30.

——. "Government, Monastic and Private Taxation in Tibet." *Tibet Journal* 11, no. 1 (1986): 21–40.

Goldstein, Melvyn. "Taxation and the Structure of a Tibetan Village." *Central Asiatic Journal* 15, no. 1 (1971): 1–27.

Grafton, Anthony. *Defenders of the Text: The Traditions of Scholarship in an Age of Science.* Cambridge, Mass.: Harvard University Press, 1991.

Greetham, D. C. *Textual Scholarship: An Introduction.* New York: Garland, 1994.

Grönbold, Guenther. "Die Schrift- und Buchkultur Tibets." In *Der Weg zum Dach der Welt*, ed. C. C. Müller and W. Raunig, 363–380. Innsbruck: Pinguin-Verlag, 1982.

——. "Tibet: Literature und Buchkunst." In *Das Buch im Orient: Handschriften und Kostbare Drucke aus Zwei Jahrtausenden*, 253–264. Wiesbaden: Dr. Ludwig Reichert Verlag, 1982.

Gyatso, Janet. *Apparitions of the Self: The Secret Autobiographies of a Tibetan Visionary*. Princeton: Princeton University Press, 1998.

Gyatso, Yonten. "Le monastère de Bla-braṅ bkra-Śis 'khyil." In *Tibetan Studies: Proceedings of th 4th Seminar of the International Association for Tibetan Studies, Schloss Hohenkammer, Munich 1985*, ed. H. Uebach and J.L. Panglung, 559–566. München: Kommission für Zentralasiatische Studien, Bayerische Akademie der Wissenschaften, 1988.

Harrer, Heinrich. *Seven Years in Tibet*. New York: E.P. Dutton, 1954.

Harrison, Paul. "In Search of the Tibetan Bka' 'gyur: A Reconnaissance Report." In *Tibetan Studies: Proceedings of the 6th Seminar of the International Association for Tibetan Studies*, ed. Per Kvaerne, vol. 1, 295–317. Oslo: The Institute of Comparative Research in Human Culture, 1994.

——. "A Brief History of the Tibetan Kangyur." In *Tibetan Literature: Studies in Genre*, ed. José Ignacio Cabezón and Roger R. Jackson, 70–94. Ithaca: Snow Lion, 1996.

——. "Preliminary Notes on a gZungs 'dus Manuscript from Tabo." In *Suhr llekhāḥ: Festgabe für Helmut Eimer*, ed. Michael Hahn, Jens-Uwe Hartmann, and Roland Steiner, 49–68. Swisttal-Odendorf: leT Verlag, 1996.

——. "Philology in the Field: Some Comments on Selected Mdo Mang Texts in the Tabo Collection." In *Tabo Studies II: Manuscripts, Texts, Inscriptions, and the Arts*, ed. C.A. Scherrer-Schaub and E. Steinkellner, 37–54. Rome: Istituto Italiano per l'Africa e l'Orient, 1999.

Heller, Amy. *Tibetan Art: Tracing the Development of Spiritual Ideals and Art in Tibet 600–2000 A.D.* Milan: Jaca Book, 1999.

Helman-Wazny, Agnieszka. "Tibetan Manuscripts: Scientific Examination and Conservation Approaches." In *Edinburgh Conference Papers 2006: Proceedings from the Fifth International Conference of the Institute of Paper Conservation and First International Conference of the Institute of Conservation, Book and Paper Group*, ed. Jaques Shulla, 247–256. London: Institute of Conservation (ICON), 2007.

Hopkins, Jeffrey. *Meditation on Emptiness*. London: Wisdom, 1983.

Howsam, Leslie. *Old Books and New Histories: An Orientation to Studies in Book and Print Culture*. Toronto: University of Toronto Press, 2007.

Hurvitz, Leon, trans. *Scripture of the Lotus Blossom of the Fine Dharma (The Lotus Sūtra)*. New York: Columbia University Press, 1976.

Imaeda, Yoshiro. "L'Edition du Kanjur Tibétain de 'Jang sa-tham." *Journal Asiatique* 270, no. 1–2 (1982): 173–189.

——. *Catalog du Kanjur Tibétain de l'Edition de 'Jang sa-tham*. Tokyo: International Institute of Buddhist Studies, 1982, 1984.

Ishihama, Yumiko. "On the Dissemination of the Belief in the Dalai Lama as a Manifestation of the Bodhisattva Avalokitesvara." *Acta Asiatica* 64 (1993): 38–56.

Ishikawa, Mie. *A Critical Edition of the Sgra sbyor bam po gnyis pa: An Old and Basic Commentary on the Mahāvyutpatti.* Tokyo: The Toyo Bunko, 1990.

Jackson, David P. "Notes on Two Early Printed Editions of Sa-skya-pa Works." *The Tibet Journal* 8, no. 2 (1983): 3–24.

——. *The Entrance Gate for the Wise (Section III): Sa-skya Paṇḍita on Indian and Tibetan Traditions of Pramāṇa and Philosophical Debate.* Wien: Arbeitskreis für Tibetische und Buddhistische Studien Universität Wien, 1987.

——. "More on the old dGa'-ldan and Gong-dkar-ba Xylographic Editions." *Studies in Central and East Asian Religions* 2 (1989): 1–18.

——. "The Earliest Printings of Tsong-kha-pa's Works: The Old Dga'-ldan Editions." In *Reflections on Tibetan Culture: Essays in Memory of Turrell V. Wylie,* ed. Lawrence Epstein and Richard F. Sherburne, 107–116. Lewiston, N.Y.: The Edwin Mellen Press, 1990.

——. *A History of Tibetan Painting: The Great Tibetan Painters and Their Traditions.* Wien: Verlag der Österreichischen Akademie der Wissenschaften, 1996.

Jackson, David P. and Janice Jackson. *Tibetan Thangka Painting: Methods and Materials.* Ithaca: Snow Lion, 1988.

Jacquart, Danielle. "Medical Scholasticism." In *Western Medical Thought from Antiquity to the Middle Ages,* ed. Mirko D. Grmek, 197–240, 380–387. Cambridge, Mass.: Harvard University Press, 1998.

Jest, Corneille. "A Technical Note on the Tibetan Method of Block-Carving." *Man* 61 (1961): 83–85.

Kanakura, Ensho, ed. *A Catalog of the Tohoku University Collection of Tibetan Works on Buddhism.* Sendai: Seminary of Indology, Tohoku University, 1953.

Kapstein, Matthew T. *The Tibetan Assimilation of Buddhism: Conversion, Contestation, and Memory.* New York and Oxford: Oxford University Press, 2000.

Kara, György. *Books of the Mongolian Nomads: More Than Eight Centuries of Writing Mongolian.* Trans. John R. Krueger. Bloomington: Research Institute for Inner Asian Studies, 2005.

Karmay, Samten G. *Feast of the Morning Light: The Eighteenth-Century Wood-Engravings of Shenrab's Life Stories and the Bon Canon from Gyalrong.* Osaka: National Museum of Ethnology, 2005.

Kieschnick, John. *The Impact of Buddhism on Chinese Material Culture.* Princeton: Princeton University Press, 2003.

Kolmaš, Josef. *A Genealogy of the Kings of Derge: Sde-dge'i rgyal rabs: Tibetan Text Edited with Historical Introduction.* Prague: Oriental Institute, 1968.

——. *The Iconography of the Degé Kanjur and Tanjur: Facsimile Reproductions of the 648 Illustrations in the Degé Edition of the Tibetan Tripitaka Housed in the Library of the Oriental Insitute in Prague.* New Delhi: Sharada Rani, 1978.

———. "Dezhung Rinpoche's Summary and Continuation of the Sde-dge'i rgyal rabs." *Acta Orientalia Hungarica* 42, no. 1 (1988): 119–152.

van der Kuijp, Leonard W. J. "A Text-Historical Note on *Hevajratantra* II:v:1–2." *Journal of the International Association of Buddhist Studies* 8, no. 1 (1985): 83–89.

———. *An Introduction to Gtsang-nag-pa's Tshad-ma rnam-par nges-pa'i ṭi-ka legs-bshad bsdus-pa.* Kyoto: Rinsen Book Co., 1989.

———. "Two Mongol Xylographs (Hor Par Ma) of the Tibetan Text of Sa skya Paṇḍita's Work on Buddhist Logic and Epistemology." *Journal of the International Association of Buddhist Studies* 16, no. 2 (1993): 279–298.

———. "Apropos of Some Recently Recovered Manuscripts Anent Sa skya Paṇḍita's Tshad ma rigs pa'i gter and Autocommentary." *Berliner Indologische Studien* 7 (1993): 149–162.

———. "Fourteenth-Century Tibetan Cultural History I: Ta'i-si-tu Byang-chub rgyal-mtshan as a Man of Religion." *Indo-Iranian Journal* 37 (1994): 139–149.

———. "A Treatise on Buddhist Epistemology and Logic Attributed to Klong chen Rab 'byams pa (1308–1364) and Its Place in Indo-Tibetan Intellectal History." *Journal of Indian Philosophy* 31 (2003): 381–437.

———. *The Kālacakra and the Patronage of Tibetan Buddhism by the Mongol Imperial Family.* Bloomington: Indiana University Department of Central Eurasian Studies, 2004.

Lange, Kristina. *Die Werke des Regenten Saṅs rgyas rgya mc'o (1653–1705): Eine philologisch-historische Studie zum tibetischsprachigen Schriftum.* Berlin: Akademie-Verlag, 1976.

Lenhart, J. M. "Capuchins Introduce Printing Into Tibet in 1741." *Franciscan Studies* 10 (1950): 69–72.

Lewis, Todd T. and Lozang Jamspal. "Newars and Tibetan in the Kathmandu Valley: Three New Translations from Tibetan Sources." *Journal of Asian and African Studies* 36 (1988): 187–211.

Lincoln, Bruce. "Culture." In *Guide to the Study of Religion,* ed. Willi Braun and Russell T. McCutcheon, 409–422. London: Cassell, 2000.

Martin, Dan. *Tibetan Histories: A Bibliography of Tibetan-Language Historical Works.* London: Serindia, 1997.

———. "Introduction." In *A Catalog of the Bon Kanjur,* ed. Dan Martin, Per Kvaerne, and Yasuhiko Nagano, 1–20. Osaka: National Museum of Ethnology, 2003.

———. "Padampa Sangye: A History of Representation of a South Indian Siddha in Tibet." In *Holy Madness: Portraits of Tantric Siddhas,* 108–123. New York: Rubin Museum of Art, 2006.

McDermott, Joseph P. *A Social History of the Chinese Book: Books and Literati Culture in Late Imperial China.* Hong Kong: Hong Kong University Press, 2006.

McKenzie, D. F. *Bibliography and the Sociology of Texts.* London: The British Library, 1986.

McKitterick, Rosamond. *The Carolingians and the Written Word.* Cambridge, UK: Cambridge University Press, 1989.

Meisezahl, R. O. "Über den Degé Tanjur der ehemaligen Preussischen Staatsbibliothek." *Libri* 10, no. 4 (1960): 292–306.

——. "Der Katalog der Klosterdruckerei A mĕhog dga' ldan čhos 'khor gliń in Ch'ing-hai (Nordwest-China)." *Oriens* 29–30 (1986): 309–333.

Meyer, Fernand. "Introduction: The Medical Paintings of Tibet." In *Tibetan Medical Paintings: Illustrations to the Blue Beryl Treatise of Sangye Gyamtso (1653–1705)*, ed. Yuri Parfionovitch, Gyurme Dorjé, and Fernand Meyer, vol. 1, 2–13. New York: Abrams, 1992.

——. "Theory and Practice of Tibetan Medicine." In *Oriental Medicine: An Illustrated Guide to the Asian Arts of Healing*, ed. Jan van Alphen and Anthony Aris. Boston: Shambala, 1995.

——. "The History and Foundations of Tibetan Medicine." In *The Buddha's Art of Healing: Tibetan Paintings Rediscovered*, ed. John fol. Avedon, 21–31. New York: Rizzoli, 1998.

Migot, André. *Tibetan Marches.* Trans. Peter Fleming. London: Rupert Hart-Davis, 1955.

Miyake, Shin'ichiro. "On the Date of the Original Manuscript of the Golden Manuscript Tenjur in Ganden Monastery." *Annual Memoirs of the Otani University Shin Buddhist Comprehensive Research Institute* 13 (1995), 13–16.

——. "Comparative Table of the Golden Manuscript Tenjur in dGa'-ldan Monastery with the Peking Edition of Tenjur." *Annual Memoirs of the Otani University Shin Buddhist Comprehensive Research Institute* 17 (2000): 1–65.

Naga, Acharya Sangyé T. and Tsepak Rigzin. *Bod dbyin shan sbyar gyi tshig tshogs dang gtam dpe: Tibetan Quadrisyllabics, Phrases and Idioms.* Dharamsala: Library of Tibetan Works and Archives, 1994.

Nishioka, Soshū. "Index to the Catalog Section of Bu-ston's 'History of Buddhism.'" *Annual Report of the Institute for the Study of Cultural Exchange, The University of Tokyo* 4 (1980): 61–92 [part I]; 5 (1981): 43–94 [part II]; 6 (1983): 47–200 [part III].

Nornang, Ngawang L. "The Monastic Organization and Economy of Dwags-po Bshad-grub-gling." In *Reflections on Tibetan Culture: Essays in Memory of Turrell V. Wylie*, ed. Lawrence Epstein and Richard F. Sherburne, 249–269. Lewiston, N.Y.: The Edwin Mellen Press, 1990.

Obermiller, Eugene, trans. *The History of Buddhism in India and Tibet by Bu-Ston.* Heidelberg: Harrassowitz, 1932.

Parfionovitch, Yuri, Gyurme Dorjé, and Fernand Meyer. *Tibetan Medical Paintings: Illustrations to the Blue Beryl Treatise of Sangye Gyamtso (1653–1705).* 2 vols. New York: Abrams, 1992.

Petech, Luciano. *China and Tibet in the Early XVIIIth Century: History of the Establishment of Chinese Protectorate in Tibet, 2nd Rev. Ed.* Leiden: E. J. Brill, 1972.

——. *Central Tibet and the Mongols: The Yüan–Sa-skya Period of Tibetan History.* Rome: Istituto Italiano per il Medio ed Estremo Oriente, 1990.

——. "Ston tshul: The Rise of Sa skya Paramountcy in Khams." In *Tibetan History and Language: Studies Dedicated to Uray Géza on His Seventieth Birthday*, ed. E. Steinkellner, Wiener Studien zur Tibetologie und Buddhismuskunde, Heft 26, 417–22. Wien: Arbeitskreis für Tibetische und Buddhistische Studien Universität Wien, 1991.

Petrucci, Armando. *Writers and Readers in Medieval Italy: Studies in the History of Written Culture.* New Haven: Yale University Press, 1995.

Pott, P. H. *Introduction to the Tibetan Collection of the National Museum of Ethnology, Leiden.* Leiden: E. J. Brill, 1951.

Quintman, Andrew H. *Mi la ras pa's Many Lives: Anatomy of a Tibetan Biographical Corpus.* Ph.D. diss., University of Michigan, 2006.

Rato Khyongla Nawang Losang. *My Life and Lives: The Story of a Tibetan Incarnation.* New York: E. P. Dutton, 1977.

Rawski, Evelyn S. "Qing Publishing in Non-Han Languages." In *Printing and Book Culture in Late Imperial China*, ed. Cynthia Brokaw and Kai-wing Chow, 304–321. Berkeley: University of California Press, 2005.

Reynolds, L. D. and N. G. Wilson. *Scribes and Scholars: A Guide to the Transmission of Greek and Latin Literature.* London: Oxford University Press, 1992.

Ricca, Franco and Erberto Lo Bue. *The Great Stūpa of Gyantse: A Complete Tibetan Pantheon of the Fifteenth Century.* London: Serindia, 1993.

Richardus, Peter, ed. *Tibetan Lives: Three Himalayan Autobiographies.* Surrey, England: Curzon Press, 1998.

Rinpoche, Rechung. *Tibetan Medicine: Illustrated in Original Texts.* Berkeley: University of California Press, 1976.

Rockhill, William Woodville. "Tibet: A Geographical, Ethnographical, and Historical Sketch, Derived from Chinese Sources." *The Journal of the Royal Asiatic Society of Great Britain and Ireland* (1891):1–133, 185–292.

——. *Notes on the Ethnology of Tibet.* Washington, D.C.: U.S. Government Printing Office, 1895.

Roerich, George N., trans. *The Blue Annals.* New Delhi: Motilal Banarsidass, 1976.

Róna-Tas, A. "Some Notes on the Terminology of Mongolian Writing." *Acta Orientalia Hungarica* 18 (1965): 119–147.

Ruegg, David Seyfort. *The Life of Bu ston Rin po che.* Roma: Is.M.E.O., 1966.

Sadhukhan, S. K. "Biography of the Eminent Tibetan Scholar 'Jam-dbyaṅs bshad-pa [*sic*] ṅag-dba˙ brtson-'grus (A.D. 1648–1722)." *Tibet Journal* 16, no. 2 (1991): 19–33.

Samten, Jampa S. "Notes on the Lithang Edition of the Tibetan bKa'-'gyur." *Tibet Journal* 12, no. 3 (1987): 17–40.

Samten, Jampa and Jeremy Russell. "Origins of the Tibetan Canon with Special Reference to the Tshal-pa Kanjur (1347–1349)." In *Buddhism and Science*, 763–81. Seoul: Dongguk University, 1987.

Schaeffer, Kurtis R. "Printing the Words of the Master: Tibetan Editorial Practice in the Collected Works of 'Jam dbyangs bzhad pa'i rdo rje I (1648–1721)." *Acta Orientalia* 60 (1999): 159–177.

——. "Textual Scholarship, Medical Tradition, and Mahayana Buddhist Ideals in Tibet." *Journal of Indian Philosophy* 31, no. 5–6 (2003): 621–641.

——. "A Letter to Editors of the Buddhist Canon in 14th-Century Tibet." *Journal of the American Oriental Society* 124, no. 2 (2004): 1–17.

——. "A Royal Nun in Fifteenth-Century Tibet: Notes on the Life of Chökyi Dronma (c. 1422–1455)." Paper presented at the 2004 annual meeting of the American Academy of Religion, Atlanta, Georgia.

——. *Dreaming the Great Brahmin: Tibetan Traditions of the Indian Buddhist Poet-Saint Saraha*. Oxford and New York: Oxford University Press, 2005.

——. *Himalayan Hermitess: The Life of a Tibetan Buddhist Nun*. Oxford and New York: Oxford University Press, 2005.

——. "The Printing Projects of Tsangnyön Heruka and His Disciples." Paper presented at the eleventh seminar of the International Association for Asian Studie, Königswinter, Germany, 2006.

——. "Dying Like Milarepa: Death Accounts in a Tibetan Hagiographic Tradition." In *The Buddhist Dead: Practices, Discourses, Representations*, ed. Bryan J. Cuevas and Jaqueline I. Stone, 208–233. Honolulu: University of Hawaii Press, 2007.

——. "Crystal Orbs and Arcane Treasuries: Tibetan Anthologies of Buddhist Tantric Songs from the Tradition of Pha Dam pa sangs rgyas." *Acta Orientalia* 68 (2007): 5–73.

——. "Death, Prognosis, and the Physician's Reputation in Tibet." In *Heroes and Saints: The Moment of Death in Cross-Cultural Perspectives*, ed. Phyllis Granoff and Koichi Shinohara, 159–172. Newcastle: Cambridge Scholars Publishing, 2007.

——. "Tibetan Narratives on Buddha's Acts at Vajrasana: Putting Hagiography in Place." In *Life of the Buddha: New Perspectives and Discoveries*, ed. Sonya Quintanilla. Leiden and New York: Brill, forthcoming.

Schaeffer, Kurtis R. and Leonard W. J. van der Kuijp. *An Early Tibetan Catalogue of Buddhist Literature: The Bstan pa rgyas pa nyi ma'i 'od zer of Bcom ldan ral gri*. Cambridge, Mass.: Harvard Oriental Series, 2009.

Scheir-Dolberg, Joseph. *Treasure House of Tibetan Culture: Canonization, Printing, and Power in the Derge Printing House*. M.A. thesis, Harvard University, 2005.

Scherrer-Schaub, Cristina A. "Towards a Methodology for the Study of Old Tibetan Manuscripts: Dunhuang and Tabo." In *Tabo Studies II: Manuscripts,*

Texts, Inscriptions, and the Arts, ed. C. A. Scherrer-Schaub and E. Steinkellner, 3–35. Rome: Istituto Italiano per l'Africa e l'Orient, 1999.

——. "Was Byaṅ chub sems dpa' a Posthumous Title of King Ye śes 'od?" In *Tabo Studies II: Manuscripts, Texts, Inscriptions, and the Arts*, ed. C. A. Scherrer-Schaub and E. Steinkellner, 207–226. Rome: Istituto Italiano per l'Africa e l'Orient, 1999.

Schopen, Gregory. "The Phrase 'sa pṛtivīpradeśaś caityabhūto bhavet' in the Vajracchedikā: Notes on the Cult of the Book in Mahāyāna." *Indo-Iranian Journal* 17 (1975): 147–181.

Schuh, Dieter. *Tibetische Handschriften und Blockdrucke (Teil 5)*. Wiesbaden: Franz Steiner Verlag, 1973.

Serruys, Henry. "On Some 'Editorial' Terms in the Mongol Ganjur." *Bulletin of the School of Oriental and African Studies* 43, no. 3 (1980): 520–531.

Shafer, Robert. "Words for 'Printing Block' and the Origin of Printing." *Journal of the American Oriental Society* 80, no. 4 (1960): 328–329.

Silk, Jonathan. "Notes on the History of the Yongle Kangyur." In *Suhṛllekhāḥ: Festgabe für Helmut Eimer*, ed. Michael Hahn, Jens-Uwe Hartmann, and Roland Steiner, 153–200. Swisttal-Odendorf: IeT Verlag, 1996.

Simon, Walter. "Tibetan 'par, dpar, spar.' and Cognate Words." *Bulletin of the School of Oriental and African Studies* 25, no. 1–3 (1962): 72–80.

Simonsson, Nils. *Indo-Tibetische Studien: Die Methoden der Tibetischen Übersetzer, untersucht im Hinblink auf die Bedeutung ihrer Übersetzungen für die Sanskritphilologie*. Uppsala: Almqvist & Wiksells Boktryckeri AB, 1957.

Skilling, Peter. "A Brief Guide to the Golden Tanjur." *Journal of the Siam Society* 79, no. 2 (1991): 138–146.

——. "Theravādin Literature in Tibetan Translation." *Journal of the Pali Text Society* 19 (1993): 69–201, at 73–140.

——. "From bKa' bstan bcos to bKa' 'gyur and bsTan 'gyur." In *Transmission of the Tibetan Canon: Proceedings of the 7th Seminar of the International Association for Tibetan Studies, Graz 1995*, ed. Helmut Eimer et al., vol. 3, 87–111. Wien: Verlag der Österreichischen Akademie der Wissenschaften, 1997.

Smith, E. Gene. *Among Tibetan Texts: History and Literature of the Himalayan Plateau*. Ed. Kurtis R. Schaeffer. Boston: Wisdom, 2001.

——. "Banned Books in the Tibetan-Speaking Lands." In *21st Century Tibet Issue: Symposium on Contemporary Tibetan Studies, Collected Papers*, 368–381. Taipei: Mongolian and Tibetan Affairs Commission, 2004.

Snellgrove, David L. *The Hevajra Tantra: A Critical Study*. Oxford: Oxford University Press, 1959.

——. *Indo-Tibetan Buddhism: Indian Buddhists and Their Tibetan Successors*. Boston: Shambhala, 1987.

Snellgrove, David and Hugh Richardson. *A Cultural History of Tibet*. London: George Weidenfeld and Nicolson, 1968.

Sorensen, Henrik. "Buddhism and Material Culture in China." *Acta Orientalia* 68 (2007): 247–280.

Sperling, Eliot. "Some Remarks on sGa A-gnyan dam-pa and the Origins of the Hor-pa Lineage of the dKar-mdzes Region." In *Tibetan History and Language: Studies Dedicated to Uray Géza on his Seventieth Birthday*, 455–466. Wien: Arbeitskreis für Tibetische und Buddhistische Studien Universität Wien, 1991.

Stein, R. A. "Tibetica Antiqua I." *Bulletin de l'École Francaise d'Extreme-Orient* 72 (1983): 149–236.

Szerb, Jânos. "Glosses on the Oeuvre of bla-ma 'Phags-pa: On the Activity of Sa-skya Pandita." In *Tibetan Studies in Honour of Hugh Richardson: Proceedings of the International Seminar on Tibetan Studies, Oxford, 1979*, ed. Michael Aris and Aung San Suu Kyi, 290–300. New Delhi: Vikas Publishing House, 1980.

——. "Glosses on the Oeuvre of bla-ma 'Phags-pa: II. Some Notes on the Events of the Years 1251–1254." *Acta Orientalia* 34 (1980): 263–285.

——. "Glosses on the Oeuvre of Bla-ma 'Phags-pa: III. The 'Patron–Patronized' Relationship." In *Soundings in Tibetan Civilization: Proceedings of the 1982 Seminar of the International Association for Tibetan Studies Held at Columbia University*, ed. Barbara Nimri Aziz and Matthew Kapstein, 165–173. Delhi: Manohar, 1985.

——. "Glosses on the Oeuvre of bla ma 'Phags pa: 4. A propos of Tolui." In *Religious and Lay Symbolism in the Altaic World and Other Papers: Proceedings of the 27th Meeting of the Permanent International Altaistic Conference, Walberberg, Federal Republic of Germany, June 12th to 17th, 1984*, ed. Klaus Sagaster and Helmut Eimer, 365–378. Wiesbaden: Otto Harrasowitz, 1989.

Takata, Tokio. "Multilingualism in Tun-huang." *Acta Asiatica* 78 (2000): 49–70.

Takeuchi, Tsuguhito. *Old Tibetan Contracts from Central Asia*. Tokyo: Daizo Shuppan, 1995.

Tarrant, R. J. "Classical Latin Literature." In *Scholarly Editing: A Guide to Research*, ed. D. C. Greetham, 95–148. New York: The Modern Language Association of America, 1995.

Taylor, McComas and Lama Choedak Yuthok, trans. *The Clear Mirror: A Traditional Account of Tibet's Golden Age, Sakyapa Sönam Gyaltsen's Clear Mirror on Royal Genealogy*. Ithaca: Snow Lion, 1996.

Thomas, F. W. *Tibetan Literary Texts and Documents Concerning Chinese Turkestan*. Londong: The Royal Asiatic Society, 1935.

Tiso, Francis V. "The Death of Milarepa: Towards a *Redaktionsgeschichte* of the *Mila rnam thar* Traditions." In *Tibetan Studies: Proceedings of the 7TH Seminar of the International Association of Tibetan Studies, Graz 1995*, ed. Helmut Krasser et al., vol. 2, 987–995. Wien: Verlag der Österreichischen Akademie der Wissenschaften, 1997.

Tsering Thar. "The Bonpo Documents and Their Assembling." In *Theses on Tibetology in China*, ed. Liao Zugui and Zhang Zuji, 325–365. Beijing: China Tibetology Publishing House, 1996.

Tsong-kha-pa. *The Great Treatise on the Stages of the Path to Enlightenment*. Ithaca: Snow Lion, 2000.

Turner, Samuel. *An Account of an Embassy to the Court of the Teshoo Lama, in Tibet; Containing a Narrative of a Journey Through Bootan, and Part of Tibet*. London: W. Bulmer and Co., 1800.

Ui, Hakuji et al. *A Complete Catalog of the Tibetan Buddhist Canons*. Sendai: Tōhuko Imperial University, 1934.

Uray, Géza. "Contributions to the Date of the Vyutpatti-Treatises." *Acta Orientalia Academiae Scientarium Hungaricae* 43, no. 1 (1989): 3–21.

Uspensky, Vladimir L. "The Life and Works of Ngag-dbang bkra-shis (1678–1738), the Second Abbot of the Bla-brang bkras-shis-'khyil Monastery." In *Proceedings of the 7th Seminar of the International Association for Tibetan Studies, Graz 1995*, ed. Helmut Eimer, vol. 2, 1005–1010. Wien: Verlag der Österreichischen Akademie der Wissenschaften, 1997.

Verhagen, Pieter C. "'Royal' Patronage of Sanskrit Grammatical Studies in Tibet." In *Ritual, State, and History in South Asia: Essays in Honour of J. C. Heesterman*, ed. A W. van den Hoek, D. H. A. Kolff, and M. S. Oort, 374–392. Leiden: Brill, 1992.

——. *A History of Sanskrit Grammatical Literature in Tibet: Volume One, Transmission of the Canonical Literature*. Leiden: Brill, 1994.

——. "Tibetan Expertise in Sanskrit Grammar: Ideology, Status, and Other Extra-Linguistic Factors." In *Ideology and Status of Sanskrit: Contributions to the History of the Sanskrit Language*, ed. Jan E. M. Houben, 275–287. Leiden: Brill, 1996.

——. *A History of Sanskrit Grammatical Literature in Tibet: Volume Two, Assimilation Into Indigenous Scholarship*. Leiden: Brill, 2001.

——. "Notes Apropos the Oeuvre of Si-tu Paṇ-chen Chos-kyi 'byuṅ-gnas (1699?–1774) (2): Dkar-chag Materials." In *Gedenkschrift J. W. de Jong*, ed. H. W. Bodewitz and Minoru Hara, 207–237. Tokyo: The International Insitute for Buddhist Studies, 2004.

Vitali, Roberto. *Early Temples of Central Tibet*. London: Serendia Publications, 1990.

Vostrikov, A. I. *Tibetan Historical Literature*. Trans. Harish Chandra Gupta. Surrey, England: Curzon Press, 1994.

Wangdu, Pasang, Hildegard Diemberger, and Guntram Hazod. *Shel dkar chos 'byung, History of the White Crystal: Religion and Politics of Southern La stod*. Vienna: Verlag der Österreichischen Akademie der Wissenschaften, 1996.

West, M. L. *Textual Criticism and Editorial Technique*. Stuttgart: B. G. Teubner, 1973.

REFERENCES

Yang, Ho-chin. *The Annals of Kokonor.* Bloomington: Indiana University Press, 1970.

Yonten, Pasang. "A History of the Tibetan Medical System." *Tibetan Medicine* (*gSo-rig*) 12 (1989): 32–51.

Yoshimizu, Chizuko. *Die Erkenntnislehre des Prāsaṅgika-Madhyamaka nach Dem Tshig gsal stoṅ thun gyi tshad ma'i rnam bśad des 'Jam dbyaṅs bźad pa'i rdo rje.* Wien: Arbeitskreis für Tibetische und Buddhistische Studien Universität Wien, 1996.

INDEX